Johnny Kling

ALSO BY GIL BOGEN

*Tinker, Evers, and Chance:
A Triple Biography*
(McFarland, 2003)

Johnny Kling
A Baseball Biography

GIL BOGEN

Foreword by Ernie Banks

McFarland & Company, Inc., Publishers
Jefferson, North Carolina, and London

LIBRARY OF CONGRESS CATALOGUING-IN-PUBLICATION DATA

Bogen, Gil, 1925–
Johnny Kling : a baseball biography / Gil Bogen ;
foreword by Ernie Banks.
p. cm.
Includes bibliographical references and index.

ISBN 978-0-7864-2414-6
softcover : 50# alkaline paper ∞

1. Kling, Johnny, d. 1947. 2. Baseball players—United States—Biography. 3. Jewish baseball players—United States—Biography. 4. Chicago Cubs (Baseball team) I. Title.
GV865.K55B64 2006   796.357092—dc22   2005037400

British Library cataloguing data are available

©2006 Gil Bogen. All rights reserved

No part of this book may be reproduced or transmitted in any form or by any means, electronic or mechanical, including photocopying or recording, or by any information storage and retrieval system, without permission in writing from the publisher.

On the cover: Johnny Kling, 1907 *(Chicago Daily News negatives collection, Chicago Historical Society)*

Manufactured in the United States of America

McFarland & Company, Inc., Publishers
Box 611, Jefferson, North Carolina 28640
www.mcfarlandpub.com

To the memory of my beautiful wife,

Rosalyn Rae Witten Bogen

who on December 16, 2004, suddenly left on a voyage.
She is now smiling down on her crew:

Four wonderful children:
Lynn, Marla,
Steve and Mark

Nine marvelous grandchildren:
Michael, Jordan,
Laura, Dana,
Helen, Andrew,
Matthew, Julia,
and
Jonathan

TABLE OF CONTENTS

Acknowledgments   ix
Foreword by Ernie Banks   1
Introduction   3

1. EXODUS FROM GERMANY   9
2. SOLACE IN CINCINNATI   13
3. THE EARLY YEARS   17
4. SETTING SAIL   27
5. A CHOPPY SEA   39
6. CHARTING A COURSE   48
7. WEATHERING STORMS   61
8. CLEARING SKIES   73
9. JUMPING SHIP   125
10. CLIMBING ABOARD   144
11. WALKING THE PLANK   167
12. TREADING WATER   175
13. A LAST VOYAGE   182
14. REST AND RELAXATION   190
15. DINNER AND THE THEATER   195
16. PEANUTS AND CRACKER JACK   198
17. SUGAR AND SPICE   205
18. THE GENTLEMAN FARMER   210

19. BREAD AND BUTTER	212
20. MEAT AND POTATOES	214
21. JUST ANOTHER DAY	219
22. JEWISH ANCESTRY, PART ONE	221
23. JEWISH ANCESTRY, PART TWO	227
24. JEWISH ANCESTRY, PART THREE	230
25. BASEBALL AND ANTI-SEMITISM	234
26. SETTING THE RECORD STRAIGHT	238
Conclusion	243
Appendix A: A Writer's Regard	249
Appendix B: Documents and Letters	251
Chapter Notes	265
Bibliography	275
Index	281

Acknowledgments

It was an honor and privilege to receive help from Johnny Kling's grandson, John Kling, who works in Buffalo Grove, Illinois. His information was invaluable because it provided a direct connection to family-held views about Johnny Kling's religion.

It was an honor and a privilege to interview the only living person who met and remembers Johnny Kling. That person is 92-year-old Helen Allen, the daughter-in-law of Bennie Allen, who was Kling's nephew and partner in the Dixon Hotel. Helen provided vital information. She also provided a story never before told.

A very special thank you to Peter Golenbock, author of *Wrigleyville*, and Peter Levine, author of *Ellis Island to Ebbets Field*. They were extremely generous in giving me permission to use information from their books.

A very special thank you to people who searched, searched and searched until they found what I was looking for. Without them, photographs and important historical information would never have found their way into this book. Thanks to Bill Boos, family service counselor, Mount Moriah Cemetery, Kansas City, Missouri; Bill Cliff of the Harold Washington Library in Chicago; Jim Dickerson, park ranger, Longview–Blue Springs Project Office, Kansas City, Missouri; Bernice Fromm of Kansas City, Missouri; David W. Jackson, Jackson County Historical Society, Independence, Missouri; Vera Gail Johnson, Mid-Continent Public Library, Independence, Missouri; Frances Leslie, customer service representative, Kansas City, Missouri, Health Department; Freya Maslov, genealogist, Morton Grove, Illinois; Steven Mitchell, Missouri State Archives; Phil Nuxhall, historian, Spring Grove Cemetery, Cincinnati, Ohio; Barbara Perkins, State of Missouri Office in charge of Corporations; Richard J. Reiman, historian, St. John's Unitarian, Cincinnati; Bill Riegel, United Jewish Cemeteries, Cincinnati; Jeffrey P. Sahaida, historian, Air Force Historical Research Agency, Maxwell Air Force Base, Alabama; Gabriel Schechter, library associate, Cooperstown Baseball Hall of Fame; staff, Jackson County Courthouse,

Kansas City, Missouri; and Alison Stankrauff, American Jewish Archives, Cincinnati.

My heartfelt thanks goes out to a fantastic bunch of guys who love baseball and helped bring this book to fruition. They went that extra mile in digging for information and gave it freely. They are members of the Society for American Baseball Research (SABR): Dave Anderson, Larry Boes, Mike Bojanowski, Ryan Chamberlain, Warren Corbett, Bill Deane, Rich Gibson, Bill Guider, Ed Hartig, Bill Hickman, Maxwell Kates, Kerry Keene, R. J. Lesch, Mike McCann, Wayne McElreavy, Stephen Milman, Mike Moose, Joe Murphy, R. "Bobby" Plapinger, Josh Prager, Chuck Rosciam, Gabriel Schechter, Ron Selter, Terry Sloope, Steve Steinberg, Dick Thompson, Stew Thornley, Bob Timmerman, Frank Vaccaro, Max Weder, Mike Welsh and Paul Wendt.

Gratitude is also extended to wonderful librarians in different states who responded to requests for books and microfilm and mailed them out as part of an interlibrary loan program. The Southwest Branch of Florida's Palm Beach County system initiated all requests.

Libraries responding were Alachua County, Gainsville, Florida; Alameda County, Fremont, California; American Jewish Historical Society; Birmingham, Alabama; Boca Raton, Florida, Family History Center; Coleman Memorial; Florida State University, Tallahassee; Dalton State College, Dalton, Georgia; Delray Beach, Florida; Ekstrom University, Louisville, Kentucky; Florida Atlantic University, Boca Raton, Florida; Henrico, Richmond, Virginia; Kansas City, Missouri; Largo, Florida; Magale/Centenary College, Shreveport, Louisiana; Miami–Dade County, Florida; Newton Gresham/Sam Houston State University, Huntsville, Texas; Oldsmar, Florida; Ramaker/Northwestern College, Orange City, Iowa; Tampa, Hillsborough County, Florida and Venice, Florida.

That I owe a debt of gratitude to Charlyne A. Sanders, senior records retention manager in the office of the Commissioner of Baseball, is an understatement, considering the magnitude of her contribution. She uncovered the 7th Annual Report of the National Commission from 1911. This report contributed an understanding of what had transpired prior to the start of the 1909 season. False rumors about a salary dispute between Johnny Kling and Charles Webb Murphy were put to rest when this report was combined with additional documented information.

I offer a very special acknowledgment to a young lady, Sheilah Kocherov, secretary at B'nai Jehudah Temple, the synagogue in Kansas City, Missouri. After asking for her help a dozen times, I stopped counting. She provided historical information about Rabbi Harry H. Mayer, about temple members long gone, about Rose Hill cemetery and the Jewish people interred there.

Acknowledgments

Also, a special thank you to Rabbi John M. Sherwood for his valuable advice. And to Rabbi Debra Eisenman, who translated Hebrew to English from inscriptions on a gravestone at the Chestnut Street cemetery in Cincinnati. And to Charles Shapiro of Boca Raton, who loaned me the book *Encyclopedia of Jews in Sports*.

Other people in Kansas City who delved into long forgotten archives and found priceless information are: Don Brink, owner of Raytown Recreation in Raytown, Missouri; Jeremy Drouin, associate special collections librarian, and Sara Nyman, special collections librarian, both at the KCMO Library; Heather Gilbride, Secretary of the Landmarks Commission in City Hall in Kansas City; and Bernice Fromm, who identified the address of Kling's home when he posed alongside his Pierce Arrow automobile.

In addition, a thank you to Frank Kling, who told of his experience in exploring the possibility that he was related to Johnny Kling, and of learning that there was no connection, and of receiving an autographed photo from the famous backstop.

Most of all, I can never adequately thank my children: Lynn, Marla, Steve and Mark. They gave me the kind of support needed to help me complete the manuscript after my wife died. Steven took it upon himself to scan all photos at 300 dpi, save them in tif files and put everything on a CD, including the letters and contracts in Appendix B.

Foreword
by Ernie Banks

As Mr. Cub, I take pleasure in writing about my favorite team. The Cubs of old were great ballplayers, a dominant team in the world of baseball, winning four pennants and two World Series championships between 1906 and 1910.

That wonderful and memorable team established major league records that have never been equaled. In 1906, the Cubs had a win-loss mark of 116–36 (.763), a record that still stands. And their combined winning percentage for 1906–1907 established the high mark for back-to-back seasons. In fact, the standard for winning percentage over a three-four-, five-, six-, seven- and eight-year span was also set by those Cubs. After 93 years, and despite the addition of more games to the schedule, the Cubs still hold all those records. Isn't that amazing!

The field general, the player who quarterbacked that team to such great heights, was its catcher, Johnny Kling. His contemporaries viewed him as one of the greatest, and possibly *the* greatest, catcher of his era.

Gil Bogen took me back to the old Cub team and its catcher and allowed me to envision actual games. I cheered as McGraw's Giants and Clarke's Pirates went down to defeat, pumped my fist as the great, arrogant Ty Cobb was picked off in the World Series, and delighted as Kling consistently frustrated would-be base stealers.

Bogen offers documented evidence that sheds new light on Kling's life and career, including his Jewish heritage. Bogen also introduces you to Tinker, Evers, Chance, Three-Finger Brown and other Cub greats. You will enjoy this well researched book.

Old Stars

'Tis fine to see old stars make good
As boosters feel that old stars should.
'Tis true a few feel rather blue
When old stars fade and pass from view.
But when an old star keeps his gait
We hasten to congratulate!
Allow us, then, this song to sing
In praise of Catcher Johnny Kling!

— William F. Kirk

INTRODUCTION

The poem "Old Stars" immortalized Johnny Kling. He was seen as a star, one of the greatest catchers of his time, and he continued to be successful in all his endeavors after he left baseball.[1]

And yet, Johnny Kling never made it into the Hall of Fame. Many say he wasn't even a marginal candidate. They point to the votes he received from the Baseball Writers Association of America: 8 in 1936, 20 in '37 and 26 in '38. He then went down hill except for 20 votes in '46. In 1953 Johnny Kling was at the bottom of the heap, receiving one vote. After that, none. Today he's in the "Who's he?" category.

Yet, in his book *Jewish Baseball Stars*, Harold Ribalow considered Kling to be "The Smartest Catcher of All."[2] Kling occupied the pivotal and most important position on the team. He was the director and transmitter of all messages, the keyboard used by the manager or pitcher to flash orders to others, and the chief wigwag station on the battlefield in the defensive game. His position was vital to the success of the team.

Johnny Kling had to direct the pitching, signal for each play made with runners on base, watch runners and signal the pitcher to make throws. He also had innumerable opportunities to throw or not to throw, when the slightest hesitancy or uncertainty could mean defeat. He handled pitchers not only with brains, but also with coolness and generalship. He had the mechanical ability to catch balls of any speed, judge distances accurately, throw from any position on the line, and — with a short snap motion of the arm — throw off the shoulder towards first base with scarcely a glance in that direction.

Kling knew the tricks and habits of every batter, knew their weaknesses and strengths, knew which men would steal and on what ball. He had a keen analytical mind that, having made an observation, knew exactly what to do to get a batter out. When Boston brought to Chicago a young outfielder with a reputation for being able to hit, Kling and Brown watched him closely during batting practice.

"He'll fish," remarked Brown.

"Anything low — in or outside," whispered Kling.

During the game, Brown pitched low curves outside the plate and low fast straight balls inside, and the new man "fished," i.e., swung at balls he could not reach. Brown, when asked to explain how he knew this, said: "He showed nervousness and pulled his left foot. I knew he would swing at anything that broke quickly."

"He held his hands with the wrists turned too high," added Kling, "and fully an inch too far apart to get a good swing at a low ball inside."[3]

Kling's powers of observation and judgment were superb. He looked closely every time a batter came to the plate — the kind of bat he carried, the position of his feet and body and how he gripped the bat. All of this told him of the batter's intentions and how to prevent him from tearing into a pitch. He was also a master at working umpires on balls and strikes and winning their friendship — no small matter when it came to getting close calls that could win ballgames. Kling's method was to be friendly with all umpires, siding with them, telling them they were right and frequently whispering to them to be on guard for a certain curve that was coming. He had to carefully conceal every signal given to prevent coaches, batters or base runners from seeing them. Frequently, when he realized he was being watched, he gave false signals to mislead the opposition. Thus one of his two nicknames was "Brainy."

An intricate part of Kling's work, and the most important, was throwing to catch runners, not when they were stealing, but while they were taking a lead off the base. The number of runners caught didn't matter as much as the throwing, which had the effect of keeping runners close to their bases and preventing them from trying to steal.[4]

Kling called the shots for such famous pitchers as Three-Finger Brown, Big Ed Reulbach, Orval Overall and left-handed Jack Pfiester. At one time or another all were 20-game winners, and there was no doubt about Kling's role in the success that these record-setting pitchers achieved on the mound.

Brown once said, "I'm not ashamed to admit that I was just a so-so pitcher before I teamed up with Kling. A pitcher can always tell you how good a catcher is, and take my word, Johnny Kling was the best."[5] At another time he said, "I don't think I ever saw Johnny call a wrong pitch." Cub pitcher Ed Reulbach called Kling one of the greatest catchers to ever wear a mask. And Brown, Reulbach, Overall and Pfiester all gave Kling much of the credit for their success.[6]

A catcher less qualified than Kling could make a pitcher "wild"; he could force the best pitcher to give bases on balls and break up all the teamwork and infield play by a moment of excitement or panic. A cool, brainy pitcher could sometimes take control of the game, but the majority of pitchers preferred to pitch to orders.

Introduction

In Donald Honig's *The Greatest Catchers of All Time*, John McGraw summed it up best when he said, "They are all very good pitchers, but the man who makes them go is Kling." And with Kling behind the bat, the pitching staff led the league in ERAs from 1905 to 1907 with 2.04, 1.76 and 1.73.

Sportswriter Grantland Rice named Johnny Kling to his "most graceful" and "smartest" teams. Pitcher Walter Johnson picked him as one of the two all-time catchers. Former Hall of Fame historian Ernest Lanigan named him as one of the three best catchers in history.[7]

With all that's been said about his ability, one player said more. One who knew him. Played against him. One that had listened to his disconcerting chatter behind the bat from 1901 through 1913, knowing that Kling was trying to distract him, to keep him from pounding the ball to the outfield and getting a hit. Thus his other nickname: "Noisy."

The great Pittsburgh shortstop Honus (Hans) Wagner knew all about Kling, and on January 8, 1924, he published "My Grand All-American Team." His pick for manager was John McGraw. Kling was his number one catcher. Then came Bresnahan and Schalk. Hans went on to say, "With the team I have selected however very little managing would be necessary. All my manager would have to do would be to make out a schedule and then come around on payday."[8]

In another article, Hans raved about Johnny Kling, "the best all-around catcher I ever saw."

> I have put him at the top of the catching staff of my Grand All-American Team, and the more I think about it the more I am convinced of being right. I have put Roger Bresnahan and Ray Schalk next to Kling.
>
> That to my way of thinking would be the best catching outfit that baseball ever has seen or maybe, ever will see. If any baseball man doesn't agree with me I'm open to argument. I'll present mine first.
>
> Johnny Kling was always aggressive and had the best throwing arm from any position of any catcher I ever saw. He was a wonder at finding batters' weaknesses and was allowed to sign the pitchers as he judged best.
>
> Kling had another facility that I have never seen in another catcher. While warming up the pitcher before the game he could tell which was the pitcher's best ball to pitch for that day.
>
> Did you ever know anybody else who could do that? One day a pitcher's fast ball might be his best; another day it might be his curve ball or his slow ball.[9]

Following these praiseworthy comments, Wagner went on to talk about Kling being "a sure hitter, a beautiful fielder of foul flies and bunted balls, a wonder at tagging base runners and on backing up plays at first base."[10]

Kling's knack of guessing on what ball a runner would attempt to steal was also a topic of conversation. And with this knack, Hans pointed out that generally, "Johnny Kling did the thinking for the pitchers." Hans then reminisced further:

Kling was a past master at breaking up the double steal. The fact that there was a man on third as well as on first never worried him. He would whip that ball down to second just the same.

Often he would freeze the man on third and then get the other runner by ten feet. That took nerve and Johnny Kling had a barrel of it.

Roger Bresnahan runs Kling a close second.[11]

It has been generally agreed that Noisy John was the brain of an immortal outfit that swept to four National League pennants and two World Series championships in five years. He threw from a squat and had an arm like a whip. He was a whiz at picking men off base. In June 1907 he threw out all four Cardinal runners who tried to steal second, and in the World Series he gunned down 7 of 14 Tiger runners, holding base stealing champion Ty Cobb to no stolen bases.

In the historic play-off contest at the Polo Grounds in 1908, which sent the Cubs into their third straight World Series, Noisy John reminded the Giants to behave on the base paths when he caught Buck Herzog off first in the opening round after Roger Bresnahan had struck out.

World Series play with Detroit was no different. Johnny stopped Ty Cobb cold on the base paths and taught every other Tiger that it was death to run against Mr. Kling. The historian of the classic put it this way: "Kling was one of the bright stars of the Series and his superiority in his position gave the Cubs a decided advantage."[12]

Johnny Kling was hailed by owners and managers alike as one of the smartest catchers the game ever produced. His knowledge of batting weaknesses of opposing teams was always "right on the money." He likewise was a veritable wonder at pegging the hit-and-run play, base stealing, and breaking up those offensive methods for the opposing teams. He was one of the first to stress the pitch-out as a means of breaking up the hit-and-run.[13]

From 1902 through 1908 Kling led the National League in fielding percentage four times, putouts six, assists twice and double plays once. Kling's reputation for throwing out runners trying to steal has not been exaggerated, as demonstrated by his lifetime record of 1562 assists, which was far more and with fewer seasons played than that of Bill Dickey, Roger Bresnahan, Gabby Hartnett, Ernie Lombardi, Johnny Bench, Roy Campanella and Carlton Fisk — all Hall of Famers.

With such style of play, with such accolades from peers who knew him and who watched him play, why then is Johnny Kling not in the Hall of Fame? There are reasons, but they are based on false information. They have been carried along for decades. Even today, the same false information will suddenly appear in a newly published text.

This book should change all that. Old rumors will be put to rest; false information will be corrected. Kling will be shown as one of the greatest catchers of the dead ball era, possibly of all time. Compelling reasons will be offered as to why he deserves to be in the Hall of Fame. The time has come to set the record straight.

1

Exodus from Germany

Johnny Kling was born in Kansas City, Missouri, the date varying from one source to another. The 1900 census tells us it was 1873. Kling's death certificate claims it was November 13, 1875. There was no birth certificate to resolve the issue because the earliest recorded birth in Missouri was October 10, 1883. Therefore, the date of birth on the death certificate will be accepted as fact.

His father and paternal grandparents were born in Bavaria, a state in southern West Germany. His mother was born in Ohio, possibly Cincinnati, and both her parents were also from Bavaria.[1]

Caroline Lorch, Kling's mother, was born February 1833. A Cincinnati birth certificate and school records could not be found. The 1850 U.S. Census shows a Lorch family of four in the 10th Ward of Cincinnati: Charles Lorch, age 50, a cooper (makes wooden barrels), "married within the year;" Theresa, Charles' second wife (maiden name unknown), age 23, born in Germany, "married within the year;" Caroline, age 17, no occupation, not in school; Charles, age 16, a painter.

The family of four suffered a severe loss. The elder Lorch died from "dropsy" on January 12, 1855. Because of freezing temperatures, the ground was too hard to dig a grave. So he was placed in a public vault at Spring Grove Cemetery in Cincinnati. When the ground thawed, he was buried February 11, 1855, in Section 48, Lot 10. Interment records show his plot to be a single grave.[2] A visit to the cemetery, a discussion with Phil Nuxhall, historian at Spring Grove, and a check of cemetery records showed Charles Lorch to be buried in a solitary plot. A later search of the public vault by Phil Nuxhall, who examined documents, letters and all pencil-written notes therein, provided nothing about Mr. Lorch.[3]

Information about his second wife, Theresa, was found. She remarried six months after Charles died. The groom was Adam Roth. The ceremony took place Sept. 9, 1855, in Hamilton, Ohio, a short distance from Cincinnati.[4]

Johnny Kling, famous for throwing runners out trying to steal (*Sporting News*).

Assuming that the first Mrs. Lorch had died, the index of death notices appearing in the *Cincinnati Daily Gazette*, 1827–1881, were reviewed. This was necessary because the City of Cincinnati did not keep any record of deaths prior to 1865, and until 1908 the State of Ohio did not require death certificates. Therefore, the newspaper was an excellent resource since it published death notices of local citizens on a daily basis. These death notices quite often included people who had previously lived in Cincinnati and Hamilton County. But no death notice was found for the first Mrs. Lorch.[5]

Old Cincinnati directories prior to 1833, the year of Caroline's birth, made no mention of a Lorch family. Therefore, it is possible that Caroline's parents arrived in America shortly before her birth. They may have come to America with other Lorch immigrants, including Theresa, who would have been about five years of age.

People left Germany in several waves of migration and settled in other countries. The first wave was 1683 to 1820, the second, 1820 to 1871.[6] German Jews first came to Cincinnati in 1817 and met with such a hospitable reception they wrote letters to their co-religionists in Germany. This stimulated the Jews to migrate. Whether any actually arrived in 1817 is not known, but they certainly came in growing numbers during the succeeding decades from 1820 to 1870.

From letters and newspaper reports that reached them prior to their emigration, many envisioned America in general, and Cincinnati in particular, as a "promised land" where economic opportunities abounded and Jews faced none of the restrictions that had so embittered their lives in the German states.

A large proportion of Cincinnati's German Jews originated in Southern Germany, particularly from the small Bavarian province of Upper Franconia and from the Rhenish Palatinate. Individual villages in these areas witnessed a great deal of chain migration; emigrants, in other words, called on their former landsmen to come and join them. They all shared a common dream — to find a "promised land" in the American frontier where Jews could settle as citizens, succeed economically, practice their religion freely and coexist happily and on equal terms with their Christian neighbors. It was a dream thoroughly compatible with the aspirations of the local citizenry as a whole.[7]

John Kling, Sr., Johnny's father, was born December 1829 in Bavaria. The 1880 census reported he was a baker. Attempts were made to obtain family records from Bavaria via the Internet, communicating with others in the U.S. who were trying to trace their Bavarian ancestors.[8] But it was soon learned that although Germans kept detailed records, there were seven districts in Bavaria and the specific location had to be known in order to search for records.

Nevertheless, it was not difficult to obtain information about the state of affairs in Bavaria and throughout the rest of Germany when the Kling family lived there. Anti–Jewish prejudice was never absent, and there were widespread anti–Jewish riots in 1819. Sometime after that, an obscure German Gentile pamphleteer, Hartwig Hundt, wrote that "killing a Jew should be deemed a misdemeanor, not a crime."[9]

Waves of German Jews fleeing to the United States reached a crescendo when they learned that their right to move about freely and settle in German lands had been severely restricted. Marriage licenses were limited and no new ones were issued unless there was a vacancy by death or removal. Moreover, no one could marry unless given domicile license, and as these were limited, marriages were correspondingly restricted. A new industrialism was a threat to their traditional economy, and the German guild system, with already severe restrictions, grew so severe that there was a general movement to the New World. This was the push that impelled Jews to emigrate. American liberties and opportunities attracted them.[10]

There were German leaders who preached a gospel of "Up and On to America." When the first wave of émigrés landed in the 1830s and 1840s, thousands of Americans were streaming westward. The Jews joined them. The balladist Henry Russell (né Levy) stirred thousands as he sang:

> To the West! To the West! To the land of the free
> Where mighty Missouri rolls down to the sea,
> Where a man is a man if he is willing to toil,
> And the humblest may gather the fruits of the soil.[11]

Such was the climate when the second wave of Jews landed in America. Ira A. Glazier, in his book *Germans To America: Lists of Passengers Arriving at U.S. Ports, June 1852–Sept. 1852*, Vol. 3, page 361, told of the arrival of Johannes Kling on board the ship *Westphalia*. It docked in New York August 16 of that year. The ship manifest listed Johannes Kling, passenger number 66, along with over ninety other Klings. All totaled, 150 émigrés had left Bremen headed for the United States. Their occupations were listed, and Johannes was said to be a tailor.[12]

But the 1900 census listed John Kling, Sr., as a baker, arriving in the U.S. in 1852 at age 22. Were there two John Klings, both age 22, one a tailor, the other a baker? Possibly. Was Johnny Kling's father a baker and a tailor? Possibly. A search was made for a ship manifest listing John Kling, Sr., as a baker, but none was found.

Be that as it may, John Kling, Sr., did arrive and headed toward Cincinnati where a 19-year-old damsel, Caroline Lorch, was quietly attending to her daily tasks.[13]

2

SOLACE IN CINCINNATI

Ohio's "wandering historian," Henry Howe, called Cincinnati "a sort of paradise for the Hebrews." Whereas throughout the world Jews faced hatred and bigotry, and many were treated as second class citizens, this was not the case in Cincinnati. The Israelites were esteemed and highly respected by their fellow citizens and a general interchange of civilities and friendships had taken place between them.

Jews and Christians interacted freely. And what may have been more important, they interacted socially. The city's leading rabbis set the pace, priding themselves on their close friendships within the Gentile community. Rabbi Mayer Wise was especially close to the local Unitarians, whom he considered "our allies." Rabbi Max Lilienthal was said to be the first rabbi to preach in a Christian pulpit, and on one occasion, he created a sensation by gratuitously attending to all the duties of Rev. Dr. Spaulding of the Plum Street Universalist Church during the absence of that minister.[1]

Beyond the leadership level there was evidence of close Jewish-Christian interactions in clubs and discussion groups. From a sociological point of view, the best indicator of Jewish-Christian relations was the intermarriage rate, evidence that the two groups not only interacted in business and formal settings but also in intimate ones as well.[2]

The German Jewish immigrants had found in America freedom of movement, of contacts, of thought, of religion; freedom from hatred and discrimination, freedom to roam and find success in a vast country abounding in innumerable opportunities.

We don't know when John Kling, Sr., arrived in this idyllic city. We don't know where he lived. We also don't know whom he met or what he did upon arrival. But one thing we do know — the elder Kling soon learned that the residents of Cincinnati wanted fresh baked bread every day of the week. So in 1855, at the young age of 25, Johannes Kling became an entrepreneur, opening the doors of the Kling J. & T. Bakery at 74 Ham Road.[3] Who T. Kling was is not known. But the two must have done quite well in delivering bakery goods to the local citizenry, for one year later, George P. Kling joined the firm. For J & T and George P., America appears to have been, at least economically, the "promised-land," the land of opportunity.

When Johan first opened the door to his bakeshop, it would be romantic to think that he knew instantly, from people coming and going, that he was on the road to success, that he was a man with a future. Then, one fine sunny day, when fragrant, scarlet carnations were in bloom along Ham Road, Caroline Lorch pushed open the door to the smell of fresh baked delicacies, and the rattle of a shiny brass bell sounded. As she edged her way to the counter, a wide-eyed, clean shaven, handsome young man, busy with another customer, kept turning his head. He stared at her. It was love at first sight. Johan Kling and Caroline Lorch were married December 30, 1855, at St. John's Unitarian Church on 12th and Elm Street.[4]

If they were Jewish, why a church? Marriage in a church was not consistent with the practices of Jewish people. Jews required a rabbi with ritualistic services such as being married under a chuppah, the canopy under which groom and bride stand side by side as they would soon do in their new household. But it must be remembered that many Jews in Cincinnati abandoned their traditional Judaism. And their abandonment of traditional Judaism was nothing unusual among the newly arrived immigrants, where religious laxity was the rule. The traveler I.J. Benjamin described the Jews he met as having "little interest in spiritual matters." According to Stephen Mostov's figures from 1851, over one-fifth of the community did not affiliate with any synagogue at all, and the majority of Jews who did affiliate attended only on an irregular basis.[5]

It should be remembered that Jews were not the only ones who fled Germany. Protestants did too. They also wanted religious freedom. Many left because of economic hardships, including unemployment and crop failures. Some left to avoid wars and military service. But the vast majority of immigrants to America were Jews. Between 1826 and 1880, 280,000 Jews came to the wonderful land of opportunity.[6]

Of Caroline's mother we know nothing, but we do know something about her father. The clue we have about Charles Lorch being Jewish was his interment at Spring Grove Cemetery, listed under United Jewish Cemeteries.[7]

The Jewish heritage issue was pursued in an interview, Jan. 1, 2004, with Richard J. Reiman, the Historian at St. John's Unitarian in Cincinnati. He said, "When a Jew marries a non–Jew, they often join a Unitarian Church. The church has no creed, so the authority for truth rests with the individual. Unitarians believe in the worth and dignity of every person and in the integral web of life. No test of belief, color, lifestyle or sexual orientation is required for membership, the church is open to all."

Richard Reiman's remarks were confirmed by Steven S. Sadleir's book, wherein he said, "Unitarians place great emphasis on individual freedom of belief, and leave each member to 'seek' the truth for himself."[8]

The religious ancestry issue became more complex after Mr. and Mrs. Kling had their first two children, Magdalene (Lena), born Oct. 14, 1856, and Caroline, Aug. 12, 1858. A year later, on August 4, 1859, Lena and Caroline were baptized at St. John's Unitarian, the church where their parents were married.[9] A search of St. John's baptismal records through 1874 failed to reveal any baptisms for the other Kling children.

Responding to questions about baptism, Mr. Reiman at St. John's said, "The baptism or christening at St. John's was to name the child and dedicate the parents to the child's upbringing." He also said, "If two of the children were baptized, it logically follows that all would be. The records could be lost, or the rite done at another church." He suggested checking other churches. Hamilton County baptismal records failed to reveal baptisms for other Kling children at other churches.

Although Jews did not believe in the baptismal rite, they desperately wanted social acceptance. And many had to buy their "ticket of admission to European culture" at the baptismal font. A tragic ambivalence characterized the spiritual climate of German Jewry at the beginning of the nineteenth century. Fully one-tenth of the Jewish population of the German states between 1800 and 1810 took the escape route of baptism.[10] And it seems reasonable to believe that this spiritual climate emigrated along with large numbers of émigrés. One such émigré may have been Johan Kling.

He became an American citizen, but the year of his naturalization was not listed in the U.S. Census. He remained in Cincinnati for many years. His family grew. In addition to Lena and Caroline, the census listed five additional children: Louise, Elizabeth, William, Charles and Amelia. All could read and write.[11] In all probability they went to school, but school records could not be found.

The documentation of important events in the lives of citizens apparently did not occur in Cincinnati, as evidenced by a Jan. 12, 2004, e-mail from Kevin Grace at the Archives and Rare Books Department, University of Cincinnati. He said, "No birth records prior to 1874 exist for Cincinnati and Hamilton County."

Records do exist as to the anti–Jewish prejudice in Cincinnati during the Civil War (1861–1865), and the rise in anti–Semitism following the war. Several local employers refused to hire Jews. Many clubs refused to accept Jewish members. There was a general tendency to exclude German Jews from Gentile social gatherings after six o'clock and many Christian homes were closed to them at night. The most prominent college preparatory school for girls likewise kept Jews out. And most serious of all, Jews found themselves frozen out of positions in certain banks and law firms. The sense of belonging that early Jews had so cherished grew more and more attenuated.

Evidence of local anti–Semitism did point out a disturbing disjunction between Cincinnati as Jews envisaged it and Cincinnati as it actually was. For a long time, Jews lived with this contradiction. They overlooked it, suppressed it, or rationalized it away. In the long run, however, it had to be confronted. In many ways, the Jewish vision of Cincinnati was simply too good to be true.[12]

It was during these times that Johan Kling and his wife Carolyn packed their things, loaded their brood onto some type of vehicle and headed west, looking for a new and better place where they could once again plant their roots.

3

THE EARLY YEARS

1875–September 10, 1900

Nothing is known as to how the Kling family decided where to settle down. A check of records revealed that a John Kling had been given 84.59 acres in Louisiana on Feb. 10, 1881, under the Homestead Act, but by then the Klings had settled in Missouri.

John and Caroline Kling arrived in Kansas City, Missouri, where John (Johnny) Kling, the youngest of eight, was born on November 13, 1875. John Kling, Sr., wasted no time in establishing himself, opening a bakery at 1825 Charlotte and listing himself in the 1876 city directory. He and the family also lived at that address.[1]

By 1884 the bakery and residence had moved to 1413 Main St., and the shop was doing well. But without warning, the family suffered an agonizing tragedy. The second born, Caroline, had married Sigesmund Z. Schutte. They had two children: Victor and Caroline (Carrie). On April 14, 1884, Carrie, at the age of two, developed congestion in her lungs and died.[2]

John Kling, Sr., and his wife Caroline had suffered the loss of a granddaughter. But what more could they do but grieve and move on with their lives. Mr. and Mrs. Schutte also moved on with their lives. Caroline became pregnant and gave her parents a grandson, Zacheriah. But this joyous occasion was not meant to be. On June 21, 1885, the 9-month-old youngster died from "Cholera Infantism."[3] The grieving mother did not recover from this tragedy. In that same year, at the age of 27, she passed on. There was no death certificate in the office of vital statistics, so the cause was unknown. Sigesmund now faced the difficult task of raising his 6-year-old son Victor while closing down his grocery business and starting up a fledgling lumber company.

The Klings stepped in. Following an idea from the Hebrew Bible, one of the 613 Laws of the Torah, law 206, which permits a man to marry a sister when his wife passes on, preparation was made for 25-year-old Louise to betroth herself to Mr. Schutte. It was preferable for the orphaned son to be raised by an aunt rather than an unrelated stepmother. In 1886 Sigesmund and Louise were married.[4]

By then, the elder Kling had plans to expand his bakery to include a grocery, and in 1887 he moved to 920 East 19th St., while he and the family lived at 1335 Highland Ave. When not baking, Johannes Kling bagged groceries. Charles and William couldn't help out. They had jobs with J. B. Bott making mattresses. But in 1889, William quit his job at J. B. and worked alongside his father as a baker.

This didn't last long. By 1890, Bill no longer cherished the idea of devoting his life to baking bread. Perhaps the heat behind the ovens was too much for him. So he again joined his brother Charles, and once again became a mattress maker.

The work in the bakery and grocery became demanding. Others joined in. Mrs. Kling sold groceries. Elizabeth (Lizzie) clerked in the bakery. With Bill gone from the bakery, Kling Sr. called upon his youngest son to come into the business, and gave him the responsibility of delivering fresh baked bread every morning to waiting customers. At age 15, John Kling, Jr., was in charge of the horse and wagon. His official title was "Bread Wagon Chauffeur."

Every morning, the clang of the family alarm sent John on his route. But the patrons on John's route didn't grow in numbers as the elder Kling had expected. And it wasn't long before he soon learned why.

An irate housewife informed the bakery proprietor that she would take bread from his competitor, as the Kling wagon never reached her house on time. One morning, Johnny's father started out on the trail of his son and found the horse meandering down the road — no Johnny to be seen. He heard a great deal of noise over in a corner field where a baseball game was in progress and these words came to the ears of the elder Kling: "Ataboy Johnny ol' horse, sticker right over the ol' oyster; dis slob couldn't hit you with a paddle."

Those were the words the catcher was flinging to the youthful Kling when Kling the elder broke up the game. Johnny, who may have experienced the paddle, then decided that driving the bread wagon on schedule and pleasing customers was more conducive to general good health than sticking it over the ol' oyster.[5] It seems reasonable to say that in spite of Johnny's love of baseball, the elder Kling instilled the meaning of responsibility in his youngest son. This lesson became ingrained as part of his character and served him well in business ventures throughout his life.

In all probability, the elder Kling didn't realize his youngest son's potential for becoming a great pitcher. If he'd been following the news he would have read about the game between the Haverlys and the Golden Eagles on

3. The Early Years

Cartoon of Johnny Kling, bread wagon chauffeur and pitcher (courtesy James Dickerson).

June 22, 1890, at Exposition Park, with batteries Kling (p) and McMahon (c) vs. Cornell (p) and Crisp (c).[6] He would've been proud to see his son win 13 to 1, thus clinching the amateur championship of Kansas City.[7]

Had old man Kling been able to take off one day a week, he may have been convinced that his "Bread Wagon Chauffeur" had a great future playing baseball. He would have witnessed his 14-year-old son pitch exciting games, like the one on June 30, 1890, when Johnny Kling had 11 strikeouts, beating the Krulls 8 to 2.[8] Or the game on July 7, 1890, when he had 16 strikeouts, beating the Krulls 9 to 5.[9]

Johnny Kling's success as a pitcher was indeed phenomenal. On July 21, 1890, the *Kansas City Journal* reported:

> The baseball game between the Haverlys and Lincoln Giants, at Exposition Park, progressed satisfactorily yesterday until the eighth inning, when it broke up in a row. The Lincolns are fine fielders, but they were unable to find Kling's curves, and had only made two hits during the game. In the eighth, one of the visitors reached third and attempted to score, but was cut off by a brilliant throw from Houlihan to McMahon. Joe Ellick, who umpired the game, called the runner out. Immediately there was a great outcry and the Lincolns refused to go on with the game. Ellick awarded it to the Haverlys by a score of 9 to 0.

The Haverlys will go to Joplin and play three games, Fri, Sat and Sun. They have had great success so far this season, winning 33 out of 36 games played.

Those were good old corner lot days, when Johnny was preparing himself for the career that awaited him. In 1891 he got on a team with real uniforms. It was with the Sibers, sponsored by John R. Siber, owner of the Hannibal Meat Market, and it has been reported that it was here "that Johnny played his first games as a pitcher."[10] Not true, as seen by his pitching for the Haverlys in 1890.

The team photo in 1891 revealed something not listed in the city directory. It reported that Johnny Kling was in the billiard hall business. But it didn't say whether he was in business for himself. Donald Honig claimed, "One of Johnny's brothers ran a poolroom."[11] It didn't say so in the city directory. But it did reveal what his brothers did to earn a livelihood and it wasn't billiards. The city directory also said that in 1897 John Kling, Jr., was a clerk for Joe and Charley. In 1898, a clerk for Charles Raber and in 1899, a manager for Charles Raber billiards.

Charles Raber went into business with Joe and Charley in 1885. Their ad in the city directory said, "Raber, Chas, with Joe & Charley, Armory Hall & Billiard Parlor, Open Day & Night, Grand Avenue, NW Corner 15th. St. The Best Equipped Pool Hall." It therefore seems reasonable to say that in 1891, Johnny Kling, at age 16, worked for this billiard hall, but neither he nor his brothers owned one.

In addition to playing ball with the Sibers, helping out in the bakery, and learning about cue sticks and billiard balls, Johnny attended grammar and high school, played on the high school nine as a pitcher and was captain in his senior year.[12] School records could not be found but based on his Charlotte and Highland home addresses and archival records on schools, he would have gone to Morse Grammar on the east side of Charlotte between 20th and 21st Street, and Central High on the east side of Locust, between 11th and 12th Street.[13]

And the same year that Johnny was pitching for the Sibers, elder brother Bill decided he had no intention of spending his life with springs and mattresses. He went off to play professional baseball in the National League, joining Philadelphia, pitching 12 games and winning four. With that kind of showing, 1892 found him at Baltimore, where he pitched two games for the year. After dropping out of professional baseball, he went home and tended bar, but returned in 1895 with the Louisville club, pitched one game and quit. His lifetime tally was 87 innings with a 4–2 record and a 5.17 ERA.[14]

By 1895, as Bill was leaving baseball, Johnny Kling was on his way to becoming a ballplayer. He listed his occupation as such in the Kansas City directory. Although the elder Kling had moved the bakery and home to

3. The Early Years

Johnny Kling (fourth from the right, standing), member of the Siber baseball team in 1891 (courtesy Don Brink).

1528½ Grand Ave., and his three sons lived with him and his wife, Charles was the only one who still helped out in the bakery. William tended bar, and Johnny focused on playing ball and shooting pool.

The literature on Kling's early baseball career is not clear; different sources have different versions. In one instance they are all flat wrong.

We can agree that in 1890, this 5 foot, 9 and a half-inch player pitched for the Haverlys. In 1891–1892, he pitched for the Sibers.[15] We can agree that at age 18 he started at least a two-year stint (1893–1894), possibly three, with the Kansas City Schmeltzers, where he served as manager, pitcher, and first baseman.[16] We can agree that in 1895 the St. Louis Cardinals may have given him a tryout, but he was turned loose because he was "too small to be a catcher."[17] And we can agree that in 1896 he went to Houston of the Texas League eager to show his stuff as a backstop, but never got a chance to do so because Henry J. Cote, from around the Troy, New York, area, prevented it.

Cote, a glutton for work, caught 126 of 132 games the Buffs played, and the chap who was supposed to be his assistant in the backstopping department—John Kling—up and jumped the club because he had no opportunity to do windpad duty. Kling engaged in 16 games as shortstop and 28 as an outfielder before taking French leave.[18] Confirmation of this can be seen in the Spalding Guide for 1897, wherein it lists Kling as shortstop and outfielder for the previous year.

We do agree without hesitation that in the fall of 1897 Kling earned his first money as a ballplayer. Emporia and Winfield were scheduled to play for the Kansas state championship, and Johnny was signed by Emporia at the munificent salary of $3 per game.[19]

The following spring, he teamed up with the Rockford, Illinois, club at a salary of $60 per month, but was released before the season ended because he was "too small."[20] The *Biographical Dictionary of American Sports — Baseball*, confirms this by saying, "His stint with this old Western Association team was short." Another source agreed: "John's 105 pounds of beef didn't look good enough to the Rockford manager."[21] Nevertheless, he did play in 14 games as catcher before being released as a failure.

In 1896, when Kling quit the Houston Buffs, the most likely thing he could do was go back home. In 1898, when fired by Rockford, he turned once again to semi-pro ball in Kansas City, playing for the Schmeltzers. He remained with the team through the 1898 season.[22]

We've come to agree with much of Johnny Kling's minor league career through 1898, but we will not agree to claims that in 1899 he played with Houston of the Texas League. We cannot agree because between 1897 and 1899 and beyond, there was no Texas League.[23] There was such a league in 1895 and 1896. And we already agreed to his playing for Houston as a shortstop and an outfielder for part of 1896. But even here reports differ.

One source has Johnny playing 44 games for Houston before quitting the team. Another has him playing in 51 games, stealing 18 bases, scoring 47 runs with a BA of .359. But this article claimed that Johnny Kling played under the name of Kline. Proof of this could not be found. Up until the end of 1898, he always played under the name of Kling, which was his real name.[24]

Donald Honig claimed that Kling used Kline in 1899 when he returned home and played on Kansas City lots, also helping his father in the bakery. Reportedly, his father opposed his playing ball and it was at this time that he used the name of Kline.[25] We know he was home because the city directory listed John Kling as "Mgr. Billiards, Chas Raber" for that year. But we don't know if he used the name of Kline. There's no proof.

In 1899, Johnny began catching. In the fall he went on a barnstorming trip with the Kansas City Western leaguers and took part in a game at Atchison. Manager McKibben of the St. Joseph club was among the spectators and thought he detected signs of future greatness in the young backstop. So Kling was signed with St. Joseph in 1900.[26]

His record with St. Jo was impressive:

G.	AB.	R.	H.	HR.	SB.	Pct.	PO.	A.	E.	Ave.
108	442	75	133	...	23	.303	441	107	28	.913

The Chicago Orphans needed a third baseman and dispatched veteran scout Ted Sullivan on a secret mission to buy Sammy Strang from St. Jo. He was so impressed with Kling, he bought him too. Thus, Chicago secured one of the greatest catchers of all time.[27] Western League play for 1900 closed September 4, and Johnny Kling was told to be in New York on September 11 to play his first National League game against the Giants.

Before going to the Polo Grounds to watch Johnny Kling play, let's listen to what he had to say about his rise to a major league career. And remember! It's a real treat to listen to him. He was probably the most difficult of all baseball veterans to coax into discussing his diamond exploits. He would parry questions calculated to furnish the interrogator with anecdotes of the catcher's thrilling years with the Cubs with the explanation that he was more concerned with present day baseball. But someone must have put a voodoo spell over him. On Oct. 4, 1910, he did talk. Page 6 of *The Chicago Daily News*, carried his story along with a photo.

How I Got My Start
By John Kling

How did I get my start? Well, if the young fellows who want to become professional players have as much trouble getting started as I did, the crop will be short. I think it was partly my own fault and partly bad luck that I had so much trouble, and the greater part of my fault was that I neither knew my position nor knew the game well enough. Perhaps I had been spoiled by too much success as a semiprofessional player before I tried to get into professional baseball. Also, I had learned wrong in many things and wanted to play my way. It took me a long time to discover they knew more about it in the organized leagues than we did in the amateur ranks.

I don't remember the time when I did not play ball. I began about the time I started to school. I discovered when I went to work that baseball helped me a lot. I got a place and was advanced faster and given better chances than the fellows who did not play, so I realized baseball was valuable as a sideline. At that time I had little idea of devoting all my time to it. I managed and pitched for the Schmeltzers, a Kansas City sporting goods house, and worked in the store when not playing.

After a time friends began telling me I was too good for the semipro game and advised me to go out as a pitcher. I was scared sick being very young, but I got a place at Rockford, Ill., and they fired me before I had my shoes broken in. That sent me back to the semipro field. We happened to need a catcher, and being the captain, I made myself catcher because we needed one and not because I was good.

I soon discovered that catching was more interesting to me than pitching. It gave me more chance to think and to study batters. I liked to try to outwit the batters, and that made caching enjoyable.

It wasn't long until they told me I was too good a catcher to stay around Kansas City. I took their word for it and went to the Texas League. The only reason I quit there was because the team refused to pay me. I returned to the Schmeltzers

Johnny Kling in catching pose (Burke and Atwell).

again and after a time signed with St. Joseph as a catcher. I had learned a lot and the biggest thing I learned was to keep cool and never lose my temper.

I believe a catcher who can keep cool can outthink any one who lets either temper or excitement get away with him. The catcher need not be brainier, but if he keeps thinking all the time he will outthink the fellow who loses his head part of the time. I noticed also that even the appearance of coolness and steadi-

3. The Early Years

Johnny Kling as a member of the Chicago Cubs (National Baseball Hall of Fame).

ness on the part of the catcher helps the pitcher and helps the infield. So even when I lost my head I tried to appear perfectly cool. After a time it became habit and part of the job.

When I learned that, I think I really was getting my start. I was at St. Joe only a short time when Chicago got me and brought me to the west-side team. There with Chance and with smart pitchers I started right.

One must have his head with him all the time, must keep cool and always look all around the field before signaling for any pitched ball. If he does this and studies batters all the time, he can get his start any time because catchers are scarce. The getting started is the easiest part.[28]

Having been ingrained with a fair amount of wisdom at this stage in his life and no major league experience, Johnny Kling, alongside his teammates, walked out of the clubhouse in center field on September 11, 1900, ready to play. The first thing he saw was Coogan's Bluff, a distinguishing feature at the Polo Grounds. It was an elevated area of land directly behind the grandstand at the home plate end. Fans were up there, looking down, waiting for the game to start. A walkway led down to areas of that grandstand which had ramps and entryways, and at the bottom of it all, up front, was home plate.

What Johnny didn't see, what could best be seen from the sky above, was the graceful sweep of a wooden ballpark whose grandstands stretched out in the shape of a horseshoe. As Johnny came close to the infield, he looked back toward the outfield. It was something! Gentry sitting in their horse-drawn carriages parked behind a rope waiting to watch the game.

4

SETTING SAIL

Sept. 11, 1900

Said game was about to start, the first of a double header against New York. Johnny Kling was in the dugout sitting between two teammates. He was aware of the cranky attitude Manager Tom Loftus demonstrated when he announced the battery: "Game one, Chance and Callahan. Game two, Kling and Griffith." Loftus was gruff. Dexter, a catcher, whispered to Johnny that the manager was steamed because of the loss of a double header to Philadelphia the day before.

Johnny had heard that Loftus had a genial nature, but it soured when the Orphans couldn't make hits when hits would have counted most. They lost the first game to the Quakers 6–0. But all the bitterness was in the second game. Bob Emslie's mistake in the fourth inning, when he miscalled a strike and let Nate Dolan walk, started Philadelphia on tallies. Chicago still had a chance until the eighth. Then came the slaughter that put Chicago completely out of the running.

Johnny Kling knew that Loftus desperately wanted to win. This was his first year with the team. His job was on the line. President Hart insisted on having a winning team, and so far the record was worse than the previous year.

Game one started with Bowerman behind the bat, Hawley pitching, McCarthy leading off for Chicago. Three up, three down. The game moved along; it was close and exciting. New York led by one run until the seventh. Then, the New Yorkers fell upon Callahan and drove the ball through every chink in the infield, piling up runs until the points of the scorer's pencils were blunt. Seven singles had penetrated the bewildered infield in rapid succession, then Selbach's two-bagger, and still more hits including Smith's homer. When the Giants finally wore their bats out, the score was 14 to 3. Time of game, 2:20.[1]

For Johnny Kling, it was more than just another game of baseball. It was the beginning of an education that he began to pursue from the moment the game started. First man up was Van Haltren. Johnny looked closely at the bat he carried, how he gripped it, and the position of his feet and body, which he could use to determine the direction of the batter's hit. As Van Haltren hit the ball solidly, Johnny began to memorize the direction he chose to hit it, and the kind of pitch he liked to swing at.

Johnny knew that the most important duty of the catcher was to know the batter. The power of observation and quick judgement involved was enormous. He also knew that once the plan of attack had been determined, he would often have to order the pitcher to pitch straight and fast toward a batter's head to force him to shift position quickly, destroying his plan of attack.[2]

Although Johnny Kling felt bad about his team being slaughtered, he felt good about being in the major leagues. He knew it would take at least three years of hard work before he had complete knowledge of all the pitchers and batters in the league, including an intimate familiarity with his own men, their capabilities and their mode of play. Johnny Kling was on his way to becoming the most valuable asset on the team.[3]

The second game started with 700 fans in attendance, still whooping it up after their team's first win. This time, the game was fast and brilliant. Carrick was on the mound. Chicago's first three batters, McCarthy, Childs and Mertes, were easy outs.

Griffith took the mound. First man up was Van Haltren. Johnny Kling crouched low behind the bat and at a glance surveyed his men: Ryan in right, Green center and McCarthy in left. Mertes was at first, Childs second, McCormick short and Bradley was at third.

The game was about to start, and in that next split second, the action would all be before him. He would be in charge of directing his men on every play. Johnny was confident that with experience, he would become a good general, possibly a great one. He instantly assessed Van, the same man he examined in game one. Griffith stood tall on the mound waiting for the sign. But before Johnny could sign him, Griffith nodded, "yes" and began his delivery. Johnny put his glove low, at the outside corner of the strike zone, and the "Old Fox" hit the mark. But at the same time, Griffith tried to fool the batsman with very little on the ball, something he was noted for. He was also noted for shaking his head "yes" or "no" before each pitch even though he was not given any sign.[4]

Van Haltren singled to right. But very quickly, Kling caught him stealing. And he did it without rising from the squat position. He just snapped his wrist and off it went, something he learned from Bruce Petway, a catcher who earned his fame in the Negro Leagues.[5]

In the seventh, the pitcher Mercer got a hit, and when he tried to make

4. Setting Sail

it home, Johnny proved his toughness. Mercer tried to ram Kling at the plate, but the collision resulted in the pitcher being carried of the field unconscious. Seymour came in to pitch.[6]

Kling and Griffith did well with the first twenty-three New Yorkers. They were out. Meantime, Loftus' men slowly gained headway in spite of Carrick's excellent pitching. Green singled in the second inning, stole second, reached third when Hickman dropped Bowerman's throw, and came home on an out by Bradley. McCormick singled. Kling ripped a two-bagger through Hickman an instant later, but McCormick was nailed at the plate trying to score from first.

In the fifth, McCormick opened with a hit. Kling bunted and reached first when Carrick and Bowerman collided fielding the ball. Griffith bunted and Carrick threw to third too late to catch McCormick. McCarthy forced McCormick at the plate. Then Kling tallied on Child's fly to Smith, and Mertes sent Griffith home with a single.

Clark Griffith had the contest in his possession, 3 to 0, up to the last of the ninth. There were no outs and men were on first and second when Van Haltren came to the plate. He hit a slow, easy bounder down toward first and it seemed certain Chicago would win. Mertes started to waltz up to the ball, then decided to wait for it to come to him. The ball struck the edge of the grass, shot crooked and low, escaped under Mertes, and rolled on down into right field. Before Ryan could get to it, one run had scored. Seymour was on third and Van Haltren on second, and the crowd went wild. Davis flied out to Mertes, and with two runs in and Van Haltren on third a tie seemed certain. But when Selbach popped a fly to Bradley at third, the crowd groaned.

Hickman, branded as the "sensation of the league," was next. Twice he whaled away at balls a yard from his bat, and Griffith, seeing the youngster's condition, aimed to give him no chance to hit. He fired up a ball four feet over Hickman's head. Kling, who was in a squat position, was taken by surprise. He leaped, stuck one hand up, managed to check the speed of the ball, but before he could recover it, Van Haltren had crossed the rubber and the score was tied. An instant later, Hickman swung at a ball a yard from the plate, but the mischief was done. Emslie then called the game because of darkness.[7]

On the following day, the *Chicago Tribune* headlined the game. The report had a short piece about the new catcher: "Kling Is a Cool Proposition." The article read, "Kling's showing was the interesting feature of the day to Chicagoans. He caught Griffith as if the Polo Grounds was his own ash heap, and he hit hard, getting three of Chicago's seven hits and scoring one run."[8]

As Chicago fans read about the team's new catcher, Johnny Kling was suiting up and putting on his spikes. Because of the 3–3 tie the day before, it was another double-header on Sept. 12, and Tom Loftus had the "Cool Proposition" catching both games. His battery mates in game one was Menefee and in game two was Taylor. After warming up Menefee, he knew the pitcher's best pitch would be a slow curve. His fast one didn't have control.

As the game was about to begin, Johnny felt a bit nervous. But as he surveyed his team from a squat position, he was certain they saw him as cool and confident. It was something he had learned to do. It was important. It helped the team settle down.[9]

Game one was going well. Chicago bunched 13 hits while New York was unable to start the ball rolling except in the seventh, when Menefee loosened up and permitted one run on hits by Grady, Van Haltren and Gleason.[10]

Playing today for the first time was third baseman Sammy Strang, who came with Kling from St. Joe in the Western Association. The two rookies put on quite a show as Chicago trounced New York 9–1.

They should also have taken game two, but a bit of bad luck spoiled the day. Chicago took the lead early in the first inning 1–0. But in the second inning, with a man on first, Ryan misjudged Gleason's fly. The ball rolled under a rope and was called a home run.

Chicago had another chance in the fifth when Kling led off with a two-bagger to right. Van Haltren's muff of Taylor's high fly gave the latter two bases and advanced Kling to third. McCarthy made three swipes at the air. Childs flied to Gleason. Davis' poor throw to Doyle of Mertes' grounder allowed Kling and Taylor to score and Mertes to reach first. Ryan forced Mertes at second. In the sixth, Chicago again tallied up 3 runs. But New York could not be deprived of a win, the final score 7–6. The *Chicago Tribune* had much to say the following day:

NEW MEN SEEM TO BE STARS

Sammy Strang of Nashville, Tenn. opened up his career by making eight hits out of nine times at bat. And Johnny Kling caught one of the greatest games seen this season. He worked plays which caused some of the alleged brainy players of the two teams to stare. In fact, if the playing and headwork of Kling and Strang can be taken as a criterion, the Western league must have been faster than the Nationals this season.[11]

The *Chicago Daily News* had more to say on the front page of its Sporting Extra. The article was headlined, "Loftus' Finds Make Good." It praised Sammy Strang's hitting, then said, "Kling won the plaudits of all the players by his steady alert work behind the bat. He caught like a veteran. He had little chance for throwing, but that is supposed to be his strong point. He made two hits in the afternoon, one a double.

4. Setting Sail

"'He is one of the likeliest young catchers I have seen in a long time,' said Loftus. He seems as good right now as many old-time leaguers. He goes about his work without any fuss, but seems to be in the game all the time. I think he will make a great catcher.'"

Johnny Kling had caught in only three games, and he was already beginning to make his presence known. He demonstrated a mechanical ability to catch balls of any speed, handled foul tips, judged distances accurately, threw from any position on the line and with a short, snap motion of the arm, he threw off the shoulder towards first base with scarcely a glance in that direction. Along with this, he remained cool, demonstrated a brainy game and continued to memorize the tricks and habits of batters.[12]

On Sept. 13, the Chicago Orphans were in fifth place with a 56–61 win-loss record. Boston held the fourth spot. And Chicago was about to play New York. The battery was Cunningham and Kling.

The Orphans took an early lead, and until the eighth inning the game was in doubt. Then McCormick singled and a shout of victory went up from the Chicago bench. McCormick's hit yielded nothing in the way of tallies, but there was a superstition among the players that when McCormick made a hit, the team couldn't lose. So when he singled in the eighth, the players regarded the game as won, and Cunningham pitched New York into a state of helplessness through the next two innings, taking the game 6–5 and moving the team into fourth place, one-half game ahead of Boston. The two rookies did well, and Kling's two-bagger provided two of the much-needed runs.[13]

On the following day, New York took the final game of the season 5–1 and Chicago fell back into fifth place. Loftus and his players left for Boston to wind up the last eastern invasion with a series of four games with the Beaneaters.

On Sept. 15, the day was cold and the spectators were uncomfortable. Chicago started something in the first, but Boston executed a startling double play, no runs scored.

Kling donned his mask and assumed the squat position with Emslie standing behind him. The outfielders were waiting. The infielders were alert and ready. Menefee was on the mound. Kling signed his pitcher and for the Orphans, the game began.

Chicago did nothing in the first, but got started in the second when Ryan's hot bounder escaped under Collins, and while Duffy loafed after the ball, Ryan stretched the hit to second. After two were out, he scored on McCormick's single. Kling hit safe a moment later but there were no additional tallies.

Menefee's pitch brushed by Lowe in the third inning. Emslie said the ball hit Lowe after he had conducted a post mortem examination and heard expert testimony on the subject. Lowe's being hit resulted in Boston's first line of tallies. Then, Dineen, the pitcher, singled, dumping the ball over second. Hamilton hit safely and Long sacrificed. Stahl hit at Childs near the second base bag. He scooped it up and threw out Dineen at the plate. Kling, in a quick play, fired the ball and nipped Hamilton at third. But Emslie, who had focused his attention at home plate, calling Dineen out, wasn't quick enough to observe the play at third. Hamilton was safe. Having one umpire, and Chicago errors, gave the Boston Beaneaters a 7–3 win and one more rung in the lead for fourth place.[14]

Kling and his teammates had a day off on the following day. There was no game. A secret meeting had been called for baseball magnates and player representatives in Baltimore, Md. The day was spent in conferences where negotiations were held regarding the formation of a new league, the American Association. Capitalists involved in the scheme brought certified checks to show good faith as to their backing for teams in eight cities, one being Chicago.[15]

It was back to baseball on Sept. 17. In game one of a double-header, the battery was Kling and Griffith. A home run by Long gave Selee's sluggers three runs early in the game. In the fourth inning, Kling injured a finger and retired in favor of Dexter. Loftus' men continued their downward slide and lost both games.

Johnny Kling was still out with an injury on the following day. It was the final game with Boston, and Chicago had the game won 5–1 when the sixth inning began. Then, the team lost it by blunders 14–5.

Johnny Kling had been watching the game from the dugout. He saw why the team lost. Dexter had been using too many signals. The infielders had a lot to watch, and the catcher kept them watching him all the time, taking their minds off their other duties and causing them to make blunders. Then and there, he promised himself to make plays when they counted and not to use too many signals.[16]

On Sept. 19, the *Chicago Tribune* carried the story:

TRIP ENDS WITH DEFEAT

After gaining a lead of 5 to 1, Loftus' men allowed the Bean-Eaters to score eight runs on one clean hit. Tonight, Manager Loftus, smiled sardonically and said: 'If they think they can play in Chicago another year, they are much mistaken.' And anyone who reads the details of the defeat, which came after victory seemed easily within the grasp of Chicago, will know whom Loftus meant. He gave no names, but the initials of those he blamed are Clarence Childs, James Ryan, Cunningham and possibly others.

On Sept. 20, the Chicago Orphans arrived in Cincinnati in fifth place with a win-loss of 57–66, no longer in contention for fourth. St. Louis was a shade behind them with 54–66 and the Cincinnati series was crucial.

On the following day, Johnny Kling was again catching; his battery mate was Garvin. During warm-up, Kling saw that this pitcher had some pretty good stuff on the ball and thought they could win today. For a time, it seemed Chicago would win, but panic came in the sixth, and before it was over, Cincinnati had piled up 5 runs on 2 hits, either of which might have been fielded, and the game was hopelessly lost.

Outside of that one inning, the game was rapidly and faultlessly played. The battle between pitchers was keen, but under punishment by errors from his own men, Garvin broke, while Chicago could not hit Hahn with any effect. Final score, 6–5.

Long after the game, Kling wondered why they lost. He examined and thought about his own play in the sixth and finally blamed himself for the loss. He broke up the team. He was responsible for stupid mistakes. He did it by throwing too much. Even though the throws were perfect, he kept the infield moving. He kept them out of position, expecting his throws and studying him instead of watching the batters. He resolved to never make any play, especially a throw, unless absolutely certain that the other men in the play have caught the signal and understood what was to be attempted. And also were prepared to make the play with him.[17]

On Sept. 22, the afternoon was dark. Clouds enveloped the field. Rain seemed imminent. Fewer than a thousand spectators watched the contest as Chicago relieved the monotony of defeat by beating Cincinnati 5–4 and getting a better grip on fifth place.

One terrific drive, a triple by Kling that yielded 3 runs, gave Loftus' men an advantage to which they clung tenaciously for many innings and then, when danger came, John McCarthy, by a great throw to the plate, shut off Corcoran, who was sliding across the rubber with the tying run, thus averting a disaster.

When Corcoran threw himself at the plate where Kling stood with the ball, the rally of the Reds ended. Corcoran arose in a fury and rushed upon Emslie, followed by half a dozen of his fellows. For several minutes they wrangled and quarreled. Presently, they subsided and went peacefully to their defeat. Menefee had profited by his narrow escape and pitched hard ball from then on. McCormick, Kling and Strang were among the Loftusites to distinguish themselves.[18]

When the Cincinnati series was over, Chicago was still in fifth place. Next was a six game series with St. Louis, who was right behind them in the standings. Rowdyism, brawls and "kicking" the umpire furnished the real "sport" of the afternoon in game one. Just before the game started, Childs climbed into the left field bleachers to chastise a spectator who wanted to steal a ball, thereby starting the excitement. And then, two fans had a fight, attracting the crowd who deserted baseball until the battle was over.

But the game was really enjoyable. The Chicagoans acted as if they had forgotten the first elements of the game. Mertes and Green let a ball thrown by the catcher roll between them, neither starting until too late. The entire infield, balled up by Bradley's lack of judgment, let a runner escape. Burkett was put out of the game for calling umpire O'Day names. St. Louis finally won it 8–1.[19]

Although Loftus' men were playing poor baseball, the same could not be said of Johnny Kling and Sammy Strang. On Sept. 29, page 7 of the *Chicago Tribune* told its readers, "The two newest Orphans, Strang and Kling, have been fighting for the batting title of the Chicago team. Strang had a BA of .327, Kling, .326, and the next highest was Frank Chance with .302."

In spite of their hitting, Chicago dropped out of fifth place after losing the first game of a double header to St. Louis on Sept. 30, 4–2. The team recaptured the number five spot by winning the second game 4–1. But the misfortune of the day was in the third inning of game one when Bradley, the third baseman, fumbled the ball. This gave Donovan new life. Wallace followed with a hit that sent Donovan to third. Keister flied to Green, and as the ball fell, Donovan made a dash for the plate. He arrived just as the ball struck Kling's hands, and collided with the catcher with terrific force. Both men were knocked out. Kling was seriously hurt and had to be carried to the clubhouse, where he recovered after a rest. Donovan had an arm injury and one crippled leg.[20]

Johnny Kling could not play on Oct. 1. He watched from the dugout as Mal Eason, a newly acquired hurler from Syracuse, was pitching the Orphans to victory, thus raising Chicago into a more comfortable possession of fifth place.

As Johnny watched, he was storing away memories of the tricks and habits of St. Louis batters. He noted the kinds of balls they hit and where they hit them. He began to see batters change their tactics. One batter who had been hitting slow balls to left field suddenly hit a slow, low one to right. Johnny knew he had to be on the lookout for subtle signs that would tell him when a batter had one intention or the other. For Johnny Kling, every game was a classroom where many lessons had to be learned.

Five days later, Oct. 6, Chicago was still in fifth place with 63–70. St. Louis had 62–72. The final games of the season were to be with Cincinnati in Chicago, and Loftus was bracing for a battle, not only with the Reds but also with his own men. He was going to undertake what Cap Anson was too weak to attempt towards the end of the nineteenth century. He was going to drive a bunch of old-time, tested players off the team. He would fill all their places with men possibly inferior in ability, but vastly superior in willingness and speed, and try to build up a team in Chicago.[21]

4. Setting Sail

Firings had already begun, even before the season ended. A *Chicago Daily News* article in Sporting Extra, Oct. 5, page 1, told the story:

> Bradley and Danny Green visited President Hart's office on Oct. 5. Tom Loftus and Kling entered a few minutes later.
> "When are you and Garvin going to Cuba," asked Mr. Hart of Bradley.
> "Guess we won't go at all," answered the third baseman. "Tim Donohue gave us our releases last night."
> "Don't you get the usual ten days' notice?" queried Loftus.
> "Oh, yes, but Tim was careful to let us know long enough ahead," was the reply.
> "Tim and Callahan are going on the trip with the Brooklyns, but I guess Garvin and I have been knocked out of it. Tommy Leach told me the last time the Pirates were here that Hanlon's men were going to play a series of five games with Pittsburgh as soon as the regular season closed."
> "Where will they be played?" asked Hart.
> "Can't tell," answered Bradley. "Leach said he didn't know himself whether they'd be played in Brooklyn or Pittsburgh. He wants them in the Smoky city, for then he believes Clarke's men can surely take three of them from the Superbas."

The *Chicago Daily News* then had more to say:

> And then Kling and President Hart fell to discussing the relative merits of the various kinds of billiard and pool games. Kling is a shark with the cue, as many of the Chicago ballplayers found to their sorrow before the last trip closed. But he says he doesn't enjoy such play, for they were all too easy.

Two days later, Oct. 7, John T. Brush, owner of the Reds, James A. Hart, owner of the Orphans, and 2,700 half-congealed fans watched the two teams go through two games at the West Side Park and divide the stingy honors.

First Hart smiled as his team won out in the ninth inning after a hard struggle. Then Brush grinned while left fielder Hartsel contributed largely to the overthrow of Chicago and put a damper on Loftus' hopes for fourth place. The final games with Cincinnati began Oct. 8, and the *Chicago Tribune* headlined the event:

LAST GAMES OF CENTURY,
GLOOMY FINISH TO CHICAGO'S
BASEBALL SEASON

> Cincinnati Wins Double-Header From the Orphans, winding Up the Year at West Side Park—Second contest terminates suddenly in an accident—Pitcher Taylor knocked out by line hit in ninth inning and the umpire calls the game.

Chicago's final three games were at Pittsburgh. St. Louis finished up at home against Cincinnati. On Oct. 15 the season was over and Chicago and St. Louis were tied for fifth place with a 65–75 win–loss record, 19 games behind Brooklyn with 82–54.

Rare photograph of Johnny Kling at bat (Acme).

It's amazing the Chicago team did as well as they did. Their four-man pitching rotation was without a big winner. Clark Griffith, who led the league in shutouts with four, was 14–13, the only regular starter above .500. Nixey Callahan was 13–16, Jack Taylor 10–17, Ned Garvin, who had a 2.41 earned run average, second lowest in the league to Rube Waddell, was 10–18. None of Loftus' other six starters won in double figures.

The club's one-time outstanding defense and its "Stonewall Infield" were faint memories. The Orphans were charged with 418 errors. Only the last-place New York Giants committed more. Third baseman Bill Bradley, in his first full big league season, drew 61 errors. Clarence "Cupid" Childs, a veteran second baseman approaching the end of his career, was next with 52 errors. Shortstops Barry McCormick and Billy Clingman had 48 and 34 errors, respectively.[22]

Although Chicago had a gloomy finish, it was glorious for Kling. James Hart released a statement to the press announcing those players who would receive a contract for 1901. Johnny Kling was one of them.[23] In addition, sportswriters had hailed him a star, and he felt good about it. He also felt good about his start in getting to know batters.

Johnny Kling finished the season playing in 15 games with 51 at-bats, 15 hits, 3 of them doubles and one a triple, batting in 7 runs and scoring 8. His BA was .294, PO 48, A 12, and he had a fielding average of .923, a great start for a rookie, and an early indication that his offensive ability exceeded that of most Deadball Era backstops.

In addition, Kling had introduced a style of play that was new for a catcher. In those days it was almost impossible to stop a man on first base from stealing second when there was someone on third. Catchers usually gave second base to the man on first rather than risk the run that seemed sure to score if they threw the ball to second. Thus, a situation of men on first and third almost automatically became one with men on second and third. And of course, this meant two runs would score instead of one if the next batter singled.

Because of his great arm, Kling was a catcher who could handle this problem. He never hesitated to throw to second even in the few games he played in the last weeks of the 1900 season. He broke up three double-steal attempts in three games, and it wasn't long before opposing base runners realized they couldn't take liberties with the rookie from Kansas City.[24]

But the season was over, and he was eager to return home to tell the family how he had done. He was also eager to see how Charles was doing, having gone back to helping papa in the bakery, even doing morning rounds as the "Bread Wagon Chauffeur," Johnny's old job. And he was more than eager to see how Lizzie was getting along, having separated from her husband. But he wasn't at all eager to hear his papa talk about his big brother

Bill, who had gone from ballplayer to tending bar to opening his own saloon, "Kling and Smith," in partnership with William Smith at 1334 E. 18th Street.[25]

Johnny knew how papa felt about smoking and drinking, something he himself looked down upon.[26] And he wondered if Bill's move away from the family to an apartment at 1743 Lydia had anything to do with the opening of this saloon.

Before returning home, Johnny put his name in the Chicago City Directory for 1901: "John Kling, baseball player, bds [boarding house] 638 W. Jackson Blvd." He knew he was here to stay.

5

A Choppy Sea

1901

The 1901 season started with a minor explosion of sorts. Ban Johnson, president of the Western League, was no longer happy with his minor league status. Waiving a committee report put together by Charles Comiskey, Connie Mack and John McGraw, he upgraded his circuit to major league status by eliminating the despicable reserve clause and "stealing" talent away from the National League by paying bigger bucks.

The National League had been behaving like any other monopoly, having imposed a $2,400 cap on salaries. National League players had had enough. They packed their gloves, bats, spikes and other paraphernalia and headed for other ballparks. Hardest hit by these defections was the Chicago team. When the dust had settled, many Chicago players had gone. Sarcastic sportswriters began calling the team "Remnants." But the *Chicago Tribune* called them Colts, so named at the time of Anson, or Orphans, so called after Anson left the team.

James A. Hart didn't care what they called the team. His only concern was attendance. It had dropped from 424,352 in 1898 to 352,130 in 1899 and 248, 577 in 1900. He had to have a winning team in order to draw fans back to the ballpark. And the 1901 season didn't look any too rosy.

Frank Chance was still with the team, but not Tim Donough. He had been let go. The only other catcher besides Kling was Dexter, but Tom Loftus now planned to use him at first. Even Sammy Strang was gone. He jumped to New York. The shortage of men was quite a problem, so much so that consideration was being given to using Chance in the outfield because he could run like the wind, and he was good with the bat. Having him in the game every day would help the team, but Frank Chance insisted he was a catcher. He refused to give up this idea, but if he did, Johnny Kling would have to do all the catching.

On the last day of March, Manager Loftus led the Chicago Nationals—

the Remnants—out of Chicago, to prepare for the season's fray by playing games against the University of Illinois team. Only six players came: Cunningham, Chance, Green, Childs, Eason and Hughes. Captain Doyle went to Hot Springs to urge Callahan to remain true. McCormick went to Cincinnati and did not return to Chicago in time to catch the train. Dexter stayed in Chicago on business. Dolan, Menefee, Kling, Delehanty and Raymer were expected the next day, and the rest would be straggling in within the next two days.[1]

Three days later, a diamond was laid out on the grassy end of the athletic field at the University of Illinois. The regular diamond was too muddy for use, and athletic director George Huff built great fires on it to dry it up. So, the improvised playing field might have to do. But in less than a week, the weather cleared. It became warm, and the regular diamond was back in use. The Chicago Nationals played as if it were midseason and made a fairly good showing, easily winning their first game at Champaign, 14–3.

On the following day big crowds came out hoping to see the varsity revenge themselves, but never once did the collegians have a chance to cheer. Still, Dr. Draper's boys kept slashing away at the ball persistently and made the Remnants hustle in every inning to head off incipient tallies.

The rapid strides made by the team were more than encouraging to Manager Loftus. The men were playing well together. They were hitting and running. They worked in unison. Every morning, a short meeting was held and teamwork was discussed. Loftus wanted the Chicago fans to see some brains on the field and was hoping for more games won if his men were mechanically able to do their part.[2]

By April 11, Chance, McCormick, Kling, Dexter, Doyle and Childs were suffering lame muscles, but the team had advanced so far in hitting and in teamwork, the university varsity were not able to cope. Final score, 8–2.

The following day was completely different. Coach Huff put the varsity team on the bench for a rest before tackling the University of Michigan, and sent in his scrubs, led by Artie Johnston. Inspired by overconfidence, the Remnants started to play in "O-this-is-easy" style, and before they knew what was going on, the scrubs had fallen upon Cunningham's easy twisters and pounded out runs.

The Chicago Nationals had a narrow escape from defeat at the hands of the University of Illinois scrubs, winning out in the ninth inning by virtue of errors and Kling's daring base running, by a score of 7 to 6.[3]

April 13 was the day to examine the Chicago team and to assess their chances for victory in the upcoming season. A staff correspondent for the *Tribune* critically reviewed the abilities of those men who were known quantities—Chance, Childs, Doyle, Dexter, Green and McCormick, and those

5. A Choppy Sea

who were practically untried, and whose qualifications were yet to be put to the supreme test—Raymer, Kling, Delehanty, Hartsel and Dolan.

In the pitching department, Taylor, Menefee and Cunningham were seen as tried, and Eason, Hughes and Waddell as experiments. Each man was reviewed, one by one, on his known capabilities, and then calculations were made as to the team's potential for taking the number one spot.

Some of the players were seen as great, and some had seen better days. When it came to catchers, Chance and Kling were seen as "the best catchers in the National League." The fans were told:

> This is the team to which the Chicago public must pin its hopes of victory in the National League, but it is not as bad as it has been represented on paper. The constituent parts of the team may appear weak but as a whole it may be strong. Teamwork will be depended upon to save the day. Loftus and Doyle have been working hard evolving plans of concerted action and these plans may avail the team much during the season.
>
> There is not left on the team a drunkard, kicker, or sorehead knocker, or alleged star. The team is composed of men willing to work and not above taking friendly advice. It looks like a good team and it may win a lot of games. At least, it will do no worse than the aggregations of supposed stars that have misrepresented Chicago for years.[4]

On April 14 the *Chicago Sunday Tribune* released a financial assessment of all the teams on page 17 of its Sporting section. "Pennant Race Is On Thursday. Outlook Is Cheerless. President Young Predicts Losing Year for All Clubs except Pittsburgh," it said.

> The prospect is at best a gloomy one from the standpoint of the club owners for following what they called a losing year last season. With high salaries, and a certain amount of divided interest this season, it will be difficult to avert a loss all around. With the exception of the Pittsburgh club, I will be agreeably surprised if any of the others pull out on the right side of the ledger, and if this should prove to be the case with the National League, with its ample capital, how can the new American League hope to survive? The Chicago and Boston National League clubs could easily drop $100,000 on the season and not feel it. In fact, I might say, any club in the National League is in a position to lose that much and survive. I doubt if the American is in a position to sink one-quarter of that amount per club in addition to its heavy starting expenses and hold its head above water.[5]

With the gloomy financial forecast for the year, and with the opening of the salary season, Loftus' men, anxious to make a good start toward earning salaries, went out on the Illinois Field on April 15 and defeated the University of Illinois team in the last game of the series, 4 to 0.

Taylor, who made his first appearance in the box for the Remnants, pitched in his best form. The collegians gave their opponents the hardest fight of the series. Kling cut loose and threw beautifully to bases, cutting down two men trying to steal. The only calamity of the day was during practice, when unlucky Chance, unable to handle a foul tip, tore a fingernail loose and was found to be unfit for several days. He had been having a problem handling foul tips since joining the team in 1898.[6]

With Chance disabled, Kling started the first game of the season against the Cardinals at St. Louis on April 19; his battery mate was Jack Taylor. From the outset, this quiet, unassuming youth off the field became a chatterbox behind the plate. He talked constantly, yelling encouragement to his pitcher, warnings to the infielders and subtle insults to opposing batters. His strategy was to get the batter into a conversation and take his mind off the pitch. With all the constant racket, he established his right to the name of Noisy John. And amidst the racket, the Remnants defeated the renovated St. Louis team by a score of 8 to 7 after an exciting struggle and a game full of wild situations.

There was a parade of the clubs in the morning: there were presents of flowers and rounds of applause for the new St. Louis team; there were jeers and hisses for the Chicagoans. Then Doyle's little band of experiments and the remnants of the team of former years went out on the field at Sportsman's Park and, by clear grit and nerve, won a game which any team of Chicagoans for the last ten years would have given up long before it was half played. Before the struggle was over, the 7,000 people in the stands cheered the Remnants and howled praise down upon them, even when disappointment was bitterest.

The lead seesawed back and forth. In the third, Powell, by catching Hartsel's vicious line drive, prevented Chicago from making tallies, and a double play, worked by Kling and Doyle, kept St. Louis from scoring too. In the fourth inning, the commencement of a struggle began which kept the bleachers in an uproar and brought the crowd to its feet in almost every inning until the end of the contest.

Doyle opened with a line hit. Delehanty was hit by a pitched ball. McCormick struck out, but Kling followed with a long drive over Heidrick's head, and after a long run, Kling reached second, while Doyle came home with Chicago's first score of the season, and Delehanty reached third. Taylor flied out to Donovan and Delehanty scored. Childs singled, sending Chicago ahead, and Hartsel flied out to center. But St. Louis came right back and tied the score.

Again, the Remnants fought their way into the lead in the fifth. Doyle and Hartsel, Dolan and Kling, McCormick and Burkett, and Heidrick and Wallace were cheered and cheered again, but the hero of the day was Taylor. He pitched a game which for nerve is hard to exceed. He batted hard and was placed in trying situations by the errors and mistakes of his fellows. Taylor pitched on, game to the core. Finally, in the seventh inning, when the game depended upon what Jesse Burkett did at bat, Taylor gave his greatest exhibition.

Burkett, the premier hitter of the National League, had made three hits. This time, he faced Taylor, determined to wrest victory from the grasp of the Chicagoans. He caught a straight ball squarely on his bat and drove it straight at Taylor. The ball struck the pitcher on the leg, knocked his foot from under him and bounded back. In an instant, Taylor was on his feet, chasing the ball, and by a desperate effort, recovered it in time to throw the fleet Burkett out at first. Then he sank to the ground with two inches of flesh torn from his leg. Even then, Taylor would not quit, but resumed pitching. And although Donovan's team fought desperately, Chicago continued to lead by one run.

When the ninth began, the crowd had been worked up to a state of frenzy. Doyle singled and, remembering the weakness of Nichols, who replaced Ryan in the seventh, Doyle started to steal. He slid straight into the base and beat the ball by more than a foot. But Emslie called him out. Doyle came to the bench telling his troubles to Loftus, and to vindicate himself, Emslie fined Doyle $5.00 and threatened to expel him from the game. Delehanty followed with a hit, which would have scored Doyle. This only aggravated the case because McCormick flied out to Heidrick.

When the Cardinals came in for their last effort to redeem themselves, the entire crowd was on its feet howling for a ninth inning victory. The mighty Burkett was to lead off, but this time Burkett struck out. In the crisis came Emmet Heidrick, who drove the sphere on a line over Hartsel's head. The little recruit turned in pursuit. McCormick tore out to help him relay the ball to the plate. It was a race for victory between Heidrick and Hartsel, two of the speediest men in the business.

Hartsel got the ball against the left field bleachers just as Heidrick turned second and tore on toward the plate. Hartsel shot the ball toward McCormick. Heidrick was turning third. Padden, on the line, was urging Heidrick to greater efforts and spurring him on toward the plate.

McCormick turned and shot the ball on a line toward Kling, who was waiting at the plate. The ball and the man came down the line together. Kling grabbed the sphere and tagged Heidrick on the back as he slid; he was out. The crowd was disappointed.

A moment later, Donovan and McCann raised the drooping spirits by cracking out hits. Then Kling stopped a low pitch. A run would have scored had it got by him. But with a man on second and third, another hit meant defeat in the eleventh hour, and the crowd was on its feet urging Wallace to reclaim the victory. Wallace hit the ball hard and far out to right, but Dolan was crouched under it and the game was over. The first scalp of the season dangled at Taylor's belt.

The playing of the Chicago club was after a style that would be new to Chicago fans. The men fought and hustled every minute, both at bat and in the field, and it was their hard work that won the game.[7]

The following day was cold. A raw wind swept the diamond. The team worked just as hard, but the wildness of Hughes, the errors of Delehanty, the luck of baseball, and a decision by Emslie drew from Loftus' men the howl of "robber."[8]

When the team kept losing, they could not just blame the umpire. The *Chicago Tribune* reported wild misplays, awful mistakes, weak defense, woeful disorganization, "hard luck" and Emslie's umpiring not favoring Chicago. It also reported, "There are some on the team who claim, that in a tight place, Emslie remembers that Doyle roughed it with him in Cincinnati last summer."[9]

By April 28, the Remnants were in last place with a 1–6 record, having lost 4 games at home to the Reds. Johnny Kling was to play on the following day and he had arrived at an important decision. He was going to be friendly with all umpires, siding with them, sympathizing with them, assuring them they were right even if it meant rebuking his own teammates. He had to win the friendship and confidence of umpires. The other players could kick, or rage, and shoot shafts of sarcasm at the umpire, but as catcher, he had to be diplomatic. Should he have any kind of objection, even one that was valid, it would be done in a low, whispered tone.

Kling knew that "getting the corners" would be invaluable to the team. He knew that some umpires called strikes on both corners, some on the outside, some the inside, and some would force the pitcher to put the ball squarely over the plate. By getting friendly with them, he would have a better chance to get a favorable call. And that certainly went for Emslie, who remembered being roughed up by Doyle. That memory would certainly not help the team. Kling knew his attitude would change all that.[10]

The day after Kling had come to this decision, the Orphans finally beat the Reds 9–6. Emslie umpired, and Kling was a gentleman behind the bat. In the fifth, Loftus' men had scored 6 runs, and then only retired on a close decision at the plate. In the ninth, Chance tried to score from second but was called out in a wild slide at the plate. Emslie was right on top of both plays. No one kicked.[11]

The season moved on. By May 7, the team was still in last place with a 5–9 record and it became clear that a major problem existed with Frank Chance's inability to handle foul tips. His injuries were frequent, and on May 20, in a game against Philadelphia, he batted for Waddell in the ninth and again tore the tip off his injured finger. He was taken to Chicago to have the bone in his finger scraped.[12]

Loftus had to have a catcher now. He was determined to get Mike

Johnny Kling at West Side Grounds following through after tossing a baseball (*Chicago Daily News*).

Kahoe, who had announced he would no longer play for Cincinnati. He telegraphed the catcher not to sign with anyone until he saw him in New York. Kahoe however, announced he was jumping to the Philadelphia American League team.[13] But on June 6, Kahoe caught his first game for Chicago, giving Johnny Kling a rest.

During Kahoe's first game, he saw the Remnants at their worst. Twice, Hartsel allowed fly balls to fall safe after preventing others from attempting to catch them. Twice, Childs threw to the wrong base. And on top of these, and several other mistakes, the Remnants added ten countable errors to their already blotted record, in addition to half a dozen more blunders. They forced a victory upon Philadelphia, 14 to 4, and Chicago got some tallies because pitcher Rhoderick Dhu Donohue pityingly lobbed up the ball, letting them make 4 runs and 6 hits.[14]

Overnight, June 7. It was as if a magic spell had been cast upon the Remnants. Page 6 of the *Tribune* reported, "Remnants Quick Form Reversal, Play an Errorless, Brilliant Game and Defeat Philadelphia, 6 to 4.

"It was bunting that turned the trick, bunting and Kling's clever base running. The Remnants needed two runs to win in the eighth, and when McCormick started off with a slashing triple, the crowd foresaw the end and began to cheer. Kling followed with a hit, tying the score. Menefee bunted to Barry, who abandoned third base to throw out Menefee. Dugglesby and Cross forgot to cover third and Kling made a dash, landing on the base in safety, and by his brainy play insuring victory, for he scored on Hartsel's fly. Green rubbed it in by smashing a home run into the right field bleachers."

June 18. The newspaper headline read, "Loftus' Cripples Go East." The injured included "Kling's split hand, Chance and Dexter going on Hobbles, Doyle's incapacitation and Delahanty [sic] out indefinitely."

While on the road, the team did poorly. On June 27, Loftus' men were still in last place and they had just lost a double-header to Philadelphia. Kling did his part, getting 2 singles and 1 triple, scoring a run and stealing a base for the day, but the team was again under a voodoo spell.

July 4. The *Tribune* said, "The fans are preparing to give Loftus' men a royal welcome in recognition of their record-breaking trip, during which they won two and lost thirteen games." The sarcasm did nothing to stir the team, to fire them up to play better baseball. They were still in last place when Pittsburgh took the flag on September 27 by nosing out Brooklyn 5 to 4.

Then Brooklyn came to town to play the last game at the West Side Grounds, and the team lost easily on Sept. 29, 4 to 1. The Remnants made their lone run in the second. After Doyle had walked, an error by Irwin and Kling's single to center scored Doyle. After the game, it was announced that

5. A Choppy Sea

the team would be given a vacation for almost a week. They then would play the last two games of the season on Saturday and Sunday with the champions from Pittsburgh.

Loftus' men were still in last place. In their final two games with Pittsburgh, the Remnants won one, 2 to 1. In New York's final two games with Brooklyn, they lost both, 8 to 0 and 4 to 2. In Cincinnati's final games with St. Louis, they took the first, 3 to 1, and lost the second, 9 to 3. These results squeezed the Chicago team into 6th place, .001 percent ahead of New York and .007 percent ahead of Cincinnati.

The team escaped the cellar by only 1 game with a 52–86 record, 37 games behind first place Pittsburgh. Chicago fans displayed their feelings by staying home. Attendance plummeted from 248,577 in 1900 to 205,071 in 1901. The loss in revenues was disturbing. James A. Hart, owner of the team, had to do something. He just had to fix the problem. And it had to be done now!

Johnny Kling finished the season having caught 69 games with a BA of .265. But most important, and a sign of things to come in his defensive play, were the 398 putouts and 70 assists. Also important was the information he now had on 122 batters in the National League, information that would be invaluable in winning games in 1902. The only player he didn't get to see was Jiggs Donahue, who played in 2 games for Pittsburgh with no at-bats. Maybe he'd get a chance to study Jiggs next year.

Johnny Kling was glad to go home, glad that Charles had gone back to the bakery, helping papa; glad that Lizzie was now running a boarding house, renting out furnished rooms; glad that Louise and Sigesmund were doing well in their new lumber company with their son Victor having joined them in the sales department. But Johnny had mixed feelings about his brother Bill, who was still selling booze. This was a constant source of irritation for Papa, who was still working hard and getting up in years.

6

CHARTING A COURSE

1902

James A. Hart desperately wanted a winner. He paid close attention to the successful twelve-year managerial career of Frank Selee, a former haberdasher and longtime skipper of the Boston Nationals who never played in a major league game. Hart was impressed by the five pennants this man had won in the 1890s while finishing only once below .500. Hart knew that Selee's contract was due to expire at the end of the 1901 season. As soon as the season ended, Hart signed him for 1902. Hart knew that his new manager had tuberculosis, but Selee seemed to be on the mend and doing well.

Johnny Kling was aware of the new manager coming aboard and kept abreast of new players being signed: Jimmy Gardner, a pitcher from Pittsburgh; and Joe Tinker, his old friend, a fantastic third baseman who played with the Bruce Lumbers, a team that beat Kling's Schmeltzers in 1898. In 1899, Johnny Kling, manager of the Schmeltzers, traded two uniforms and a bat for Tinker. The two played together and became friends.[1]

When the players arrived at the 1902 spring training camp in Champaign, Illinois, they were greeted by a slender man with a thick, shaggy, walrus type mustache bidding them welcome. They suited up and went onto the field, tossing and batting the ball around. As he watched them, Selee knew that the only way to build a team was to focus on the young. He wanted his youngsters to be aggressive and high-spirited, so that's exactly what he looked for. He knew each player's background and potential.

In talking with sportswriters who visited the camp, Selee emphasized youth in rebuilding the team. One newspaper liked the idea of youngsters playing the game and began referring to the team as Cubs. Selee didn't want that name. He liked Colts, as in the days of Anson, and was happy that the *Chicago Tribune* continued using it.[2]

Selee knew talent. He had a keen sense of knowing what position a player should play and why. To play for Selee, a player not only needed to

6. Charting a Course 49

be aggressive and high-spirited, but he had to be bold and smart as well.

As Selee watched the team practice, he began to size up each man. He was determined to whip the team into shape, starting immediately. Selee knew about Joe Tinker, a 5-foot, 10-inch, 175-pound third baseman who helped Portland win the pennant in the Pacific Northwest League. He knew about his brilliant fielding and his solid .290 batting average. Watching Joe at third, he noted his ability to cover a wide expanse of ground, his sure hands, his quickness and his strong arm as he fired the ball to first. Selee knew Tinker would be one great shortstop. After a lengthy discussion, Joe agreed to give it a try with the understanding that if he didn't do well, he'd go back to third.

Selee turned his attention to Kling. He was keenly aware of his ability to throw with accuracy and speed from a crouched position. Behind the plate, he appeared calm and confident; he was relaxed and seemed comfortable in the squat position. He handled foul tips with aplomb, and he sure had hustle. Kling was also smart, knew how to handle pitchers and could hit well and run. Kling had everything. But there were other catchers: Kahoe, Chance and Zalusky. They too wanted a shot at the backstop position.

Shifting his thoughts to other positions, Selee believed Bobby Lowe had second sewed up. Dexter could be used at third until a better man was found. Jimmy Slagle, who had just been brought up from Boston, was solid in center, as was Miller in left. Congalton or Jones could be used in right until a better man was found. As for pitchers, time would tell.

Selee arranged practice games with the University of Illinois in Champaign, and one game with the pennant winners of the Terre Haute "Three Eye" league. Chance and Zalusky were used as backstops for most of the games, and it became evident early on that Frank Chance would never learn to handle foul tips. As for John Zalusky, he was unable to throw well to second — an absolute must for a catcher. Zalusky had to go.

Chance, when asked to play first, insisted he was a catcher. At first he refused to back down. Selee reasoned with Chance. He praised his hitting and his ability to steal bases, and explained the need for the team to have him in every starting lineup. Selee emphasized the contribution he would make to the winning of games. As a last resort, Selee offered to pay him more money to show he was really needed.

Finally, a deal was struck. Chance agreed to play first if he was also allowed to catch. Selee agreed, instinctively knowing that once Chance saw how great he was as a first sacker, nothing would ever tear him away from that position.[3]

Selee now had Kling as his starting catcher. Kahoe would be a backup. As the practice games progressed with the Illini, the Remnants began to shape up and win games in grand style: 13 to 6 on April 9, 14 to 6 on April 11, 6 to 5 on April 13 at Terre Haute and 4 to 1 back in Champaign. And Frank Chance started some of the games as backstop.

"Tinker played at his new position and handled himself in great style,"[4] the *Tribune* reported. As for Kling, he was pounding the ball hard, getting hits — singles and a triple — and scoring runs.[5]

On Tuesday, April 15, Charley Dexter found himself on the bench during the last Cubs' practice game while Germany Schaefer assumed the responsibilities of the third base position.[6] Dexter had not been doing well at third, showing weakness and making errors that were sure to lose games.[7]

Frank Selee watched the last valedictory game with interest. His scholars completed their preliminary schooling and he now had to select the best pupils and to pit them against Biddy McPhee's Reds on Thursday.

Sportscasters predicted a runaway race with Pittsburgh taking the flag because its team of veterans was left intact in a circuit that had been riddled by the rival American League. But the war between the two leagues was over and from the opinions expressed by the other seven managers, the aggregation put together by Manager Selee was looked upon as the most promising candidate for second honors.[8]

President James A. Hart agreed. "I think we have a team that should be well up in the race," he said. "The youngsters, from present appearances, look to be excellent players and the club may prove to be a winner."[9]

The season opened in Cincinnati on April 17; the batteries were Taylor and Chance for Chicago, Swormstedt and Berger for Cincinnati. Although Kling was on the bench, he began to study the opposing batters as he did in 1901. First man up was Dummy Hoy, a center fielder from the American League, a player he had never seen before. For 1901, Hoy had a BA of .293. With 23 doubles, 11 triples and 2 homers with 60 RBIs and 30 stolen bases, he was a formidable foe. Kling knew he could not distract this man with behind-the-bat chatter because Hoy was deaf and mute. Dummy would have to be defeated by figuring out the pitch that he would not be able to hit.

As the game moved on, Erve Beck, another player he had never seen, came to the plate. He was with Cleveland in 1901 and had a wonderful year with the lumber. Kling studied his grip, his hold of the bat and his feet in the box, and he knew this man's intentions. He also knew that if the pitcher were to throw at Erve's head, Beck would have to change his plan of attack.

Johnny Kling had studied all the other players the previous year and began to understand how to sign the pitcher, how to keep opposing batters from getting hits. But as he watched the game, he knew there would be times when strategies would not be so crucial. His teammates were clobbering the Redlegs and won the game 6 to 1.

The sportswriters summed it all up with, "Chicago's Youngsters Hit

Ball Cleanly and Make Brush Outfit Look Cheap. The Twentieth Century Colts Played Rings Around McPhee's Men."[10]

Although they won, the game again pointed out the weak spot at third. The Reds scored their only run because Dexter picked up Hoy's grounder and had so much time to spare that he didn't know what to do with it, so he tried to hit the grandstand and bound the ball back to O'Hagen in time. Hoy reached second and was sacrificed to third, and scored when Jake Beckley bruised Jack Taylor's shin with a sizzler.

The club was beginning to shape up but it still had many frayed edges. Selee knew he had work to do. He would ask George Huff, his friend and athletic director at the University of Illinois, to find star players to shore up the weak spots. Huff was one of the best baseball scouts around and Selee knew the job would get done.

As he watched his men finish the series with the Reds, they had a 3–1 record, and Chance continued to have problems behind the plate. Yet, Selee continued to put him in as backstop. The only time Kling played was in the third game, April 19, in the ninth inning when Chance was thrown out of the game for kicking on a strike. Kling proceeded to get a hit, but in the last game with Cincinnati, Chance was again catching.

Johnny Kling's first start was April 24 against Pittsburgh. And the team beat the Pirates 5 to 3, taking over the first slot with a 6–1 record. But Selee continued to use Chance behind the plate. For the future, however, Selee knew Chance would handle first. Although it was 1902, Frank Selee was experimenting. He was gearing up for 1903.

Hal O'Hagen was tried at first even when Chance was not catching. Schaefer took over third. Dexter was tried at first and in the outfield. Joe Tinker settled in at short and seemed to have that position sewed up. He instinctively knew where the ball was headed the moment it struck the bat. He became a fighter, no longer the genial and good-natured guy when off the field. The transformation was remarkable.

The season moved forward. By May 10, the team was in second place. The game with New York was going quite well with Kling having hit two doubles and having made two double plays, Kling to Lowe and O'Hagen to Kling, on the way to beating the Giants 5 to 0.

On June 6, Chicago was still in second place with a 23–14 record, trailing the Pirates, who had 32–7. The youngsters beat Brooklyn that day by a terrific batting streak in the fourth. After Congalton had been retired, Kling doubled to deep center and Schaefer pasted out a triple. Captain Lowe followed with a single and stole second, and then little Tinker did not do a thing but make a home run. This quartet of runs proved enough to win 6 to 3. When the opposition threatened to produce more tallies, a double play from St. Vrain to Kling to Dexter smothered the attempt.

August 14 saw the Chicago Colts in third place with 51–44, trailing Brooklyn with 55–44. That day saw the youngsters beat the Beaneaters 6 to 2 with Kling pumping out a nice three bagger and scoring on Dahlen's fumble of Ward's return throw.

But their winning ways did not continue. On August 20, the *Chicago Tribune* headlined an article, "Colts Still on the Down Grade." Two days later, they were in fourth place with a 51–51 record, Boston having moved into third with 52–47.

Nevertheless, the team was doing better than the year before. Carl Lundgren, a new pitcher, was doing fairly well, winning one, then losing one in spite of a low ERA. Jack Taylor as usual was the workhorse, doing far better than in 1901 when he was 13–19 with an ERA of 3.36. If he kept up his current pace he would have a great year.

As for infielders, Chance was solid at the plate. He showed his speed by leading the team in stolen bases. Best of all, he didn't object when Selee started putting him at first on a more frequent basis, allowing Kling to take over behind the plate full time.

Tinker was something else! Although his batting average was not that great, he did much better in a clutch, always getting a hit with men on base. Late in the season, he and Kling were neck and neck with 46 RBIs, far ahead of the rest of the team.

Bobby Lowe, the captain and second baseman, continued his excellent glove work at second. He also showed some power with his 11 doubles, 1 triple and 3 homers. In the final weeks of the season, Lowe sustained an injury but still could play. Selee demanded another infielder just in case. At this time, a number of big league scouts were trying to appraise the value of Troy's star pitcher and a Chicago scout received Selee's urgent request on August 31.[11]

Johnny Evers had just finished a game, but his thoughts were not completely on baseball. He had buried his father on August 24. He'd been feeling down. But when offered the opportunity of reporting to the Chicago team, he said goodbye to his teammates and left Troy with only a handbag. He dozed in the uncomfortable "smoker" all the way to New York. When the train came to a stop at the Forty-second Street station, Johnny leaped out and found his way to the Pennsylvania terminal to Jersey City and boarded a train for Philadelphia.

The Chicago team was concluding a series in Philadelphia. When Johnny was dropped off, he was met by an emissary from Manager Selee. Without a moment for rest or food, he was hurried to the Junction Hotel, where he slipped into an oversized uniform. On September 1, he boarded a bus to join the team.

Frank Selee wanted to get a look at this nineteen-year-old shortstop

6. Charting a Course

who threw right-handed and batted left, this scrappy little kid from Troy weighing a little over 100 pounds with a wet towel around his waist. This frail wonder boy, skinny as a rail, had powered a triple only yesterday. As Johnny's name was put down on the roster, some of the older players wondered if Selee had gone wacky, putting in a kid destined to be carried off the field on a stretcher.

Selee saw it differently. He was impressed by what he had heard about little Johnny Evers, and he needed another infielder. So he juggled his lineup. Johnny was to play short, Tinker moved to third, Lowe remained at second to see if he was still fit to play and Jocko Menefee took over first. Chance was out with an injury.[12]

The two double-headers with Philadelphia resulted in Selee's men taking only one game, and on September 5, Tinker was back at short, Evers was at second and Lowe was given a rest. The team had slipped to fifth with 57–60 and Selee's hope of finishing above .500 was rapidly going downhill.

Johnny Kling had been hitting, stealing and scoring, and had been moved up to the number three spot in batting. But in spite of this, the team did not win. His three hits on September 3 against Brooklyn resulted in a whitewash, Chicago losing 4 to 0. By September 12, the team was still fifth with 60–64 and on their way home.

The Colts celebrated their return home by giving the St. Louis Cardinals an awful drubbing at the West Side Grounds, 12 to 0, Kling leading the way with 3 hits, including a double. But a twin bill with the Reds on September 14 resulted in a twin loss and a slim chance of finishing in the first division.

With Kling slamming the ball, Selee moved him into the cleanup slot for the last game with the Reds on Sept. 15 and Johnny proceeded to lead the team to a 6–3 victory, getting 2 hits, including a double, and scoring 2 runs.

On Sept. 28, in the last two games at the West Side Grounds, Selee was still experimenting. Tinker was moved to third, Evers to short and Schalfaly was tried at second. Chance was now at first full time. Menefee, a pitcher who covered first when Chance was out with an injury, was now in right field. Kling continued to bat fourth.

The Colts won the double-header 4–2 and 4–1, Kling again leading the way. In the first game, he scored one run and his timely double in the seventh scored Dobbs and Chance. In the second game, Kling's double in the fourth drove in Dobbs and Slagle. For the day, Kling had 5 hits and scored 1 run. He turned out to be a good clean up hitter.

The season was rapidly coming to a close and Chicago could not move into the first division. In their final two games at St. Louis on Oct. 5, Chicago won game one, 11 to 4, and won an agreed upon five inning game two, 6 to

5. Kling got 4 hits for the day and scored 1 run, the last tally being made in the last of the fifth.

Chance started the fifth with a double and went to third on a passed ball. Kling's safe fly to right scored him. Kling started to steal, and a wild throw by Weaver sent him to third. Smoot fumbled the ball and it was then too late to catch Kling at the plate.

The game was interesting in that Selee continued to experiment to the very end. In the first game, Kling batted in the cleanup spot, but in the second game, he batted ninth and the pitcher, Williams, batted fourth.

Overall, the team did better than in 1901 when they finished a miserable sixth. And Selee was pleased even though he did not achieve a .500 win-loss, having missed it by .004. Chicago fans must have also been pleased since attendance climbed from 205,071 to 263,700. The increase in revenues made owner James Hart happy. He readily agreed to have George Huff, at the University of Illinois, scout around for new players and Selee knew there would be new youngsters on the field in 1903.

The 1902 club showed solid contours taking shape. Frank Chance was now at first full time, a position he at first disdained. Joe Tinker, a brilliant fielder, was at short, and tough, aggressive Johnny Evers was solid at second. The backstop position was firmly in the hands of Johnny Kling, having caught 112 games during the season.

Kling's stats, when compared to other starters, were impressive:

	G	AB	R	H	2B	3B	H	RBI	SB	BA
Chance	73	236	40	67	8	4	1	31	28	.284
Lowe	119	472	41	116	13	3	0	31	16	.246
Tinker	133	501	54	137	17	5	2	54	28	.273
Schaefer	81	291	32	57	2	3	0	14	12	.196
Jones	64	243	41	74	12	3	0	14	12	.305
Dobbs	59	235	31	71	8	2	0	35	3	.302
Slagle	115	454	64	143	11	4	0	28	40	.315
Kling	113	434	50	124	15	6	0	57	23	.286

The games played were in more than one position.

Having caught more than 100 games in 1902, Johnny Kling was now a premier catcher. His defensive play can be judged by his 477 putouts and 160 assists. But with the baseball season over, his thoughts were elsewhere. Shooting pool. Once back home, that is what he focused on as he prepared for tournament play. And on December 7, 1902, page 36 of the *Washington Post* reported, "Johnny Kling, the Chicago National's backstop, and T. Heuston, are in the thick of a 750-point pool match at Kansas City for $250. Heuston is the champion of St. Louis and Kling is the best conjurer of the ivories among the ball-playing contingent."

The outcome of the match could not be found in future editions of the *Washington Post*. But what was found were numerous articles clearly demonstrating Kling's ongoing involvement and expertise in handling a cue stick. He seemed as fond of billiards as he was of baseball. Both sports earned him a livelihood. But would the demands of one sport interfere with the demands of the other? If so, would this create serious problems? Time would tell.

1903

Johnny Kling must have greeted the new year with a measure of contentment and absolute joy. Papa and mama were doing well in the bakery and grocery. Charles decided to become a baker, and with papa's help was doing well. Liz seemed satisfied running the boarding house and had adjusted to the separation from her husband. Although Bill continued running his saloon, there was less tension between him and papa. And best of all, he had fallen in love with a 22-year-old beauty, a pretty thing from Salena, Kansas. Lillian May Gradwohl had captured his heart the moment he saw her. Johnny knew that she was the one. He didn't want to rush things, he'd wait awhile. From the way she had cozied up to him he knew she'd say yes.

Then there was baseball and billiards, the two things he loved. Everything seemed to be falling into place. Reporters were even writing flattering articles about him. Others were calling to verify a rumor. Almost overnight, it seemed as if he had become famous. One article said, "Johnny Kling, the star catcher of the Chicago National league has been signed by Manager McKibben to play the coming season with Tacoma in the Pacific-Northwest league. Kling is rated as one of the best catchers in the business."[13]

Another article six days later in another newspaper said, "Reports from Tacoma assert that Johnny Kling, the clever backstop of the Chicago Nationals has signed with Tacoma. Kling is rated as one of the greatest catchers in the baseball business and last year caught nearly all the games for the 'Windy City aggregation.'"[14]

These rumors were set straight when Johnny Kling was interviewed. The headline reported, "Kling Denies He Has Jumped. Brands Story That He Will Play Baseball at Tacoma Next Season as False. Will Stay Here."[15]

Rumors about Johnny Kling were abounding. On Feb. 5, the *Chicago Tribune* floated a story on page 7 saying, "Johnny Kling, the baseball catcher who has signed for the next season with the Chicago National league club, has almost decided to retire from the game and open a tailoring establishment in Kansas City." But the rumors subsided, and Kling began participating in the two things he loved.

On March 25, 1903, a news item said:

> Johnny Kling, Chicago's crack catcher, who has been opening wide the eyes of local sports by his remarkable skill as a pool player, went down to defeat last night in the presence of a crowd of enthusiastic spectators at the Hoffman club in a match game of three-cushion billiards with Walter Johnson, a local saloon man. The game was for 50 points, $50 a side. Quite a bit of money was put up by the onlookers in side bets. Johnson beat Kling 50 to 43, the game lasting two and one-half hours. The best run was 4, and both men scored it.
>
> After the billiards, Kling and Johnson played a match game of bank pool, Kling giving Johnson odds of 25 to 21. Kling won by a score of 25 to 17. The game was for $25 a side, and about $100 was wagered by spectators.
>
> Kling bars nobody on pool, and Johnson is known on the Coast as a crack billiard player.[16]

A week later found the now famous backstop in Colorado catching in the first exhibition game against the Denver Western league, batting third, getting 2 hits, scoring 2 runs and leading the team to a 6–3 win.[17] After polishing off Denver, the team moved to Omaha and Kling continued pounding the ball, getting 2 hits, including a triple, scoring 2 runs and leading the team to a 9–0 win. The team continued winning. The Colts looked good as April 15 and the regular season opener drew near.

The team as a whole had become closer, and Johnny Kling, in addition to his old friend Joe Tinker, had become friendly with other players, including Frank Chance. His familiars jocularly called him the Jew and saw their backstop as one of the shrewdest catchers of all time. He was a fine thrower, and it was positively uncanny the way he would trap unwary runners off the bases, especially when working in collaboration with Johnny Evers and Joe Tinker, the keystone guardians of the team.[18]

On April 15, the weather vetoed baseball plans in St. Louis and the Colts went off to the races, attending the inaugural at Kinloch. Johnny Kling and Chance did the heavy gambling and both were losers up to the final race when Dick Padden, of the St. Louis Browns, steered them on to Pay the Fiddler at 7 to 1 odds. The "tip" put Kling and Chance to the good. In the evening all the players were well distributed among the various theaters. Manager Selee remained around the Southern Hotel where the Colts were staying.

"This is tough," he declared after dinner. "This cold spell is doing us no good."[19] But the drop in temperature didn't hurt the team one bit. They won more than they lost, and after hammering three Reds' twirlers on April 27, the team was in a tight race with New York who was first with 6–2, then Pittsburgh 7–3 and Chicago 6–3.

Yet, in spite of playing good ball, there may have been a problem on the team. On April 29 it was reported that "Jack Menefee will not be in shape to work in any of the series. He hurt his arm in a little boxing bout with

Kling at the Chicago clubhouse some days ago. His wing hurt him, so yesterday he went to Dr. Walker, who diagnosed his trouble as a slight strain."[20]

The newspaper account offered no explanation for the incident. Was the fight in jest? If not, it had to have been about something serious. Kling was not known as a man to resort to fisticuffs, and it would have taken a fair amount of provocation to push him over the precipice.

But it had become common knowledge that Johnny Kling was being regarded as the most important cog in the Cub machine. A greater amount of responsibility rested on his shoulders than any other player on the team. By working every day he had learned the peculiarities, the weaknesses and strengths, of opposing batsmen better than the pitchers who performed every fourth game or so. With men on base, not only did he have to keep his mind on the batsmen, but he also had to watch the runners like a cat to detect the next move of the attacking team. In essence, he had to be the brainiest player on the team. And the "little boxing bout" may have been due to a disagreement between the catcher and pitcher. We will never know.

Be that as it may, the team moved on and Johnny Kling was catching every day. By May 12, Chicago held the number two spot with a win-loss of 14–8, trailing New York's 14–4. On that same day, page 9 of the *St. Louis Star* said, "Johnny Kling has broken up more games at St. Louis than any other man on the Chicago team. He strikes out when the bases are empty. But in a pinch he has a bad habit of spoiling nice games by tearing off a long hit. He certainly plays the game behind the bat and on the bases."

Johnny Kling lived up to his reputation. On May 13, he again led the team to a 6–2 win against Brooklyn, getting 3 hits, including a triple and homer, and scoring 1 run. In addition, he was still cutting down traffic on the base paths with a double play from Harley to Kling to Wicker.

Page 8 of the May 14 *Tribune* said, "Selee's Colts continue to sweep everything before them, and today won their eighth consecutive victory by defeating Brooklyn in the second game of the series by a score of 3 to 1." Notes of the game said, "Strang stole a base today, the first one made on Kling." Imagine! After a month of season play, a base had finally been stolen against Johnny Kling. This attests to his ability to mow down runners trying to steal, a very big factor in winning ball games.

May 19 saw the Colts in the number one spot with 19–9, Johnny Kling continuing to play good ball. President James A. Hart was ecstatic. Attendance was rising. To show his appreciation, he had Selee take his young men to the best hat store in town and had them pick out the best Panama in the place with his compliments.[21]

The Colts continued winning and Johnny Kling led the way. On April 25, the team captured the final game against the Phillies, Kling getting 3 hits, including a double, and scoring 2 runs. Away from home the Colts had now won 16 out of 17 games.[22]

On June 5, page 9 of the *Washington Post* reported, "Johnny Kling has done all the back-stopping for Chicago this season, and his all-around clever work has been a big factor in the team attaining its present high position." But New York had been keeping pace with Chicago, and on June 12 they climbed into first place.

The Colts continued to slide. On July 23 they beat Cincinnati 5–2 with Kling getting 2 hits, including a triple, and scoring 1 run. The team ended the day with 50–33, still in third place behind second place New York's 47–30. Three days later the Colts inched up into the two spot with 52–35.

By August 6, Chicago was still in second place, and Johnny Kling was playing at his best. In the eighth, when Wagner foolhardily tried to steal third with one out and his team seven runs behind, Kling threw him out. Wagner made such a kick, he was chased from the game. The Colts won 9–2. Kling had 2 hits and scored 2 runs.

August 22 saw a struggle between Chicago and New York for second place, and Kling continued to use his talents in winning games. In the sixth, Mertes was thrown out trying to steal second, and for the day Kling had 2 assists. With Chance and Jones on base in the third, Noisy John tripled, driving home two runs. The Colts ended the day with an 8–3 win, still in second place.

On Sept. 11, page 8 of the *Chicago Tribune* reported, "Manager Selee and his Colts returned yesterday from their trip to Pittsburgh, happy in the possession of the scalps of the champions, whom they have beaten out in the season's series, confident of winning out in the fight with New York for second place." But it was not meant to be. In spite of Johnny Kling's continued prowess at the plate and his great defensive plays, the Colts could not keep pace with New York's momentum.

On Sept. 24, Johnny Kling was unable to play. He went back home to Kansas City because his injured finger proved too painful to permit him to catch, but he was expected back for the White Sox series.[23] Kling's absence was sorely felt. On Sept. 26, with Tommy Raub behind the plate, Sunday's *Tribune* Sporting section reported careless running by Boston basemen and "getting away with it on account of Raub's ineffective throwing to bases, seven bases being stolen off him," the Colts losing by a score of 4 to 3.

Chicago finished the season in third place with 81–56, two games behind New York's 84–55, but Chicago's record in 1902 was 68–69, and the rise in the standings reflected Selee's hard work in rebuilding the team. The fans were happy. Attendance climbed from 263,700 to 386,205 and President Hart wasted no time in issuing a press release: "President Hart of the Chicago National league club yesterday announced that he had offered a

6. Charting a Course

John Kling waiting for his turn to bat at West Side Grounds (*Chicago Daily News*).

substantial prize for the Colts if they win the coming Series with the White Sox. The announcement was made to the players in a letter to Manager Selee."[24]

The series ran 14 games, each side winning seven. Some of Jack Taylor's losing performances were suspect. Had he thrown games? Although never proven, Selee traded him that winter to the Cardinals as part of a deal that brought the Colts the man who would become a remarkable pitcher: Mordecai "Three Finger" Brown. His nickname came about as a result of an accident with a corn shredder that had no mercy for this young man. That nasty piece of equipment tore off his index finger and damaged his pinky and middle finger. But fate took a strange turn. As a result of this injury, "Three Finger" Brown was able to throw a curveball with an exceedingly sharp downward break, forcing batters to hit ground balls that Johnny Kling would use to advantage in his defensive style of play. He and Brown would soon become battery mates and new records were on the horizon.

Kling's stats when compared to the other starters were very impressive:

	G	AB	R	H	2B	3B	H	RBI	SB	BA
Chance	125	441	83	144	24	10	2	81	67	.327
Evers	124	464	70	136	27	7	0	52	25	.293
Tinker	124	460	67	134	21	7	2	70	27	.291

	G	AB	R	H	2B	3B	H	RBI	SB	BA
Casey	112	435	56	126	8	3	1	40	11	.290
Harley	104	386	72	89	9	1	0	33	27	.231
Jones	130	497	64	140	18	3	1	62	15	.282
Slagle	139	543	104	162	20	6	0	44	33	.298
Kling	132	491	67	146	29	13	3	68	23	.297

Johnny Kling was once again a premier catcher, having caught 132 games. His 565 putouts and 189 assists demonstrated great defensive play. But the season was over and it was time to head back home where his sweetheart, Lillian, was waiting.

7

WEATHERING STORMS

1904

On January 3, 1904, a news item under "Baseball Gossip," page ES 12 of the *Washington Post*, listed "Players Who Do Not Idle Away the Winter Months but Engage in Lucrative Business." One such player was Johnny Kling. It said, "The crack catcher of the National League is one of the best pool experts in the country, and doubles his diamond income by winter exhibition with the ivories."

Although busy with the cue stick, Johnny still found time for romance. On Jan. 19, Chicago fans learned that their famous backstop had fallen victim to the contagion for marrying that had attacked other players on the team. "Invitations had been received that announced the wedding of the noted backstop to Miss Lillian May Gradwohl in Kansas City on Jan. 27," the *Tribune* reported.[1]

On that date, Johnny and Lillian were married by Rabbi Harry H. Mayer, the spiritual leader of B'nai Jehudah Temple in Kansas City, Missouri. The newlyweds then hurried off to Los Angeles for their honeymoon.

Manager Selee and his team also headed toward Los Angeles. It was time for spring training and the newspaper carried the story. It told of new players joining the team: catcher O'Neil, and pitchers, Brown, Corridon and Briggs. It also informed its readership that "Johnny Kling, when he arrives, will bring a wife with him, having married a Kansas City girl."[2]

Lillian Kling, the Kansas City girl who was born in Salena, Kansas, certainly enjoyed her honeymoon. It was fun and frolic, and getting to know Johnny Kling during weeks of spring training. She also watched her husband shoot pool in the much talked about Kling-Carney match. After that, she returned to Kansas City as the team headed out for a series of exhibition games.[3]

The first game was in Denver. Although Kling was in the game for a short time, "he seemed to be as well as ever," a news item said. The *Chicago*

Marriage license for John Kling and Lillian Gradwohl (Jackson County, Missouri, Courthouse).

7. Weathering Storms 63

Daily News began calling the team "Cubs" as it told of their first win on March 28 by a score of 11 to 9. But the *Tribune* continued calling them Colts.

The Colts were doing well, but on April 2 they were beaten by Denver 2 to 1. Chance attacked umpire Davis for calling him out at second, and it took the other players to put an end to the battle.[4] Johnny Kling knew this was no way to win the friendship and confidence of umpires, no way to win ball games. He remembered the incident where Doyle had roughed up umpire Emslie, and in a tight situation the umpire favored the other team. Being friendly, siding with them, sympathizing with them and assuring them they were right even if it meant rebuking his own teammates had become a routine for Kling. But he did not rebuke the husky first baseman who had a way with his fists.

Selee's men were shaping up as they won the last exhibition game from Omaha 8 to 2. The one mishap was in the fourth inning when Miller slid for the plate feet first. O'Neil, who was catching, put him out, but was badly spiked. The fourth toe on his left foot was nearly cut off and Kling finished the game.[5]

Immediately after the game the Chicagoans hustled to catch a 5:50 train for Chicago. Arrival time was 7:30 the following morning and the team was scheduled to leave in the evening to open the season.

On the train, Selee talked of Chicago's chances for the pennant and thought his players had a great chance for the flag. "We are strong in batteries," he said. "Our staff of pitchers is a good one. It is stronger than last year, as is the team generally. Every one knows the fight we made then. We shall make a harder fight this year.

"The Chicago men are all in fine shape physically and are working well and harmoniously together. All the men are anxious to open the season and begin the fight for the pennant."[6]

The players were all primed for the long race with the exception of O'Neil, who had been spiked and would remain home for at least a week. But it wasn't long before the team found themselves incapacitated. McCarthy, Corridon, Wicker and Brown were down with bad colds. Kling hurt his back in Cincinnati and on top of that, he had a split finger. Slagle too had a severe finger injury to his catching hand. Chance was hardly able to get around with his right leg in bad shape and Selee needed a catcher, so Frank Chance had to stand behind the bat even though it was painful, and Frank Corridon, a pitcher, had to cover first.[7]

Mrs. Kling and Mrs. Tinker joined the team for a short stay, coming from Kansas City.[8] Joe Tinker was ill, as were others, and the two wives may have wanted to render tender loving care (TLC). In fact, the entire team could have used TLC, including Manager Selee. His tuberculosis had flared up again. Needing more rest, he began handing the reins of authority over to his first baseman.

When snow hit the ground in St. Louis, Manager Selee hustled his players out of bed in the morning of April 20 and told them to make ready to go home at noon. Not one had a word of objection to the offer. Selee wanted them home in the evening to get a good night's rest. He was hoping that the St. Louis snowstorm would find its way to Chicago and give his men at least two additional days of leisure.

"The weather man has certainly come to our rescue," Selee said. "The team is in such a dilapidated condition that defeat was the inevitable result for every game played. Doc Casey was slated to do the back stopping today but he has caught only two games in six years."[9] Yet, the third baseman was put behind the bat. He did so poorly that a local man, named Holmes, had to take over the backstop position. By April 24, the team was tied for sixth with a win-loss record of 3–5, one game ahead of last place Philadelphia's 2–6.

Kling was back April 27. The premier catcher had completed three full seasons of play in the National League. He had experience. He knew every batter in the league, and knew what he had to do to get them out. He knew his own infield. The Tinker to Evers to Chance double play combination had drawn the attention of fans and sportscasters alike. And he knew his pitchers. All he had to do now was put it all together into a winning combination.

By May 10, Chicago was in third place with 10–7 and its catcher was praised. "There are few backstops in the business today who show up better than Kling, the star catcher of the Chicago National League team," the news item said. "When one considers his catching, throwing, coaching and hitting, he is almost in a class by himself."[10]

On May 15 Manager Selee was juggling the lineup, using his men as best as he could. O'Neil was back catching. Wicker, a pitcher, was in center field, Kling was in left. Juggling of positions continued and on the last day of May, "Manager Selee reported that the team was pretty much crippled up. O'Neil and Kling were suffering from injuries and Capt. Chance had a badly bruised head from being hit by a pitched ball in Cincinnati.

"Manager Selee announced that he expected Alec Smith, the old time catcher, to join the team and would play at once."[11] The new backstop reported but Selee decided to use him only if Kling and O'Neil could not manage to play even with their injuries.

In spite of colds and all the other maladies, Selee demonstrated his genius as a manager by using his men in positions they customarily did not play. He kept the Colts near the top. And on June 3, the team moved into first place after beating Philadelphia 4–3. But they lost the lead on June 6.

7. Weathering Storms

The team dropped to third, edged up to second and by July 5, Selee's men were in bad shape once again. Injuries and other handicaps were back again, with Kling and Tinker finding it difficult to play a good game.

Nevertheless, the team pushed on. By July 30, the Colts and Reds were fighting for second place. In the fourth game of their series, they battled for eight full innings without a run. Then, Selee's men broke ground, and with three errors in the ninth, tossed victory into Cincinnati's basket by a score of 2 to 0.

Huggins, who was entirely recovered from his hard knock in the head of the day before, led off in the sorry ninth with a pretty bunt, which Casey grabbed and shot to first in time. But Otto Williams tried to catch it on a slippery spot in his mitt and dropped the ball. Seymour followed with a sacrifice. Peitz was passed. Brown steamed up here and put the ninth strikeout to his record by fanning Odwell. As Manager Kelley had already struck out twice in previous rounds, it looked safe enough, but Joseph fooled them all by driving a hot roller between Casey and Tinker, which broke up the game. Slagle came tearing in to cut off Huggins at the plate but the hit went through him. Before the dust settled, Peitz had also scored from first. Tinker fumbled on Corcoran's grounder, which did no damage, as Kling ended the round by working the hoary old bluff throw trick on Manager Kelley, nailing his runny feet off third base when Corcoran started to steal.

Williams opened Chicago's last half with a fan out. McCarthy raised false hopes with a single, only to be forced at second by Evers after Kling had lofted an easy fly to Seymour.[12] On July 31, the *Tribune* published the Colts' batting averages on page B2. The team had been doing poorly compared to 1903:

	1904	1903
Chance	.300	.327
Jones	.275	.282
Evers	.268	.293
Kling	.250	.297
McCarthy	.236	.277
Tinker	.214	.291
Casey	.249	.290
Slagle	.248	.298
Williams	.161	.223

In spite of the team's drop in hitting, they were fighting it out for second place. But August 7 brought the boys a day of respite. They welcomed it as they hustled out to Brooklyn's Bath Beach and took to the water for some relief from the heat and the sun. The only absent member of the team was Manager Selee. He left early in the day for Newark, N.J., where he wanted to watch a ballgame in order to get a line on the playing of Frank Schulte of the Syracuse team.[13]

The day of relaxation continued into the evening, and Johnny Kling loosened up. He became more talkative. This side of the backstop was an uncommon occurrence. Everyone knew that Kling was stingy with anecdotes. It was almost impossible to get him to talk.[14]

But talk he did. He even told a tall tale that reached the ears of a sportswriter. It became known as:

Kling's Elephant Story
Chicago Catcher Tells an Improbable Tale of Animal Instinct

John Kling, catcher of the Chicago Cubs, is not only a crack ballplayer, but a pool shark — one of the cleverest pool players in the business, and able to hold his own against any of the professionals. Kling is also a fairly good raconteur, and one that he sprung some weeks ago shows that the pool-playing catcher deserves a high niche in the Prevaricators' Union.

"I heard a great deal," said John, "about the intelligence of elephants, but I was dumfounded by a Hindu palmist whom I know who said that an elephant could always recognize his own ivory — that if you took an elephant's tusk away from him, and showed it to him again, no matter how many years after, no matter how the tusk might be carved and altered, the elephant would know it instantly. Well, I had a chance to test the truth of this statement soon after it was handed to me. There is a little circus which winters at Kansas City, and two years ago one of the elephants had his tusks sawed off. The proprietor of the billiard hall where I spend some of my time bought a tusk and had it turned into billiard balls. He was very proud of these spheroids, and they were really much better than the average.

"Well, when the Hindu told me these things about the sagacity of the elephants, I decided to test old flap-ears, and so I went to the billiard hall to borrow one of the balls. The proprietor was as much interested in this scientific experiment as I was, and so we went to the circus quarters together. We found the elephant from whom the tusks had been sawed, and I reached out a hand to him, with one of the balls in the hand.

"Did he recognize it? Why, sir, it was the most wonderful thing you ever saw! He smelt that billiard ball half a moment, then took it in his trunk. Then he hit me on the head with it, and knocked me dizzy. That showed that the elephant not only recognized his tusk, but was still sore about losing it, and demonstrated the wonderful sagacity of the beast beyond all denial."[15]

The time for relaxation and stories was soon over. Frank Selee was back. He had signed Frank Schulte, a youngster with a BA of .331, and it was back to baseball.

Page 6 of the Aug. 9 *Trib* reported a Colts' win by 4 to 1, Kling getting 3 hits, including a double. By Sept. 1, the *Trib* said, "Colts Send Brooklyn Back East with a Nestful of Goose Eggs." Selee's youngsters were in second place.

The ride toward the top was not a happenstance event. It was in large measure due to Johnny Kling, who had learned a great deal about his own pitchers. He had learned how to use their particular pitching skills to defeat opposing batters with understandable weaknesses. This was the part of the game that fans could not see and could not appreciate. It was the inside game and Kling had become a master of it.

One pitcher who must have marveled at his sudden success with Kling behind the bat was Buttons Briggs. He had an abysmal record before joining the Colts:

	G	W	L	IP	H	HR	BB	SO	ERA
1896	26	12	8	194	202	6	108	84	4.31
1897	22	4	17	186	246	6	85	60	5.26
1898	4	1	3	30	38	0	10	14	5.70

Buttons was so dismayed with his record he quit baseball. And he didn't return until joining the Colts. Why Selee signed him is a mystery, but he must have seen something in this 28-year-old, 180-pound right hander. With Kling behind the bat, Buttons Briggs was having a fantastic season, possibly a 20 game winner with an ERA far below his prior years.

His rise continued. On Sept. 16, in a pitchers' battle against "Noodles" Hahn of Cincinnati, Briggs held the Reds to 1 run and 5 hits before Kling broke up the game with a two-bagger in the twelfth, driving in Tinker with the winning run, final score 2 to 1. On Sept. 28, with Kling as his battery mate, Buttons defeated the league-leading Giants 7 to 2 on their home grounds. He allowed five hits but only one of these had anything to do with run making. When the locals found they could do nothing with Briggs, they let up in their efforts and the 8,000 rooters began "roasting" them considerably for not trying, although the game was hopelessly lost.

The same was true on the following day when Bob Wicker defeated the New York team 7 to 3. His ability to win with Kling as his backstop had been and continued to be phenomenal. At St. Louis his best win-loss was 5–12 with an ERA of 3.19. After joining Chicago in 1903, he had a 20–9 with an ERA of 3.02. At the pace he was now going, another 20 game winner was a possibility.

Johnny Kling knew these men and was dedicated to them. Not once did he ever showboat for the fans or anyone else. Not once did he ever pop off in the clubhouse, trying to impress everyone with his own knowledge by criticizing his pitchers. They knew him, and had absolute confidence in him. That relationship was essential for the winning of games.[16]

As the season neared its final games, new men joined the team: Harry McChesney and Solly Hofman, outfielders from the Western League. Manager Selee signed them, and wanted them aboard before leaving for a series in the east.

The Colts were still in second place and Selee was determined to finish the season that way. Chicago firmed up its position by taking three straight from Boston, shutting them out 3–0 in the final game on Oct. 5. Kling led the way with 3 hits, including a double. The season closed with a loss to the Pirates, but Selee had firm hold of second place with a 93–60 record, thirteen games behind the Giants, who were a sizzling 106–47.

The Chicago manager expressed pleasure over the work of his youngsters, and had words of praise for all three of the new outfielders, Frank "Wildfire" Schulte, Solly Hofman and Harry McChesney.[17] Selee knew that next year could be the year his boys would make it to the top. The only thing he wanted was to be around to enjoy it.

The season was remarkable for the number of players Manager Selee had in the game at one time or another, also for the great number of substitutions necessary. Players like Otto Williams and Jack Barry played nearly every position on the diamond, and although Johnny Kling played in 120 games out of the 153, 10 were in either left or right field and 6 were at first base, leaving 104 behind the bat, 28 fewer than in 1903. Nevertheless, by catching over 100 games, he was still a premier catcher.

The juggling of men in different positions, the frequent changes in batting order and the never ending attempt to bring new players into the club was a manifestation of Manager Selee's determination to counter the effects of illness and injury that had plagued his team. His efforts paid off. The Chicago fans showed their appreciation by flocking to the West Side Grounds, attendance jumping from 386,205 to 439,100. This made President Hart smile; his bank deposits had become quite sizeable.

Johnny Kling headed home. He too had banked his earnings. Although small, he had ideas about investments and wanted his meager savings to generate other income. His wife was in full agreement, so when Lillian suggested they live in the family home in back of the bakery, at 1528½ Grand Avenue, he readily agreed. Although it was not spacious, and although he wanted more privacy for himself and his wife, Johnny was looking forward to sitting around the dinner table, chatting with his brother Charles and his sister Lizzie. As for Mama and Papa, all he had to do was be a good listener since Papa did all the talking. He was hoping there wouldn't be too much talk about Bill, who was still a saloonkeeper, even though Papa's emotions was at an all time low.

But Johnny may have talked to Papa and others about business. His ambition to become a capitalist had somehow reached Chicago. It was hinted at on page A4 of the *Chicago Tribune* on Nov. 13. It told the Chicago fans about reports of Kling's flirting with a magnate's job in the American Association by buying up the Kansas City club together with "Kid" Nichols. But the *Trib* added a comment, saying that these reports were of doubtful origin. It then went on to say: "It is doubtful too, if President Hart would consent to release Kling. The backstop is the mainstay of the West Side club and there would be small chance of filling one of Kling's shoes, to say nothing of both of them."

Page 7 of the Dec. 25 *Washington Post* gave Colt fans a Christmas present when it first talked about Kling managing the Kansas City team in 1905, and of how Selee began worrying because his catcher "was about the best backstop in the league." But the Chicago manager "was rendered extremely happy when Kling signed."

Johnny Kling too must have been happy. He would soon be playing ball again, the game he loved. He would be studying men at bat and working with his pitchers, trying to help the team make it to the top.

1905

Frank Selee had done an excellent job rebuilding the team. But the skipper was afraid he would not reap the harvest he had so diligently worked for. TB had taken hold of him. He knew he would have to turn more and more to his first baseman for help.[18]

Nevertheless, Selee continued to weed out players he no longer wanted and add new men to the roster. Jones and McCarthy were gone. Billy Maloney, an outfielder, and Jeff Pfeffer, a pitcher, had joined the team. He also asked his friend George Huff at the University of Illinois to find him a 20-game winning pitcher.

Prior to the start of an exhibition game, the players congregated in the clubhouse to elect a captain of the team. Praise was voiced for three men. Votes were collected and the final tally was Chance 11, Casey 4 and Kling 2.[19]

A piece of hard luck hit the Chicago National League club. They were playing the Kansas State Agricultural College team. It was the sixth inning. Chance was on third, taking a big lead. The pitcher whirled to throw, and the new captain of the team ran back to the base. He hit the bag with his left foot and fell, wrenching the instep so badly, he had to be helped to a carriage and was driven back to the hotel. It was announced that he would not be able to play for at least two weeks.

Chicago won the game easily, 15 to 0, Kling leading the way with 4 hits, including a double, and scoring 1 run. Although Selee's men continued to play a snappy game, winning the exhibition games and the opening game against St. Louis on April 14, their fortunes were soon reversed and on May 3 they found themselves in fifth place with an 8–8 record.

The game on May 3 against the Reds went poorly. A wild throw by

Charles Webb Murphy, new owner of the Chicago Nationals (*Chicago Daily News*).

Kling let in the winning run, while it was Kling's failure to bunt in the seventh inning, when there were two men on and nobody out, that spoiled the chances for at least a tying run. Chicago lost 3 to 2.[20]

It was then learned that Kling had received a telegram summoning him home, telling him his mother was dying.[21] That evening, he boarded a train at Grand Central Station that left Chicago at 6:30, scheduled to arrive in Kansas City at 3:30 in the morning. It was a Twin Cities-Chicago-Kansas City route and Johnny Kling desperately wanted to be home before his mother died.[22]

He didn't make it. And he didn't get back to playing ball until May 16. His long stay at home can be explained by the Jewish tradition of sitting *shivah* for seven days, a demonstration of grief at the loss of a near relative, and a way of honoring the deceased while family and friends visit, never leaving the bereaved alone. There is no proof that Johnny Kling sat *shivah* other than the fact that the family did practice other Jewish traditions, as already mentioned.

On May 16, it was Chicago at New York; the batteries were Reulbach and Kling for the Colts, Ames and Bresnahan for the Giants. Big Ed Reulbach had been tracked down by Selee's friend, George Huff, and was hailed as a fantastic pitcher with a blazing fastball. Kling had never seen him before but soon saw his wild, fast deliveries. He could not be calmed down. He walked men, and even punctured McGann in the ribs with one of his sweet benders, losing 4 to 0. The Colts had suffered their third shutout and hadn't scored a run for twenty-seven innings.[23]

On the following day, Chance was back playing first. There were days when he had to take on more of the managerial responsibilities because Selee's TB was becoming progressively worse. It was at these times that he began to make his opinions known.

As Johnny Kling sat in his squat position behind the bat eyeing the team, he saw that his captain and acting manager was a firm believer in fines whenever anything was done detrimental to the winning of games. He saw a stern disciplinarian, someone who was running the club with a clenched fist, someone who came down hard on any player who gave less than 100 percent. He was a fighter, not in the sense of pugnacity of temperament, but he was the boss and insisted his men give the best that was in them.[24]

By June 3, the team was still in fifth place. Kling was the backstop in most of the games, getting to know his new pitcher and new men on the team. A reporter stopped by and interviewed him. Page S 1 of the June 4 *Washington Post* then reported: "Johnny Kling, the Chicago National backstop says he will catch his customary 100 games this season, barring misfortune."

In addition to catching, Kling's hitting began to improve. By June 11, the Colts had won five straight and Johnny Kling was once again pounding the ball hard, scoring 2 runs in a 7–0 win against the Beaneaters. The Colts had climbed into fourth place with a 26–24 record, 3 games behind the 29–21 third place Pirates. On June 27, the team was still doing well, having won 16 out of the last 21 games with Johnny Kling leading the way. But Selee's men were still in the number four spot.

Four days later Selee's physician ordered him to bed. The players found it hard to go on without him, and it took Selee's encouragement to help them out of it.[25]

Selee's men soon learned that their manager would never again be able to help them out of anything. Tuberculosis had eaten away his lungs. On August 1, he was forced to resign and advised Jim Hart to put Chance in charge. The owner willingly agreed.

Spurred on by the new manager's leadership and Kling's ability to play in every game, the team won 40 of their last 63 games to finish a strong third at 92–61.

Sportswriters increasingly referred to Chance's men as Cubs. That name took hold as the new manager led his boys against Comiskey's White Sox for the city championship, winning 4 games to 1. This broke the tie for the crown that had existed since 1903, and the Cubs were now the champions of baseball in the city of Chicago.

Johnny Kling was once again a premier catcher, his fourth year in a row, with 106 games behind the bat. His assists tallied 136 and his total for major league play was 702, a record setting pace.

With the season over, Kling was eager to get home. His wife was pregnant. Her delivery was due in December. In addition, family members had taken brother Charles to court, claiming he "was wrongfully withholding money, and chattels of Caroline Kling, deceased; $9,300 in money and a note for $1500 payable to Caroline." They wanted their share of their mother's estate.[26]

That winter, Charles Murphy, seeing that attendance had climbed to 509,900, jumped at the chance to purchase the Chicago National League franchise and the West Side Grounds. He made Chance manager and rented an office on the eleventh floor, room 1115 of Chicago's Masonic Temple at State and Randolph's North East corner. It was a prestigious location with 22 stories. It had shops on the first nine floors, offices above and meeting rooms for Masons on the uppermost floors. The Temple was his office from where he planned to conduct all of his baseball business.[27]

The first order of business was to deal with John Kling, who wanted more money for the 1906 season, and to tell him why the answer had to be no.

8
CLEARING SKIES

1906

John Kling greeted the New Year with joy. He was the father of a baby girl, Virginia, born Dec. 5, and his wife was doing fine. But his joy was far from complete. He was still troubled by not knowing if his brother Charles had benefited financially from his mother's estate. Brother William, sister Amelia, and his nephew Victor Schutte claimed that Charles had all of Mama's money in his possession and kept it. But sister Elizabeth sided with Charles, claiming there was no money.

The case was dismissed when Public Administrator R.S. Crohn submitted his final report to the Court. He said, "Charles Kling and Elizabeth Kling made the statement that when Caroline Kling died she did not leave any personal property of any value whatsoever."[1] Nevertheless, for Johnny Kling, the issue remained questionable.

Another issue that soon surfaced was Murphy's refusal to give him the raise he had asked for. A Jan. 1, 1906, letter said: "My dear John: ... I have, after much thought, decided to tender contracts with the figures of 1905. Your salary is a bit more than others, but you are a hard, faithful and loyal worker, willing to work at any and all times. This must of course be taken into consideration."[2]

A series of letters followed, and on Feb. 1, Charles Webb Murphy continued to refuse Kling an increase in salary and cited reason after reason why the backstop should get less than what had been offered (see Appendix B, item A).

A confidential letter was sent on Feb. 25, wherein Murphy claimed:

> Since our club won the local championship, invidious persons have attacked me viciously in a campaign of misrepresentation and abuse. The victory of the Cubs last fall in which you shared liberally, was a severe blow to some folks, who have doubtless inspired libelous stories about me....
> No contracts were sent to the members of our team until I had given several

months thought to the subject and our Board of Directors had considered the matter. Your salary, being so much larger than that of other players, caused comment and it was the sense of the meeting that $3,000 would be big pay for you, in the light of what others get....

I want the members of the Chicago club to know that I intend that they shall be liberally treated. It is not my desire to have a cheap team. I want a successful one. Now, John — you can take it from me that there is no more chance of your getting a contract from the Chicago Club calling for $4,000 for a season's work than there is of me becoming the next president of he United States.[3]

Murphy's letter of March 26 appeared to terminate all discussion. It said:

Your communication of Mar. 24 was received today, so as far as the Chicago Club is concerned, the incident of your refusal to sign your contract is closed.... We will carry your name on our reserve list, but shall not expect you to be with us in 1906....

It is true that you have worked hard for the Chicago club in the past, but I must assume that you have been paid for that service. The present management cannot pay you for work done in the past. If you were not a sober, painstaking player, the club would not want you. Your earnings for 1905, I understand, are as follows: —

    Salary -$3,500.00
    Free uniforms -30.00
    Post season money - - - - - - - - - - - - - - - - -425.00
    Emblem -40.00
    Won at billiards on the road - - - - - - - - -1,800.00
    [Total submitted by Murphy] - - - - - - - -$6,155.00

[Author's Note: The total adds up to $5, 795.00]

"You are a good catcher and a nice fellow and I would like very much to see you on the team but we have arrived at the parting of the ways...."[4]

But President Murphy did not end the discussion. On the very next day, March 27, he wrote Kling a derogatory letter.

Notwithstanding the fact that we do not regard you as any longer an active member of the Chicago team ... I shall not insult your intelligence by saying that we will not avail ourselves of your services some time in the future in the event that you report in fit condition to play ball. I understand that at present you are fat and out of condition and that you have made no effort to get in shape to play ball....

We feel that you have passed the stage when you were at your best and we do not wish to purchase your past reputation....

I have received unsolicited verbal advice that you are afraid of base runners coming in from third base and that you do, as an anonymous writer says, catch nearly all balls on the first base side of the home plate. I have also been informed that you have missed foul flies many times because of a fear of colliding with the grandstand and that your batting has fallen off because of your fear of being hit by the ball....

8. Clearing Skies 75

Understand, I do not say that the above is true, but it has been said to me just the same. Manager Chance and myself both consider you as good as ever, but we can't prevent critics from saying what they think....[5]

On March 22, the *Chicago Daily News* put out a Sporting Extra, headlining the dispute over salary: "John Kling Holds Out, Chicago National Catcher Thinks New President Should Pay More Than Old—Threatens to Start a Billiard Hall in Kansas City."

"I feel that I am worth more money than the Chicago team paid me last year, and unless I get it, I'll quit baseball," said Kling. "I asked for a raise last year, and when it was not forthcoming, I made up my mind to get it this year or retire to the simple life. This is not a baseball player's bluff. I've received three contracts from President Murphy and I've returned all of them unsigned. Many persons may be of the opinion that I am the highest salaried catcher in the business, but they are greatly mistaken.

"I joined the Chicago club in 1900 and have caught a majority of the games for the team since that time. In 1902 I caught all but two games. In 1904 I caught 122 games and last season I was behind the hickory in 116 games. I've certainly earned my pay. I've never shirked and have caught games when I should have been on the bench. But that has nothing to do with the case. It's more money I am after and if I don't get it I will retire from baseball. I will stay right here in Kansas City."

Kling has leased space in a building in Kansas City and whether he signs his contract or not, he will open a billiard and pool hall next fall. If he fails to sign with the club, he will start to work on his new plans immediately.

March 26, another Extra, "Kling Remains Obdurate":

John Kling reported for practice at Association Park in Kansas City this morning and said he was going to get into condition, no matter whether he goes to Chicago or not. He will coach Manager Murphy's young pitchers and will probably play in the exhibition games.

Kling said this morning that he would not pay any attention to any telegrams from Manager Chance or President Murphy. "Chance is my friend, and if I play with Chicago this year, I'll give him the best I have. But I'm not going to play ball unless I get what I think I am entitled to. That is final."

March 28, another Extra, "Kling 'Holds Out' on Chance."

Johnny Kling received another telegram from Manager Chance this morning from Vicksburg, Miss., asking him if he was going to report. Kling replied that he would never play baseball again unless his demand for an increase in salary was met. Kling is practicing daily with the Kansas City team.

March 29, another Extra, "He Aims to Bar Kling. President Murphy Dislikes to Have Catcher Coach Kansas City Pitchers. Writes Letter to Blues.

Secretary Shriner of the Blues ball club received a letter from President Murphy of the Chicago Nationals asking him to refuse Johnny Kling the privilege of practicing with the Kansas City Blues. Murphy said in his letter that he did not care to have Kling coaching pitchers unless they were under contract to Chicago.

Shriner said that he would pay no attention to the letter.

March 30, another Extra, "Gets Kling Signed Up. Ted Sullivan Guides Hand of Murphy's Backstop and He Will Report."

John Kling has formally signed his contract to catch for the Chicago club this coming season. Chicago must thank no less a man than Ted Sullivan for the capitulation. Now the burning question is "Did he get his raise?"

"It is presumed that Ted in his soulful way, got John 'between bases' and went after him something like this:

"You're in bad, Johnny. You know what you are getting and you know you're aching to play. You're getting enough on which to live at least a year and a half at your present rate. Billiard tables will do for a bluff, but when it comes to the real goods, pass them by until you get too old to catch as a permanent business.

"It brings tears to my eyes to see the real goods like you wasting your talents on Kansas City. A little switch of the hand and it is done. You will please the thousands of fans camped around the telegraph wires in Chicago, anxious to hear from you. Sign, John, sign, and then always remember on pay days to be glad you took Ted Sullivan's advice."

"I'll sign," said John cheerfully, almost like a man who has what he went after and sign he did. Then Ted Sullivan shot a telegram to President Murphy saying, "It is done and signed."

"Did you get the raise?" was asked of Kling this morning. He did not reply. President Murphy was also asked. His reply, "It is a closed incident. Forget it."

The question of the raise did not immediately go away. But the final conclusion appeared on page 8 of the *Chicago Daily News* on March 31 in an article titled, "Kling a Much Talked of Man:" "Whether Kling was able to get his $500 raise from President Murphy will remain a secret perhaps, but at any rate, Kling got out of the predicament without backing down. His silence since the contract was signed and his remark of 'I am satisfied' is meant to indicate that he did get his raise."

The much-talked about man never did say another word about getting the $4,000 salary he was asking for. Nor did he say whether or not President Murphy backed away from the staunch position of cutting his salary from $3,500 to $3,000. But reporters still pursued the story. They still tried to find an answer to that nagging question. After some time had passed, they stopped trying and the question died away. Both men carried the secret to their graves.

Johnny Kling kept this secret safely tucked away. He may have known that the day would come when it would finally surface. When Johnny died, his wife Lillian became the custodian of that document. After she died, it was handed down to the next generation. Imagine! A secret lying dormant for over 90 years.

This hand-me-down occurrence could have gone on and on. But a

8. Clearing Skies

happenstance incident occurred that allowed a non-relative to see the March 29, 1906, contract that Johnny Kling had signed. It was then donated to a public facility where it became available to the public. That document and its long held secret about the $500 raise can be seen in Appendix B, item B.

The contract was signed March 29. Johnny Kling received $3,500, the same salary as in 1905. As witness and signatory for the Chicago club was Ted Sullivan, the man who was sent on a secret mission to purchase Sammy Strang for the Chicago Orphans from St. Jo of the Western League in 1900, the man who was so impressed after watching Johnny Kling play, he bought him too. Kling signed his contract with a stipulation. It said, "This contract is signed understanding that no fines is imposed for not reporting."

When the controversy was over, Chicago fans were given a glimpse of the kind of remarkable man Kling was. "Kling does not smoke, drink, chew tobacco or swear," a news article said.

> He has never lost his temper but once or twice since being a member of the Chicago ball team.
> When it is taken into consideration that a ballplayer is surrounded on all sides by people who are continually tempting him to indulge in more of these habits, the fact that a man has been able to keep himself clear of these habits is considered remarkable. Kling's not having any of these flaws is the reason for his always being in condition and being able to work in so many games during the hard season.
> Another characteristic of one of the greatest catchers in the business, is that he always keeps cool under the most trying circumstances. His nerve never fails him and he is the same calm dispassionate person in defeat as he is in victory. His cool calculating disposition is what makes him so strong as a pool player. He ranks just under the championship class in this game and in most all of the cities of the National League circuit. Kling has at some time or another "cleaned up" the local champions in games so that they will remember him.
> Kling is well fixed in the world's goods also. He purchased a small farm just outside of Kansas City last year. The city is building out toward his property and it will make him a fortune in a short time according to the best informed real estate men.[6]

Stories about Johnny Kling must have had a significant effect on the circulation of the *Chicago Daily News*. The reporter followed him to Champaign, Illinois, where Kling joined the team for the second exhibition game with the University of Illinois varsity nine and Chicago fans continued to read about their hero:

April 3: The Cub squad was re-enforced this afternoon by the arrival of Johnny Kling, catcher, who said he was in good shape. Mordecai Brown was mighty glad to see the backstop.

April 4: When Johnny Kling dropped in yesterday, smiling and debonair, as if there never had been such a thing as quibbling over baseball contracts, he had no suit. George Huff loaned him an Illinois uniform, and the crowd, all through the game, in which Kling starred, were under the impression that he was a college recruit. Wherever Johnny has been practicing, he certainly has his batting eye.

April 5: John Kling, the star backstop of the National League who has been assigned to do duty with the second team of the Cubs, because of his tardiness in reporting for practice, is making up for his error in a way that brings joy to the heart of Manager Chance. Kling is hitting the ball with a vengeance that would indicate that he got more than the five hundred that he asked for. His throwing to bases is excellent also, and he is stealing and playing the game with more energy than he has displayed for two years.

There is some speculation as to whether Manager Chance will give Kling his place behind the bat in the opening game of the season next week or whether Pat Moran will be given the honor. Kling's refusal to join the team at once this spring displeased the Cub leader considerably and it may be that he will keep from Kling the honor that comes from the catching of the first game.

With the exhibition contests over, the team moved on to Cincinnati for the opening game of the season. Frank Chance knew his team was ready. All they needed was a winning attitude. After his talk with them, they knew that every opposing team was the enemy. Every time they played they were at war, not at a pink tea.[7] If a player shook the hand of a member of the opposing team, it would cost him $10. From now on there were fines if you didn't follow the rules.[8]

Johnny Kling was in the lineup for the first game on April 12. His battery mate was Carl Lundgren. A record-breaking crowd of 17,241 fans crowded into the ballpark, eager to see the Reds win the opener. There was nothing to cheer about for the first two innings. In the last of the third, Overall cracked a single past Steinfeldt and wandered around to third on Huggins push to right center. Barry sent Slagle back to the fringe of society after his long fly and it scored the first run of the game. Huggins tried out Kling's arm and was stopped at second for his temerity. Carr fanned.

Chance's men got busy and the Reds soon began struggling madly to tie up the game. Seymour opened Cincinnati's fourth with a single, but after watching two men fly, he tried to steal second and failed. Carr led off in the sixth with a double, but Lundgren made the next three hit the ceiling for easy flies.

The seventh inning found Kling crouched low behind the bat. In an instant, he surveyed his men: Sheckard in left, Slagle center and Schulte in right — the finest outfield; Chance at first, Evers second, Tinker short and Steinfeldt at third — a perfect infield; Lundgren, on the mound, looked great. He was pitching a fantastic game and could end up being a 20 game winner. With himself behind the plate, and all the other superb pitchers,

8. Clearing Skies

Johnny Kling knew the team could make it to the top. He also knew that should he be laid up with an injury, there were three new catchers — Pat Moran, Pete Noonan and Tom Walsh — to give him a hand. But down deep, Kling had every confidence that he would be able to catch his 100 games for the season and then some.

For the last three innings, the Cubs gave the fans a "no ands, ifs or buts" message that they were not to be denied victory, and trounced the Reds 7 to 2. Johnny Kling did his part by bagging a double, scoring a run, and throwing out two men trying to test his arm, chalking up two more assists to his numbers.

On the following day, the *Chicago Tribune* published photos of "Players who starred in the Opening Game." Besides Tinker, Slagle, Schulte and Huggins, Kling was shown behind the plate as Barry dropped the bat and headed toward first.

The Cubs continued to play excellent ball. New men had strengthened the team. All of them had adopted the new attitude and played as if there was an all out war. They would let nothing go unnoticed, even if it meant throwing a few punches.

April 16, in another game with the Reds, Chicago was leading 2–0 going into the last of the eighth. Lundgren was pitching another great game. He looked like a sure winner. Suddenly he disconnected. He hit a batter with a wide curve, issued a walk and then let a few hits change the tally. It was a mad bunch of Cubbies that came in off the field, especially the manager and Evers, whose sharp tongue bedeviled umpire Jim Johnstone nonstop.

Things had not been going smoothly between Johnstone and the visitors earlier in the fray and now they reached a climax. Walking over toward the Chicago bench, Johnstone waved Chance and Evers off the field. The final score was 3–2 in favor of Cincinnati, but further excitement was yet to come.

There was a fight between Joe Tinker and a spectator following a talking match as the Chicago bus was about to leave. The man was too much for the shortstop, and Tinker would have sustained a severe beating had Manager Chance not come to his rescue. Luckily, the police got wind of the affair and three of them came running up. They soon put a stop to hostilities and the Chicago team was allowed to drive out of the grounds. There must have been joy on that bus, for the Cubs had won 3 of their first 4 games.

President Murphy hurried home. He wanted publicity for his club. He wanted attendance at the West Side Grounds to keep going up. What better way to do it than to prepare for an extravaganza on opening day at the ballpark. But working people sent in many petitions to Murphy to hold the flag raising on Saturday, not Tuesday. So the day for celebration was changed to a non-working day.⁹

Opening day on April 17 was an auspicious occasion. Over 14,000 enthusiasts welcomed Chance and his men to Chicago. The weather was perfect, the crowd happy — except those who had to pay 50 cents to get into seats that formerly cost only 25 cents — and everything was lovely except the playing. The Cubs lost the first home game 6 to 3.

The person with the best seat in the house watching it all was Johnny Kling, who sat in the dugout. He watched Pfiester, the Cub pitcher, trying to nip the corners of the plate. He finally lost control, became wild and had to be replaced by Wicker.

Johnny knew that it was best not to demand too many corner pitches from the man on the slab, especially early on, and to call for such a pitch as part of a strategy. Too many attempts at corner pitches had placed a burden on Pfiester. It made him anxious. He lost his focus and the Reds took an early lead, then went on to win the game.

By Saturday, April 21, Cincinnati had won 2 out of 3, and Kling was again in the lineup with Lundgren as his battery mate. Before the game, the Cubs were presented with a monster red bat inscribed with the names of the men who helped win the 1905 post-season series. The pennant raising followed. The Cubs watched the new flag being hoisted to the top of the flagpole, bearing the inscription "Champions of the City of Chicago," and the band played. The silence that followed the raising of the pennant, was broken suddenly by the outburst of an exuberant fan who rose in the bleachers and shouted, "Oh, long may she wave o'er the park of the Cubs and never fall into the hands of those dubs."¹⁰

This shaft of humiliation aimed at the vanquished Comiskeyites met with the smiling approbation of all who heard it. Then, the players hurried onto the field to get the proper amount of practice before tackling the Cardinals in the final game of the series.

The game was grandly played. Lundgren's control was marvelous, allowing 7 scattered hits and 2 runs. Kling was marvelous. First inning: Bennett struck out. Shannon popped a short fly to Steinfeldt. Grady was given his base on balls but was out attempting to steal second, Kling to Evers. Second inning: Smoot went out on a long fly to Slagle. Beckley lined to Tinker. Himes singled to left and was out stealing, Kling to Tinker. Third inning: Arndt was walked. McBride popped out to Kling on an attempted sacrifice. Brown fanned. Arndt was out stealing, Kling to Evers.

After three Cardinals met sure, instant death trying to steal, the team gave Kling no further worries. Besides adding 3 additional assists to his numbers, the premier backstop also added 2 hits and kept his batting average at a very respectable range. The Cubbies won the game 5 to 2.¹¹

8. Clearing Skies

Kling had another great day on April 22. In the seventh with a 1–1 tie in the game, he slapped a single to left, driving in Evers, who had been on first, and the game was cinched. In addition to another hit for the day, he added 3 additional assists to his totals, and Chicago trimmed Pittsburgh 3 to 1. Wicker pitched a beautiful game, allowing 6 hits, holding Hans Wagner to a single hit for the day. But in spite of their wonderful day, the Cubs were in fifth place with a 5–4 record.

Johnny Kling's work was equally stunning as the Chicago Nationals took a close one from Cincinnati 7–6 on April 27. For the day, he had a double, scored 1 run and had 3 more assists, moving the team into third place with an 8–6 record. But in five days, with 4 straight wins against St. Louis, the Cubbies climbed into the number two spot with a 12–6, not far from New York, the 1905 World Champs, who had 14–3.

Besides working well with his pitchers and infielders, Kling demonstrated excellence with the lumber, as shown in the last game of the St. Louis series. With 4 at-bats, he got 4 hits including a clean two-bagger. He scored 2 runs and continued to pile up his assist numbers, leading the team to victory.[12]

On May 3, a press release from Pittsburgh said: "There is no weak spot on our team at present," said Chance tonight. "And our pitchers are all working well again. We will not claim any of the games until we win them, but the Pittsburgh team will know we are in the game. We have never had an easy time in Pittsburgh, and even with a badly crippled team, the Pirates are a hard bunch to beat."[13]

Frank Chance was wrong. The Pirates were not a hard bunch to beat. With Kling behind the bat in all four games, the Cubs beat them handily, and on May 7, Chicago was in first place.

Kling had pounded the ball steadily, slammed 2 homers on May 3 and 4, and added 4 more assists to his record. Best of all, his work with the pitchers was masterful. He had put a crimp in Pirate batters by having them reach in vain for the offerings of his right and left handed pitchers.

It is not difficult to understand Kling's ability to work successfully with his pitchers when you consider his five years of experience. He knew the peculiarities, the weaknesses and strengths of the Pittsburgh batsmen better than his pitchers who performed every fourth game or so. They had confidence in him because with men on base, he was able to keep his mind on the batsmen, and at the same time, watch the runners like a cat to detect the next move of the attacking Pirates, in advance if possible. When Kling became a baseman, he defended home plate against a runner, seldom slipping, seldom giving up an irrevocable run to the enemy.

Fans who watched the game probably never knew that Johnny Kling had more chances to make mistakes than any other player, not only because he handled the ball more often, giving himself more frequent opportunities for mechanical slips, but also because he had to do more thinking in the ordinary nine-inning game than anyone else on the team. And a wrong guess by him could have upset the whole works.

Every defensive play started with Kling. If he did not actually order the play, he would have gotten it from Manager Chance and would have had to repeat it so the other men became involved. In essence, Johnny Kling was the most important cog in the Cub machine.[14]

He continued slamming long balls, getting a homer and triple on May 18. He continued raising his number of assists when opposing runners tested his arm, and the pitchers continued winning games. But tragedy struck on May 22 in a game against the Giants. Kling was injured by a foul tip from Dahlen's bat in the ninth. It broke a wire in his mask, and a bad cut over his eye took three stitches. He could not play. The location of the wound would not allow him to don a mask until the wound was healed.[15]

On May 24, as Johnny Kling watched from the stands, Carl Lundgren was no longer effective as he issued pass after pass. McGraw's Giants took the game 6 to 5 and recaptured first place.

The loss of Johnny Kling from the lineup, even for a short period of time, was a severe blow to the team. Not only was he regarded as the best backstop in the league, he was also one of the leading batsmen for the Cubs. On June 2, page 6 of the *Chicago Daily News* came out with the batting averages for the club. The top two hitters were Steinfeldt with .349 and Kling with .314. The loss to the Giants by one run on May 24 may not have occurred with Noisy John in the lineup.

In early June, Manager Chance and his men headed for New York for another series with John McGraw's 1905 World Champions. June 5 saw Kling again in the lineup and the Cubs took the game 6–0, proving that "Iron Man" McGinnity was no riddle. Chance's men were once again in first place.[16] But it was on the following day, June 6, that Johnny Kling proved how essential he was to the winning of games. Although not in the lineup, he batted for Harper in the second inning and pushed a two-bagger into left, scoring the first two runs of the game.

After the game, the *Chicago Tribune* proudly reported that the Nationals trimmed the champions 11 to 3. Chance's men couldn't stop hitting as they collected 18 safeties off Dummy Taylor, driving the Giants down to third place.

June 7 witnessed the third game of the series. After it was over the Chicago fans had every reason to be proud as they read the bold headline of the sports page in the *Chicago Daily News*, "Chance's Men Get Awful Revenge." It read:

8. Clearing Skies

> Not content with the humiliation of the Giants on two previous days, Chicago's Nationals, remembering what McGraw did to them in Chicago, set out to annihilate the world champions today in the third game and succeeded. A score of 19–0: 11 runs in the first inning, 22 base hits and the scalps of McGraw's two crack pitchers, Mathewson and McGinnity, was the harvest of the Cubs. And they might have made it more.[17]

Whitewashed and disgraced again, the world's champions were hooted and jeered at by "loyal fans," who for three years have hooted and jeered all visiting teams alike at the Polo Grounds. They never dreamed of seeing McGraw at the head of as dilapidated and lifeless a band as the Giants looked today. The farce lasted considerably over two hours and at least half of the 8,000 spectators left long before the end. Chance's men had to allow themselves to be put out on the bases after making their hits in order to get the game over.[18]

For John McGraw it was shame. After the Giants had won the pennant and World Series in 1905, he claimed to the day he died that his team was the greatest team he ever managed. The shirts of the road uniforms the Giants wore bore the legend "World Champions." The legend was repeated on the yellow blankets that adorned the horses that drew the open carriages in which the Giants rode in splendor to the ballparks in the hostile towns.

But McGraw had become overconfident. He failed to see the feud that was to come. It was the Cubs against the Giants and Chance against McGraw. And on his side, Chance had the finest outfield and infield in the league and Johnny Kling, the brilliant field general whose signals bound the individual players into a coordinated team effort. As soon as the Cubbies took the field on June 7, with Kling behind the bat, it was as if a voodoo spell had been cast over the world champions. The rest was history.

By July 13, the Cubs were in first place with 56–24, having pulled away from the rest of the league and still climbing. In a game against the Phillies, the Cubs rallied in the ninth and fairly swept away Duffy's men by a score of 4–3. It was a brilliant rally after Chance's men had been put down for eight innings, having made only three safeties and one run. It set the rooters crazy with something they would always remember.

Schulte faced Duggleby for the last time. He smashed one on the ground straight at Doolin and it looked a cinch out. But the shortstop hesitated, backed away a step, and was lost. The ball shot past him and, while Thomas and Magee were falling over each other after it, Schulte reached third base. Chance followed Schulte's lead by jammin' a hard one to Doolin's right. The latter blocked the ball but fumbled an instant, and Chance beat the throw to first while Schulte scored.

A whirlwind had started full blast. Steinfeldt laid down a bunt toward first. Bransfield stood stock still, but Duggleby by rapid work fielded the ball and touched Harry out. Tinker bounded one to Doolin, who tried to head off Chance going to third, but threw wide of the bag and everybody was safe. Evers pounded the ball for a liner to right, on which Chance registered the run, which tied. Tinker scampered to third on the drive and Johnny reached second on the throw in. Then Kling finished it with a swat over Courtney's head into left, sending Tinker home with the winner.

Yet, it wasn't really Kling's swat that won the game. Besides driving in the big run, Kling's fielding was the feature of the day. The Phillies had been up against St. Louis for four days and imagined they could steal eight or eleven bases every day. Kling stopped them. Three times he nailed men at second, twice he cut thieves off at third, and when Gleason capped the climax by trying to steal home, Johnny tagged him a half yard from the rubber, chalking up six assists for the day.[19]

On July 17, Noisy John did it again in a game against McGraw's men when he prevented disaster. In the sixth, the Giants found Brown for two singles and a pass, but could not score. Strang got the first hit but was nailed trying to steal second. Shannon drew the pass and reached second on Seymour's safe rap, then tried to steal third and was out by a city block. Brown put a fitting finish on the round by fanning McGann, winning the game 6–2.

The July 18 *Chicago Tribune*'s "Notes of the Game" said: "The value of a catcher's work was illustrated in limelight yesterday. If Kling had permitted Strang or Shannon to catch him napping with their unexpected steals in the sixth inning New York surely would have broken the tie in its favor and given Chicago an uphill fight. If Bresnahan had been able to stop Chicago's stealing, the Cubs would not have scored a run except in the ninth."

And so it went until August 7 when Kling was telegraphed in New York where he was playing, telling him his father died. He left immediately for the funeral. The *Chicago Tribune*, in addition to brief information about his father, reported something never before revealed: "A year ago, Kling's mother died and the catcher came home for the funeral. The Chicago club docked Kling for the absence and the catcher refused to join this year until the amount taken was refunded."

The *Trib*'s article must have troubled James Hart, who owned the Chicago club at the time Kling's mother died. He wasted no time in contacting the *Chicago Daily News* on August 8 and issued his side of the story, published on page 6: "I asked to have a statement corrected, that the Chicago club had docked John Kling at the time he left the club to go to his mother's funeral last year. Kling was not only not fined or his salary docked, but he was away from ten to fifteen days although he reached Kansas City after the funeral of his mother," said Mr. Hart today.

A Kansas City reporter's comments must have been of concern to Chicago fans: "The loss of Kling at this stage of the game is likely to prove serious to Chicago. He has a faculty of steadying the pitchers and his timely batting will be sadly missed for a few days."[20]

On August 15 Noisy John was again behind the bat in a game against Brooklyn, having been gone eight days. Considering travel time to Kansas City from 6:00 p.m. to 3:00 a.m., or eighteen hours round trip, and seven days to sit *shivah* in honor of his father, this would explain his absence for eight days.

Kling was gone somewhat longer when his mother died, but back then, his father was alive, and it seems reasonable to assume that private time with Papa was a must for Johnny Kling. Now that Papa was gone, he hurried back to the team.

By Sept. 1, the Chicagoans had pulled far away from the pack, leading second place Pittsburgh by 13 games. On the following day, the *Chicago Tribune* startled the baseball world with a short article in part two of the Sporting section:

KLING MIXED UP IN WILL CASE

A suit was brought in the Circuit court today to break the will of John Kling, who died July 14. William Kling, Lena Dahl, Louise Schutte, and V.E. Schutte, a grandson and other children, are suing Charles Kling, Elizabeth Kling and John Kling, also children.

Charles and Elizabeth Kling lived with the father before his death, and their brothers and sisters say they persuaded him to favor them in the distribution of his property.

John Kling, a son, is a professional baseball player. He is a member of the Chicago National League team.[21]

After reviewing the elder Kling's last will and testament, it was evident that the newspaper article had it wrong. The only two defendants in the suit were Charles and Elizabeth Kling. Johnny Kling was not being sued.

The elder Kling bequeathed five of his children $5.00 each. To his grandson, Victor Schutte, he gave $5.00, and to his son-in-law, Sigesmund Schutte, $1.00. He gave the rest and remainder of his estate to his son, Charles Kling, and his daughter, Elizabeth, to be shared and shared alike.[22]

Case number 7944 was settled, and the Probate Court of Jackson County in Kansas City, Missouri, was so notified. The estate was divided into equal portions, with each of the children and the grandson, all plaintiffs in the suit, to receive $732.65. All of the parties receiving money were required to acknowledge, in writing, that they received their share. The only plaintiff to receive nothing was Sigesmund Schutte, the son-in-law, but he did not protest.

Johnny Kling acknowledged receipt of his share of his father's estate and wondered why Papa had left everything to Charles and Elizabeth to start with, and why it had to go to court in order to settle the dispute.

Kling's acknowledgement was on Baltimore Hotel stationery.[23] But records were not found indicating that he was in any way connected to the hotel business in September 1906. Nevertheless, the 1907 Kansas City directory listed "Kling, John G. Billiards at 1102 Baltimore, the address for the Baltimore Hotel." He was therefore using hotel stationery temporarily, until he had his own. This is supported by a news item that was published after the Cubs arrived in Springfield, Illinois, on September 11 for an exhibition game. It said that Johnny Kling was on his way to Kansas City to arrange for the opening of his new poolroom in the fall.[24]

After the game, the team ran over to St. Louis. They were in a happy frame of mind, feeling that they had the pennant all but safely tucked away. Every man on the team just knew they were going to set a new record in games won that would stand for many seasons. One hundred games had already been tallied in the win column. And the team had twenty-two more to play. Chance and all of his men believed they could win at least 15 of the remaining games without trouble.

The local fans were almost as enthusiastic over the Cubs as the west siders in Chicago were. People in all of the towns in Illinois felt the same way. They were proud of the team and were pulling hard for them to keep on winning.[25]

And win they did. On Sept. 19, the team rejoiced over winning the pennant after a 3–1 victory over Boston, giving them 106 wins for the season, thus tying the all time record for wins in a single season. And they still had 15 games to play.

The Cubs, under Frank Chance, had put together a juggernaut that no team, not even McGraw's mighty Giants, could stop, and he was praised highly for this. But at the same time, he should've been severely criticized for what he did to Johnny Kling.

The rest of the games were very important to Kling. He had still not reached the century mark, and had held the belief that he would once again do so, thus extending his premier catcher status from four to five straight seasons. But when the team cinched the pennant on Sept. 19, Moran was catching and Kling was on the bench — watching.

Manager Chance had arranged the assignments of his men so as to take away the opportunity for Johnny Kling to once again become a premier catcher, a status that he held since 1902. The *Chicago Tribune* published Chance's schedule:

8. Clearing Skies

Game	Catcher	Right Field	Center Field
Sept. 19	Moran	Schulte	
Sept. 20	Moran	Kling	Gessler
Sept. 21	Kling	Gessler	Moran
Sept. 23 Exhibition Game			
Sept. 24 Double Header:			
Game # 1	Moran	Kling	Gessler
Game # 2	Moran	Kling	Gessler
Sept. 25	Kling	Schulte	Gessler
Sept. 26	Kling	Schulte	Gessler
Sept. 27	Kling	Schulte	Gessler
Sept. 28	Kling	Schulte	Hofman
Sept. 29 Double Header:			
Game # 1	Kling	Schulte	Hofman
Game # 2	Moran	Schulte	Gessler
Oct. 1 Double Header:			
Game # 1	Moran	Schulte	Hofman
Game # 2	Moran	Schulte	Gessler
Oct. 4	Kling	Schulte	Gessler
Oct. 7	Moran	Schulte	Hofman

Johnny Kling finished the season having played in 96 games as catcher and 3 as a right fielder. In the final three double headers, Moran caught five times and Kling once, and although Frank Wildfire Schulte was fit to play, Chance had Kling play right field in three games. If a right fielder was needed for whatever reason, why didn't Chance put in Gessler as he did on Sept. 21? Or Hofman, who was a great utility man? Why did he not put Noisy John in as catcher for four more games?

It would have been simple. Instead of playing in right, Kling could have been catching, giving him 99 games as a backstop. Instead of having Moran catch five times in three double headers, the assignment could have been divided equally, giving Kling a total of 101 games as backstop for the season, thus allowing him to be a premier catcher.

The answer to this seeming injustice lies in understanding Frank Chance. He was a strict disciplinarian. His motto was, "do it my way or meet me after the game." When on March 26 the press reported that Kling would not pay any attention to a telegram from Frank Chance asking him to report for spring training, it could easily have been predicted that the day would come when Chance would get his revenge. After all, though he was a great player and leader, a vengeful spirit was a distinct part of his personality.

Every player on the team knew the Jack Harper story. He was a pitcher for Cincinnati. In the early part of 1906, this pitcher deliberately hit Chance in the head with a beanball. Chance showed Charles Murphy the kid's record, 23 wins in 1904, 10 in 1905. Chance convinced Murphy that Harper would be an asset to the club. Having been convinced that the new pitcher would help the team win games, Murphy traded for him.

When the kid arrived, Jack Harper found himself looking at a contract with a $3,000 cut in salary. Chance told him to sign or quit baseball. After he signed, Chance kept him in the dugout. He refused to let him pitch even though Harper threatened to go to the National Commission. Harper had no way out. He knew it. So he finally quit.

It seems fair to say that Johnny Kling did not reach the century mark because Frank Chance wanted revenge. It also seems fair to say that Kling was somewhat put out by being put in the outfield. But he continued to give his manager everything he had.

On Sept. 21, he got 3 hits, slamming two of them for doubles, driving in runs and scoring 1 in a 5–4 win over the Giants. Besides pounding the ball consistently, he continued chalking up assists as he mowed men down trying to steal. In addition, he worked with his pitchers, calling every pitch, signaling strategies to the infield and guiding the team to a record setting pace for victories.

Just before President Murphy left New York for Chicago to make preparations for the beginning of the World Series, he talked to a reporter: "It's real luck that I bought the Chicago Cubs when I did," he said. "I feel like a man who has fallen overboard and on being fished out of the river finds his pockets filled with gold, a diamond necklace around his throat and his fingers loaded with valuable rings. I don't consider myself any shrewder than the ordinary mortal—only luckier."[26]

After the team had the pennant sewed up, the *Chicago Daily News* did a biography on each of the players. For Kling, it said: "John G. Kling is the leading catcher of the league and his friends are all willing to back him for the championship of the country. As a batting catcher, Kling has no peer and his long drives have brought the crowds to their feet more than once this year."[27]

When the season ended with the Cubs setting a new win-loss record of 116–36, the newspapers gobbled up every bit of information they could find on "Three Finger" Brown, and Chicago fans cheered wildly as they read laudatory statements about him:

> Chicago has produced this year a pitching wonder, greater than the great Mathewson, even at Christy's best. Mordecai Brown, of the new National League champions, with only three working fingers, is the man who has beaten Mathewson's record of last season.
>
> Brown has won twenty-seven and lost only six games this year, giving him the lofty percentage of .818. Mathewson's 1905 percentage was .775.
>
> The work of the great Chicago slabman has been remarkable. Brown has pitched in two games in which his opponents made only one hit, one game in which he allowed only two hits, and five games in which only three hits were

made off him. Eight of the twenty-seven victories to his credit have been shutouts. No pitcher in his league has approached that record of effectiveness on the slab against all comers.[28]

It is important to put these praiseworthy remarks into a broader context. This can best be done by remembering the remarks made by Mordecai Brown. He once said, "I'm not ashamed to admit that I was just a so-so pitcher before I teamed up with Kling. A pitcher can always tell you how good a catcher is, and take my word, Johnny Kling was the best." At another time he said, "I don't think I ever saw Johnny call a wrong pitch."[29]

Brown's laudatory remarks about Kling becomes even greater when consideration is given to his 1906 record, and it seems fair to say that had Kling played instead of Moran in some of the games, the Cubs would have an even greater win-loss record.

	AB	R	H	2B	3B	HR	RBI	SB	BA
Kling	343	45	107	15	8	2	46	14	.312
Moran	226	22	57	13	1	0	35	6	.252

Kling's bat alone could have made it happen. His BA was third highest, behind Steinfeldt with a .327 and Chance with a .319. His number of assists for the season was 126, but enough with numbers. It's time for the World Series.

The Chicago Cubs were about to be tested by the "Hitless Wonders." The name was given to the Chicago White Sox because they were seen as a fluke winner of the American League pennant with a flimsy batting average of .230.

In contrast to the mighty Cubs, the Sox were a so-so team that should never have won a pennant. For most of the season they seemed doomed to stay in the second division, but with a sudden outburst of superb pitching, they won 19 consecutive games in August and rose to the top. The national debate favored the Cubs to win the World Series.

The Sox outfought the Cubs through an intermittent snowfall, pushed across an unearned run and won the opener 2–1, Nick Altrock beating "Three Finger" Brown. Most people dismissed the Sox win as another fluke.

Chance's men came back strong the next day and evened things out. Reulbach pitched a beauty, giving up 1 hit and winning, 7–1. Sox fans pointed to 2 Sox errors and 5 unearned runs and the plummeting team morale that gave the Cubs an easy victory. They claimed the Sox should've won it.

To prove their point, spitball pitcher Ed Walsh took the mound for game 3 and did what Reulbach had done the day before. He completely shut down the Cub machine, giving them 2 measly hits, beating Pfiester 3–0.

Fortunately for the Sox, their starting shortstop had been injured and

George Rohe, a player they were planning to get rid of, was forced into game 3. He came to bat in the sixth inning of a scoreless tie with the bases loaded. As he stood at the plate waving a menacing bat, chatterbox Johnny Kling tried to confuse him, saying, "You're the guy who likes fastballs, well, you won't see anymore." But Rohe looked for a fast one, got one shoulder high and hit it solidly on the line, clearing the bases with a triple, giving the Sox a 2–1 lead in the Series.

Again the Cubs bounced back as Brown delivered a 2-hitter, nipping Altrock and the Sox 1–0. The Series was knotted 2–2 and the majority of fans firmly believed that the moment had arrived for the Cubs to finally assert their power and their dominance in the Series. Most baseball writers agreed.

It wasn't to be. The Sox suddenly exploded. They astonished the baseball world by cranking up their hitting, pounding out 12 hits for an 8–6 win in Game 5. The Sox followed this up with a 14-hit slugfest in Game 6, driving "Three Finger" Brown from the mound in the second inning, en route to an 8–3 win and the world championship.

After struggling with just 11 hits in the first four games, the White Sox came alive with their bats and pounded out 26 hits in the final two games, proving they were no longer "Hitless Wonders."

Baseball gurus continued to express their wonder at what the Sox had done. The *Sporting News* said, "Who would have thought that the Sox would show up the Cubs the way they did?"[30]

"They simply came out and beat us," Chance said, "that is the nature of baseball. It was fair and square." That was his statement for the record but privately he hated the Sox and hated admitting defeat. The skipper told "Three Finger" Brown, "How that goddamn ball club beat us, I'll never understand."[31]

Nevertheless, Johnny Evers had an explanation and put it down in writing:

> Though we were overwhelming favorites to beat the "hitless" White Sox, we lost the series four games to two, through the great pitching of Nick Altrock and Ed Walsh — aided and abetted by a trick that the White Sox had worked all season and that, so far as I know, has never been mentioned in connection with the playing of the "hitless wonders."
> The White Sox had their outfield fences painted in several contrasting broken colors, with signs in huge white letters, so that the sunlight, shining on this broken and glaring background, blinded the batter. The White Sox, having a weak hitting team anyway, didn't suffer so much from this bad background as a stronger hitting ball club, so it gave them a big advantage by serving to equalize the hitting.
> The figures show that during those years the hitting by visiting ball clubs to the White Sox park was always light.

8. Clearing Skies

In one of the games in this series, Walsh shut us out with two hits and set a new World Series record by striking out an even dozen. In another game each side made only four hits, while in two other games Reulbach held the Sox to two hits in one game, and Brown beat them 1–0 in the other.

There is no question in my mind that an important part of the strategy of Fielder Jones's "hitless wonders" of 1906 was that blaring, blazing, blinding background on the outfield fences at the White Sox park.[32]

In spite of the Evers explanation, Frank Chance must have known why he lost. His pitching staff, those marvelous pitchers who had recorded an incredible combined ERA of 1.76 during the regular season, had lapsed. They allowed the Sox 22 runs in six games.

With the baseball season over, Johnny Kling wanted to hurry home. He wanted to see how his brothers and sisters were getting along. Since the suit was settled, were they on friendly terms? With Charles taking over the bakery and now a full time baker, was he doing as well as Papa? Then there was Lizzie, still separated from her husband and still renting out rooms. And Bill, still running a saloon in spite of Papa's admonitions about the evils of whiskey.

1907

Johnny Kling celebrated the New Year with a sense of satisfaction. His brothers and sisters were on speaking terms with one another even though some of them did not trust Charles where money was involved. But none of them complained about Charles taking over the bakery since he was now the baker, doing the work that Papa had always done, and he was entitled to whatever he earned.

Lizzie was getting along with her rooming house and Bill seemed content behind the bar. As for himself, Johnny felt financially secure for the first time in his life. He had opened up a billiard parlor in Kansas City at 1102 Baltimore. It was doing well. He had also hired an attorney to negotiate for a piece of real estate, and to find a buyer for a racehorse that looked like a sure winner.

Then there were the many opportunities to play pool, and he was already scheduled to meet former champion Alfred De Oro in February in Kansas City.[33] All in all, he did not have to take any more guff from "penny pinching" Murphy. Nor did he have to put up with or be humiliated by his manager's need for revenge. The idea of putting him in the outfield, preventing him from being the backstop, ruining his chance of again becoming a premier catcher was crazy! No! He didn't have to take it any more.

Johnny Kling let it be known that he would prefer playing for Cincinnati rather than Chicago.³⁴ Five days later, Feb. 9, page 8 of the *Washington Post* followed this up by saying: "Kling said nothing would please him more than to be transferred from Chicago to Cincinnati. Few players go voluntarily to Cincinnati. His friends are thinking of employing a sanity expert to examine him."

What his friends did not realize is that President Murphy had started a series of letters on Jan. 27. These letters were no different than in 1906, giving Kling reason after reason why the club could not increase his salary even though Murphy said, in a Feb. 5 letter, "About your work in 1906, it was simply great."³⁵ In spite of his remark Murphy had the audacity, on March 19, to send Kling a contract for $3,000 (see Appendix B, item C).

The *Chicago Tribune* soon learned of the squabble and got in on reporting what die-hard fans wanted to read about:

March 8: Chance is not worrying over the absence of Kling and is waiting for the pool shark to be waked up without being called. Kahoe, a new catcher, is in pretty good shape. Pat Moran will report in another week.

March 23: Manager Chance declared himself in the Kling case: "If I do not hear from him within a week, he will be traded. I have deals on for two young backstops, either one of whom will develop into a star in fast company. The way Kling has behaved the last three years in the matter of reporting disgusts me. Kling is a grand catcher, but he isn't too good to be traded. The deal I have pending will be delayed one week to give him one more chance. If Kling does report and is not in condition to play the opening game I will keep his money until he is ready to work."

April 2: Mr. Murphy has wired Kling at Kansas City to go to Chicago for a conference, and says that he can at least talk the matter over with Kling. "I will discuss terms with Kling when he meets me," said Mr. Murphy, "and if we find it impossible to agree on terms perhaps something in the way of a trade can be arranged."

April 3: Regarding the reported efforts of Cincinnati to buy or trade for Catcher Kling, Manager Chance says: "We wouldn't take $50,000 and the pick of Hanlon's catchers for Kling. That is how much chance he has to get him."

April 8: "Kling and I discussed his plans today," said Mr. Murphy, "and he did not sign. He seems to think there is a better future for him in the billiard business which he has established in Kansas City. He said he thought there would be more money in it for him than in baseball and that he ought to stick to it."

April 9: Johnny Kling is back in the fold, and in all probability will be behind the bat in the opening game of the season at the West Side Grounds on Thursday. The return of Kling will bring joy to the fans with whom he always has been a popular idol and they will be more than pleased to know that he will catch the opening game against the St. Louis Cardinals.

8. Clearing Skies 93

President Barney Dreyfuss was after Kling and yesterday sent President Murphy several telegrams asking for terms. Mr. Murphy's reply was: "You can have him for $1,000,000 in real money."

The Pittsburgh magnate came back asking Mr. Murphy to stop joking. To this the Cub magnate answered: "We will take Hans Wagner and $80,000."

When asked how he and Murphy got together and if he was satisfied, Kling replied, "I can't tell you anything about the terms except that they are satisfactory to me."

The *Tribune* reported information from "a reliable source." It said, "Kling wanted $4,800 and a three year contract." But the salary reported was $4,700 for a period less than three years.

On April 11, the opening game with St. Louis found Pat Moran behind the bat, not Johnny Kling. The Cubs won 6–1. A blizzard then hit Chicago, putting the second game with St. Louis on the shelf. But with additional delays and a slight rise in temperature, Chance's men took two more games with Moran catching, giving Chicago a 3–0 record before moving on to Pittsburgh, where the team met their first defeat.

Sheer luck turned the tide by the narrowest possible margin of 1–0. A muff by Jimmy Slagle, which was not a muff, yet was a muff, was all that stood between Mordecai Brown and a shutout, with at least a drawn decision.

In the third inning Phelps started with a rainbow fly, for which Slagle hardly had to move. It was a cinch, and Jimmy, with the habitual desire to get rid of the ball as soon as possible, caught it and started to throw with the same motion, but the ball slipped out of his fingers and dropped behind him.

Slagle and the Cubs claimed Jimmy had held the ball long enough to constitute an out, but O'Day ruled otherwise. Phelps saw the break in time to advance to second on it. A sacrifice put him on third, and Anderson squeezed him over the plate with a perfect slow bunt to Chance. It was a tough lemon to hand Brown, and a squeezed lemon at that.

In spite of Slagle's error, was he the only one responsible for the loss of the game? What about Chance? It was he who did not let Noisy John into the game.

Kling was good with the bat. He often came up with a hard hit long ball when it was needed, driving in and scoring runs. But true to his vengeful spirit, Frank Chance had Johnny Kling on the bench, wasting an opportunity to win a close game. Snow hit the ground to cancel the game on April 19, but Kling was in the lineup on April 20, his first game of the season. The team beat the Pirates 5–1. From then on, Noisy was in the lineup a bit more frequently, and by the end of the month, the Cubs found themselves in first place with a win-loss tally of 13–2, one half game ahead of the Giants, who had 13–3.

As the season moved forward, Noisy John found himself behind the bat more often. He gave the team everything he had. The pitchers—Brown, Fraser, Lundgren, Overall, Pfiester and Taylor—knew they'd be in capable hands, knew they'd be winning more than losing, just knew they'd be heading toward another pennant. The news media wrote about the relationship between pitcher and catcher in an article, "Depends on Catcher: First-class Backstops Needed to Win Pennants Must Be a Field General. Headwork Behind the Bat an Essential. All Flag Winners Have Had Great Receivers."[36]

But pitcher and catcher took time out when a howling blizzard blew into town hours after the Cubs arrived home. The Pittsburgers, who came to Chicago seventeen strong, were forced to remain indoors and the games were rescheduled for July 1.

Kling and his best friend Joe Tinker couldn't stay cooped up. They broke away and went to see *David Warfield*. In the attic scene where pop and daughter come together and weep, Tinker felt some manly tears welling up inside. Furtively he reached for his handkerchief, wiped away his own tears, and took a peek at Kling. There sat the noted pool shark. He had thrown back his head, his eyes and mouth wide open like a rube inspecting a tall building. Some of the largest tears seen in public rumbled down on either side of John's nose, turned the corners and fell into his mouth with a dismal splash. The sight of this emotion was too severe for Tinker. He let out a merry squawk that awoke Kling and dammed up a lot of moisture in various parts of the house. John felt stung. He reached for the handkerchief in his side pocket and said any man who had a heart would weep at the scene. This was a noble tribute to Warfield and a fearful slam at the boisterous Tinker, who could laugh out loud at the real tears of a fellow athlete.[37]

Relaxation time was over and the team began playing ball. Fierce competition greeted the team at the Polo Grounds on May 21, where Johnny Kling got 2 hits and scored 1 run to lead the team to a 3 to 2 win over the Giants. The fans then started a riot.

The play that touched off the fuse was simple. Bresnahan drew a pass in the ninth. McGann hit to Evers, and Bresnahan ran out of line to avoid a touch. Emslie allowed a double play on the throw to first. Dahlen flied.

With his eyeballs blazing green fire, the Giants' catcher made a run at Emslie and talked so fast he telescoped his words. This action and the loss of the game primed the mob for the regular explosion. The rowdy crowd went after Emslie, who had started for the dressing room under the stand. Then two cops dragged out guns and fired at the setting sun. A lot of loose cops outside the grounds heard the cannonading, and they came and helped haul Emslie away. At the end of the day, the Giants and the Cubs were tied for first place, both teams having a win-loss of 24–5.

8. Clearing Skies

Chicago pulled a half game away from the Giants when they beat the Reds 5 to 0 on May 25. Besides getting 2 hits and scoring 1 run, Kling was applauded in the *Chicago Tribune* with a paragraph titled "Kling's Eye Working." It said: "The pegging of Kling was a feature. He stopped two stealers and nipped McClean a box car length off second in the round of that number."

The last day of May saw another *Trib* headline: "Kling Leads Rally," telling how the Cubs won a double header from the Pirates, 6 to 4 and 7 to 1.

On June 1, the team was in first place with 29–9, the Giants trailing by 1 with 28–10, but New York soon pulled into a tie and inched ahead. The Cubs, nevertheless, were not to be outdone. On June 8, in a game against New York, "Three Finger" Brown triumphed for the second time in the series, 4 to 2, the game being saved in the ninth: "In response to the howls of the multitude, Ames passed Evers. Kling bunted and Ames made a two base wild heave over McGann's head. Brown walked filling the corners. With the infield up and the outfield on the heels of the infield for a possible Texas leaguer, Slagle put a liner between right and center and the Giants flew the Coop."[38]

But the real feature of the day was Noisy John's two doubles and his scoring one run when Bresnahan tried to block home plate: "The Giant catcher had Kling blocked away from the rubber in the fifth. When John made his slide, one arm was poked between the shin guards while the fingers clawed madly for the goal. The efforts of Bresnahan to recover the lost ball raised the blockade and the gallant Kling inched home."[39]

Johnny Kling was a dangerous man at the plate, especially so when runs were needed to win games, and one such game was against Brooklyn on June 15. *Trib* headlines on the following day read, "Score Tied in Ninth, but Evers and Kling Bat Out a Victory for Chicago."

Headlines on June 18 said, "Cubs Continue Onward March." The story then went on to tell Chicago fans how Kling kept three Boston runners from stealing, thus winning a close game 2 to 1.

The June 19 *Tribune* also told fans about Kling's business dealings. In the "Notes of the Cubs" game section, page 10, it reported: "Last March Mr. Kling purchased a large slab of property at old K.C. Mo. He received a 4 × 9 inch envelope yesterday containing a letter with the request that John pay the taxes from November 1906 to March 1907. The idea is preposterous. He did not own the slab during that period."

Apparently, the *Trib* was willing to intermingle Kling's baseball exploits with his ventures into the business world, and there is no question about his being heavily involved in both.

Amidst the hectic pace of the baseball season, Noisy John conducted business in Kansas City from afar. Besides his pool hall that was in operation, being managed by who knows who, a June 17 letter from Dale Gear, an attorney, clearly demonstrated Kling's involvement in a real estate deal on the verge of closure. It also demonstrated that the multifaceted backstop had a racehorse that he was trying to sell (see Appendix B, item D).

Interest in Kling was not happenstance. Fans idolized him. He almost always came through in the clutch. June 23 saw an example in a game against the Cardinals.

Karger choked the champions to three safties in seven rounds. Like Reulbach, he was great. The game itself was a lulu. With the enemy possessed of one run, and hanging on to it with tooth and nail, things looked dismal for the Cubs. But there was Mr. Kling. Don't forget Noisy John. He was a potent factor. Noisy poled a triple in the eighth and came home on a fly, tying the game. The team went on to win it in the tenth 2 to 1.[40]

By June 26 Chicago was in first place with a win-loss record of 45–12, ten games ahead of New York's 34–21, a comfortable and commanding lead.

Johnny Kling, a very potent factor in the race for the pennant, continued playing splendid ball. On July 6 the *Chicago Daily News* published the batting averages of the 101 players in the National League. Johnny was tenth with .286. The only two Cub players who had higher averages were third place Steinfeldt with .302 and fifth place Hofman with .292. Pat Moran was fifty-seventh with .232.

Fate dealt a serious blow to Noisy John in a July 12 game against the Phillies. He had the thumb on his right hand knocked out of joint and it was likely to be some time before he could go behind the bat to catch again. Chicago's *Daily News* had this to say: "It was my own fault that I was hurt," said Kling. "I became careless and the ball caught my thumb right on the end, pushing the first joint back over the second. I expect to be in shape to work again by the time we get to Boston, at least."

The *Chicago Daily News* went on: "One of Kling's greatest assets as a catcher is his ability to work regularly. He is always in condition and seldom gets hurt. He frequently plays in 100 or more games in a season and that is hard work for any backstop. Coupled with his throwing, batting and head work as a catcher, Kling stands pre-eminently at the head of the list of back-stops in the major leagues today. His absence from the game, even for a few days or a week, cannot help but weaken the team to a certain extent."

On July 19 Kling was again in the lineup in a game against the team's favorite foe, McGraw's Giants. The team celebrated his return by pounding out twenty-five hits, dealing New York a cruel blow with a score of 12 to 3. Johnny got his share of the enjoyment by slamming 2 hits, one a double, and scoring 1 run.

But fate again intervened in Noisy John's play. On July 30, in a game against Brooklyn, a dispute arose that was responsible for three runs in the opening round. Alperman started with a scratch hit past Overall. Casey bunted and Steinfeldt threw to second too late to get "Alpy." Lumley sacrificed both runners ahead, then Batch hit to Overall, who tossed the ball home, cutting off Alperman. Kling ran him back to third base, where Casey already was. "Noisy John" touched Casey and then Alperman, both standing on third. Emslie called Casey out, of course, but Alperman, with a ballplayer's usual carelessness about rules, thought he was the man out and started for the bench.

So far the facts are unquestioned. Kling claimed he touched Alperman again after he left the base and both umpires were willing to take an oath he did no such thing. At any rate, somebody on the bench wised up "Alpy" to the fact he was not forced off third, and he ambled to the plate without anyone trying to stop him. The ump allowed the run to count. They argued Alperman, not being out when he was touched while on third base, was not touched afterward, hence he was not out. Kling and his pals gathered in constantly shifting bunches around the two arbitrators and took repeated solemn oaths that Kling did touch Alperman again while off the base.

First they would talk to Klem awhile, then scurry over to Emslie's stamping ground and converse with Bob, until finally Kling asseverated Klem was a prevaricator, for which he was ordered off the lot. Slagle walked up and remarked: "Whatever you called him, John, that's what he is."

Klem replied, "That goes double, to the clubhouse for you, too."

Finally Klem exhibited his ticker and play was resumed with Moran behind the mask. Jordan immediately walloped an awful one to right, clearing the *Tribune* signboard by several feet and landing in the alley outside. It was the longest swat seen there for years and it sent Batch home ahead of the home run hitter.

That pretty nearly cost the game, and all the runs could have been saved if the Cubs had taken the trouble to put Alperman out twice. Luckily, Chicago won 7 to 6.[41]

Noisy's three day suspension came to an end, but on his return, the team was not in the best shape for a stiff fight, owing to injuries, but the men were battling bravely and winning as well as when the club was in tip-top shape. Chance himself was out. Hofman was out. Slagle was limping. Steinfeldt was under the weather with a heavy cold and some of the others were not in fine trim. But Johnny Kling felt fine, and he continued his style of play, helping to win close games when disaster seemed a certainty.

August 18, in a game against the Giants with Christy Mathewson on the mound, a game which had already been awarded him by the vast majority of a big Saturday crowd, Hofman, Schulte, and Chance participated in and shared the glory of tying up the score after two men were out in the ninth.

Then came the twelfth, still tied, and Johnny Kling stepped up to the plate. He hammered the lid onto the first game of the final Cub-Giant series with a home run drive into the left field bleachers, thereby putting a stopper on twelve innings of boiling, bubbling trouble. Final score: 3 to 2, Cubs.[42]

There was no letup from Noisy John. Aug. 22 saw him as a "batting fiend," so the *Trib* said.

> Noisy John packed away a perfect average. He was up 4 times, made 3 hits, two of which were stinging three-baggers, and dumped a sacrifice the other time up. To the man up a tree it looked as if Kling beat out his bunt when he sacrificed, but as Carpenter was in much better position to judge than if he had been sitting on the limb of a tree, only casual mention is made of the incident.
>
> Kling is using, when he dares to, a bat which was presented to Manager Chance by 'Spike' Shannon while the Cubs were in 'Gotham.' It was given to Chance before the twelve-inning battle, with the understanding, Chance was not to use it in the New York series. Manager Frank lived up to the agreement, all right; but Kling, who didn't know anything about it, discovered the new bat in the pile when his turn came to bat in the twelfth inning of the memorable scrap. He poked the ball into the bleachers and did not discover the identity of the stick until the next day.
>
> Chance left the bat in Kling's care and Johnny never lets it out of his sight, except when he is sleeping. He has asked Pat Moran to bring down a Boston bull dog from his home in Fitchburg to guard the stick. He does not dare use it in every game for fear the opposing pitchers will get sore and hire a gang to smash it with dynamite. But he used it in today's game all right and the 9 to 3 win over Boston tells the story."[43]

Kling's bat was not the only weapon he used in the battle for the pennant. On Aug. 27, John demonstrated another method of attack in winning the opener against the Dodgers 1 to 0.

All three of Brooklyn's hits were made in the first five rounds and did no damage. In the second, Kling saved Lundgren. Jordan drew the first of three passes but was nailed stealing. Maloney scratched a lob into center and also was caught stealing by Kling's deadly aim. Ritter got the only healthy single but died on first. The rest of the game went smoothly.[44]

All was going well until Johnny Kling wrenched his back on Aug. 28, and together with the cold he had caught on the train from Boston to Brooklyn, that combination put him on the hospital corps because he was unable to move about freely. With Moran back home on account of his mother's recent death, acting boss Sheckard had to rush Catcher Hardy from Nashville into harness before the young man had recovered his land legs after spending forty-eight hours on trains to get to Brooklyn.

The quick substitution did not go well for the Cubs. Pitchers were wild

8. Clearing Skies

and could not be steadied. The return of Moran to the lineup in early September didn't help, and the Champs lost a double header to St. Louis, 6–0 and 9–0.

On Sept. 7, a Staff Correspondent for the *Chicago Daily News* reported:

CUBS ARE BADLY CRIPPLED

Chicago's National League baseball champions, in their present badly crippled condition are meeting with some heart breaking reverses. Neither the pitching nor catching departments are in shape. When these two go wrong the main strength of the Cubs is lost.

John Kling is needed right now worse than at any previous time this season, but he is home nursing a wrenched back. Chance received the joyful intelligence from President Murphy last night that Kling would be in shape to work in tomorrow's double-header with the Pirates at the West Side Grounds and the Cub leader will welcome his return.[45]

On Sept. 24 the Cubs clinched the pennant after winning their 101st game, and were again champions of the National League. Chance did not forget the World Series of the previous year when the "Hitless Wonder" defeated his team. He was not going to allow it to happen again. With time to spare before squaring off with either Detroit or Philadelphia, that race soon to be decided, Chance allowed himself to be interviewed by a *Chicago Daily News* reporter.

On the following day Chicago fans read: "Tomorrow is an open date for the champions, no game is scheduled. Manager Chance will not permit his players to spend it in idleness however, for he plans two sessions of hard practice at the West Side Grounds, one in the morning and another in the afternoon. The work will be given to keep the men keyed up to the highest pitch for the coming struggle in the World Series."[46]

The Cubs remained keyed up. They closed the season with a 107–45 record, seventeen games ahead of second place Pittsburgh, which had 91–63. It was a crowning achievement for Manager Chance, but a disappointment for Johnny Kling. Once again, for the second year in a row, he failed to achieve the status of a premier catcher, an honor denied him by his skipper who would not put him in the lineup as catcher just two more times.

Noisy caught 98 games and was a first baseman twice. Moran caught 59 games. Mike Kahoe played in four games for the entire season, catching in 3 and taking over the first base sack on one occasion.

Kling finished the season with a BA of .284, third highest for the team, Chance having a .293 and Schulte .287. In regard to assists, Johnny had chalked up 109.

With a fair degree of certainty, it can be said that Noisy John's bat was in large measure responsible for the Cubs winning the pennant. A review of 1907 games in the *Chicago Tribune* showed him getting hits consistently, driving in and scoring runs when they were needed to win a game.

As batsmen, the catchers in both leagues were not known for their exceptional hitting ability. The BA of catchers in both leagues were:

American League	BA	*National League*	BA
Detroit — Schmidt	.244	**Chicago — Kling**	**.284**
Philadelphia — Schreckengost	.272	Pittsburgh — Gibson	.220
Chicago — Sullivan	.174	Philadelphia — Dooin	.211
Cleveland — Clarke	.269	New York — Bresnahan	.253
New York — Kleinow	.264	Brooklyn — Ritter	.203
St. Louis — Spencer	.265	**Cincinnati — McLean**	**.289**
Boston — Criger	.181	Boston — Needham	.193
Washington — Warner	.256	St. Louis — Marshall	.201

It's now time for the World Series.

Prior to the Series, "penny pinching" Murphy must have lost his sanity amidst wild celebrations, for it was announced that his team would go into the World Series in brand-new uniforms of a striking pattern. The new regalia was of a dark-gray hue, with a green longitudinal stripe. On the breast was a small "C," and on each arm, a diamond with a "C" inside it. The suits were cut specially for each player on the team, and for each one, the name of the player was sewed in silk. The names were also sewed in silk on the caps. But in regard to a new pair of baseball shoes, every member of the team had to purchase his own.[47]

Opinions varied as to who had a better team and who would win, and across the country, sportswriters had a glorious time typing one column, then another. On October 4 the *Washington Post* had an article headlined "Kling Better Catcher." The Cubs had a great advantage because of Kling's ability to stop the Tigers on the bases. The *Chicago Daily News* had agreed with this assessment on the previous day when it said, "For Chicago, catching is head and shoulders ahead of Detroit."

But Manager Hughey Jennings didn't give a hoot about Kling's ability when he told the *Daily News* reporter, "The Tigers are the best ball team the world has ever seen. Our pitchers are all good. Every man on the team is fit. Cobb and Crawford are batting at their best. Now what more would be necessary to make them look like real champions."

That reporter had more to say:

> Will Cobb outgeneral such men as Overall, Brown, Lundgren, Pfiester, Reulbach, Fraser, Kling, Chance and Evers? Or will they get Cobb as they have gotten other fast experts like Beaumont, Wagner, Clarke, Leach, Devlin and the others?
>
> Cobb is a phenomenal base runner and the promised duel between him and John Kling will be the feature of the series.

8. Clearing Skies

If the Cubs should defeat the American League entry for the world's series this week, it would be the first time on record that a Chicago National League club has emerged victoriously in a set of games for the supremacy of the country. Pop Anson's Grizzlies twice were contenders in world's series play and each time failed to win the laurels.[48]

A Chicago victory did indeed depend upon Noisy John's ability to stop Cobb from stealing bases, something the Georgia Peach had been doing all season. He had stolen 49 sacks, the highest number in both leagues except for the 61 thefts credited to Honus Wagner.

Early in the afternoon of October 8 Manager Chance and his champions, resplendent in their new uniforms, marched on the field of the West Side Grounds amid the loud and prolonged buzzes of the multitude. Every movement of the champions brought spontaneous outbursts of applause.

Jennings led his band of confident warriors steadily and straight to home plate, where it broke, and in an instant the preliminary practice had begun. Every move of the catlike enemy was watched with eager eyes by the huge crowd; a brilliant stop, a clever catch, or a hard, long throw elicited an abundance of applause.

Ty Cobb was the center of admiring eyes from all. The question "What will Cobb do to the Cubs?" was on every lip. The tall, handsome Georgian, who had in a single season jumped from an unknown utility man to the highest pinnacle of fame in the baseball world, was looked over from every angle. Every move was studied. The fans were more than pleased with his grace and style of movement, easy yet determined and swift.

Game one began. In the first, Noisy demonstrated his deadly aim by nailing Schaefer stealing, Kling to Tinker. It was a pitcher's duel until the fourth, when it looked like Detroit would take the lead, but it was not to be. Evers made a sensational fielding play that undoubtedly shut off a run. Chance walked in the Cubs' half of the fourth and was moved to second on a sacrifice by Steinfeldt. Kling drove the Cub leader home for the first run of the game. Kling, however, was nipped trying to get to second. It was a bit of tough luck because Evers laced out a single, which was ammunition wasted.

The 1–0 lead was shattered in the eighth when Detroit jumped into the lead scoring three runs, but Chicago bounced back in the ninth with two. Thus reprieved, the Cubs went on to play a 3–3 tie, the game being called in the twelfth because of darkness.

The Cubs then ran away with the series. Jack Pfiester made short shrift of Detroit, 3–1 in Game 2. The Tigers' attempt to switch to a new catcher, Freddie Payne, didn't work. He couldn't stop the Cubs from stealing five bases during the victory. But Kling stopped the Tigers cold. The *Chicago Daily News* had this to say:

In one department alone the Cubs, champions of the National League, so far outclass the Tigers, that critics who watched the work of two contestants for world's championship honors in yesterday's battle figure Chance's men ultimate winners with an even break of baseball luck.

That one department is John Kling.

Kling never in his baseball career shone with greater brilliancy than in yesterday's game against the Tigers. Jennings' bunch from the jungles of Detroit had been touted as world beaters on the bases, fast, wonderful sliders, invincible. Ty Cobb, when sitting in the press box at St. Louis last Sunday, voiced the supreme confidence of the Detroiters that they could run rings around the Cubs when he said:

"I can go from first to third on any bunt we lay down on that slow infield."

Cobb has yet to make good his statement: he failed utterly yesterday to show any of his boasted speed.

John Kling was the stumbling block that tumbled over the Tigers whenever they dared attempt to purloin a bag.[49]

Fans whooped it up one day later as they watched their team maul Detroit, 5–1. Before the game started, Chance and his men got their batting eyes in practice, hitting southpaw Pfiester's curves. Two scratchy hits were all the Tigers got off Reulbach in five innings, but the Detroit squad started what seemed to be an inning of possibilities in the sixth. Three hits were bunched, Ed Killian, the pitcher, getting one of them. The Cubs broke up the Tigers' chances with a fast double play. Only one run scored.

The series now moved to Detroit. Manager Chance said, "They have only Wild Bill Donovan to rely upon now and we will get him tomorrow. We are going to make it four straight if we can, and wipe out our defeat of last year by the White Stockings for the championship." The 1906 defeat by the Sox was still gnawing away at Manager Chance.

"We're still in the saddle, though slightly disfigured," replied Detroit Manager Jennings. "We will show them a thing or two on our home grounds tomorrow. The boys are not downhearted and believe they will get their batting eyes back when they return home."[50]

Day one of the out of town games found the *Tribune*'s efforts to entertain Chicago's fans fully appreciated. Long before the hour for the game, three big halls—the Auditorium theater, the First Regiment armory and Studebaker hall—were besieged by crowds eager to watch the electric scoreboards report the game play by play. Women stood up and waved flags and banners as the Cubs emerged several times from perilous situations and the men rose up, shook hats, sticks, and papers and even danced in the aisles as each succeeding inning added to the lead of their favorites.

When the game ended with a 6–1 win for the Cubs, the fans let out cheer after cheer of joy and filed out of the auditoriums perfectly satisfied with the game and the *Tribune*'s method of affording them an afternoon's entertainment.

8. Clearing Skies

"Three Finger" Brown finished the series by inflicting a humiliating shutout on Detroit, winning by a score of 2–0. But a greater humiliation was inflicted upon the apoplectic Cobb when he took a lead off second base. Kling, the first Jewish player in the twentieth century, was catching. Tinker said to Cobb, "Don't get too far away from that bag or the Jew will nip you off." With that, Tinker in some mysterious way gave Evers a signal to take the throw. Tinker knew that Kling had also received the message. As Cobb turned to sneer at Tinker, Evers rushed to cover, took the throw and tagged Cobb out before he could get back to the bag. This one play helped win the game and the Series.[51]

Saturday evening, after the show was over, "Wild Bill" Donovan was standing in the lobby of the Cadillac hotel in Detroit, talking over the series with Manager Murray of the Philadelphia National League club and a couple of fans. A Detroiter ventured to say: "It was too bad that the Tigers weren't in their best shape to play the Cubs in this series. It might have turned out differently."

"That's where you're wrong," answered Donovan. "The ball the Cubs played against us in this series would have beaten the best game the Tigers ever played. It was not a question of condition or luck. It was simply that Chicago outplayed us all the time."

"I know that ball club from the bottom up," said Bill Murray. "I played twenty two games against it this season and I know it's a wonderful machine possessing the brains that goes with mechanical skill. The only way to beat the Cubs, I learned from experience, is to score runs just as often as they do, and then you may have a chance of getting the final one that wins the game. If Chance's team ever gets a lead of two or three, the opposing team has its work cut out for it if it is going to win out with a tally. I never saw a team that was better at smothering rallies than these same Chicago Cubs."[52]

Chance praised the Cubs, praised Del Howard who played in the final game, praised "Steiny," the name given to Steinfeldt by his teammates, and praised Three Finger Brown, calling him his star twirler, but in the lengthy statement he gave to the press about his players, not once did Chance mention the name of Johnny Kling, not once did he refer to the playing of the man behind the bat that outdueled the mighty Ty Cobb.[53]

It was time for Noisy John to head back home to spend time with his beautiful wife, to play with his daughter, to play pool in his own billiard parlor and to explore real estate possibilities, but definitely no more racehorses. Surprisingly, it took time to find an interested buyer for the one he had owned.

Then there was Charles, who did not seem happy baking bread, cakes and other delicacies. The working hours were brutal and he had no help.

He was not like Papa, who seemed happy behind the ovens, who took delight in boasting that he was the best baker in town. As for Lizzie, she was doing okay renting out furnished rooms and at times helping Charles in the bakeshop. As for William, he was destined to be a bartender until the day he died. After all, what else could he do? Johnny knew that deep down, his brother Bill's spirit had been shattered. He felt like a failure after leaving baseball.

Johnny Kling wanted to help his brothers, and knew that if he were a successful businessman, he might be able to do that.

1908

Johnny Kling no longer had to respond to letters from Charles Webb Murphy, no longer did he have to read derogatory remarks about his being fat and out of shape, no longer did he have to keep his feelings in check when the "penny pinching" President gave him a long litany of ridiculous reasons why his salary should be less and not more.

Noisy John had asked for a 3-year contract in 1906, and signed one for more than one year, but the exact number of years was not released. So, instead of busying himself in squabbles with Murphy, he devoted himself to his passion with pool.

J. Ed Grillo told it best when he wrote about the famous backstop:

"Johnny Kling is not content with being the best catcher on the best team in the world, but is seeking more laurels.

"Among ballplayers, Kling is regarded as the greatest pool player in the profession. Having gobbled up just about all the baseball honors possible, the Cubs' great catcher desires to pick up a bit of glory in the world of pool.

"Kling has issued a challenge to meet Champion Heuston, of St. Louis. He has put up $250 as a forfeit and side bet for the match. The Chicago catcher runs one of the finest pool and billiard rooms in Kansas City, and he naturally wants the match to come off there. He is willing to meet Heuston at any time between now and March 15.

"Kling is supposed to report to the Cubs on March 3, but he feels sure he will be allowed to stay at home if the match is arranged. Heuston will, in all probability, accept Kling's challenge for the championship."[54]

The match never came off. Noisy John reported for spring training and made no fuss about it when he did not receive permission to show up a week or so late. This kind of obedience must have pleased Manager Chance.

When Hughey Jennings took it upon himself to say that Johnny Kling was not to be classed with men like Bennett, Ewing, and Mike Kelley, he touched a tender spot somewhere in Frank Chance's make up. He came back in defense of his backstop in terms that could not be misunderstood.

8. Clearing Skies

Chance pointed to the fact that Kling did his work without ostentation, and did not make false motions or attract attention to his work by sensational plays. But he did display the rarest of judgements in sizing up the opposition's offensive play, and instead of having to throw his arm out to catch men trying to steal, his strategy allowed him to make the plays easily.[55]

Chance might have gone a bit further. He could have pointed out the fact that Jennings was not in a position to make the comparison. In the first place, he only saw Kling in one series, the last one for the world's championship. He never saw Ewing, Bennett or Kelley when they were in their prime. This trio of stars was going out when Jennings broke into the game. So how could he possibly say they were better men than Kling? It was not based on personal observation.[56]

Johnny Kling now had the skipper on his side, and it didn't hurt Noisy one bit when he helped the Cubs slaughter the Dayton team in an exhibition game 8–1 by pounding out a homer.

It also didn't hurt Noisy when he was given a souvenir postcard contract for the spring training trip. He was required to mail one card per day to each of twenty friends. The physical labor of writing addresses kept the great backstop hustling most of the time between games.[57]

April 14 saw the opening game of the season in Cincinnati with a crowd of 19,000, the biggest opening ever. Mayor Markbreit tossed out the first ball. The batteries: Overall and Kling for Chicago; Ewing and Schlei for Cincinnati.

The Reds opened the first round with 5 tallies, but Manager Chance and his pards hacked and chopped away at the commanding lead. By persistent pounding they tied in the sixth and won out in the ninth, 6 to 5.

Five runs loomed up big as a handicap early in the doings, but the Cubs took a brace and went after Ewing in the second, pounding in 2 runs with four singles, all in the same place. Steinfeldt had retired on a fly to left when Evers, Tinker, Kling and Overall shot off successive safeties to right. Slagle fouled out and Sheckard hoisted a long fly to the busy Lobert.

Another Cub tally was made in the fourth when Kling's single scored Evers from third. The Cubs continued to whittle down the Reds' lead in the fifth. Slagle was walked. He stuck to the bag while the next two passed away on flies, but went to second on a balk. Chance singled to right, driving in a run. He then perished trying to steal. At last those demon champs tied her up in the sixth due to the fact that the Reds stood still after their grand splurge in the first.

Steinfeldt opened with a triple into the left field crowd. Evers' third safe wallop put Harry across. Tinker sacrificed. Pretty soon Campbell caught John napping off second and Kling fouled to Ganzel.

To the bold and fearless Zimmerman belongs a great deal of credit. With Evers on second in the ninth and two men gone, Heinie went to bat for Overall and poled John home with a superior wallop over second base. Brown took the slab for the finish and held it superbly while the miserable Reds chanted their little swan song.[58]

Following a Cubs' win of game two on April 16 by a score of 7 to 4, the press accused Mr. Kling of conspiring to open a hall containing forty pool tables and ten bowling alleys. The news item said, "John denies all allegations, but says he would like to open such an institution in Chicago."[59]

On the very next day, April 17, the Cubs once more humbled the Reds, 1–0, and page 14 of the *Chicago Tibune* continued making what appeared to be wild accusations about Kling's plans: "Kling has telegraphed ahead to St. Louis for a ten year lease on city hall in which he intends to open bowling alleys during his three day stop. Fraser is a silent partner in the well known firm of bull conners. They expect to have a chain of phantom pool parlors and alleys around the baseball circuit before the middle of July."

Details about Kling's accomplishments as to pool parlors and bowling alleys were never mentioned in the St. Louis press. It reported only his baseball exploits, and the fact that he and the team were on their way home to open their first game at the West Side Grounds.

The opening game was scheduled for April 22, and President Murphy announced that there would be large doings on the field where the Cubs would dedicate their new World Series flag. It was to be an afternoon of music, parading and flag raising prior to the battle between the Cubs and the Reds. It was also to be like a pink tea function, with potted flowers and palms, and a couple of showcases filled with cigars and candy.

Painters were busy aloft putting the last coats of various colors on the statues and fancy frill around the office roof. The improvements had to be in, and were promised to be in by early afternoon. Jim Hart, owner of the Cubs, Garry Herrmann, owner of the Reds, and Ban Johnson, president of the American League, were to be among the notables attending the game. The batteries were Chick Fraser and Johnny Kling for Chicago; Andy Coakley and Larry McClean for Cincinnati.[60]

The combat was illuminated by individual exploits. Notable among them were the marvelous stops and stunts of the agile Evers and the plunking of difficult foul flies by Kling and McLean. And don't forget Hans Lobert, the "Finely Trained Athlete." His home run blow and the way he sprinted around the sacks won for Hans the admiration of the left field sun gods, who showered peanuts and small coins upon the F. T. A.

The Cubs were back in the game in the fourth when Kling singled to right. Fraser dittoed with one to left that sounded like a small cannon. Slagle worked the hit and run idea, scoring Kling from second. Sheckard's rap to Hulswitt forced Slagle.

In the local eighth, Evers walked and Tinker sacrificed. Kling's beauty-double to left sent in the run. Fraser's wallop to left bounded away from Lobert, scoring Kling and giving Chick an extra base. Slagle skied. Sheckard singled through the box. Huggins got the ball back of second, relayed it to Mowrey, and they stopped the runner at the plate.

The Cubs took the opener 7–3, Kling leading the way with 2 hits, including a double, and scoring 2 runs.[61] The team went on to play grand baseball but lost some close ones. On May 9 they continued to hold first place with a 12–4 record, two games ahead of Pittsburgh after winning a close one from the Pirates, 1–0.

Fraser's two-hitter was the feature of the day, but he may not have been able to claim victory if Noisy John had not used his noodle. The Cub pitcher was in a hole in the first round when Becker walked and Leach singled before a man was out. But Kling caught the minor leaguer napping off second, so Evers' fumble of a nasty bounder from Clarke was not costly. Wagner's grounder forced Clarke, but there were still Pirates on second and third. Then Kling came to the rescue when he caught Leach napping off third and retired the side.[62]

In four days the Pirates were hot on the Cubs' trail with only 1 game separating the two teams and New York inching up close as Chance's men went into a batting slump. The skipper sought to remedy the problem by "shaking up" the team.

Slagle was out and Hofman in, and the batting order was changed for the upcoming game with the Phillies. The lineup was to be Evers leading off, then Sheckard, Schulte, Chance, Steinfeldt, Kling, Hofman, Tinker and the pitcher.[63]

Weather stopped all play, and on May 16, "The World of Sports" section of the *Chicago Daily News* headlined a feature article "Close Race in National." It said, "There is going to be a hot race in the National League for the championship pennant from the present prospects. Five clubs are now within three games of each other, and today's results could easily bring them all within two games and at the same time provide a tie for the leadership. That is about as close as most leagues can run their races at this time of the season. The Cubs must win today to hold undisputed possession of first place."

And win they did. Mordecai Brown pitched a one-hitter, beating Brooklyn 5–0. The most fun came in the fourth. Hofman started it with a short fly to left that fell safely. The visitors played Kling for a bunt to advance Artie. Instead, John walloped a mighty fly into the farthest corner of right field and sent Hofman all the way home, making three bases himself before

Lumley got the ball back. Tinker got in line with a swat to left for two cushions, on which Kling registered leisurely. There were no outs, so Brown was up to sacrifice. He caught the Brooklyn infield twisting itself all out of shape to get Tinker at third, so he pushed his bunt through where the shortstop ought to have been and Tinker scored all the way from second. Some bunt! Evers tried to chop another hit into short left but Lewis got under it. With that, Rucker steadied himself and struck out Sheckard. Schulte's fly ended the comedy.[64]

With Chicago on top, its heels still being nipped at by Pittsburgh, the May 20 edition of the *Chicago Daily News* told its readership:

> Yesterday was an open date in the schedule of the Cubs and Manager Chance had his men [were] out for practice twice, both morning and afternoon. Johnny Kling was the only absentee, being in Cincinnati. Reports from that city say he bought some property there on which he will build a billiard and pool hall, with bowling alleys, to be ready by the opening of the season this fall. The additional report that Kling would buy his release and play with Cincinnati to be near his business and give it all the time possible is denied by Manager Chance.[65]

On May 27, 1908, John G. Kling wrote a letter to August Herrmann expressing his desire to be with the Cincinnati club, hoping that a satisfactory trade could be worked out with Manager Chance (see Appendix B, item E).

Although Kling was busy trying to establish himself in Cincinnati, he continued to give the Cubs the best he had. On May 28, one day after sending a letter to President Herrmann, he led the Cubs in stick work, hitting 3 singles in four times at bat and scoring one run in an 8–2 win over St. Louis. The win put Chicago 3 games ahead of Cincinnati, which was now in second place. He also continued mowing down opponents trying to steal and was an ongoing steadying influence on the pitching staff.[66]

Page 6 of the June 13 *Chicago Daily News* listed the B.A. for every player in the National League. Kling was twelfth with .280, and for the Cubs he was second to Steinfeldt's .296. Nevertheless, by the last day in June, the team was battling Ganzel's Reds to maintain their hold on first place.

The Cubs lost, and the bold headline on page 14 of the July 1 *Trib* proclaimed: "Fans Joyful in Pittsburgh: Defeat of Cubs by Reds, Boosting the Pirates Into First Place Makes Rooters Glad — Parade in Streets."

The same newspaper had a bit of good news and another bit of bad news. Although it was sad that Mordecai Brown's mother died at his home in Rosedale, Indiana, and he had to leave the team to attend her funeral, he was due back that day. He was badly needed.

The bad news had to do with the state of affairs that surrounded Kling's poolroom ambitions in Cincinnati. Johnny and Chick Fraser were both eager to get on with it. Garry Herrmann had offered to back John in a

$75,000 enterprise and the catcher wanted a contract. So did Fraser, who was going to manage the chop suey roof garden connected with Kling's pool and bowling palace. So far, nothing had been signed.

Two days later, July 3, Chicago fans were handed more bad news. In the sixth inning of the first game of a double header at Pittsburgh, Kling's right thumb was knocked out of joint by a foul tip off Leache's bat. The flesh was lacerated and an artery ruptured. A surgeon stitched up the wound using three stitches to draw the flesh together. It would be three weeks before John could work again, which kept him out of the entire series with the eastern clubs coming to Chicago.

President Murphy arranged a deal with St. Louis and brought catcher Doc Marshall aboard. He was expected to do most of the backstopping with help from Moran if needed. The Chicago champions now had a weak spot on the team.[67]

Other injuries plagued the team, and by July 8 the Pittsburgh Pirates inched up into first place. The Cubs would move up, then down again, struggling to maintain their lead, waiting for Kling to again resume his position behind the bat.

Every player knew that Johnny's position was a thankless job. It was physically wearing. Crouching all day seemed, at times, to take some of the spring out of his legs. He had been part of every play, called every pitch and was the only man on the team who was aware of the weakness of every batter on the opposing teams.

Foul balls bounced off his chest, and he was always in danger of a split finger. When runners slid high into home plate, with their spikes high, this too posed a danger. He could never relax as players did in other positions. After all, he was the brains of the team. They needed him and missed him.[68]

On July 15, page 12 of the *Chicago Tribune* told the players that Kling's thumb was not yet healed and that his doctor could "not allow the star backstop to work for at least another week." But Noisy came back in three days, played right field, and with 3 at-bats got 2 hits, including a double to help the Cubs win a close one from the Giants 5–4. This moved Chicago into second place in the standings, one-half game ahead of New York and 3 and one-half games behind Pittsburgh.[69]

Johnny Kling's exploits as a right fielder caught the attention of the *Trib*'s sportswriter when the backstop again played right field on the following day, July 19. He said, "Mr. Kling is not a Jew. He is a professional pool shark and backstop with a bum thumb, trotting a few trial heats in right field for his hitting. He got three hits yesterday."[70]

That remark was an unusual way of praising Noisy John. It was as if the sportswriter was saying that Jews were not known to be remarkable athletes, and that it was hard to believe that Kling was Jewish because of his extraordinary accomplishment both in billiards and in baseball.

But July 20 found Johnny Kling, this extraordinary ballplayer, being ordered out of the game, being ordered to the bench by his physician. "Kling's thumb has healed," the doctor said, "but the middle joint is stiff."[71]

The standings on July 24 showed Chicago in third place, 1 game behind New York and 2 and one-half behind first place Pittsburgh. On July 27, Johnny was back catching and page 6 of the July 28 *Trib* praised him highly: "John Kling returned to the arena with all of his old time speed in throwing and nailed every runner who tried to steal anything. He was given a hearty round of applause by the local rooters when he first came to bat."

On the following day the *Trib* applauded John Kling after headlining their feature sports article in bold, black type:

KLING'S HOMER SAVES CUBS

There were gobs of blue around the Cub bench in the eighth but not for long. Kling scattered them like chaff before the gale with a whale of a drive far out into left field. So far, that Burch never got near it, and had to chase it to the bleacher fence out there. John never stopped running, and although it seemed like taking long chances when he rounded third base with the ball ready to be relayed to the plate, he took them. Ball and runner arrived at the plate at the same instant, but the throw was high, and Kling slid under to safety in true wild western fashion. That run and the runner ahead of it were all that proved necessary to hold the lead the remainder of the way, Chicago beating Brooklyn 4 to 2. The Cubs now moved into second place.[72]

It was nip and tuck for three teams—Pittsburgh, Chicago and New York. On July 31, in a game against Boston, Johnny Kling again led the way to a 3–1 win, getting 3 hits, including a tremendous slam over the left field fence for a home run. One more victory and a Pittsburgh loss was all that was needed to put the champions in the lead.[73] But a Cub downward slide pushed the team into the third slot, and by mid–August, all calculations showed that Chance had to win 33 out of 53 contests to have a shot at the flag.[74]

One week later, Aug. 21, saw the Cubs come out in brand new black hosiery, with no rings or marks of any kind. It improved the appearance of the uniforms, making them look cleaner cut, and they worked well with the ballplayers' superstition that good luck went along with black. The black sox were to remain in high favor if the team made a spurt and climbed to the top just when both New York and Pittsburgh thought they had the Cubs blocked off for good for the rest of the year.[75]

With their lucky hosiery neatly in place, the Cubs defeated Boston on Aug. 21 in the rematch of an eleven inning draw, 2 to 2, fought on July 22, which was called at that time to permit the champions to catch a train.

At the start of the makeup game, Ed Reulbach's wildness kept the big

Cub twirler in a peck of trouble early on. He was replaced by Overall. From then on, the game was grandly played.

The Cubs regained the lead in the fourth and held it the rest of the way. Evers started the winning attack with a pass. Steinfeldt nearly beat out his own bunt, advancing John. Howard was the hitting kid right there with a double along the left foul line that scored Evers with the tying run. Tinker popped out, but Kling, who had replaced Moran, drove Del across the plate with a single to left. Overall grounded out. The press picked up on the win by telling Chicago fans: "By keeping persistently at it, Chicago's National League ballplayers are slowly gaining on the leaders in the flag race. One whole game was gained on Pittsburgh through Thursday's victory and a half a game was made up on the New York Giants yesterday when the Cubs took their third straight from the harmless Doves from Boston by a score of 5 to 3."[76]

Chance's men continued winning. With renewed vigor, and coming from behind with an irresistible rush, the Cubs handed Brooklyn their third defeat on Aug. 24. Leading the way was Johnny Kling. With 3 at-bats, he got 2 hits, including a three-bagger, and scored 2 runs in the 4–2 win.[77]

On the following day, Manager John McGraw issued a statement to the press:

> Tell the fans at home that we have hit our stride and the pennant is safe in old Gotham. I never feared the Pirates. As I have said all along, it is the Chicago Cubs that we must beat to win the pennant and it's there that our fight will be made. The team is in grand shape and ready for the series with the Cubs. Mathewson and Wiltse are better than ever right now and can keep up the pace they've been going without a let-up. In fact, they can stand a lot of grinding if necessary.
> When we get through with the Cubs it will be easy sailing and as we finish up at home and in the lead, they will never take it from us. New York will float two standards from her flagstaff and you can say for me that it looks like the best bet of the baseball year.[78]

All roads led to the West Side Grounds and all these roads were packed and crowded with baseball enthusiasts flocking to the enclosure where the contest was to be staged. Outside the ballpark was a jam of humanity almost equal to the mob packed about the gates. At noon the gates of the park were thrown open and fans who had been patiently waiting in the sun rushed into the stands seeking the best vantage points, to wait three more long hours until time for the game to begin. It was the biggest crowd ever, estimated at close to 25,000. Half an hour before the scheduled time for the game to begin, every stand was packed to the utmost, and the overflow went out on the field. As long as possible the fans were massed on foul territory from third to first, back of the plate, but this space was quickly packed

> # CUBS
> ## vs.
> # GIANTS
>
> The crucial series in the National League begins today, when the first of three games between the Cubs and McGraw's Giants will be played at the west side ball ground.
>
> *The Tribune, recognizing the intense interest of the people of Chicago in these battles, will install its automatic electric scoreboard in front of The Tribune Building beginning this afternoon and will report each game of the series, play by play, as it occurs.*
>
> Every movement of every man on the field is faithfully and instantaneously reproduced on a miniature diamond so accurately that but little imagination is needed to picture the scene itself.

Front page "Extra," Cubs vs. Giants, August 27, 1908 (*Chicago Tribune*).

twenty deep and then they spread around the outfield, thousands watching the battle from that distance.

It was a scoreless game until Chicago's fourth. Bridwell threw Chance out at first on a slow bounder over Wiltse's head. Evers hit a double over third into the crowd, giving him two bases. Steinfeldt singled to right, sending Evers to third, and he scored on Donlin's momentary fumble. Howard fouled to Devlin. Tinker singled. Kling hit to the bleachers in left center and completed the circuit before the ball was recovered. Under the ground rules O'Day sent him back to second and Tinker to third, with Steinfeldt alone scoring. Pfiester was out, Devlin to Tenney — two runs.

In the fifth, Barry scored for the Giants a run on a sacrifice fly by Wiltse, but the Cubs came right back and pounded out three more runs. The final score was 5 to 1.[79]

Game two was a front page headline in the Aug. 30 B-1 section of the *Chicago Sunday Tribune*: "Triumph of Cubs Over Giants, 3–2. One Delirious Inning Results in the Downfall of the League Leaders"

Chicago was now tied for the number two spot with Pittsburgh, each one and one-half games behind New York. On the following day, the world champion Cubs completed a brilliant and sensational series of ball games with the Giants when they won the third consecutive contest from "Muggsy" McGraw's band from the Polo Grounds, thereby pulling within half a game of the league's leader.

It took one more day for the Cubs to practically tie it all up when Overall's great slab work defeated St. Louis 2 to 0.

The standings were New York, 69–45, and Chicago, 71–47, with the Giants .003 percentage points in the lead. But the Giants had to catch up with their schedule or it would tax McGraw's small pitching staff to work overtime. The win over St. Louis was highlighted by the remarkable feat of two players: Hofman and Kling made 80 percent of the putouts in a nine-inning game.

The Cubs could not maintain the pace. By Sept. 10 they had slipped to third place, 1 and one-half games behind second place Pittsburgh and 4 games in back of New York. But they gained a game on the leaders two days later when Johnny Kling depopulated the bases with a home run clout in the twelfth. Four tallies bustled in, breaking the tie at three, and the Cardinals were so disgusted they didn't try to tie it up again in their half of the twelfth.[80]

On the following day, the champions whitewashed the Cardinals 3–0 and inched up into second place. Besides reporting on the game, the press noted: "Kling is negotiating for a twelve story building in St. Louis full of pool tables. John has given up the Cincinnati idea."[81]

The Cubs then lost a ten-inning game to the Phillies while the Giants won twice over the Pirates. The loss was a hard jolt, for Overall pitched one of his greatest games of the season. It was lost, as so many had been during the season, through errors in the field. The tying run in the eighth inning should never have been scored; Zimmerman should have gotten McQuillen's grounder that started the inning, and then the pitcher should have been out at second when Kling caught him off first, but Tinker lost sight of the ball on Chance's throw as the ball just escaped the runner's ear, and then Joe muffed it. "Had he been caught, the side would have been retired before Titus had a chance to make his hit that scored the tying tally,"[82] the *Daily News* maintained.

Page 10 of the Sept. 21 *Chicago Tribune* painted a gloomy picture when it wrote: "Cubs Hoping Against Hope. Meanwhile Those Giants Order Their Coronation Robes."

But miracles happen; there was ghoulish glee in the cub camp as the champions took a double win over the Phillies while the Giants lost to Pittsburgh 2–1.[83]

Then, on Sept. 22, Mighty Mordecai came to the mound. He snatched the first game from the clutch of the Giants, 4–3, and won the second, 3–1. In each contest the Cubs were given a battle royal by McGraw's hostilities, but his men were destroyed on the base paths when they tried to steal. Johnny Kling chalked up 6 assists. Chicago was now in a tie with New York except for a .006 mathematical difference because the Giants had not played three postponed games.

Sept. 23 saw a very close race. Everyone's nerves were on edge. In the final game of the Giants-Cubs series, Jack Pfiester started for the Cubs against Christy Mathewson. A large crowd of 20,000 filed in knowing the importance of every game. The crowd took their baseball with a deadly intensity.

It became a pitching duel between Mathewson and Pfiester. It was a scoreless tie going into the fifth. It was then that Joe Tinker took advantage of the long center field power alley at the Polo Grounds to leg it out for his sixth homer of the year. The Cubs took the lead 1–0.

With one man on in the last of the sixth, Turkey Mike Donlin singled over Evers' head to tie the score 1–1. Three New York rallies threatened to take the lead but they were felled by the Cubs when Kling called for low, inside corner pitches that were quickly gobbled up into double plays from Tinker to Evers to Chance.

A feeble attempt was made by the Cubs to regain the lead. Kling hit a slow roller to Devlin and beat the throw. Pfiester attempted to sacrifice, but it became a double play made by Mathewson, Bridwell and Merkle. Heyden struck out.

In the last of the ninth the score was still knotted, 1–1. There was one out and tension was rising. Art Devlin singled to center to get the Giants going. The winning run was on first. Moose McCormick hit a slow grounder to Evers, who relayed it to Tinker in time to get Devlin at second, but too late for the double play that would have retired the side. Up to bat with two out and McCormick on first came a nineteen-year-old rookie first baseman Fred Merkle. Pfiester studied the right-hand hitter and delivered. Base hit, right field. McCormick raced to third.

Al Bridwell was the next batsman. He took Pfiester's first pitch and lined it to center for the game-winning single. McCormick raced home with the winning run. The fans poured onto the field yelling their elation at the Giants' 2–1 triumph. Merkle, seeing the crazed New Yorkers heading his way, stopped running toward second and made a beeline for the clubhouse beyond right field.

Evers, known for having one of baseball's most agile minds, began screaming for center fielder Solly Hofman to throw him the ball. Hofman's throw went over Tinker's head and rolled to where Joe McGinnity, the Giant pitcher, was standing. Joe raced for the ball. He realized what was happening, outwrestled the Cub shortstop for the ball, and with Tinker on his back, he heaved the ball into the crowd.

Rube Kroh, a second-line Cubs pitcher who was not even in the game, saw who caught the ball: a tall, stringy, middle-aged gent with a brown bowler hat. Rube demanded the ball. When he wouldn't cough it up, Kroh hit him on top of that stiff hat, drove it down over his eyes and as the gent folded up, the ball fell free. Kroh grabbed it, tossed it to Tinker who fired

8. Clearing Skies

it to Evers who was yelling and waving his hands out by second base. Evers stepped on the base and made sure Hank O'Day saw him.

When the hit was made the crowd swarmed upon the field. O'Day, remembering the Pittsburgh game several weeks earlier where the same play had come up, raced toward second base. He saw Merkle turn and go to the clubhouse, waited until Evers received the ball, then saw the second baseman touch second base.

"The run does not count," O'Day said, as the crowd swarmed over him. Fans shrieked, struck at him, pulled him and threatened his life. He made no attempt to continue the game because of the confusion.

When hundreds of drunk and angry Giants fans learned what the Cubs were trying to pull, they headed for the Chicago clubhouse intent on revenge on both umpires and the Cubs. Chance was the target. The crowd would have treated him harshly but for two fat policemen. Surrounded by them and some of his players, the Chicago manager argued that he would protest the game and called for O'Day. He complained that because the New York fans invaded the field and prevented the continuation of the game, the Cubs should be declared winner by a forfeit. Umpire Bob Emslie refused to take a stand for or against O'Day. "I didn't see the play," he insisted. That was all he said on the matter.

Mathewson and a couple of the Giants had dashed for the clubhouse and tried to get Merkle back to second, but Evers was standing there with the ball before they got him out of the door. They saw it was too late. McGraw kept screaming bloody murder, hollering that the Giants had won. A couple of cops McGraw had scattered around to protect the visiting players took a few pokes at Chance under the guise of keeping the crowd back. Fistfights were going on as the team finally got out of the Polo Grounds.

When the umpires emerged in their dress clothes, Bob Emslie repeated that he hadn't seen anything. Hank O'Day shouted back over his shoulder, "Merkle didn't run to second, the last run doesn't count. It's a tie game."

When Giants Manager John McGraw began to protest with his customary vitriol, O'Day told him if he didn't like the decision he could take it up with National League President Harry C. Pulliam. The next day, the furious Giants appealed to Pulliam. So did Chicago. Giants owner John T. Brush wanted O'Day's out call nullified, giving the Giants the victory. Chicago owner Charles Murphy demanded the Cubs be awarded the game by a forfeit. The world waited for Pulliam's decision.[84]

Regular season play continued, and Chicago fans had every reason to dance in the streets when the *Tribune* flashed its headline on Sept. 25: "Joyous Day for Champion Cubs Victory Over Brooklyn and Double Defeat of Giants by Reds Cut Lead. But One Point from Top."

Overall's great pitching gave Chance's men the game. But Noisy John was recognized for his contribution. The Cubs were unable to break the 1–1 tie until the seventh. Then, hits by Kling and Overall and Slagel's sacrifice fly induced the winning run to flicker across. The luck held out until the eighth and the Cubs compiled one more tally. Tinker skied, but Kling singled and stole. Overall smashed a safety, putting John on third. Slagle again produced a sacrifice fly to center, and Kling ambled home from his corner pocket. Overall was nipped stealing. Two more tallies came across in the ninth, giving the team a 5–1 win.

The Cubs took two more games from Brooklyn on the following day, 5–0 and 3–0, and the B.A. for all players in the National League were published. Kling occupied the fourteenth slot at .274 and was fourth highest on the Chicago team.[85]

Sept. 29 was a glorious day for Chicago fans, as indicated by the *Trib*'s headline: "Cubs in Lead by One Point. Defeat of Reds and Other Doings of the Day Give Them a Margin. Cincinnati Beaten, 6–2."

The "other doings of the day" referred to the Phillies winning one game in a double header with the Giants, knocking McGraw's men down to second place. But the real news of the day was in the Sept. 30 *Chicago Tribune*, tucked away in "Notes of the Cubs." It reported that Evers, Kling and Steinfeldt were going to retire from the game for good at the end of the season. "Evers is to sell shoes at Troy," it said. "Steinfeldt will manufacture bread pans on a large scale in Cincy, and Kling is to open a chain of international pool parlors extending entirely around the civilized globe."

The loss of Evers, Steinfeldt and Kling would devastate the Cubs, but next year was a long way off and maybe it wasn't true. Of immediate concern was Pulliam's decision regarding the game of Sept. 23 that umpire O'Day had declared a tie.

That decision was still in the making. The only thing Mr. Pulliam did say was that "the Cub-Giant tie game imbroglio would be decided by him in the natural course of events— namely, when he had looked over the documents submitted by New York. When he has rendered his decision, either side will have the privilege of appealing to the board of directors of the National League."[86]

On Sept. 30, with the decision still pending, the Reds landed a blow that hurt the Cubs. Trailing 5–4, they pushed across two runs in the ninth for a 6–5 win that forced the champions into third place. Two days later, Pulliam handed down his ruling. He upheld the umpire's decision citing the O'Day report. "The people had run out on the field," the umpire stated. "I did not ask to have the field cleared, as it was too dark to continue play." Pulliam said he was upholding the umpire on a question of fact. O'Day had ruled that the game had ended in a 1–1 tie. So it would stand. As neither club had an open date, Pulliam ruled that the contest would not be continued. The Giants appealed Pulliam's decision to the board of directors.

On October 3 the Cubs beat the Reds 16 to 2, Kling getting 3 hits on 3 at-bats and scoring 1 run. He was unharnessed after three rounds of combat to let him rest up and compose his intellect for the coming games that meant so much.[87]

One of those games was on the following day, Oct. 4, against Pittsburgh. With the race being so close, it was do or die for either team. Manager Chance decided to send Three Finger Brown against Clarke's crew even though, in the desperate attempt to pull up to the Giants, he had been used twice in Cincinnati. But "Brownie" was never known to welch at a critical moment, and was known to have more nerve in a pinch than any other pitcher in the business. He told Chance his arm was fine and that he was ready to fight the Pirates for the final game. And he did.

Chicago newspapers played it up big. The *Trib* headline boldly proclaimed: "Cubs Jump to Top, Beating Pirates. Trouncing of Pittsburgh Leaves Only New York as Opponent for National League Pennant. Giants Must Win All Contests Remaining to Tie; Brown Is Victor in Great Pitching Battle."[88]

The World of Sports section of the *Chicago Daily News* gave a detailed analysis of the 5 to 2 win by the Cubs:

> Brown was master of the situation all the way by his teammates getting a lead of two runs, scoring in the first and fifth innings. This was tied up by the Pirates in their half of the sixth through a bit of luck for the visitors, and one hard hit by Wagner. But even then confidence was not shaken in the great three-fingered hurler who stood upon the mound within view of the largest crowd that ever witnessed a professional game of baseball either here or anywhere else in the land.
> Backing the superb pitching of Brown was the equally able catching of Johnny Kling. In the tumult that followed the victory of Brown, upon whom so much depended, the sterling services of the greatest backstop of them all were passed over. It was Kling's headwork in outguessing batters, it was his good right arm and accurate throwing that killed off base runners attempting to steal and get in position to score on hits that made possible Chicago's great victory.
> The whole Chicago team should come in for praise for the great fight it showed yesterday. Every man played brilliantly in the field. The batting was timely, especially Schulte's. The defense was strong and the offense irresistible.[89]

On Oct. 5, the Board of Directors of the National League met for the second straight day. A decision regarding the Cubs-Giants 1–1 tie was not released. On that day the Giants beat Boston 4–1. With the Cubs' season over, the Giants still had one game remaining against the Boston Braves. If the Braves won, the entire matter would be moot.

In Chicago, the *Tribune* was offering prayers that the next day's Giants-

Boston game be rained out, preventing the Giants from finishing in a tie with the Cubs. Such was not to be. The season ended with the Giants and Cubs in a tie, both 98–55.

The board decided to replay the Merkle game. There were choices to be made. They could play a single game or the best out of five. Charles Murphy liked the idea of five games because of the extra money a series would bring. He didn't want to risk everything on a single game against Christy Mathewson, the best pitcher in baseball. So, he opted for five games. McGraw didn't give a hoot about money. He cared only about winning. He had Mathewson and chose to play one game.

On October 7, the *New York Herald* wrote: "The coming showdown is going to be a war. Never before have two teams been tied at the end of a season. Never before has the race been so close. Never has it been necessary to play off the tie of six months' baseball in a single gigantic battle. That the game will be a struggle to the death is certain."

Johnny Kling came near to being left behind. He went to Kansas City on business and knew nothing of the club's trip until 10 o'clock the night before. He had barely one hour to catch the 11 o'clock train. That train was three hours late, reaching Chicago only about half an hour before the team left for the east. Chance heaved a sigh of relief when he saw the catcher come through the gate at the LaSalle Street station.[90]

When Frank Chance led the Cubs into New York the morning of October 8 to meet the Giants that afternoon, Mordecai Brown had a half dozen letters in his coat pocket. "We'll kill you," these letters said, "if you pitch and beat the Giants."[91]

It wasn't the only Giants hanky-panky afoot. McGraw planned to cut the Cubs' batting practice time from thirty to fifteen minutes. Then, if the team protested, he would send his three toughest players charging out to pick a fight. The wild-eyed fans would riot! Blame would be put on the Cubs for starting it and the game would be forfeited to the Giants. As McGinnity stepped to the plate under orders to begin knocking grounders to the Giants for fielding practice, Chance tried to brush him away and the "iron man" raised his bat menacingly. For one instant it looked like the beginning of a riot. But players rushed in and surrounded the belligerents, smoothing out the incident quickly. When the thing was explained to Chance, he smiled contemptuously and acquiesced. The Cubs proved later that they didn't need the extra fifteen minutes of batting practice.

The game was one of the most fiercely fought in the history of baseball. It was Mathewson versus Pfiester, the same pitchers that dueled it out during the 1–1 tie in the Merkle game. Fully sixty thousand fans were aquiver with excitement.[92]

The Cubs started with their first three men making easy outs. In the

8. Clearing Skies

Giants' half of the first, the first ball pitched by Pfiester was a sign of disaster. Tenney was hit on the arm. With two strikes on Herzog, Pfiester lost control and passed him, putting Tenney on second. Bresnahan struck out, but Kling dropped the third strike. Bresnahan was out anyway because first base was occupied. Seeing Herzog taking a long lead, Kling fired a throw to Chance, nailing Herzog for a double play.

Despite Kling's play, the Giants scored the game's first run. Mike Donlin pulled a liner over first base near the foul line, scoring Tenney. Chance argued the ball was foul. The crowd hooted and the tensions rose to such a high pitch, a fireman out beyond center field fell off a telegraph pole and broke his neck. Seymour was given a base on balls. Chance removed Pfiester from the slab and Brown replaced him. Brown's first act was to strike out Devlin, leaving two men on base.

Frank Chance came to bat in the second. The fans met him with a storm of hisses. He responded with a single. The ball came back to Mathewson. He looked at Bresnahan behind the plate, then wheeled and threw to first, catching Chance off guard. Chance slid. Tenney came down with the ball. Umpire Klem threw up his arm; Chance was out.

Frank ripped and raved in protest. Most of the Cubs rushed out of the dugout. Solly Hofman called Klem so many names he was ejected. The stands went into a panic. The roar became even wilder when Matty went on to strike out Steinfeldt and Howard.

Chance was grim when he came to bat in the third. Tinker had led off the inning with a long ball to center over Cy Seymour's head. Kling then singled on a line to left center, sending Tinker across the plate. Brown bunted toward first for a sacrifice and was retired by Tenney unassisted, putting Kling on second.

Johnny Evers came to bat and Mathewson deliberately pitched four wide balls, sending Evers growling on his way o first. Schulte was next. His fighting Dutch was just as good as Johnny's Irish—he hit a liner over third base into the crowd in left field, giving him two bases and scoring Kling with the run that put Chicago ahead and driving Evers to third.

It was now Chance's turn and the crowd was howling. Gripping the bat, he put into his swing all the vim and vengeance that had been welling up in his heart, all the enmity and disgust for the petty tricksters who had been yapping at his heels trying to do him out of a pennant. He met a curve squarely in the middle of its break, driving the ball far out of reach of Mike Donlin. With that swat two more Cubs crossed the plate, borne by Evers and Schulte. Frank made it to second with a great slide that beat a great throw by Donlin. As Chance stood on second with a smile on his face, the Cubs were ahead 4–1.

The battle ran along smoothly, as if the great stakes had been forgotten. Then in the seventh came the Giants' final rally and the final successful repulse. Devlin started the attack with a whistling single to left center. McCormick poked a grounder just beyond Evers' reach into right field, and Bridwell would not let Brown outguess him at the plate. Instead he drew a base on balls to load the bases with nobody out.

Once more the raging mob, which had been chewing the bitterest cud known to baseball fandom, rose to the occasion. Once more they saw a new pair of pennants floating in center field in place of the torn and stained emblems of 1905 when the Giants were the whole thing in baseball and then some. The yelling was rasping and raucous, with the anger of hope deferred and of anxious moments of fear and dread.

Here, Manager McGraw seized the opportunity by sending Larry Doyle to bat in place of Mathewson, to try to bring home the runs and complete the downfall of Brown and the Cubs. Instead of sticking his hip into a pitched ball, as this same Doyle had done once before to steal a game from the Cubs, he hit only a pop foul.

As Kling went to catch it, the fans sailed derby hats, bottles, paper—anything and everything—to confuse him. But Kling had nerve and he corralled it. That was one out, but those three Giants still panted on the bases and unless they were kept there, Chicago's lead would be wiped out.

Tenney was next. He lifted a fly so far into right field that Schulte was content with pulling it down and made no effort to stop Devlin's score. Instead, he fired the ball back to Evers to hold McCormick on second. Two were out and only one run of Chicago's lead had been lost. Still, there were Giants on first and second and the gate was still open. Herzog grounded out, Tinker to Chance.

New York could do nothing against the great "Three Finger" Brown in the last two innings. After four pitched balls in the ninth the game was over. For the third successive year the Chicago Cubs were the National League champions.

As the ninth ended, the Cubs ran for their lives. Some of the boys were roughed up, but they made it to the clubhouse and barricaded the door. Outside, a wild crowd looked like a lynch mob. Police came, formed a line across the door and pulled revolvers to hold the crowd back. When safe, Chance and his men rode to the hotel in a patrol wagon with two cops on the inside and four riding the running board and the rear step. That night, they left for Detroit and the World Series by slipping out the back door. They were escorted down the alley in back of the hotel by a swarm of policemen.[93]

Chance had put Johnny Kling behind the bat in 117 games, thus allowing him to once again become a premier catcher. Kling's stats for the 1908 season were:

8. Clearing Skies 121

G	AB	R	H	2B	3B	H	BA	A
149	424	51	117	23	5	4	.276	149

Noisy John's BA of .276 was second highest for Cub regulars, Johnny Evers topping the list with .300 and Frank Chance third at .272.

With the season over, Frank Chance issued a brief statement on the following day. "My boys were nervous at the start of the game. But they braced up and you know the rest. The team is the finest in the history of the sport."[94] Praise for the Cubs poured in from the baseball world. Even President John Brush of the Giants had something nice to say. Bellyaching comments from John McGraw, however, showed he would never forget.

Cubs' owner Charles Murphy was delighted at the publicity. It meant higher ticket prices for a World Series that was certain to be a complete sell-out. He was, however, incensed at John McGraw's bellyaching that the Giants had been cheated out of the pennant. Deciding to rub salt on the Giants' wounds, he issued a press release referring to Fred Merkle's failure to run to second base on a base hit. He said, "We can't supply brains to the New York Club's dumb players." The complaints from McGraw suddenly vanished from the sports pages and were replaced by World Series news.[95]

Prior to the first game, fans were asking, "What chance do the Tigers have with the Cubs?" The *Chicago Tribune* attempted to answer that question by comparing the two teams. "The Cubs are the greatest baseball machine of modern days," the *Trib* said, "not the greatest machine in every department of the game with its various ramifications, but the best balanced with a grand pitching staff, a terrific impetuous attack and a brilliant defense."[96]

In comparing players on the two teams, the *Trib* focused their attention on the catchers. "Kling is without a peer in the backstopping department," the newspaper said. "His accurate throwing to bases is invaluable to his pitchers when a pinch arises and the enemy becomes daring on the sacks. His batting, naturally strong, is not likely to be affected by the nervous tension of a crucial struggle, and, while comparatively slow as a base runner, he knows what is required and has the niceties of judgement which any team playing scientific baseball must possess."[97]

October 9 found the three-time champions hopping off their train in Detroit as chipper as a bunch of 10-year-old lads. They were glad to have escaped with their lives from the maelstrom of angry, disappointed Giants fans they left behind in New York. They were anticipating with great delight the prospect of one quiet, restful night's sleep before doing battle for the second World Series championship with the Tigers on the following day.[98]

October 10 brought out a Detroit crowd to root for the home team in Game 1. For eight innings they had something to scream about. The Tigers were ahead 6–5 going into the ninth. Three more outs and Ed Summers, a rookie knuckleball pitcher, would have put one away for Detroit.

With Evers out, Schulte sped down the path, beating out a hard drive to deep short. Then came Chance with a vicious single to center, putting Schulte on second. Steinfeldt came to the plate and lined a single to McIntyre in left. So quickly did he field the hit, the fleet Schulte had to hold third. Solly Hofman, a great utility man, took two strikes and waited for three balls. It was a guessing match between batter and pitcher. It came, a fast one over the heart of the plate, and away it sailed into left, scoring Schulte and Manager Chance, Steinfeldt taking third on the throw.

Joe Tinker bunted on a squeeze play. It worked. Steiny scored. While they were trying for Steinfeldt at home, Tinker got to first. Hofman was on second. Then Tinker and Hofman worked a double steal. The Cubs were playing rings around the discomfited Tigers. There seemed no way of stopping them. Kling delivered a single to center to score Hofman and Tinker. Brown sacrificed and Sheckard, the man who got three hits the first three times up, flied to Sam Crawford.

The agony was over. The Tigers were subdued. The first game, which carried so much with it in a short series like this, was won 10–6. A happy bunch of Cubs left the field to prepare for the next day's game in Chicago.[99]

Meanwhile, back in the Windy City, where crowds had been watching the electric board in Orchestra Hall, pandemonium broke loose when the defenders of Chicago's preeminence pounded out five runs in the ninth. The *Tribune* gave an account of the reaction.

> "Are we downhearted?" called a small boy in the gallery.
> "No!" thundered the fans' chorus, from ushers to millionaires.
> "Why?" queried the boy, feigning ignorance.
> "One! Two! Three! Four! Five! Six! Seven! Eight! Nine! Ten!" counted the throng in answer, the deepest note of the organ was sounded in sympathetic triumph. All of this was a clear demonstration of public happiness throughout Chicago.[100]

Prior to the second game, Charles Murphy infuriated Chicago fans by raising World Series ticket prices. Usually, a team charged double the regular season price. Murphy charged five times as much. Instead of the sellout crowd of 25,000 that was expected, only 17,760 showed up at the West Side Grounds.

For seven innings they saw Orval Overall and Bill Donovan duel it out in a scoreless game. With one out in the eighth, Hofman beat out an infield hit, Chicago's second hit of the day. Donovan threw Tinker a waist high ball which was so close he had to step back from the plate. Meeting it squarely, the shortstopper sent the ball soaring on the wings of the wind out into the cavernous blue depths of right field and over the fence. It was the first Cub home run in World Series play.

Kling followed that home run smash with another of similar dimensions into left field. It sailed into the overflow crowd in back of the temporary fence. That constituted a two-bagger only, but it unnerved Donovan and he allowed 2 more runs in what became a 6–1 loss.

After the game, Cobb blamed the wind for the defeat of the Tigers. He said that Tinker's hit would have been a sure out had it not been for the wind in back of the ball, and there would have been no runs scored in that terrible eighth inning.

"Tinker's hit was a high one," he said. "And I rushed back and got set for it. I saw the ball sailing on over my head and I rushed back to the fence and backed up against the wire netting, believing that I would surely get it. I was surprised when the sphere went on over the fence. I jumped for it but could not touch it. On an ordinary calm day the ball would never have gone so far and I could have easily caught it and held Hofman on first. That would have made two outs and Kling's two-base hit would not have resulted in two more runs. The inning would have ended in a tie at the most, and we could have gone on to win.[101]

Manager Jennings also found reasons for the loss. He vowed the Tigers would come from behind and take the lead as they had done in the past. In Game 3, there was a hint they would when Ty Cobb banged out 4 hits and the Tigers beat Jack Pfiester 8–3.

The Series returned to Detroit. Tiger fans were confident that they had now seen the real Tigers and were expecting more of the same. But Mordecai Brown took the slab in Game 4, and he was nearly the whole show.

Trouble started in the fourth when O'Leary started a rally with a single over Tinker's head. Crawford followed with one much like it only faster into left field. The crowd grew violent in its spasms of joy and anticipation, for the mighty Cobb was next.

Cobb came close to breaking up the game with a little bunt toward third. Brownie did some fast thinking while racing across the grass after that roller. Steinfeldt was ready for a play at third. But O'Leary was tearing for that bag like a March hare while Cobb was dashing to first with such speed, only the quickest action could retire him. Brown had nearly no time at all to think it all out and make a decision knowing full well the wrong play probably spelled defeat.

He elected to get O'Leary if possible and there was steam on the shot he fired at Steinfeldt after picking up the ball. Steiny didn't mind the steam, but held the ball and the decision was so close that the rooters fairly gasped and held their breaths until they saw Klem wildly waving his arms to signal that the man was out. Brown had decided and Brown had won the crucial verdict.

But the enemy was dangerous. Two fleet ones were on the bags and Roseman was at bat, but Kling and Tinker came to Brown's rescue by catching Crawford napping off second base. Kling's throw had little speed on it but it went straight to the mark, and Tinker had Sam blocked off the bag, getting another remarkably close verdict.

Thus was the threatening situation turned into one of comparative safety by use of brain matter concealed in the skulls of Chance's warriors and their machine-like ability to pull off plays.

Roseman completed the inning by striking out as Cobb started to steal second. The Tigers were never dangerous again and the Cubs recorded their third victory of the World's Series, 3–0. The Tigers now had to win three straight to win the Series and even the most loyal Detroiters believed this to be an impossible feat.[102]

So it was. Overall took the mound for the Cubs and proceeded to toss another shutout over the American League champions by a score of 2–0. Manager Jennings was the first to congratulate Manager Chance, rushing to the Chicago bench the minute Kling caught Schmidt's foul fly in the ninth inning.

It was a brilliantly played game, full of pretty fielding and timely hitting on the part of the Cubs. Johnny Evers figured prominently in both runs, scoring the first run in the initial round and bringing Kling home in the fifth with his clean two-bagger. On October 15, the *Tribune* said it all: "Cubs Supreme in Baseball World."

The players were overjoyed knowing they would soon receive another championship medal with rubies and diamonds in addition to a nice piece of cash.

As for Johnny Kling, he immediately headed for the train station on his way home. He wanted to see and talk with family about how fed up he was with Charles Murphy, who blocked his plans to establish a chain of pool and billiard parlors. He was going to let them know about his plan to open a second such establishment in the heart of the business district in Kansas City, not far from his other pool hall at 1102 Baltimore Avenue that was already proving to be a very successful enterprise. Other business ventures were already bouncing around in his daily thoughts, and he wanted family to be involved.

9

JUMPING SHIP

1909

The year 1909 was one of momentous occasions. Celebrated that year were the achievements of Charles Darwin, Elizabeth Browning, Alfred Tennyson, and Robert Fulton. Americans planned to rejoice anew their citizenship in America.[1] And later on, Americans would note 1909 as the birth year of Abraham Lincoln, Oliver Wendell Holmes and Edgar Allan Poe.

New Year's eve found Johnny Kling already rejoicing. On Dec. 21, he had beaten D.J. Loney in a six-night pool match, 600 to 481. He, John Kling, the undisputed Western champion, had beaten the Eastern champion. The prize was $200. But more important was proving to the world that his ability as a cue artist was second to none.[2]

Another reason for celebration was his planned opening of the finest billiard hall in America. After months of remodeling, the first floor was ready and set to open January 6 in the Heuston building at 1016 Walnut. In three weeks, Kling's Kansas City pool hall would be complete. He had already spent $40,000 and was pumping more money into the establishment, but fourteen tables in each section was seen as a good investment.[3]

Suddenly, amidst the gaiety, calamity! The press reported, "Johnny Kling, backstop for the Chicago Cubs, will not be with the champions when the team starts on its trip to begin spring training Monday. Johnny is not holding out, but luck has gone against him in the past 30 days, and he is forced to look after business interests before departing for the training grounds. Kling believes he will not be able to join the Cubs until they have assembled at Shreveport for the first exhibition game.

"The crack backstop has been beaten in two pool matches, was robbed, and his place of business was practically destroyed by fire. This looks like a pretty tough streak of luck, but it is said Kling has the business well insured, so that the loss won't be so great after all."[4] Johnny Kling didn't mind much being robbed, but when Rube Waddell, the erratic pitcher for the St. Louis Browns, singled him out and beat him in six successive pool games, that was real mortification.[5]

This feeling passed quickly. He was deeply concerned about the fire and far too busy attending to details in arranging for the insurance company to pay for his loss, so Kling said. But was there ever a fire at all? Ray Elder, historian for the Kansas City Fire Department, was interviewed on August 20, 2004, and said no record exists for a fire at the Heuston building at 1016 Walnut as reported by Kling. To verify Mr. Elder's report, *Kansas City Star* newspapers were reviewed on microfilm at the Kansas City Library:

Jan. 26, 1909,	"Johnny Kling is practicing daily in his pool rooms at 1016 Walnut street in preparation for his match with B. Allen, the 'kid' pool expert of this city" [p. 8].
Feb. 11, 1909,	"Bennie Allen will meet his uncle, Johnny Kling, in a 650-point match for the championship of K. C. Kling holds the trophy of Kansas City and Allen, who is considered one of the best young pool artists in the West, is very anxious to capture the title from his uncle" [p. 8].
Feb. 13, 1909,	"Johnny Kling and Bennie Allen will meet for the city championship beginning next Monday night. Both cue artists are now in condition to put up a first class game. Allen is probably in better shape than Kling, as he has been cueing for the ivories regularly for the last six months, while the Chicago catcher has been spending most of his time in building his pool hall" [p. 8].
Feb. 15, '09 headline:	"The pool players will start championship match at 1016 Walnut St" [p. 6].
Feb. 16, '09 headline:	"Kling off in the lead, 'Uncle John' Beat Bennie Allen in First Block of Pool Match at Kling's New Academy" [p. 8].

But Bennie Allen overtook his uncle and on page 15A of the Feb. 21 *Kansas City Times* a headline reported: "Allen Won the Pool Match, Johnny Kling Lost the Championship of Kansas City, 625 to 590."

Following the Allen-Kling match, other tournaments were held at Kling's Academy: Williams vs. Strom, Ingram vs. McWhorter, Kling vs. Dillon.[6] And yet, Charles Murphy, Frank Chance and Chicago fans were led to believe that their catcher, who was said to be the very best in baseball, was unable to report to the team because of a fire that never took place. What motivated "Noisy John" to say this?

Briggs, a caricaturist for the *Chicago Tribune*, startled Chicago fans when on Jan. 31, he announced: "Kling will not be in the line up this year." Briggs may have thought he was being clever with his "Low Comedy Monologue Stunt," but his portrayal of the Cubs backstop was a slap in the face to African Americans and an insult to Kling.

9. Jumping Ship

Kling jokingly teaching his nephew to play after losing a title match to him (*Kansas City Star*).

On Feb. 26 Johnny Kling announced he would report to Frank Chance on April 10, shortly before the season started. When asked about his physical condition, he said, "Don't ask me that. I always report in condition to play ball, and I'll be on the job ready to get in the game on the jump." Kling told the press he would work out with George Tebeau's Blues.[7] In fact, he had been working out for the past month, playing indoor baseball at the Hippodrome in Kansas City. He had his own team called the Klings.[8]

Two days later, Sunday, Feb. 28, Chicago fans turned to the Sporting section of the *Tribune* and read about a letter that had been sent to Manager Chance and Charles Webb Murphy: "Johnny Kling officially stated it would be impossible for him to go in the first squad to West Baden and Hot Springs and asked for a leave of absence until a few days before the start of

Caricature depicting Kling as a comedy stunt on stage (*Chicago Tribune*).

the season." Nearly three weeks later, March 20, Chicago fans learned that Frank Chance had been asking Kling to report, and that a final notice would be served on the Cubs catcher, "ordering him to report immediately to the club."[9]

Johnny Kling knew Frank Chance. Once the skipper arrived at a decision, he never backed away. He ran the club with a clenched fist. "Play it my way or meet me after the game" was his motto. He came down hard on any player who didn't play it his way.[10] So, on March 20, Kling quit. The

Sunday, March 21 edition of the *Tribune* told the story: "John Kling, world's champion catcher, has quit the Cubs. This body blow to the team's chances for a fourth straight National League pennant was received in the form of a telegram from the star backstop, whose words carried conviction and have been taken in deadly earnest by Manager Chance and the players who knew Kling best. The message was a reply to a wire from Chance, ordering John to report at once."

Kling's reply said, "Don't expect me this season, as I find it impossible to trust my business here in other hands. No question of salary, but my manager here is not capable of handling my affairs in the proper way."[11]

After questioning the players, a *Trib* reporter, rightly or wrongly, had a new slant on the story:

> He is still "sore at" President Murphy on account of the latter's alleged effort to balk his plan of securing a billiard hall in Cincinnati. It will be remembered that Kling was thinking of buying a place in Redland last spring, that Murphy accused Garry Herrmann of tampering with the catcher, and that the deal fell through. Kling holds the club President responsible for his failure to secure the Cincinnati property. Several times last season he told his friends he never would play for Murphy again.
>
> This spring he asked for permission to stay at his Kansas City home during the training trip, saying his business interests required his presence there. The permission was given by President Murphy, a fact that did not please Manager Chance at all.
>
> Manager Chance tonight dictated the following statement after telegraphing Kling his regrets at losing him:
>
> "The loss of Kling unquestionably will be a great blow to the Cubs, but it will not put us out of the running. Kling's loss may weaken us. I am willing to admit it does, but I do not for one moment believe his loss will be a vital one. We will win the pennant of the National League just the same.
>
> "The Cubs were not prepared for such a blow. I consider Kling the greatest catcher in baseball today. Next to Kling, I consider Pat Moran the best. I believe I had the two greatest catchers in the business when I secured Moran from the Boston team. His stay with us has not weakened him in any regard. The Cubs are strong enough to win without Kling and the Chicago fans need lose no sleep by his desertion.
>
> "The Cubs were busy rejoicing over their first victory of the season at Shreveport and then all the joy was knocked out of them by Kling's telegram. They are now a gloomy lot. All of them realize Kling's value to the team and all of them share their Manager's anger. The significant words in the telegram, 'this season' do not carry any comfort for them. The Cubs want Kling now — want him to help them break all records for championship winning, and care little about what happens after the season is over."[12]

The players had reason for gloom. They knew that without Kling, the Cubs would not be as strong as they were a year ago, and with that handicap against them, their advantage over the other national league contenders was just about nullified.[13]

Chicago fans learned why the loss of their premier catcher was such a devastating blow. "The classy catcher is a rare breed," the *Kansas City Star* said.

> He is the mainspring of the baseball machine. Being stationed behind the batsman, he has greater opportunities than the pitcher for observing what a batter can and cannot hit. Knowing the man with whom he works, he can tell if his curves are breaking right, can make him work slowly when inclined to hurry and can make him hustle when he inclines to slowness.
>
> The catcher is the chief watcher of the bases when occupied, passes the signals for the pitcher, throwing to catch runners too far from the bags and signals the proper time for delivering the ball to the bat. He must have a keen eye and a strong, accurate arm to keep opponents from stealing bases.
>
> Aside from all this mental effort, he must snatch any sort of curve the pitcher lets loose, must dig up wild pitches that go into the ground and must chase the elusive foul fly. He must block runners who slide into the plate and must take his turn at bat. These few things are calculated to keep a man of average intellect and physical ability quite busy. Catching is a difficult and thankless job, and good catchers are scarce.
>
> How often has it been observed that many young pitchers go along as only ordinary performers until some smooth, heady catcher commences to work with them, and then suddenly they blossom out as stars.
>
> If you offer John Kling and Mordecai Brown for sale, clubs would go for the catcher. For he could take a lot of ordinary pitchers and get good work out of them.[14]

The swirl of emotions and controversy forced the press to publish another article:

> "I have quit the Cubs for a year for no other reason than, that my business here is worth more than I can make in baseball," was what John Kling, the Cub catcher, said today regarding his decision. He says he would rather play in Chicago than anywhere, and asserts that he has nothing to be "sore" about and that his determination to quit for a year cannot be altered by a raise in salary.
>
> "Chance is a good fellow and Murphy is a good fellow," said Kling tonight, "But business is business, and I've simply got to pass up the game for one year. I haven't a kick coming and it isn't a question of salary. If I played ball, I would be perfectly willing to return to Chicago at the same money I received last season. But I've got a proposition here that will make me $150,000 in ten years. I have been figuring for a long time and have come to the conclusion I must remain here this summer.
>
> "You see, I've got an investment of $75,000 here, and that's a lot of money tied up. Every winter, I come back and work up a good billiard business. In the summer I leave and the business drifts. I come back and have to start all over again. I believe I can remain here this summer and keep my trade. And I will be right here to keep an eye on my billiard business. I have found that my manager cannot handle the game. That's the secret."[15]

The news item went on, "Kling admits that a year out of the game may be enough for him. In that case, he says he will again don a Cub uniform and give Murphy and Chance the best he has.

"But I've got to try this thing for a year," he said, "and you can tip it off straight to Murphy and Chance that John Kling won't be on the job with the Cubs this season."[16]

The *Trib* gave Chicago fans more.

> He has leased a large building and uses the second floor for his billiard rooms. His lease has ten years to run, and he has sublet the rest of the building at a good profit.
>
> However, Johnny's decision doesn't necessarily mean he intends to pass up the national game. The hero of two world's championships will continue to play baseball in Kansas City where he took his first baseball hurdle.
>
> Kling is going to organize a semi-professional team and play in the city league, which will be formed at a meeting tomorrow. He proposes to organize a six-club league to play games on Saturdays and Sundays. "Kid" Nichols, another former National League star, says he will have a team in the city league. A good semi-professional league of six clubs will have a chance.[17]

A Fort Wayne newspaper had something else to say. "Kansas City fans have been clamoring for a baseball organization such as Kling is about to start, and present indications are that it will be a great success."[18]

Johnny Kling demonstrated responsibility toward his business venture, something he learned from his father when, as a youngster, he had deserted his post as the bread wagon chauffeur. Delivery of bread came first, then baseball. His love of the national game was steadfast, as demonstrated by his clear intention of playing ball in Kansas City.

A news release in Kansas City on March 27 summed up Kling's financial condition.

> John not only says he is worth close to $150,000, but gives the details. He says he has made it all himself. He estimates that in the last six years, he has saved $18,000 from baseball, has $75,000 tied up in two billiard halls, and that in the last three years he has made at least $15,000 in the billiard business.
>
> Five years ago, Kling bought a fifty-acre tract of ground just outside the city limits here. He paid $5,000 for the tract. Today, the city is figuring on extending the limits beyond Kling's property and John values fifty acres at $30,000. He has other real estate, which he values at $8,000. The total comes to $146,000.
>
> Several months ago, Kling leased the second, third, fourth, and fifth floors of the Heuston building on Walnut Street in the heart of the business district. He spent a lot of money on improvements and put in a billiard hall on the second floor. He has the figures to show that the rent from the other three floors will be sufficient to give him the billiard hall rent-free and $150 a month to boot. Kling has worked up an excellent billiard business in which he figures to make $150,000 in ten years. And that is the reason Kling has decided to cut out the baseball. He desires to stay here, keep the trade going in the summer, and watch the shekels come in.
>
> Last Saturday, John reached his final decision. He is done with professional baseball. If the proposed city league is organized, Kling will captain the Missouri Athletic Club nine. Sunday ball will be played. John will catch and he says he

has a hankering desire to do some pitching. So Kansas City fans may have the opportunity to see one of the greatest backstops in the history of baseball in a new position — on the rubber. John says he has a lot of fancy shoots.

Asked if he thought the Cubs could win the pennant without him, John said, "Sure they can. They can get along without me. Moran is a grand catcher. But I have contended all the time that the Giants will have a great chance for the next pennant. That St. Louis deal strengthened McGraw's team and, with me in the game or out of it, the Giants will be hard to beat this year."[19]

The latest newspaper article appeared to put a lid on the Kling issue. Chance and Murphy announced they would not go after him, that they would win the championship without him. Murphy told the press, "If he is after more money, I do not know it, for he has not written to me. We want him to play with Chicago, for the Cubs can win the flag easier with 'Noisy' John behind the bat than without him, but his absence will not make it impossible for us to win our fourth successive championship of the league."[20]

On April 8, the *Tribune* headlined an article, "Chance Says Kling Can Go." It went on to say, 'Let Kling do the worrying,' said the Peerless Leader. 'His absence won't wreck the club and I am sincere when I say I don't care what he does. If any club will give me the men I want in exchange, it can have him. We may put through a deal with Cincinnati.'

Murphy followed up with another press release: "Kling signed a three year contract," said Murphy. "I don't think there can be any sympathy for a contract breaker. Having his signed contract, we depended upon him, but when he announced his intention to stay in Kansas City, we purchased Tom Needham for $1000 to protect the catching department in Kling's absence. If he decides to play this year after all, it is only just, to expect him to reimburse the club. He need not buy a ticket to Chicago to report unless he is prepared to do so.

"Regarding a trade, it's up to Manager Chance. I'll trade Kling just as quickly as anyone else for value received. We can win the pennant without him."[21]

Chicago fans saw it differently. They implored John to return. Some demanded his presence in a Cub uniform. One letter was pathetic. It was from a lady. She could see nothing but disaster if the "peerless Cub" failed to report. "What will we do without you? Who will nail the flying runners at second base? Who will drive in the runs that win for the Cubs? John, please return," she said. "Save the day for your friends."[22]

One Chicago gentleman got peevish. His spiel was: "You've got a contract with Chicago, ain't you? Well, no good man would break his word. Get in line, Johnny. Don't join the holdout crowd."[23]

Chicago fans knew what they were talking about. They had a reason for pleading, almost begging and demanding that Johnny show up. They remembered the *Trib* on Jan. 31, where it listed the RBIs for all players on both Chicago teams during the '08 season. Kling was third with 65, three behind Steinfeldt, who had 68. They also remembered the last paragraph of that article: "Johnny Kling was the only player in the two big organizations who twice slammed out a four bagger when all the cushions had tenants. The Cub made his first rap of this kind on June 6 in Boston and his second on Sept. 12 in St. Louis. Kling's second cleanup four bagger gave the Cubs a twelfth inning victory over the Cardinals."[24]

In spite of the favorable publicity and the hundreds of letters from Cub fans, Kling ordered uniforms for his city league team and paid real money for the suits. "That doesn't look like I am going to Chicago, does it?" he said.[25]

In reply to the $1,000, Kling laughed. "Murphy might as well make that $1,000 fine $1,000,000," he said. "He is trying to give out the impression I am holding out for more money, but Murphy knows better.

> I am perfectly satisfied with my contract as far as the financial end of it is concerned. He can't injure me by knocking me. I always gave Chicago my best and would rather play there than any other place, but I am through for the year at least.
> I understand Murphy says I am not going to be in on that $10,000 bonus that he is going to "cough up" for advertising purposes. Murphy can keep that too. I never really expected it.
> I hope the Cubs win another pennant and another world's championship. It's a great team and a grand bunch of boys. Murphy says they can win just as easily without me and I hope so—but if they can, I don't see why he is yelping so hard.
> As to my being traded, that is a joke. I am not going to play ball and no manager is foolish enough to trade something for nothing.[26]

Beneath the "niceties" of Johnny Kling's language, there must have been a sense of anger and antagonism toward Charles Murphy and Frank Chance, as revealed in the seemingly innocent headline and story in the April 17 *Tribune*:

KLING'S NINE MAY PLAY HERE

> Further evidence—take it for what it is worth—that "Noisy" John Kling will not be seen in a Cub uniform this season developed at yesterday's meeting of the Chicago Baseball League, when a suggestion was received from Claude Johnson, Kling's partner in his semi-pro venture, that John's Kansas City team exchange games with the clubs of the Chicago League.
> Kansas City has organized a semi-pro league of six clubs with three parks, which play Saturday and Sunday games. Kling acts as catcher and Kid Nichols is pitcher for one of the teams. It was thought a series of weekday games between the Kansas City club and some of the locals would prove great attractions both here and in Kansas City.[27]

Kling and his KC All Stars in Chicago to play a series of games (*Kansas City Post*).

Johnny Kling's desire to return to Chicago, to play once again before Chicago fans, where he had been playing for more than eight years, reveals unspoken feelings. Returning as owner and manager of a Kansas City team would give him a large measure of satisfaction.

This satisfaction was greatly enhanced two days later when the *Trib* reported: "The Reds expect to secure John Kling." The *Trib*'s announcement was supported by *The Kansas City Journal* on April 19. It reported "whisperings" from Cincinnati to the effect that Garry Herrmann had started negotiations for the services of the great backstopper.

But President Murphy called it a rumor and squelched it quickly. He announced: "There wasn't a chance for Kling to be traded or sold by the Chicago club under any circumstances. This decision was made irrevocably at a conference between himself and Manager Chance."[28]

This announcement showed the Chicago fans the kind of quandary Charles Webb Murphy was really in. Just eleven days earlier he told the *Trib* reporter, "I'll trade Kling as quickly as anyone else for value received. We can win the pennant without him."

Chance also told the *Trib* reporter that Kling could go, that he might just put through a deal with Cincinnati. But Chance knew baseball. And deep in his bones, he must have had doubts about his chances of winning the pennant without "Noisy" John.

For both men, their position as to ridding the team of Johnny Kling had been a show of bravado. It was meant to influence Chicago fans. But they knew better.

The situation became more complex when Charles Murphy wrote a letter dated April 26. It said, "This is to notify you that you have been granted an indefinite leave of absence by the Chicago National League baseball club."[29] But such permission had been granted at the start of Spring, on March 4, 1909.[30] And Frank Chance had not been too pleased about it. Why send Kling another indefinite leave of absence?

Did Murphy forget about the first one? Or, did he come to believe he had acted hastily, without prior discussion with Chance? And now, after discussing it with his manager, and obtaining his approval, a leave of absence was issued as if it had never occurred. Or, could there be other reasons?

Regardless of the reason, the entire affair should have made Johnny Kling angry. And it is not difficult to understand why he decided to take a year off.

He had given his heart and soul to the Cubs ever since he broke into major league baseball. He had become known for cutting down runners trying to steal and hitting the ball well when runs were needed. He alone had won many a game. He had been the backstop behind the bat, the general who led the team to record setting years, wonderful years. And now, when for whatever reason, he wanted time before reporting to the team, the answer was "report immediately," even though he had promised to report by April 10, days before the start of regular season play. Was this the thanks he deserved?

If so, then what about Joe Tinker? He was doing his thing on the vaudeville stage, earning $3,000 a week. He didn't report on time for spring training. Joe was close to finishing up his contract in Cincinnati and only then did Chance order him to come straight to Shreveport — upon completion of his work on stage.[31]

What about Chance himself, the manager who demanded obedience from his players? On Jan. 24 he paid $46,500 cash for a California home and orange groves for himself and family, and he expected to realize $10,000 yearly from the property. Now, he declared positively that he would stay in California unless Murphy kicked in to his demands. Although the details were not released, Chance soon reported because Murphy caved in and gave him what he wanted.[32]

Then there was Johnny Evers. He notified the club he was going to take the year off and rest up, but changed his mind and notified Chance and Murphy that he would report about the middle of June. No fuss was made about it.[33]

Why all the fuss about Johnny Kling when Chance and Murphy knew he would be with the team and ready to play by April 10? It didn't make sense. If Johnny Kling's decision to take the year off was his way of objecting to the way he had been treated, it seems fair to say he was justified in taking this position.

But in taking this position, Johnny did not endear himself to his teammates, as seen by events surrounding a June 2 gala day on the Cubs' calendar. The flag that the Cubs had won in 1908 was hoisted on the newly painted flagstaff. Just before the game, President Murphy presented a $10,000 check to Manager Chance in one big lump without ceremony. The check was to be cashed by the Cubs' leader and divided into twenty-two equal parts; each player was to receive $454.54. Kling was to receive nothing even though he had aided materially in bringing the flag to Chicago.

Murphy had talked with Kling by phone the day before the event and invited him to participate. He declined the invitation and declined his share of the bonus. The Cub boss then informed him that he had much to do in bringing the third flag to Chicago, but the players on the team objected at dividing the prize among players who were not members of the team at the present time.[34]

The baseball season moved forward. On July 19 Murphy announced, "President Ebbets made me an offer of $20,000 for Kling but I have done nothing in regard to it."[35]

By September 2, Kling was still hanging in the wind, going nowhere, and the Cubs were still trying to catch Pittsburgh. Ed Grillo, a sportswriter, took a dim view of the Cubs' chances to catch the Pirates. He said, "The Chicago Cubs have sadly missed Johnny Kling this year, notwithstanding the fact that the new man, Archer, has apparently filled the veteran's shoes.

"But Archer is not Kling. Kling's strategy did much to win games for the world's champions, and his stick work also cut a figure. His refusal to join the Cubs has cost every man on the team, as well as the club, dearly, and it is a safe prediction that if the Cubs fail to win the flag this year, which is most likely, it will be blamed on Kling's absence."[36]

9. Jumping Ship

On September 3, the rumor mill had it that Murphy had given up hope of his team's winning out. This statement was attributed to him in an alleged interview in Cincinnati. "There is no truth in it," Murphy said, "and I cannot imagine where it came from. We are not out of the race by any means, and I never even hinted that we were. Our team is going well enough to suit me, and I am convinced we will be on top at the finish."[37]

Weeks earlier, a sportswriter had given a different view.

> The failure of the Chicago Cubs to come to terms with Johnny Kling promises to be a most costly experience for the team which has won three consecutive pennants. The Cubs are not playing up to their old form with Kling out of the game. Kling demanded an increase of salary, though he gave it out that his personal affairs would prevent him from playing ball this year. Had the Chicago club made any effort to have him join the team, there is no doubt that he would have done so, and, instead of Pittsburgh leading, Chicago would no doubt be on the way to a fourth consecutive pennant.
>
> When a team has a great catcher, it cannot afford to lose him. Too much depends upon this position to figure it can be filled by any man who is able to handle a mitt or throw to the bases. Kling was the directing general of the Chicago team, and it is a noteworthy fact that since his absence the Cubs have not been playing their former intelligent game, nor have the pitchers shown that same consistent effectiveness.
>
> Of course, Kling may be a loser by his holding off, but his losses will be nothing to those of the club and the other members of the team, for there is but a slim chance now of their figuring in the world's championship pie.[38]

The Cub boss was only putting on a good front. He must have known that his chance to make it to the top was slim. His three catchers were not doing well. In fact, Needham, the catcher that had been purchased to replace Kling, hadn't played. He had been sitting on the bench most of the season.

President Murphy had a knack for making statements that could not be backed up, as seen in his remarks when Johnny Kling arrived in town with his Kansas City All Stars, scheduled to play a series of games the following week with local semi-professionals. Murphy tried hard to keep Kling from performing in Chicago. He pointed out that Kling was still under contract to the Cubs, and that he would take the matter to the civil courts and secure an injunction, restraining Kling from playing in the Chicago area.

"Kling couldn't play here without my permission," said Murphy, "and I am not going to grant it. I would consider it an insult to patrons of our park to allow him to take part in a game anywhere in the city. I will not allow him to appear in uniform. Kling belongs to the Cubs, and he will play with them here or else he will not play at all."[39]

Days later, Kling's Kansas City youngsters drew a peppery reception at Logan Square Park when Callahan's nine defeated the visitors by a score of 11 to 3. That same evening, Kling was shooting pool, and he made the headlines in the *Chicago Trib*: "Kling Again Wins at Pool. Johnny Kling, ex–Cub catcher and Kansas City Baseball Magnate, added another game in the pennant aspirations as a pool player by defeating Harry Dell 125 balls to 59 at Hemmer's rooms last night. The Missourian scored a high run of 41 in one inning, enough runs to win a dozen ball games for his semi-pro team. Tonight the holdout backstop will meet Dick Richards, the New England champion."[40]

Playing ball during the day and pool at night was a treat for Chicago fans. They hadn't seen Noisy John all season. And they finally had a chance to see him play ball. On the following night, Sept. 8, Kling had his third straight victory at pool, defeating Richards at Hemmer's rooms 125 to 61. Kling played perfect position with a high run of 27. Richards proved no match for the Kansas city expert.

Die-hard Kling fans had a never-to-be-forgotten baseball experience on Sept. 9, when pitcher Campbell, of Kling's All Stars, pitched a no run, no hit game at Logan Square, winning by a score of 8 to 0.[41] Campbell had everything and Callahan's men walked past Johnny Kling to and from the batsman's box in a steady procession. Come evening, Johnny traded in his catcher's mitt for a cue stick and chalked up another victory, defeating Lescher 125 to 61.

Sept. 10 was a busy day for the *Trib*'s sportswriter. He had to pound out four stories that were certain to capture the attention of Chicagoans the following morning.

"Kling's Warriors Beat Ryan's Team" was story number one. It told how the "Rogers Park boys bowed to former Cub's Kansas City boys by a score of 6 to 2, and of how Johnny Kling started the run getting in the first inning with a single, driving in Kneaves who had been given a pass.

"May Bar Kling for 3 Years" was the second story. "Johnny Kling, former catcher of the Chicago Cubs may be declared ineligible to play with any national agreement club for the next three years as a result of playing with his Kansas City team of semi-professionals against the semi-pro teams of Chicago, which are said to contain several ineligible players.

"When his attention was called to a report from Chicago today that Kling had played against Chicago semi-pros, August Herrmann, chairman of the National Commission, said, 'If it's true that Kling played against ineligible players, and the reports from Chicago indicate that he has done so, he has made himself liable to suspension from organized baseball for a term of three years.'"

"John Kling Plays Good Pool," said number three. "Johnny Kling forgot all his troubles with organized baseball at Hammer's billiard rooms by defeating two men, Senske and Wilson, 125 to 46, and made a run of 45, the highest of the week."

"Klings vs. Leland Giants" was the finale to the backstop's saga. "Johnny Kling's All Stars will play their last game in Chicago today when Kansas City meets the Leland Giants at West End Park. The Giants expect to spring a surprise on Kling in the shape of base stealing, five of the fastest men on the club having spent the week in sliding to second base: Wright, Hill, Harris, Payne and Green were the ones selected to test the former Cub's arm."

"Kling Winds Up with Defeat" was the *Trib*'s Sept. 12 headline. "Although losing by a score of 6 to 1, Johnny Kling showed the fastest men on the Leland Giants that trying to steal a base off him continued to mean instant death. Harris stole the only base, but a bad stop by Kling gave him the theft. The backstop also showed the Giants they had to be on their toes. Kling's whip was in action twice, each time the runner being caught asleep."[42]

Overall, Kling's boys did good, having won four out of six games. Chance's men, on the other hand, weren't doing too well. A headline read, "Miracle Only Will Keep Flag on West Side."[43] And it didn't take long before Pittsburgh had the flag sewed up.

It was only then on Sept. 28 that Johnny Kling called in the Kansas City press. His interview was telegraphed to Chicago, ready for Chicago fans on the following morning as they sat at their kitchen tables, eating breakfast and sipping coffee.

KLING GLAD CUBS LOST FLAG.
Former Chicago Catcher De-e-e-lighted
Because of Trick He Claims
Murphy Turned on Him.

Probably the happiest man in the United States over the fact that the Chicago Cubs lost the National League pennant is Johnny Kling, the former world's champion catcher, who has been in this city all season tending to his billiard business.

He refused to join the club last spring because he claimed Charles W. Murphy had cheated him out of a chance to manage the Cincinnati team and also to own a big billiard hall in Cincinnati, which would have been financed by Garry Herrmann if Kling had taken hold of the Reds.

After he found that Pittsburgh had clinched the pennant today, Kling said: "Well, I'm tickled to death. That suits me exactly. At the beginning of the season I was pulling for New York, but I am glad Pittsburgh won it and not Chicago. Revenge is sweet and I have got it. Murphy did not treat me right when he cut me out of that good billiard business in Cincinnati and a chance to manage the Reds. It is the best news I have heard this year. If Murphy had not treated me as he did, I would have been glad to have played with the Cubs."[44]

Had Johnny Kling played with the Cubs, there is no question as to the record the team would have set by winning their fourth straight pennant. Compare the stats of the team's three catchers in 1909 with that of Kling's for 1908.

	G	R	H	2B	3B	HR	RBI	SB	BA	SA
Archer	80	31	60	9	2	1	30	5	.230	.291
Moran	77	18	54	11	1	1	23	2	.220	.285
Needham	7	3	4	0	0	0	0	0	.143	.143
Kling (1908)	126	51	117	23	5	4	65	16	.276	.382

Pittsburgh won the pennant with a win-loss of 110–42. Chicago had 104–49. A review of all games for 1909 demonstrated that the Cubs could have won the pennant and may have broken their 1906 win-loss record of 116–36 — a record that still stands.

If anyone is to be blamed for this unnecessary and tragic loss, it is Charles Webb Murphy and Manager Frank Chance. Both witnessed what Johnny Kling had done for the team. He had always been a warrior. He had played for the Cubs and only for the Cubs since becoming the team's regular catcher in 1902. He played in 765 games, an average of 109 games a season. That made him a premier catcher. And he had been one of those day-in and day-out catchers who do better and better by doing a great deal of work. As backstop, he was the recipient of more battering than any other man on the team, so it is surprising that he was able to do so much work and do it so well.

What thanks did he get? How long was he to endure what he considered to be bad treatment? So he finally rebelled. And the Cubs were forced to make do with the three catchers they had. But they were not Kling. Examine a few of their records: April 18 *Tribune*, Moran, no hits. Notes of game: "They stole three bases on Pat Moran yesterday." Cubs lose 4–1. April 24, Moran, no hits. Cubs lose 6–3. May 5, Moran, no hits. Notes: "Moran made a careless heave to Chance in the third inning after dropping the third strike." Cubs lose 1–0. May 9, Moran, no hits. Cubs lose 3–1. May 10, Moran, no hits. Notes: "It looked like a Cub run in the seventh. With Hofman out, Tinker was safe on Hulswitt's fumble. But Moran struck out reaching for a wild pitch that ought to have given him first base." Cubs lose 5–2. May 14, Moran, no hits. Cubs lose 4–1. May 31, Game 1, Moran, no hits. Cubs lose 4–2. Game 2, Moran, no hits. Cubs lose 5–4. And so it was for the rest of the year.

Jimmy Archer was no better. He repeatedly failed to get a hit in close games, even as the season moved along with the Cubs trailing the Pirates. Johnny Kling's bat alone would have made a difference. But considering his ability to keep opposing players close to the bag, mowing them down if they tried to steal and keeping his pitchers in control, what kind of record might the Cubs have set? Unfortunately, we will never know. But we do know that August Herrmann, chairman of the National Baseball Commission, issued a press release to the *Washington Post* on Sept. 11, informing the baseball world: "Kling Will be Punished. For playing with his Kansas City All Stars against a Logan Square team of Chicago who had ineligible players on the team, and that Kling had violated the rules of organized baseball."

Throughout the clamor and the calls for retribution, "Noisy" John went about his business in a methodical and seemingly unperturbed way. He was determined to set a record for himself, something dear to his heart, something he had thought about when growing up, something he had been preparing for, striving for, something he now felt within his reach.

On Sept. 30 Johnny Kling took on "Cowboy" Weston in a pool match for the world's championship in Kansas City at his academy. The place was packed. All eyes were glued to two men standing alongside a brightly-lit pool table holding cue sticks. On the green cloth was a rack of colored balls—waiting.

The contest was to be held on three successive nights, lasting through Oct. 2. And from the outset, it promised to be a closely fought contest. When it was over, headlines told the Kansas Cityans:

John Kling wins world championship, October 2, 1909 (National Baseball Hall of Fame).

J. G. KLING, POOL CHAMPION
From the First Night's Play Until the Finish
Last Night Kling Was Always in the Lead

John Kling is now the pool champion of the world. In a hard fought match of 800 points which lasted four nights, the Kansas City challenger finally wrested the title from "Cowboy" Weston by a score of 800 to 783. When the play began last night, Kling had a lead of twenty-two points, but at the end of the eighth

> **John Kling Baseball Supply Manufacturing Co.**
> John G. Kling, President, Kansas City, Mo.
>
> ## APPLICATION FOR STOCK
>
> John Kling Base Ball Supply Mfg. Co.,
> 1010 Commerce Bldg., Kansas City, Mo,
> Gentlemen:—
> I hereby subscribe for............shares of the capital stock of your company at the par value of $10 per share.
> I agree to pay my subscribtion as follows: Twenty-five per cent of total herewith; twenty-five per cent in thirty days from date, and fifty per cent in sixty days from date.
> This application is subject to the approval of the Board of Directors.
>
> Date................................
>
> Name................................
> (Write plainly.)
>
> Address..............................
>
> City..............State.............

Application for stock in Kling's baseball supply manufacturing company (*Kansas City Post*).

frame, Weston had passed him and had a lead of three balls. From there on to the twelfth frame they see-sawed back and forth, each leading at intervals by one ball. In the fourteenth frame Kling "cleaned the table" and from there on until the finish he always maintained the lead.

The match from the beginning Wednesday night has always been close with Kling's finishing each night's play in the lead. At the end of the first night's play the Kansas Cityan had a lead of forty-two points, but Thursday night when the game was over his margin was only eleven points. Friday night he increased his lead to twenty-two points. According to the rules of the game Kling is now the champion of the world. The match was played for a bet of $250 and 75 per cent of the gross receipts.[45]

"Cowboy" Weston was interviewed right after the match. He said, "Kling has a better stroke than De Oro. His execution is wonderful. All he needs is the inside work. There is more to pool than merely pocketing the balls. Safety play is the wheel upon which champions revolve. Kling lacks safety work. This will come when he gives up baseball and devotes his entire attention to pool. Kling is the best in America today on long shots. That's his eye."[46]

Having won a world title, Johnny Kling could now turn his attention to his most recent business interest, the Johnny Kling Baseball Supply Co., Inc.[47]

He was the largest stockholder and chose to distribute a portion of the stock to several hundred enthusiastic baseball fans—men who would advertise the Kling Glove, the Kling Ball, the Kling Mitt and the Kling Bat—men who would advertise these things because they had a vital, monetary interest in them.[48] Stock was offered.

Beneath Kling's outer facade of peace and tranquility, as he busied himself with business interests there simmered a burning desire to get back into baseball, don his mask, crouch low, eye the batter, signal his pitcher, raise his mitt and begin his chatter while Three-Finger Brown began his wind-up. Would he ever be able to do that again?

10

CLIMBING ABOARD

1910

J. Ed Grillo, sportswriter for the *Washington Post*, started off the new year with nothing but praise for Johnny Kling. He said:

> Had Johnny Kling been with the Cubs during the past campaign, it is not likely that the Tigers would have met the Pirates in the world's series. The absence of Kling made all the difference and proves the great importance of having a first-class catcher behind the bat.
> Gibson, of Pittsburgh, is a good catcher, but he is not a Kling. Yet he is so much better than any man Detroit could use. There was no comparison between them. Even with most of his pitchers out of form, Jennings would have stood a grand chance of winning the series had he had a capable man behind the bat. Nothing so unnerves a team, and the pitcher, as to have a catcher who cannot throw, for his inability to throw also affects his judgement, and it is the catcher who should do most of the thinking for a ball team.[1]

Johnny must have felt pretty good about Grillo calling him a first class catcher, and it seems fair to say he had regrets at not having played with the Cubs in 1909. The thought of winning a fourth straight pennant and beating Detroit for the third straight time in the World Series would have been something special. The idea of cutting down Ty Cobb trying to steal would have made him feel wonderful, just as it did in '07 and '08.

Losing, on the other hand, gave him a bad feeling, one that took time to ease up and go away. Like losing his world's championship title in pool to Thomas Heuston on Nov. 12. And here it was more than six weeks later and he still felt bad.

But good news caught Kling's eye. His spirits soared! He suddenly learned of talk calling for his reinstatement. Of all people to do that, it was Charles Webb Murphy, his old nemesis. Murphy wanted Kling restored to good standing inasmuch as the Philadelphia National League club stood ready to pay $15,000 for his immediate release.

"If Kling wants to play ball," said Murphy, "he should not be prevented

Caricature expressing Kling's desire to get back into baseball (*Chicago Tribune*).

from doing so. He is not a contract jumper, and has done nothing dishonorable. He did not play with the Cubs last year because he had a leave of absence in order to devote his time to a private business venture in Kansas City. Personally, I do not know where Kling wants to play ball next season, but I do know that if he has a chance to play with any other team outside of Chicago, and the Chicago club is willing, the Commission should not stand in the way."[2]

One day later, Jan. 5, the "Supreme Court of Baseball," the National Commission, met to take up the case of catcher Johnny Kling. The three man "court" came to no decision, but Fogel, of the Philadelphia club, insisted he had an agreement with Murphy by which Kling's release could be purchased by the Quakers for $15,000. John McGraw of the Giants, meanwhile, declared that Murphy agreed some time ago to let him have first call on the great Chicago catcher, and that the New York club stood ready to close the deal at Murphy's terms.

When asked, Kling declared he would never play with the Cubs again and that he preferred New York to Philadelphia.[3]

Baseball became a strangely confusing business. As soon as John McGraw finished talking to the press, it then became Murphy's turn. He took on an angry, bitter tone when he allowed himself to be interviewed:

> Once and for all, he said, let it be understood that catcher John Kling is not for sale. He is the property of the Chicago National League baseball club, and will ever remain so under the laws of organized baseball, unless he can be traded for some player or bunch of players regarded as equal to his athletic worth. Fifty thousand dollars in cash — real, hard dollars — cannot purchase the release of the holdout backstop. President Murphy, of the Cubs, says so, and in such an emphatic manner that there can be no doubting his sincerity.
>
> Hardly a week passes but there is a report from somewhere that John Kling is to be purchased from the Cubs for $15,000, or even $20,000. But the truth of the matter is that Kling is not for sale at any price.
>
> If the president of the richest bank in the United States should walk into my office and place $50,000 upon my desk as the purchase price for the catcher, I would refuse the offer.[4]

Murphy's squabbling over Johnny Kling can be seen as the bind he was in. On the one hand, he desperately wanted his catcher back. Kling was the best. With him, he could recapture the flag in 1910, perhaps another World Series. There was money to be made, and everyone knew that Murphy loved money.

On the other hand, Kling hated Murphy. He had ruined a good business deal for the catcher, a moneymaking deal in Cincinnati that would have been backed by Garry Herrmann. But Murphy knew Herrmann was only being nice because he wanted Kling to manage and play for the Reds. It seemed as if everybody wanted the great backstop. Everybody wanted to steal him away from Chicago. And he was just not going to let it happen. Johnny Kling belonged to him, and that's the way it was going to be.

Poor Johnny Kling. He was in the middle of the squabbling. All he wanted was to play ball once again. He told this to a Kansas City reporter who came to interview him, and who then went back to his office and wrote up the story:

KLING WANTS TO PLAY

Kling wants to play ball this year, and he is not concerned about money. He likes the game of baseball. There's the secret, and that's the reason John is in a receptive mood. He fears that if he lingers beyond the pale of organized baseball another season, he'll never be able to come back.

John doesn't figure that he is in bad with the National Commission. He has a paper signed by Charles Murphy, granting him a leave of absence for the entire season. With this document tucked safely away in his strongbox, Kling doesn't see how he can be under the ban of baseball's highest tribunal.

"Where would you like to play ball this year?" was asked of Kling, after it became certain that John was willing to be approached in a baseball way.

"Oh, any old place," he said.

"Would you play for Murphy?"

"Well, now I don't — oh, yes I would, of course, if he'd pay me everything he owes me." But John refused to mention just how much Charles W. is indebted to him and for what.

"How would you like to play in New York, for McGraw?"

"Oh, fine: McGraw is all right; I'd play there. Wouldn't mind playing in Boston too. There's a great town for you. I believe they're going after a better team. I wouldn't mind playing in Boston."

"How about Philadelphia, John?"

"All right," replied Kling. "I'd play in Philadelphia. Good ball club there; good town, too."

"How about Cincinnati?"

"Oh, Cincinnati's all right, too," he said. "I wouldn't mind playing ball in Cincinnati. I'd go there, all right."

"Would you play ball under Griffith?" Kling was asked. "Would it take more than that $9,000 offer of Herrmann's that you turned down?"

Kling hesitated. Evidently that $9,000 bid looks good to Kling now. "Sure, I'd play for Griffith," he said. "I'd play for $9,000 now."[5]

Johnny Kling became the focus of national attention. Baseball fans followed the drama on an almost daily basis. On Jan. 18, "Kling was of the opinion today that Murphy is trying to make a deal with Cincinnati, and that he will figure in a trade. He also believes it is possible that he might be traded to New York or Philadelphia and is willing to play in any of these cities."[6] Jan. 20, Kling wrote to the National Commission and inquired as to his standing in organized baseball and was informed he was an ineligible player.[7]

Jan. 22, "The old cry for John Kling to return to the Cubs has been raised by the West Side fans. The followers of Chance's team think that "Noisy" John must be behind the bat if the 1910 pennant is to float from that championship flagstaff. Plans are now being made for the circulation of a monster petition to the National Commission, praying for Kling's reinstatement.

"Sentiment against the proposed trading of Kling to any other club, should he make peace with the supreme court of baseball, is strong, and it is quite likely that when that point is reached, President Murphy will be given to understand that the West Side fans will not stand for any such trade."[8]

Jan. 27, "Catcher Kling has patched up his differences with Charles W. Murphy and says he will play with the Cubs this year, providing he can be reinstated by the National Commission."[9]

Jan. 27, "Johnny Kling, perhaps the greatest catcher of recent years, was said to have refused to report to the Chicago club because he could not get the salary he wanted, and yet the obstacle between him and the club was of an entirely different nature.

"It seems that Kling had the promise of a lease for a billiard hall in Chicago which owner Murphy controlled. He had agreed to take it at a certain figure, but before he got ready to make needed repairs and renovations the price went up three or four different times. This so disgusted Kling that he declared he would not play for Murphy again, and the present breech between the two resulted."[10]

Feb. 2, Kling applied to the commission for reinstatement, stating in his application among other things that he had "not knowingly violated any of the rules of organized baseball."[11]

Feb. 8, "The National Commission has picked Joe Flanner, one of President Johnson's chief lieutenants in the American League, as the man who will investigate the case of Catcher Johnny Kling and report to that body in a few weeks as to the merits of Kling's application and Kling's breaking of the rules."[12]

Feb. 8, "If Murphy will agree to give me my release at the close of the 1910 baseball season, I would be glad to play with the Chicago Cubs this season for nothing. An absolute release would mean $15,000 to me." The reporter then asked Kling: "What do you believe Murphy will do with you if you are reinstated?"

"I believe he'll trade me," Kling replied. "That's what he's engineering on."

"If you had your choice, which team in the National League would you rather play on this season?" was the next question shot at John.

"Well, you see," — and Kling drew a bit closer, and spoke in a confidential way — "I wouldn't mind playing in Chicago. Those Cubs look awful good."[13]

Feb. 13, "Wants Kling Back. Owner Murphy Working for Catcher's Reinstatement. Is En Route To See Lynch."[14]

Feb. 16, "Murphy said tonight that if Kling was reinstated he would not sell him to any club. 'Why,' said the president of the Cubs, '100,000 Chicago fans sent me a letter demanding that Kling be kept in Chicago if he was reinstated. If I let him go, I might as well put a padlock on the park gate.'"[15]

Feb. 28, "Captain Chance says if Kling is placed in good standing the Cubs will win the championship; in fact, they will lead the National League race from start to finish. Chicago fans are clamoring for a decision in this famous case."[16]

March 3, "Evidence Against Kling," the headline screamed.

> New and unlooked for evidence has just reached the members of the National Commission against the reinstatement of Johnny Kling. It concerns the organization in Kansas City, of an Inter-City League, formed by the Missouri Athletic Club, which Kling controlled. He was the secretary and treasurer of that organization, and therefore fought the American Association when his team, the Kansas City All Stars, played other Inter-City League teams on Saturdays, Sundays and Holidays on its home grounds there.
>
> Information has come to the Commission from members and officials of the American Association. They say that inasmuch as Kling was an official of the baseball league there, a league that openly competed with the Kansas City Blues, a team that belonged to the American Association, they feel that Kling has done organized baseball a serious injury.
>
> He advertised himself as the star attraction. Not only did he deal a body blow to baseball in this way but he took many hundreds of dollars away from the Kansas City Blues, and at times, the amounts were of major proportions. In doing this he used his personal popularity in Kansas City to cripple the American Association.
>
> Since this matter has been directed to the attention of the members of the National Commission, and it has been shown that Kling was one of the ringleaders of the organization in Kansas City, his trouble has taken on a very serious turn.
>
> The Commission has so far failed to hear from President Murphy, who was to provide within five days a concise statement of his side of the case. Therefore, the clouds begin to grow dark again, and it now looks as though Kling will be asked to remain out of baseball for four years.[17]

March 19, "Kling Threatens Suit" was the only way to move the Commission members off their backsides. "Catcher John Kling has lost about all his patience in waiting for the National Commission to take action on his case. If the supreme body of baseball does not reinstate him next week he plans to take the case into the civil courts for settlement. It is said he has put his case into the hands of a lawyer in Kansas City, and if nothing is done by the committee next week, he plans to file suit against the dictators of the national pastime."[18]

March 20, "To Decide Kling's Case" was the reply in just one day. "National Commission to render decision this week."[19]

March 23, "'I understand that there have been rumors that the Kling case has been decided,' said Chairman August Herrmann of the Commission. 'These are false. There has been no agreement reached and there will be none reached until the members of the Commission, Mr. Johnson and Mr. Lynch meet here. Even then the decision may be delayed. I wish it understood beyond all question that a decision has not been reached.'"[20]

March 24, "Within the next few days it will be known whether Johnny Kling is to remain under the ban of organized baseball or whether he is to re-enter the ranks of the Cubs. Murphy, the owner of the Chicago club, is making the plea that his star catcher had permission to remain away from the team, and if he can make the Commission see it in this light, there is no reason why Kling should not be reinstated, though he will be fined for having played semipro ball in Chicago last summer.

"The strange feature of the case is that during the early periods of Kling's absence, he and Murphy engaged in a rather animated wordy war through the papers in which accusations and threats were made. And yet Murphy contends that Kling had permission to stay at home even at that time."[21]

March 26, "Chance Blames Ban Johnson." The Cub Manager then went on to say, "The American League President is responsible for delay in announcing a decision in the Kling case. Johnson doesn't want Kling to get in condition by the time the season opens. Otherwise, the National Commission would announce to the world what it has decided without any further delay."[22]

March 29, "Catcher Kling to Be Reinstated," was a welcome headline for many people.

> Catcher John G. Kling will be penalized, but reinstated into organized baseball some time during the next week, but it will not be with the consent of Ban Johnson, president of the American League.
> The report of the findings in the Kling case will be signed by Garry Herrmann, chairman of the National Baseball Commission, and by Thomas J. Lynch, president of the National League, who, with Johnson, compose the Commission.
> For the good of organized baseball, President Johnson will not submit a minority report along with the findings of Herrmann and Lynch. He has demanded that his name be taken off the Commission report.[23]

March 30, "Kling Must Return to Cubs and Pay $700" was the *Trib*'s headline. The club was prohibited from trading him or raising his 1908 salary of $4,500.

Manager Chance wasn't about to trade his backstop. "I will be glad to have Kling back with the team," he said, "for he is one of the most valuable

Caricature questioning Kling's ability to play as he once did (*Chicago Tribune*).

men the game has ever produced. With Kling back and in the shape he was two years ago, I am confident no club on earth will ever stop us."[24]

April 2, "Kling Still on Fence" had to be explained. "I have received no communication whatever from either Chance, Murphy, or the National Commission," said Kling. "And what is more, I have not paid the fine assessed against me. Officially, I have no knowledge that any decision has been reached in my case."[25]

April 4, "By next Friday John G. Kling expects to be fully reinstated into organized baseball. Today he received official notice of his having been fined $700 by the National Commission."[26]

April 6, "Order Kling to Report." At last, it appeared to be over. Murphy telegraphed Kling ordering him to report at Indianapolis on April 6 or 7, but he couldn't leave immediately. He replied he would join the team in Columbus April 10.

"It's a great day for me," Kling said. "I'm happier now than I've been any day since I caught the final game in the championship series in New York in October, 1908.

"Can I come back? That question makes me laugh. I know that I shall regain my old form within ten days after I join the squad. By April 20, I'll be doing the heavy end of the catching for the team. Just watch me come back."[27]

Kling's return to the Cubs meant that the team would now have four catchers—Archer, Kling, Moran and Needham.

The inside story of how Kling was influenced to return to the Cubs was not widely publicized. The *Chicago Tribune* and the *Daily News* made no mention of it, and probably knew nothing about it. On April 10, the *Washington Post* did a special titled:

BROUGHT KLING BACK.

The part Joe Tinker played in influencing John Kling to apply to the the National Commission for reinstatement and to make his peace with President Murphy has not been related to the fans.

"No man on the Cub team is more anxious to win the pennant this season than is the actor-shortstop. Joe has been burning with a desire to knock Pittsburgh from its pedestal ever since the close of the 1909 race. To be on another world's championship club means as much to Tinker as to any of the other Cubs, and perhaps a little more, for Joe's vaudeville act naturally would be twice as much of a drawing card if his team again takes the highest honors in baseball.

Joe, realizing this, set his brains to work last fall, and finally came to the conclusion that the Cubs' chances would be increased immeasurably if Kling could be persuaded to get back into harness.

One day in January he visited President Murpny's office and told the magnate that his theatrical bookings would land him in Kansas City the following month. He asked the Cub President for permission to talk to Kling about coming back, and Charles Webb, knowing the friendship which exists between Joe and Kling, gave his consent, figuring that Joe would have more influence than any other man he could secure for the purpose. But the vaudeville dates were changed, and Joe's Kansas City booking was postponed until March. Knowing this would be too late, and having a week off in the middle of January, Joe volunteered to make a special trip to Kansas City to see what he could accomplish with his old pal.

Caricature depicting Kling's return to the Cubs (*Chicago Tribune*).

So President Murphy paid the shortstop's expenses to the Missouri town, and Joe arrived there on January 18. On the following day he took Kling out to lunch, and while the catcher was eating, Joe was arguing with him.

"Don't you realize," asked Joe, "that your billiard and pool business will be twice as profitable if you are a big league ballplayer once more? If you won't come back and play with us, at least ask the Commission to reinstate you, and then you will be ready to play when you make up your mind."

The upshot of the matter was that Kling consented to hold a long distance telephone conversation with President Murphy, and at 2 o'clock on the afternoon of January 19, catcher and owner were talking business.

Thinking it was too early to publish Kling's intentions, Joe, on his return to Chicago, was obliged to say that he thought Kling was through playing ball, when, in reality, he knew that John would be back on the Chicago club if the Commission would act favorably on his application.

"Kling is going to play this season for two reasons," said Joe. "In the first place, he knows he can make good money in baseball and that his business will be much better for his return to the Cubs, and, in the second, he is like most professional ballplayers. He loves the game, and is unwilling to stay out of it any longer.

"And you may be sure he'll be in shape. He has the advantage of being a careful person. He doesn't drink, smoke or chew, so his condition is certain to be all right. Then Kling is a man of pride. Whatever he does, he wants to do well, and he wouldn't think of getting back into a Cub uniform if he didn't know he could fill the bill.

"I took some trouble in the Kling case, but I feel I am well repaid, now that he is sure to play with us, for I believe we have the pennant as good as won with him on the club. I like the honor of being on a championship ball team, and I also like the money that we will make if we win this year, so I won't figure I did that work for nothing if the Cubs come back into their own."[28]

The almost daily newspaper articles must have had some wear and tear on Manager Chance, for he talked to a reporter on April 19 and his feelings poured out:

Chance Sore on Kling

"Johnny Kling's signed statement that he would start playing as soon as he joined the club is all rubbish," said Manager Frank Chance. "Of course we will give Kling a uniform and a chance to play ball if he does pay his fine and come back to us, but it is a matter of indifference to me. If he wants to stay in Kansas City it is his own lookout. You may be sure the Cubs will not beg him to get back into the game. I am sick and tired of the whole Kling business.

"Kling has a motive in not reporting to us," continued the Cubs' leader, "and his motive is a regular stick-up game. He seems to think we are clamoring for his return. He knew his old salary was $4500 and he was out to get a raise. As a member of the Chicago club Kling picked up the sum of $7500 in baseball during the season of 1908."[29]

Although Johnny Kling was happy to be going back to the game he loved, he had strong feelings about, and was not happy about, the $700 fine. After talking with W. A. Thompson of the American Music Hall in Chicago,

Kling agreed to go on the vaudeville stage with Cap Anson and play a game of fifty points balkline billiards at each performance. He would thus recoup the fine that had been imposed upon him.

President Lynch, of the National League, heard about it and sent the following telegram to Chairman Herrmann: "I suggest that you take steps to stop Kling appearing in vaudeville. He cannot make a burlesque of the national game. Insist on his reporting to his club at once or the Commission will take further action in his case. If Kling defies the Commission, President Lynch will ask to have the case reopened."[30] August Herrmann wired Kling, saying that if he did not report to the Chicago National ball team Monday, his recent reinstatement would be suspended for one year.[31]

When Johnny Kling was told of President Herrmann's threat of suspension, he told the Associated Press, "I will leave for Chicago Saturday night and report for duty as soon as I arrive."[32] Saturday night, Kling was at the train station, mitt and mask inside his suitcase. To a little group of reporters who were at the station to see him off, Kling said: "Boys, I'm glad I'm going back. While I believe the team would have won the pennant without me, I feel more certain now. I am in fair condition and will report to Manager Chance tomorrow morning."

"What about your salary, John?" was asked.

"It's like this...," Kling said, but before he could finish, the rear lights of the train were down the platform.[33]

Kling arrived in Chicago Sunday morning and was shaking hands with Manager Chance in the afternoon at the ballpark. He greeted President Murphy and told his player friends he was here for good. When asked about his fine of $700, Kling refused to say whether or not he had paid it.[34]

Four days later, April 29, the *Chicago Tribune* answered the question:

NATIONAL COMMISSION GETS
$700 CHECK FROM J. KLING.

Johnny Kling of the Chicago National League club has made peace with the National Commission. Secretary Bruce today received a check for $700 covering the amount of the fine imposed on Kling for violating his contract with the Cubs. The check came in an envelope bearing a special delivery stamp and was mailed in Chicago at noon Thursday.

Kling is now free to play with the Chicago club any time Manager Chance wishes to use him. It was thought for a time that Kling was making sport of the Commission by refusing to pay up for such a long time after this body reinstated him.

The fine paid by Kling was the largest in the history of baseball. A couple of years ago Hal Chase was fined $200 for jumping the New York Americans. This was the largest previous fine. Chairman Herrmann of the Commission would make no comment other than Kling had paid his fine and was eligible to play with the Cubs.

A fine of $200 was also imposed against the Cubs for tendering Kling a contract before he had been restored to good standing, a violation of Rule 47. Murphy pleaded guilty, and said it had been done to protect the team's interests and that the Commission had due notice of his action. The fine was therefore suspended.[35]

On May 5, page 13 of the *Tribune* reported: "Kling Signs Contract with Cubs for Next Three Years. Catcher John Kling of the Cubs, yesterday signed a three-year contract in President Murphy's office. The salary, which Kling will receive, was not made public. The verdict of the National Commission ordered that Kling should return to the Cubs and receive not more than $4500 for the year.

"Kling was also awarded his share of the prize money for assisting in winning the world's championship in 1908. Kling asserted he was ready to go behind the bat at any time. He may be seen in action in tomorrow's game with Pittsburgh."[36]

Although the press reported that a three-year contract had been signed, it wasn't true. The contract began on April 14, 1910, and ended October 15, 1910. This period of time constituted the life of the contract, but it gave President Murphy the right to fire Johnny Kling at any time with ten days' written notice without any explanation for such termination of the contract (see Appendix B, item F).

On the day "Noisy" signed, the Pirates trounced the Cubs, 8–3. Mordecai had an awful eighth inning when six runs were chalked up against him. The team found themselves in fourth place.

On May 5, Chance was notified that Kling could start work at any time since his contract had been signed. The manager told the press, "Kling will be catching this afternoon." And yet, Needham did the catching.[37]

On the following day, Johnny Kling worked behind the bat during the Cubs' fielding practice and fans cheered when John pegged perfectly to second. Some were not at all pleased when Kling wasn't sent in to catch the game after Chance promised that he would be. Needham again did the catching, and the Cubs were dosed with bitter medicine, losing 6 to 1 against the league leading Pirates.[38]

Morning rains came down on May 7 and continued most of the afternoon. This caused manager and magnate to call the game off. But on the 8th, the fans could hardly believe their ears when Umpire Klem announced the Chicago battery—Cole and Kling.

The *Trib*'s sportswriter, R.W. Lardner, took a swipe at Kling. "When the truth was finally pressed home that Kling was going to catch," he said, "the gang yelled joyfully, showing there was still a warm place in many hearts for the truant of 1909."[39]

Even if R.W. thought he was being "clever" calling Johnny Kling "truant" was bad PR for Johnny. But he gave Kling some good PR when he headlined an article: "Kansas City Cue Star Catches in Old Polished Form. Manager Chance Sick in Bed."

Lardner then went on to let the fans know that "a combination of grip, pleurisy and lumbago" were the culprits keeping Chance in bed. He made this diagnosis before telling the die-hard Chicago Cub fans, "None of the Pirates tried Kling's arm, so he had no chance to show what it would do in a pinch." What R.W. reported next showed an underlying problem Kling would have to overcome if the Cubs were to recapture the flag.

> Tommy Leach opened the disastrous eighth with a clean single to left, and Manager Clarke was passed. Since Manager Chance was sick in bed, Samuel James Tilden Sheckard was bossing the job. Sheck extracted King Cole and brought in Rescuer Brown, but the yelps of delight soon changed to a groan of despair when Mordecai failed to put on the brakes in his usual precise manner.
> Wagner was up when Brown entered. Instead of sacrificing or hitting it out of the lot, Honus hit a high bounder, which Brownie nailed with his gloved hand. He had time sufficient to force Leach at third and threw thither, but the ball hopped out of Steiny's hands and the bases were full. John Miller immediately brought in a pair of runs with a clean shot to right. Schulte kicked it when it came by him, and before he had recovered, Wagner was at third and Miller at second. The score was tied and there was more to come.
> Jack Flynn, a young upstart from the American Association, who had a nasty habit of doing things you don't want him to do, saw the overflow crowd in left field and aimed a blow at it. His hit not only reached the throng, but sailed over it and into the covered stand, far enough inside the foul line to have no doubt in anyone's mind. Of course, Honus and Jocko strolled home ahead of him. The Cubs lost 7 to 4."[40]

Jack Flynn was a new man. Johnny had never seen him before. He didn't know the kind of pitch he liked, or the one that would keep him swinging at air. He didn't know Flynn's intentions when he saw the grip on the bat or the way he planted his feet in the dirt. Johnny had to learn about this man before he could tell Brownie how to pitch to him. In fact, he had to learn the little tricks and habits of 58 new men on all of the teams in the National League before he could lead an effective defense and offense against opponents. And he had to learn fast.

With the team in fourth place, 3½ games out of first, they boarded a train that evening for Chicago. They were scheduled to play New York, who had suddenly pushed Pittsburgh out of the top spot. Those New Yorkers looked good with a win-loss of 13–5, and the Cubs were about to be tested. So was Kling.

The *Tribune* said, "If Kling is as good as he ever was, [Chance] will alternate Archer and Kling behind the plate. By working these two, he will have the strongest catching department in the National League."[41]

The season moved forward and the Cubs won many more than they lost. June 1 saw the team in first place after routing Boston, 5–1. Chicago now had a 23–12 record, New York was second with 24–14 and Pittsburgh was third, 18–16. The team had been energized, and continued playing at a sizzling pace. In the mid–June series with the Giants, a lot of Cubs believed the lead was theirs to keep.[42] On the last day of the month, June 30, they played a grand game against St. Louis.

Kling did some great throwing in the second round when he caught Mowry stealing, and also made himself conspicuous with his whip in the fourth when Koney fanned and Oakes was doubled stealing. Evans got on a little later and was out stealing, Kling to Tinker.

Noisy John also helped push across runs when the team began to score in the sixth. Reulbach fanned for a starter. Evers slipped one over on Koney at first and beat out a bunt. He advanced to second on a wild pitch. Sheckard hit to Mowry and Evers was caught between the sacks, but landed on third when Huggins dropped a throw. Sheckard moved to second on the play and Hofman followed with a neat two-base chop to left field that counted both runners. Chance fouled to Koney and Steinfeldt bounced a hot grounder off Hauser's shins, on which Hofman tallied. Tinker waited for four balls.

At this time, Chicago had only a one-run lead over St. Louis, so Kling's duty was to sacrifice. He bunted and beat it out. Reulbach sacrificed both men ahead. Evers hit to Koney, but Tinker easily slid under Bresnahan's effort to tag him. Sheckard's single counted Kling. Evers stole home a few moments later, but O'Day called him out, claiming Steinfeldt interfered with Bresnahan. This he did not do, as Evers slid right into him and toppled him over inside of the diamond.[43]

Chicago's momentum continued. The feats on the diamond were stunning. The cork center ball began to pay off with four-baggers, Wildfire Schulte pacing the way. The Cubs had a commanding lead in July, and Johnny contributed to that lead with his bat, as evidenced by the July 9 headline on page 10 of the *Chicago Tribune*: "Kling's Home Run Gives Cubs Game. 'Noisy John' Clouts Long One Which Sends 'Zim' Ahead of Him to the Plate."

They had just beaten the Reds, 3 to 2, and were still in first place with a win-loss of 43–24, 2½ games ahead of New York, and 8 games ahead of Pittsburgh. With almost three months into the season, the questions raised about John Kling had been answered.

"When Catcher John Kling rejoined the Cubs this season," the news article said, "the question was asked, 'Could he regain his old form in batting and throwing?' That query was in the mouth of thousands of Cub fans that watched his work with the keenest of interest."

> For the longest while there was a doubt of his being able to return to the same condition he was in when Manager Chance's men finished the year of 1908 with

the championship of the National League. But he showed he was steadily approaching his former trim. At present there need be no doubt about it. He is as good as he ever was, critics say.

Second baseman, Johnny Evers, said today, he believed that the year's rest had done the backstop a world of good, that he looks as good, if not better, than he did in 1908. And one thing the rest did for him was to revive some of the pepper he had many years ago. He seems more active behind the plate than heretofore, as he is continually talking now, which is a good indication that he is himself again. Besides that, he has more ginger on the bases and seems to take more interest to his work than when he quit the club. Up to that time, Kling had been playing many years and felt a little tired of the game. It was as if he needed rest. And it seems to have done him a whole lot of good.

When he first returned it was a task for him to move around with alacrity. Now it is the opposite. He chases after foul fly balls and bunts with the speed that made him so prominent in contests of years gone by.

Kling's batting average alone indicates he is back in shape. His records for the last thirteen games shows he has been to bat forty-three times. In that time, he secured sixteen hits which gives him a batting average of .372. He is credited with five extra base hits, one of which was a home run and the others doubles, and has scored eight runs.

His throwing, which was not quite perfect, is grand now, and he gets the ball away with more snap. Manager Chance need not worry about rival clubs stealing many bases with him backstopping, as he is lighter than in 1908 and stronger.

In addition, his mental faculties are clear and keen. When he came back, he had to get used to all the new players in order to get his judgement back. And he sure did that mighty fast. Kling will be a great factor in our winning the championship.[44]

The Evers prediction appeared to be coming true. Nearing the end of August, "Noisy John" was still helping the team win ball games.

"Giants Given Awful Drubbing," the headline said. Kling's two hits helped drive in runs in that 6–1 drubbing. And the Cubs now had a win-loss of 76–35 — 8½ games ahead of second place Pittsburgh and 12 games ahead of New York.[45]

But the month of September saw the Cubs go into a slump and the hated New Yorkers began inching their way back. They never made it. By Sept. 29, Chance's boys needed only three more victories to win the National League pennant, and they had fourteen games yet to play.

But the team suffered a crippling blow on October 1 in a game with the Reds, as described by the *Cincinnati Enquirer* on October 2, 1910: "With Evers on second, Hofman cut a clean single through to center and Johnny Evers set sail for the plate. Miller's throw home was slow and Johnny saw, while still a few feet from the pan, that it would not be necessary for him to go to the ground. He was all ready to slide however, and the change of mind cost him the use of his leg. As he checked himself, his spike caught in the hard earth near the plate and he toppled over on his side. Even in that position, and with sharp pains shooting through his broken leg, Johnny's first thought was to touch the plate and score his run. The bone protruded through the flesh and Evers was carried off the field on a stretcher."

Although Evers' injury was a most unhappy event, the following day, Oct. 2, saw an event in another game with the Reds that allowed for some rejoicing. It was on this day that the Cubs cinched the 1910 flag. Kling came back. And they all came back.

When Chance's great team of veterans cinched the 1910 championship of the National League by defeating Cincinnati on October 2, 1910, they finished the accomplishment of a feat unequaled in the annals of the organization to which they belonged. Never before had a National League team of champions come back in the short space of one season after surrendering their title of champions.

At the close of the season, the Cubs did not touch their own world's record of 116 games won in a season, but they passed the century mark in victories and thus established another record in the quantity of wins to their credit in five successive years. Never before had a team won 500 games in that space of time and the Cubs were way over it.

The news media spoke of the twelve men who accomplished this feat and placed them in the "500" club. The twelve men selected were Frank Chance, John Evers, Joseph Tinker, Harry Steinfeldt, Mordecai Brown, Orval Overall, Edward Reulbach, Jake Pfiester, John Kling, James Sheckard, Arthur Hofman and Frank Schulte.

John Kling had not played with the Cubs those five successive years, having been missing and missed during the entire season of 1909. But as he was technically and legally a member of the team while absent, he was considered eligible. Without him there would be no backstop in the Five Hundred Club.[46]

Kling's 1910 stats were:

G	AB	R	H	2B	3B	H	RBI	A	SB	BA
91	297	31	80	17	2	2	32	118	3	.269

It was time for Chance to prepare for the World Series between his team and Connie Mack's youngsters. He had sent Johnny Kling to scout the Athletics, and on his way to Philadelphia, "Noisy" stopped by at Jack Doyle's billiard-and-betting parlor in New York. It was an unambiguous assignment. The A's had clinched the pennant way back in the summertime. *Newsweek* reported this conversation:

"How do you figure the Series?" asked Mr. Doyle politely.
"We won't lose a game," said Mr. Kling.

A few days later the spy touched at Doyle's again, on his way home from enemy territory.

"How do you like the Series now?" asked Doyle.
"We won't win a game," said Mr. Kling bleakly.[47]

William G. Weart, baseball editor of the *Philadelphia Telegraph*, compared the two teams. "Many concede," he said, "that the Cubs outclass the White Elephants in catchers and rate both Kling and Archer better than the best that Mack can show in the way of backstops. Kling undoubtedly outshines them all. But in pitching, the Athletics more than offset the advantage which the Cubs have in backstops."[48]

Mr. Weart's evaluation of the pitching staff proved to be true. The Chicago team charged into the World Series as heavy favorites. On the other side of the diamond sat the Philadelphia A's, featuring the "$100,000 infield" and four pitchers, each having won more than 15 games that season. The Athletics needed only two pitchers, Jack Coombs and Charles "Chief" Bender, to dispose of the Cubs in 5 games.

Bender was in the best possible condition in game one, his pitching being faultless throughout. It was easy to note that he was familiar with nearly all of the Cubs' hitters, and such men as Hofman, Chance, Sheckard, and Kling, who as a rule could be depended upon to hit with regularity, were entirely helpless before the Indian's pitching.

To show how good Bender was, it is sufficient to state that only twenty-four men faced him in eight innings. He was in trouble only once. That was in the ninth, when Tinker hit a fast ball to center for a single and went to second when Strunk let the ball roll past him. Kling then hit a curve ball on a line over Bender's head for a single, scoring Tinker. There was no further hitting.

The team fielded in their usual perfect manner and no criticism whatever can be made of their defensive play. Kling's swift and accurate throws easily caught all the Athletics who tried to steal second, and were the most marked fielding stunts of the day. The principal cause for the Cubs' 4–1 defeat was their inability to hit.[49]

When A's pitcher Jack Coombs took game two by a score of 9 to 3, sportswriter, Fielder Jones summed it up by saying, "It is another case of youth against age. It is speed and enthusiasm against the listlessness that follows continued success. In some such way must we explain two successive defeats of that perfect baseball machine, the Chicago Cubs, by Connie Mack's bunch of lively youngsters."[50]

The prevailing odds on the series made the Athletics 5 to 3 and 7 to 5 choices. Some offered 1 to 5 that the Cubs would not win a single game. But Manager Chance was still optimistic. He expected to win the world's title despite the two game handicap and was eager to get home and play on his own grounds.

But with Coombs again on the mound, the Athletics made it three straight, 12–5. They knocked Reulbach and McIntire off the slab and hit Pfiester hard. The assessment made by Garry Herrmann, chairman of the National Commission, was, "They were not only beaten, but disgracefully beaten."[51]

A rabid Cubs fan took out an ad in the *Chicago Tribune*: "WANTED— AT ONCE. FOUR CONSECUTIVE VICTORIES over White Elephants by Cubs. B. F. Budinger"[52]

All he got was one victory. The Chicago team avoided a clean sweep by pulling out a tight win in Game 4. Trailing 3–2 going into the bottom of the ninth, they knotted the score on a triple by Chance before putting the game away in the tenth with a two-out single by Jimmy Sheckard. The Series was over. The Cubs were defeated. Suddenly the Cubs appeared to be an aging team. They seemed to have lost the confidence and the dash that had been theirs prior to the 1910 World Series. The Cubs had grown old, seemingly overnight.[53]

Then again, perhaps it wasn't aging. Perhaps it was a matter of picking up Cub signs and knowing in advance what was coming. Kling pitched Brown out many times in the hope of catching his man at second or of breaking up the hit and run play. He had been doing this all season and it worked. But in every case, the Athletics disappointed the Cubs' play by failing to do as they were expected to do.[54]

Frank Chance always had to have a reason for losing, like when the "Hitless Wonders" beat the Cubs in the 1906 World Series. For the record, he said, "They simply came out and beat us." But privately, the skipper told Three Finger Brown, "How that goddam ball club beat us, I'll never understand."[55]

And now that the Cubs were again losing, Chance believed that Johnny Kling was allowing Mack's boys to steal his signs. How else would they know what to do, or know what not to do? Suddenly, Manager Chance "scarred the veteran's pride by refusing to allow him to conduct his own campaign behind the bat, and removed him from the last two games." Kling was thus singled out as the scapegoat for the loss.[56]

Christy Mathewson had a great deal to say about this:

> When the Philadelphia Athletics unexpectedly defeated the Chicago Cubs in the World's Series of 1910, the National League players cried that their signals had been stolen by the American League team, and that because Connie Mack's batters knew what to expect, they had won the championship.
> But were the owners or any member of the Philadelphia club charged with grand larceny in stealing the baseball championship of the world? No. Was there any murmur against the methods of Connie Mack's men? No, again. By a strange

kink in the ethics of baseball, John Kling, the Chicago catcher, was blamed by the other players on the defeated team for the signs being stolen. They charged that he had been careless in covering his signals and that the enemy's coachers, particularly Hartsell, a clever man at it, had seen them from the lines. This was really the cause of Kling leaving the Cubs and going to Boston in 1911.

After the games were over and the series was lost, many of the players, and especially the pitchers, would hardly speak to Kling, the man who had as much as any one else to do with the Cubs winning four championships, and the man by his great throwing had made the reputations of a lot of their pitchers. But the players were sore because they had lost the series and lost the extra money which many of them had counted as their own before the games started, and they looked around for someone to blame and found Kling. One of the pitchers complained after he lost a game:

"Can't expect a guy to win with his catcher giving the signs so the coachers can read 'em and tip the batters."

"And you can't expect a catcher to win a game for you if you haven't got anything on the ball,'" replied Kling, for he is quick tempered and cannot stand reflections on his ability. But the pitchers chance remark had given the other players an excuse for fixing the blame, and it was put on Kling.

"I honestly do not believe that Kling was in any way responsible for the rout of the proud Cubs. The Chicago pitchers were away off form in the series and could not control the ball, thus getting themselves 'into the hole' all the time. Shrewd Connie Mack soon realized this and ordered his batters to wait everything out, to make the twirlers throw every ball possible. The result was that, with the pitcher continually in the hole, the batters were guessing what was coming and frequently guessing right, as any smart hitter could under the circumstances. This made it look as if the Athletics were getting the Cubs' signals.

"Why, I changed signs every three innings, Matty," Kling told me afterwards in discussing the charge. "Some of the boys said that I gave the old bended-knee sign for a curve ball. Well, did you ever find anything to improve on the old ones? That's why they are old."

But the Cubs still pointed the finger of scorn at Kling, for it hurts to lose, I know it, I have lost myself.[57]

There was no proof that the A's were able to steal signs from Johnny Kling. In a discussion with Josh Prager, a SABR member who is knowledgeable about stealing signs, he cited remarks made by Eddie Collins, second sacker for the A's who talked about how good his team was at stealing signs from the pitcher by noting what he did before throwing. Nevertheless, Kling was the fall guy, and bad PR was something Noisy did not need. Be that as it may, the players divided more money than any two other championship clubs ever did, each Cub receiving $1,315.

And with money in hand, Johnny Kling was on his way back to Kansas City, perhaps disappointed. Besides losing the World Series, he was the backstop in only 86 games during the regular season, and the status of premier catcher had once again eluded him. Nevertheless, he had things to do. Important things.

First, after hugging and kissing his wife Lillian, then hugging his four-year-old daughter, Virginia, they would sit down and talk about three very important birthdays—his own, November 13, Virginia's on December 5 and Lillian's, next year, January 16. The women had agreed to do all of the planning, including sending out invitations.

Next on the agenda was to sit down with brother Charles and go over the books for his two billiard parlors. Hiring his brother after he grew tired of being a baker was fortunate for both of them. Charles had a job. And Johnny Kling had a brother that watched over and kept track of all the money coming in. At first, there had been a question about Charles being trusted, but he had proven himself over the past two years.

Now, a project dear to his heart, the Missouri Valley Athletic Club, a new organization formed by businessmen in Kansas City for the purpose and promotion of indoor and outdoor sports, had chosen John Kling as president. One of the goals was to immediately establish a gymnasium to be used exclusively in the daytime for school children in Kansas City. A physical director of national reputation would be in charge and girls and boys alike would be given physical instruction free of charge.

Plans were already being drawn up for the gym, which, when completed, was to be one of the most up-to-date in the country. Grounds were now under option and the deal was scheduled to be closed within 60 days.

The club was designed to also maintain rooms in the downtown section for the benefit of members. These quarters were to be maintained separately from the gymnasium, but during the evenings, club members would be permitted to exercise and play games in the gymnasium.[58]

Another project dear to his heart, and most exciting, was a partnership with his nephew, Bennie Allen, his sister Amelia's 19-year-old son who had the audacity to beat his uncle John at pool, thus retaining his crown as the champion pool player of Kansas City. Although Bennie had no money, his father, Holly, invested heavily and became a partner, then allowed his son to take over.

Yes! He and Bennie could really pull it off! Build a hotel with the finest pool and billiard emporium in the world. Bennie was for it. Johnny was for it. He already had a place picked out in a downtown section of Kansas City, had signed a 99-year lease for the lot, and planned to lay it all out for his nephew.

In all probability, while Johnny Kling busied himself with family, business and philanthropic endeavors, he gave no thought, none whatsoever, as to why Ban Johnson demanded that his own name be taken off the commission's report after it had been decided to allow Kling to return to baseball. Ban wanted a more severe penalty, but he refused to say just what it was he wanted.

"A mistake has been made," he said, "but it is best that I remain silent, especially in connection with the views of President Lynch, a new man in baseball. I have no desire to speak harshly of any error he may make at the beginning of his administration."[59]

Knowing the history of Ban Johnson, it seems fair to say that he was not a man to impose caution in his remarks or in his behavior. And he was never one to be silent. He had been president of the Western Association from 1894 through 1888. In 1899 he changed the league's name from Western to American — the same American Association that Johnny Kling was supposed to have "crippled" by selling tickets to baseball fans in Kansas City. They came to see Johnny's team play instead of the Kansas City Blues, which was an American Association team. Selling tickets meant money.

Ban Johnson operated the American Association as a minor circuit in 1900, but he wasn't happy with his minor league status. In 1901, with strong franchises in Chicago, Boston, Detroit, Baltimore, Cleveland, Philadelphia, Washington and Milwaukee, he announced a second major league, the American League. Mr. Johnson then eliminated the despicable reserve clause and raided the major league clubs, "stealing" talent away from the National League by paying bigger bucks.

The Nationals had been behaving like any other monopoly, having imposed a $2,400 cap on salaries. National League players had had enough. They packed their gloves, bats, spikes and other paraphernalia and headed for other ballparks.

Ban Johnson had fired the first volley and war had been declared between the Nationals and the Americans, but these kinds of battles cost money. Large amounts of money were drained from the coffers of baseball magnates, one being Mr. Johnson.

And now, along comes this upstart, Johnny Kling, establishing franchises, heading up the formation of another league, "stealing" money away from the Kansas City Blues, a team under the protection of the American Association. Noisy John had dealt a "body blow" to that organization, "crippled" it, and Ban Johnson was not going to sit idly by and watch Kling do what he himself had done. The fear was that John G. Kling could possibly be successful.

So Ban Johnson wanted a more severe penalty, not just a fine of a measly $700. It seems fair to say that Mr. Johnson wanted Johnny's head, and he wanted it under the guillotine.

Although Noisy John was now back in baseball, the publicity that was generated did not serve him well. His photograph at home plate holding a bat waiting for the ball to be pitched was published in a leading newspaper. Beneath the photo it said: "Johnny Kling, Chicago Catcher, who has made more trouble and discussion in big league ranks than any other player in years."[60]

Noisy John didn't know it, but this was the start of bad PR that would follow him as long as he lived, and beyond.

11

WALKING THE PLANK

1911

Coming into another baseball season, Johnny Kling had no reason to expect anything different than in 1910. Chance's refusal to allow him to conduct his own campaign behind the bat in the World Series was still on his mind. And he knew that if the manager could figure out a way, his position on the team would get even worse.[1]

Although quiet and unassuming, not one to easily express feelings, Kling opened up a bit to Fred Tenney, manager of the Boston Nationals when he last visited that city.

"He told me he couldn't seem to work up the old time interest," Tenney said. "A change of scene would work wonders for him, though I hope to see him back in his old splendid form, as it is certainly a pleasure to watch a finished artist."[2]

But there was no change of scene. During spring training, and prior to a scheduled game with the Louisville Colonels, Johnny Kling witnessed the harsh, dictatorial demands doled out to pitcher Lew Richie and third baseman Heinie Zimmerman by the skipper. And there were no ands or ifs about it.

Whatever their crimes, Richie had to pitch good baseball all through the summer, go through a probationary period with no upsets, and if he did this to the satisfaction of Manager Chance, he would suffer only a little financially. As for Heinie, he had only one chance in the world to continue on as a member of the team. From now on, he had to live in the straight and narrow in addition to playing top-notch baseball. Chance demanded moral and athletic achievement from the husky German. Anything less would mean that someone else would be doing the regular third basing for the champions.[3]

On April 8, the Cubs were ready for the 1911 season and President Murphy came out with his prediction:

The Cubs again will win the National League pennant as well as the world's championship or I will be mightily mistaken. Manager Chance has picked up five of the likeliest recruits it has been my good fortune to look upon. Toney and Griffin are top notch pitchers. Saier has the making of a corking good first baseman. Doyle is a heady as well as a handy infielder, and Shean is a known quantity. The return to perfect form of Kling and Sheckard is a revelation. All the other players are in perfect trim after one of the best training trips ever taken by a club.[4]

April 12 opened the 1911 baseball season and it hosted the wives of eight Cub players at the West Side Grounds. Occupying box seats were Mrs. Frank L. Chance, Mrs. Mordecai Brown, Mrs. John Kling, Mrs. James Archer, Mrs. James Sheckard, Mrs. John Evers, Mrs. John Kane and Mrs. "King" Cole.

Threatening clouds did not prevent fans from turning out for the game with St. Louis. There was almost a parkfull of people there before the teams had begun their preliminary practice. A brass band livened things up before the games started, and Mayor-elect Carter H. Harrison, from an upper box, tossed out the ball that started the contest.

It was the gayest opening ever held on the West Side. Still, there was an air of despair over all, for the St. Louis players wore crepe on their arms, and the Cubs' pennant hung at half mast from the flag pole in memory of the late Stanley Robison, former owner of the Cardinals.

The Cubs played a wonderful game. But the hole they were thrown into at the start, because of the wildness of Ed Reulbach, seemed to take a bit of their baseball sense away from them for a time. Reulbach was not right because he did not warm up long enough. The bell for the Cardinals' practice was rung too late and as Umpire Cy Rigler insisted that the game start promptly at 3:30, Reulbach had only seven minutes in which to practice. It was not enough for him. As a consequence, he went into the game cold. He was unable to locate the plate and issued ten consecutive balls without getting a strike over the plate. He passed Huggins and Ellis and had two balls on Mowry when Chance took him out and called Weaver to his rescue.

During the fray, Kling was cheered repeatedly by the fans for his excellent throwing to the bases. And when he made the first steal of the game and pounded out a long double, this too invited the admiration of Chicago fans.

The game lasted two hours and forty-four minutes, which carried it past the dinner hour of nearly everyone present. There were only a few who left before it was over or even thought of the time, so intense was the contest from the start to the finish. But it ended in a 3–3 tie and the game was called because of darkness.[5]

As the season moved forward, Noisy John found himself on the bench more often than not. It seems fair to say that he felt humiliated. Possibly devastated. And most certainly, his passion and enthusiasm for the game would have dwindled to a low point. The element of depression could easily have set in, thus robbing him of the ability to focus and to play as in the past.

Oh, there were times in a game when a faint glimmer of his former self shone through. Like on April 27, in a game against the Pirates, when he hit a triple. But even then, his thoughts were not completely on the contest as Leach darted for third on Miller's foul to the catcher close to the stand. The ball was not thrown until he was half way down the line. Then it took a bad bounce in front of Zimmerman and rolled about fifteen feet away allowing Leach to go all the way.

By the end of April, the batting average of all the players in the national League were listed on page C-2 of the *Chicago Tribune*. Kling was number 59 with .187, not anywhere near his former self. In fact, the lowest ever. It didn't make him feel any better when Jimmy Archer was listed as number 65 with .156. And from the number of games he was playing, it could have been predicted that he would not come near the 86 games he caught in 1910.

Then it happened. Johnny Kling was working out in the morning of June 9. The practice session was in preparation for a game against Brooklyn that afternoon. The batteries decided upon were Brown and Kling vs. Rucker and Bergen. Early in the fray, Three Finger had to be removed after two innings and Fred Toney replaced him. But the Cubs came up short, 4 to 1.[6]

One day later, June 10, Johnny Kling was again behind the bat, but he was no longer playing for the Chicago Cubs.[7]

Overnight, and without any prior notice, Noisy John had been traded. How did he feel about not being notified in advance, about having the deal dumped in his lap? Imagine playing before Chicago fans one day as a Cub, then crouching low behind the bat the next day as a member of the opposing team. If that wasn't a slap in the face, what was? And it could only have happened with the approval of Frank Chance.

The news media picked up the story. Interviews were conducted. And the immediate remarks published were from Johnny Kling: "John Kling, who has been a member of the Cubs for 11 years before he was traded to Boston Saturday, refused to put on a Boston uniform yesterday, and is now supposed to be on his way to Kansas City."[8]

"Kling Retires from Game" was the headline that caught the attention of baseball fans everywhere. They went on to read that "Catcher John Kling is said to have given as his reason that Boston is too far from his private interests in Kansas City."[9]

On the following day, June 14, 1911, a headline read: "Kling Changes

The score:

BROOKLYN.	AB	R	H	PO	A		CHICAGO.	AB	R	H	PO	A
Tooley, ss.	3	1	1	2	3		Sheck'd, lf.	2	0	0	1	0
Daub't, 1b.	4	1	2	6	0		Schulte, rf.	3	0	1	3	0
Wheat, lf.	4	1	1	3	0		Archer, 1b.	4	0	1	9	1
Hum'el, 2b.	4	0	1	2	3		H. Zim, 2b	4	0	1	1	1
Burch, cf.	4	0	1	3	0		Doyle, 3b.	4	1	1	0	1
Coulson, rf.	4	0	0	2	0		Tinker, ss.	4	0	0	3	3
E Zim., 3b.	4	1	1	3	1		Kaiser, cf.	4	0	1	0	0
Bergen, c.	3	0	0	3	0		Kling, c.	4	0	0	10	2
Rucker, p.	3	0	1	0	2		Brown, p.	0	0	0	0	1
							Toney, p.	3	0	1	0	4
Total	33	4	8	27	9		Total	32	1	6	27	13

Error—Hummel.

Brooklyn ....3 1 0 0 0 0 0 0—4
Chicago ....0 0 0 1 0 0 0 0 0—1

Three-base hits—Wheat, Hummel, Rucker. Home run—Doyle. Hits—Off Brown, 6 in 2 innings; off Toney, 2 in 7 innings. Double plays—Tooley and Daubert; Kling and Tinker. Left on bases—Chicago, 7; Brooklyn, 3. Bases on balls—Off Rucker, 3; off Toney, 1. Struck out—By Brown, 3; by Toney, 4; by Rucker, 3. Time of game—One hour and thirty-eight minutes. Umpires—Messrs. Finneran and Rigler.

Chicago vs. Brooklyn, June 9, 1911 (*New York Times*).

His Mind." The story followed with this: "After a conference with President Russell, of the Boston club, Kling started for Pittsburgh with the Boston team."[10]

On June 15, the headline explained why Noisy John had changed his mind: "Kling to Be Captain." The article said, "President Russell announced that John Kling would be made captain of the team. Russell said that he thought that a hustling, heady player like Kling would steady up the Boston players, and that in Kling we secured a good catcher, and one of the best baseball heads in the business."[11]

The June 17, 1911, issue of *Sporting Life* talked about the motive for the trade: "Frank Chance may not play again this season, and perhaps never. As a result he figured out that he must have a first-class outfielder to take Hofman's place in center, it being necessary to put Artie on first base. He

```
CHICAGO, June 10.—Chicago defeated Bos-
ton to-day, 6 to 3. The locals bunched hits,
and with the assistance of daring base run-
ning, bases on balls, and costly errors, had
little difficulty in winning. Kling and Kaiser,
and Graham and Goode, who figured in the
big exchange of players to-day, participated
with their new colleagues. Score:
        CHICAGO.              |       BOSTON.
         AB R H PO A           |        AB R H PO A
Sh'kard, lf. 4  1  1  1  0 |Sw'ney, 2b. 4  0  1  4  5
Schulte, rf. 3  0  0  4  0 |Tenney, 1b. 4  1  1  9  1
Archer, 1b. 3   1  2 10  1 |Herzog, ss. 4  1  3  1  2
Z'm'm'n, 2b.3   1  2  5  3 |Miller, rf.  4  0  0  2  0
Doyle, 3b.  4   1  1  0  3 |Ing'ton, lf.,
Tinker, ss. 3   2  1  2  4 | 3b.  ......3  0  2  1  1
Goode, cf.  3   0  1  0  0 |K'ser, cf.,lf.4 0  0  2  1
Graham, c.  4   0  1  5  0 |Sprat, 3b.. 1  1  1  0  0
Brown, p.   3   0  2  0  1 |Pfeffer, cf.2  0  0  2  0
                           |Kling, c..  4  0  1  2  2
 Total..   30   6 11 27 12 |Mattern, p. 3  0  0  1  1

                            Total... 33  8  9 24 13

Errors—Tinker, Tenney, Herzog, Kaiser,
Mattern.
Chicago ..............2 1 0 0 1 1 0 1..—6
Boston  ..............0 0 1 1 0 1 0 0 0—3
```

Chicago vs. Boston, June 10, 1911 (*New York Times*).

tried, but could not land a good first-sacker and keep Hofman in the field. Chance has a mysterious injury of the head. "The new Cubs and Doves appeared in new uniforms Saturday, Kling catching for Boston and Graham for Chicago. It took four hours to pull off the deal."

As part of the trade, Chicago received "Peaches" Graham, a catcher who was to take Kling's place. But the trade brought back anew Johnny's background: "In 1909 he refused to report and the Cubs failed to win the pennant. This desertion did not help Kling's popularity in Chicago, either did it help him as a player. Last year he rejoined the team, but caught only about half the games. This year he has shown up poorly with the stick."[12]

This was bad PR for Kling. Combined with bad PR from the past, a decision had been reached by corporate heads of Turkey Red, Old Mill and Fez Cigarettes. It was standard practice for companies to use famous athletes in selling their products. So it was with cigarette companies. They made baseball cards with a picture of the player on front and information about him on the back. In a 1909–1910 series of baseball cards, John G. Kling had such a card. His autograph was boldly written on the front. He was a prominent player. Laudatory information about him was on the back of the card. But after he received bad press, his name was no longer used in cigarette ads.

In 1911, a No. 17 baseball card was made for Clark Griffith. The back listed 75 prominent players, and any one of them could be obtained for cigarette pack coupons. But the list did not have Kling's name. He was no longer a prominent player.

His teammates Tinker, Evers, Chance and others were there. Contemporary catchers like Bresnahan were there. But John G. Kling had been scratched. In all probability, he had no knowledge of this, and players on the list did not pay any attention as to who was on or who was off the list, but the fact that he was no longer there was an ominous sign for his future in baseball.

Nonetheless, Kling was now being given an opportunity to turn his future around. He was captain of a last place team, and a confidential letter to a friend in Kansas City was leaked to the press revealing possibilities for upcoming seasons. "Kling, it will be remembered," the news item said, "refused to join the Beaneaters after he was traded by Chicago and sulked for several days. After a little chat with the president, he came around, donned his mask and glove, and has been in the fray ever since. Kling now declares he was assured that he would be the manager of the team next year. Fred Tenney will finish the season and then retire."[13]

Not long after Kling donned his mask behind the bat, it became apparent that the Beaneaters were doomed to remain in the cellar. They had a long string of pitchers and three of them were out with arm injuries. Of the remaining 15, not one of them had the makings of a 20-game winner. In fact, the way the team was losing, it would be a miracle if one of the 15 pitchers won 10 games.

Boston fans had become accustomed to turning to the sports pages and reading: "New York Beats Boston, 2–1." "Doyle won today's game for Chicago, 5–3 in the eleventh inning." "Pittsburgh won twice from Boston today, 6–2 and 9–5." "Chicago won both games of a double-header with Boston today, 4–1 and 7–2," and on and on it went.

At the close of the season, Boston had a win-loss record of 44–107; its winningest pitcher was Buster Brown with 8–18 and an ERA of 4.29. The team's ERA was 5.08, and Johnny Kling was reportedly going to manage this bunch in 1912.

After the close of the season, tragedy struck. Page 13 of the *New York*

11. Walking the Plank

Times ran the story on November 22 with a bold headline: "W. Hepburn Russell, Lawyer, Dead at 54." William Hepburn's will left everything to his wife, Mary G. Russell, that document being admitted for probate in the New York County Court.

On the very day of Russell's demise, John G. Kling was fiddling around with his big, new, 7-passenger, 60-horsepower Oldsmobile that had just arrived in Kansas City. The Boston catcher, fearing that damage might come to the $4,000 car if he attempted to pilot it without instruction, engaged someone to teach him the art of cutting sharp corners, tooting a horn and changing speeds. After three days, the instructor left and John took over.

"I'll show my friends a little speed," he told his brother-in-law, H. B. Allen.

"I'm with you, John," said Allen. "I'll try anything once."[14]

So John invited Charles McCourt, a billiardist from Pittsburgh, and his sister-in-law, Miss Julia Gradwohl, with two of her young women friends. Everything went nicely. John drove his car around Scarritt's Point just to see if the machine would obey him. It seemed docile enough. Then the car neared Thirty-first Street and Wabash Avenue.

"I tell you, Allen, in two weeks' time I'll push Barney Oldfield off the racing map," Kling confided to his brother-in-law. "I believe that I'm going to be a wonder at this game — better than I am at baseball. It's all — — —"[15]

But just then, John sighted a streetcar coming west. The Oldsmobile was running south. John didn't finish his sentence. His motor was going about eighteen miles an hour and the streetcar a little plus. The Oldsmobile stopped with the front part of the motor intruding in the path of the streetcar. Feeling compassion for the bright new motor and the scared owner, the streetcar brushed it from the track, adding a thousand dollars, not to the value, but to the cost, of the Oldsmobile. In the evening, John said, "None of us hurt. But say, it'll take a long time to fix that motor car, won't it."[16]

After that incident, John found out about the death of his boss, President Russell, and the damaged Olds was a thing of the past. He mobilized his energies, contacted friends and almost immediately began to gather up offers of financial assistance. His plans leaked out to the press, who gobbled up the story:

"KLING AFTER BOSTON CLUB. THE CATCHER WORKING TO FORM A KANSAS CITY SYNDICATE. Ownership of All the Stock Contemplated in Negotiations Now Pending — Will Know the Result in Two or Three Days."

"I will know in two or three days," Kling said, "whether I can put the deal through. It looks like a pretty big undertaking, but I believe the Boston club can be made an excellent paying proposition — and a better paying proposition than it has been in the last few years."[17]

On December 6, John Kling was on his way to a meeting in New York to negotiate a deal whereby he might be able to acquire control of the 1911 National League tailenders. Bona fide bids had been received and control of the club was expected to take place within a week.[18]

Since John Kling was reported to be on his way to New York where the meeting was being held, it seems reasonable to believe he had financial backing of Kansas City businessmen for the acquisition of the Boston club, and that he would be making an offer.

But on December 9, a statement was released on behalf of President Russell's widow to the effect that offers for the club had been received by Pittsburgh interests, Charlie Dooin, manager of Philadelphia Nationals, Hugh McBreen, treasurer of Boston Americans, L. Coues Page, Dan Lane (formerly state senator), Felix Hanlon, a wealthy Philadelphian, James E. Gaffney and J. G. McGill, owner of the Denver club.

It was then learned that John M. Ward, former shortstop for the world champion Giants in 1888 and 1889, had an option on the club, and exercised his option with the assistance of James E. Gaffney, a millionaire contractor and an associate of the leader of Tammany Hall politics. The asking price was $200 a share with 945 of the 1,000 shares being sold, but they were sold for $174,000.[19]

The perplexing aspect of the sale was the absence of John Kling's name as one of the bidders. Yet, we know the meeting was in New York, and that he had gone there.[20] Kansas City, Chicago, New York, Los Angeles and District of Columbia newspapers did no follow up on the story that said Kling was on his way to Boston to submit an offer.

There was a hint from Beverly Winslow, the former partner and closest friend of William Hepburn Russell, that the Boston offers were considerably lower than those of Boston outsiders.[21] But there was no explanation as to why the higher bid was not accepted. And no comment was made about which of the Boston outsiders had the higher bids. Be that as it may, Ward announced that manager Fred Tenney would be released and that either John Kling or Bill Sweeney would be the manager.

One of Ward's first acts was to contact John Kling, who was in New York at the time, and signed him to a contract for 1912. Ward reported that he had no difficulty in signing the great catcher. "Kling," he said, "was really enthusiastic over the prospects of the team, and he believes we will have a much stronger club than the one which represented Boston in the National League last season."[22] He also reported that "a new park will be found and the team thoroughly overhauled. Modern stands will be erected at a cost of more than $500,000."[23] This must have been wonderful news for Noisy John. It was his future in baseball with bright horizons, a future he could once again enjoy.

12

TREADING WATER

1912

Johnny Kling had good reason to celebrate New Year's eve, feeling good about all that had transpired. His sister Lizzie was content renting out furnished rooms, as was brother Bill pouring drinks in his saloon. And brother Charles took special delight in balancing the billiard hall books to the penny. He was so proud of his achievement as a bookkeeper he wanted to spread out, take on more responsibility, so Johnny put him in charge of maintenance and repairs. It was his job to keep the place looking beautiful.

Another accomplishment bringing joy to Kling's heart was the partnership between his nephew and himself in a luxurious hotel with two of the floors to be devoted to billiards. His 21-year-old nephew didn't have much money, so his father was backing him. A call for bids to build the hotel was published on January 3, 1912.[1]

Three days later, January 6, baseball fans learned that John G. Kling was the new skipper of the Boston Doves. While his salary had not been disclosed, "it was probable," the news item said, "that he would get $9,000 for next season's work."[2]

On January 11, the *Sporting News* announced, "Boston Under Way. Owner Gaffney had looked over the old South End Park and concluded it won't do for major league ball. Mr. Gaffney hoped to have a new ballpark for the 1913 season."

Noisy John cranked up his managerial abilities and showed the fans he meant business. In company with President Ward, Treasurer James Gaffney, Charles Meyer, and a New York engineer, he hustled out to the Walpole Street grounds and spent a couple of hours deciding what changes to make for the coming season. Despite the fact that the team would have a new ballpark for the 1913 season, Kling felt that the Boston fans would appreciate improvements in the present grounds. He planned for changes of the playing field to accommodate a larger crowd in the grandstand.

"Believe me," said Kling, "the more I see of this city and its prospects the better it looks for having a good team this year. A couple of good pitchers and a good infielder would bolster up the team in great shape, and if they are obtainable we will get them."[3]

John Kling began talks with President Murphy, who told the press that a trade with Boston was possible but no names were mentioned. When asked if Ed Reulbach was one of the players, President Murphy refused to answer. It was known however, that Boston needed a seasoned pitcher, and Kling knew of Reulbach's desire to be traded.[4]

Nothing came of these talks. Noisy John tried other team owners and was encouraged by their willingness to make what seemed to be fair trades. But on February 8 the *Sporting News* ran a headline on page P-3 telling the baseball world: "Offers to Help Him Prove but Empty Promises. Instead of Aiding Boston, Fellow Magnates Block Every Move Made That Might Strengthen Braves."

The story went on, "Manager John Kling will meet President Ward at the National League annual meeting in New York next week where other clubs will learn that the new Boston owners have not been treated as friendly as Messrs. Gaffney and Ward were led to believe they would be. 'It looks like a case of every man for himself, and the Old Boy take the hindmost,' said Ward, speaking to the National League magnates."

Nevertheless, Manager Kling and President Ward forged ahead. By February 15, seventeen Boston players had been signed and a decision was reached to hold spring training in Augusta. New bathroom facilities were to be installed close to the ballpark to avoid the one-mile trip to the Y.M.C.A. where players had to go to bathe after practice.[5]

At the end of the month, Kling signed Joe Crisp, a catcher from the Topeka Western League, and left for the east with the hope of making a few trades.[6] With all of his busyness, Kling kept the Augusta pocket-billiard sharks busy, beating them as fast as they met him.[7] He also found time and delighted Boston fans by introducing his 6-year-old daughter to the players. By unanimous vote they elected her mascot for the team.

The March 23 newspaper gave the youngster top billing in an article titled "Miss Kling, Honorary Mascot, Is the Real Life of Pilgrim Party." It said:

> The Pilgrims have a new mascot to furnish new luck for the new 1912 team. Little Virginia Kling, six years old daughter of "Noisy John" Kling, the new manager of the Boston Nationals, has been elected mascot by the unanimous vote of the players.
>
> She inaugurated her reign over the destinies of the club by posing for a series of pictures for the *Boston American* while performing some of her new duties.
>
> If you fancy this little six-year-old girl doesn't know anything about baseball,

Manager Kling and 6-year-old daughter Virginia, mascot of Pilgrims (*Boston American*).

you're wrong. She knows every player on the team, is the most self-reliant person in the Pilgrim squad and is the real "life" of the "camp." She is out on the field for an hour every day.

When she was informed that she was expected to have some pictures made, in honor of her election as mascot of the Pilgrims, she picked out the poses, went out alone and found the baseball material that was needed, and as a reward, demanded the right to borrow the camera so she could "go out and snap Buster Brown." And the camera man had to make good too.[8]

The start of the season was getting close and the press was kept busy reporting the goings on in the baseball camps. For the Pilgrims, one item said, "The other National League club which promises to spring surprises is the Boston club, now owned by James E. Gaffney and John M. Ward of this city. With Johnny Kling, the former Cub catcher as manager, the club is aiming to get into the first division. Kling has a great team of sluggers, five of them being able to bat better than .300. With this foundation to work on and a pitching staff of promising twirlers, the Boston Braves expect to make a big noise."[9]

Sportswriter Hugh Fullerton did not agree. He predicted the standings for both leagues at the end of the season, and put Boston at the tail

The 1912 Boston Nationals. Starting line-up: Houser 1B, Sweeney 2B, McDonald 3B, O'Rourke SS, Titus RF, Campbell LF, Jackson CF, Kling C (*Chicago Daily News*).

end of the National League. "He said, 'The National League race looks to be the most promising, for there are seven clubs with a chance to win that pennant, and Boston is such an oddly built ball club it may turn the race upside down, even if it remains eighth. That club is going to muddle everything because it is just as likely to beat a strong team as it is to beat a weak one. It can hit terrifically and whenever a pitcher lets down an inning or two it will be all over.'"[10]

After five games had been played, Kling's men were doing well, with a win-loss of 3–2, one-half game behind St. Louis and Cincinnati, who were tied for first at 3–3. On the following day, April 15, the *Chicago Tribune* headlined an article on page 15: "Boston Humbles New York Giants."

It stated, "New York, with Mathewson pitching his first game of the season, fell before Boston today, 3 to 0. Perdue pitched a steady game. Boston scored its first run in the sixth when Sweeney, who had been passed, went to second on Campbell's infield hit and to third on Meyers' wild throw, scoring on Miller's single. Kling's home run added another tally in the seventh, and in the eighth, Campbell, who had doubled, scored on Miller's single after reaching third on a passed ball."

This win captured the attention of other sportswriters because it was the great Christy Mathewson who had been pitching for New York. One headline said: "Boston Youngsters Pummel Matty."

> That audacious lot of youngsters who are enlisted under the Gaffney-Ward-Kling banner, made acquaintance with Christy Mathewson today, or it might be better to say that he made their acquaintance. Few of the Braves, for so they are called, had ever seen the great pitcher, but they showed no signs of stage fright and tackled him as though he had been one of their own bush leaguers. The score does not begin to tell how hard and how ofter they hit the ball. There were several flies caught in the deepest field and long and lofty fouls were almost innumerable.[11]

Hugh Fullerton was correct in at least one respect, the Boston youngsters sure could hit. Manager Kling, although not a youngster at the ripe old age of of 37, had joined the hitting squad. His BA was at a clip beyond .300 and his swats were solid. It was as if his batting eye and passion for the game had flared anew.

After interviewing Boston players, a sportswriter had this to say on April 16: "Kling is working his head off to make good. He was never stronger as a winning ballplayer. His throwing arm is as good as ever. His cool style of handling pitchers has a certain effect on the members of his team. Kling is a modest fellow, sociable to the writers, a favorite with the fans. The players have everything good to say of their leader."[12]

One day later, April 17, the *New York Times* turned it all around when they printed a story on page 14 as to how "the so-called Braves were introduced to Rube Marquard," a Giants pitcher who mystified them, allowing three measly hits. New York won 8 to 2. By June 1, Boston was in last place with a win-loss tally of 13–26.

As the Pilgrims continued to lose games, Johnny Kling's attention was momentarily diverted by exciting news from Kansas City. A building permit had been issued for the erection of a seven-story steel and concrete hotel building he and his nephew, Bennie, had planned for. A contractor, Flannagan Bros. Mfg. Co., had been hired, the cost being $87,000.[13]

The hotel was an investment in his future whereas baseball was not. By the end of June, Boston was still in last place with 19–43. The team had won only 6 games that month while losing 17. In spite of Noisy John hitting well above .300, the youngsters, and their oldster manager, continued losing.

James Gaffney was upset at losing. He sent a letter to Kling, who was in Chicago with the team. Gaffney had had it. He was tired of talk and wanted action. But Kling had a problem. He had been handicapped since the start of the season. President Ward had been interfering with his running of the team, and continued to do so.

Ward was an old timer whose career in baseball began in 1877. He had been a pitcher as well as an infielder and outfielder. His fame grew, as did his confidence when playing the game.

As president of the club, he was operating with ideas that were used when he himself was in baseball back in the last century. Rudimentary pitch calling from pitcher to catcher evolved into a duty for the catcher by 1887, after which time only a few stubborn old-time pitchers insisted on being the signal givers. And here he was, trying to play the defensive game from the bench. Kling didn't like it. The players didn't like it. And the fans sure seemed to object to the way the game was being played. But Ward was the boss.[14]

The team could not gain ground. Hugh Fulleron's prediction proved accurate. In spite of excellent hitting, the pitchers caved in when the going got tough. Gaffney knew a change was needed. As owner of the club, he gave Ward an ultimatum, a definite amount of time to buy or sell. Ward sold, but it was too late to produce much improvement in a tail-end team.

Gaffney thought highly of Kling. He wanted him to stay on, but the catcher talked of quitting the game altogether in favor of his billiard emporium.[15] A leak to the press then told of Gaffney's decision to install George Stallings, former manager of the New York Americans, as manager of the Boston Nationals in the coming year.

Noisy John was on his way out. He let it be known that he was through with major league baseball, and that he would become manager of the Kansas City American Association Club in 1913.[16]

The season ended with Boston at the bottom with a 52–101 record. Its pitching staff had an ERA of 4.17, the top pitcher being Hub Perdue with a 13–16 win-loss and an ERA of 3.80. Kling finished with a BA of .317, fourth highest for the team. He worked behind the plate in 74 games and had 108 assists.

On October 17, after the dust had settled, the *Sporting News* came out with an article titled "Majors in Review." It said, "The Braves deserved better. Perhaps they would have made somebody take notice had John Ward kept his hands off Manager Kling all season."

The *Sheboygan Press* didn't agree. It said, "Johnny Kling did all in his power to bring Boston higher in the race, but the material he possessed was unable to respond."[17] Yet, after Ward left, the team played better ball than either St. Louis or Brooklyn.[18]

Regardless of why the team did poorly, or who might have been at fault, James Gaffney announced that he was cleaning house, that he would have a new manager, a new secretary and new players for the next season.[19]

Following that announcement, the sports pages in Decatur, Illinois, carried a small news item titled

"John Kling Is Sought by Cards." "Johnny Kling," the news item said, "the peer of all the catchers of a few years ago, and manager of the Boston Braves last season, is likely to be a member of the St. Louis team in 1913."[20]

> **Grand Formal Opening**
> **—of—**
> **KLING'S**
> **BILLIARD PARLOR**
> *Saturday, Nov. 2*
> SOUTHEAST CORNER TWELFTH AND BALTIMORE.
>
> Most elaborate and perfectly equipped parlor in America.
>
> 39 Circassian Walnut Inlaid specially designed Tables.
>
> You are cordially invited.
>
> MUSIC, KELLY'S ORCHESTRA

Opening of Hotel Dixon billiard parlor, 1912 (Kansas City Library Special Collections).

But who cared what anyone said? Certainly not John Kling. He and his nephew were joyfully excited. They were busy opening their billiard parlor in a brand new hotel.

John G. Kling was through with baseball. He was determined to become a successful businessman. The opening of the Dixon now gave him the title of hotelier. More hotels would follow. But the man he could not tolerate, Charles Webb Murphy, indirectly brought Kling back to the game when he fired Chance and made Evers manager of the team.

13

A Last Voyage

1913

Before going into events that brought Kling back to baseball, one should know why he was stubbornly resistant toward Murphy, the man he was forced to deal with.

In dealings with Murphy, Kling received letters haggling about salary. When Kling refused to sign, a letter from Murphy said that if Kling died, the team would have to get along without him, implying he wasn't really needed. Another called him "fat and out of condition."[1] These and other remarks were rude and insulting.

When the Cubs lost the city championship to the White Sox in 1912 after leading three games to one, Murphy came down to the bench and fired Chance. Chance fired back. "In all the time I have been with this club I have had to fight to get players," said Chance. "Murphy has not spent one-third as much for players as have other magnates. How can he expect to win championships without ballplayers?"[2]

According to Chance, when he told Murphy what other owners were spending, Murphy said, "If they want to be suckers and pay for it, they can, but I won't."[3] Chance also said that he had to operate under Murphy's cheap reign for the past three years. He said his players would often complain of the low salaries that Murphy was paying them.

Chance told how in 1906, the year the Cubs won 116 games, he was making $5,500 a year when his less successful rivals John McGraw ($18,000) and Fred Clarke ($10,000) were making far more money than he was.[4]

This was the man Kling was up against, and why he often said he was quitting baseball. But it was hard for him to stay away. Even in November 1912, when his new billiard parlor opened, he wanted to play ball. And it was Tinker, his best friend, who enticed him back. And Murphy's firing of Chance led to the actions taken by Tinker.

After Chance was fired, Evers took over. Joe Tinker didn't want to play under his management, so he left and became manager of the Cincinnati Reds. Tinker wanted Kling. Reds owner Herrmann wanted Kling. On February 4, Joe wrote a letter to Herrmann telling him that he had abandoned all efforts to obtain Kling, that he was convinced that Kling would not play ball in the coming season.⁵

Herrmann knew Kling. Previous discussions and communications had convinced him that Noisy John loved the game. So President Herrmann, desperately needing and wanting a catcher of Kling's caliber, joined Tinker in trying to change Kling's mind.

A plan was hit upon. Tinker interviewed Kling's partners. They admitted it was a matter of money — that Kling's name and Kling's presence in the billiard rooms formed a large part of their visible capital. They were asked about compensation for the loss of their drawing card. But Kling replied that he couldn't in fairness ask that extra money be paid to his partners. Negotiations seemed to stop there, but August Herrmann had one more card to play.

Holly and Bennie Allen were offered a guarantee of salary to anyone hired to manage the billiard parlor from March to October, allowing Kling to play ball. President Herrmann went so far as to offer extra money thought necessary to cover the situation.⁶ But just to make certain of the thing, the news media suggested that the Cincy President offer Bennie a year's supply of free gasoline to run his motor wagon.⁷

John G. Kling finally signed a contract but tore it up. He wrote August Herrmann and explained why he was forced to do so: "I was unable to see my way clear to leave my business" and "for the past ten days I have tried in vain to get my partner to consent to my leaving."⁸

Herrmann did not want to take no for a final answer. He encouraged Kling to keep trying. So, he did. Kling again talked with Bennie Allen, but saw that his nephew was scheduled to play in a number of billiard tournaments and they were not all in Kansas City. Bennie's father, Holly, had his own business to attend to. So he again tried to hire a manager to run the billiard parlor for the entire summer. When it looked as if he had found his man, it all fell through. With regrets, John Kling again wrote August Herrmann and explained why he could not sign a 1913 contract.

"As I wired you last night, it is simply out of the question to leave here and join your team at this time. I have exhausted every effort to secure the only man here capable of handling my affairs, but he insisted upon a five year contract at such an exorbitant figure, that it was absolutely impossible to do business with him" (see Appendix B, item G).

August Herrmann and Joe Tinker gave up on the idea and made no further efforts at signing Noisy John. But Kling had not given up. The urge to don his mask, grab his mitt and squat low behind the bat was still with him, and on April 17 another letter was on its way to Mr. Herrmann. "I have at last arranged my business so that I could join your club about the 25th should you still desire my services," it said (see Appendix B, item H).

May 2, 1913, was a happy day for thousands of fans as they turned to the sports pages and saw the headline about Kling's return to baseball: "Catcher Kling Signs Cincinnati Contract." The story said, "Manager Joe Tinker, of the Cincinnati team, today signed John Kling, the catcher, who will report for duty next Monday. In exchange for Kling's release Tinker gives C. McDonald, an infielder, and a cash consideration to Boston.

"Kling was at the local ballpark in Kansas City 'working out' when informed that the account of signing with Cincinnati had been confirmed. He had nothing to say."[9]

Cincinnati fans responded with delight and expressions of future anticipations. The owner of the Cuban Cigar Co. had to sit down and type a letter to August Hermann almost immediately, telling him of his delight in the acquisition of Kling, and that "if there is anything in a pitcher he will get it out of him" (see Appendix B, item I).

When Johnny Kling signed on, the Reds were in last place with a 2–12 record, having lost the day before to St. Louis 7–5, their fifth straight loss. The pitching staff had been doing miserably, including Three Finger Brown, Kling's old battery mate.

Noisy didn't get to play until May 13 in a game against Brooklyn and although he scored 1 run, getting 3 hits for 4 at-bats, Dahlen's men trounced Cincinnati 9–3.

The team continued to lose more than they won, and Clarke continued to work behind the bat more than Kling in spite of the fact that John had been cranking out hits at a sizzling pace.

On June 8, the National League stats were published. To make the list, a player had to have a BA of .250 or better. Johnny Kling was third with .379, Tinker was 18th with .305 and Bates was number 20 with .299. Tommy Clarke, the regular backstop, wasn't on the list.

Club batting records showed Cincinnati to be fourth with a .262, but the pitching records were dismal, including that of Mordecai Brown, who wasn't even listed because he didn't win at least half his games.[10]

The season moved forward. Kling continued hitting quite well but his BA dropped from .379 to .318. And the Reds kept losing close ones. On June 23, they lost to the Pirates 5–4. Pittsburgh scored its first run on a base on balls to Byrne and singles by Carey and Wagner. They scored the second on a base on balls to Coleman and a two-base hit by Carey. The other three runs were scored on singles by Adams, Byrne, Carey, and Miller, and a base on balls by Wagner. Cincinnati made its runs in the second inning when Dodge, Groh, and Kling doubled, Devore singled, and Bescher tripled.[11]

Although Kling had not been catching as often as Clarke, he did receive favorable comments from the press: "The value of an inexperienced catcher," an article said, "is being proved by the Cincinnati team. With Johnny Kling catching, the Reds have been winning a better percentage of its games. With Kling behind the bat the young pitchers are all showing better form, and the team is in a fair way to gain a more respectable position in the race if it can keep up its present gait.

"Kling, by the way, appears to be in better form this year than he has been in several, and this is particularly true of his throwing, which is said to be the best he has done in some time."[12]

Toward the end of July, it was a seesaw battle for last place. Boston and St. Louis had been jockeying for the sixth and seventh spot while Cincinnati had sole possession of eighth, but the race became tighter when the Reds began to win some.

Page 5 of the July 30 *New York Times* reported a rise in the standings of the Redlegs in a game against Brooklyn. The headline said: "Reds Win in Eighth. Cincinnati Rallies and Captures Last Game from Brooklyn." The article continued, "With two men on bases in the eighth inning and two runs needed to win, Johnny Kling pasted a single to center field, scoring Packard and Sheckard, and Cincinnati won the last game of the series from Brooklyn by the score of 6 to 5."

This win inched the Reds into seventh place with a 37–59 record while St. Louis dropped down a notch with a 36–58. Boston's 39–51 gave them a comfortable lead.

A bold headline again caught the attention of Cincinnati baseball fans. "Emerged from the Dingy Cellar."

The story followed, "John Kling played a very important part in the auspicious events of the day looming largely at all stages of the pastime. His throwing was extremely accurate, and he stopped man after man who tried out the trusty wing which has been killing them off for many seasons. John's hitting was also a supreme factor, as he drove in three runs, including the tying and winning tallies in the eighth round. His performance was in his best style. He looked like a fast youngster rather than a veteran playing his last year of baseball."[13]

Moving up one notch didn't make Manager Tinker feel any better. He was inclined to take a far from rosy view of the future. He frankly admitted to a reporter from the *Cincinnati Enquirer* that he did not have a strong team with which to make a strong fight in the league race, and that he saw no bright light for the next season. He blamed President Herrmann's policy of cutting down his squad to the smallest limit, without securing arrangements with minor league clubs for obtaining new players for the Reds.[14]

On the following day, Manager Tinker received a wire from the boss informing him that he had violated baseball law by talking to a reporter from the *Enquirer,* and requested that he await the arrival of a letter before submitting to further conversation with the terrible scribes.

Joe declined to take this advice. "I don't know what law I have violated," he said. "If there is a law requiring nothing but pleasant compliments to be handed out about the officials of the club, perhaps I am a law breaker. The showing of the team has been a great disappointment. I have held off as long as I could. But when I found that our players were being sold outright to minor league clubs without options, and that I was constantly being urged to cut off players against my best judgement without waiting for a chance to make a trade which would help the team, I decided to take a stand.

"I would rather go out to my fruit farm in Oregon than try to handle a club when I am not backed up by owners."[15]

This tirade didn't go down well with President Herrmann. The team knew that Joe wouldn't be around much longer, and Kling knew that he too had to go. He would soon be 38 and it was time to move on.

With this kind of team evaluation from Manager Tinker, and the antagonism between manager and owner resulting therefrom, the morale of the team may have nose-dived, but the Reds held on to the seventh spot with a 64–89 record as the season closed.

Johnny Kling finished the season with a BA .273, having played in 80 games, 63 as backstop with 94 assists, not too bad a season.

But for him, the season was a definite disappointment. When he signed his contract in May, and was on his way to join the Reds in Cincinnati, he met with the press at the Kansas City train station. They had reported: "Before leaving, Kling once more said this would be his last year in baseball. 'I am in good shape,' he went on to say, 'and I expect to end my career in a blaze of glory.'"[16]

It seems fair to say that his work as a backstop was superb, and if his hitting had remained at the .379 or even at .318, as it had been, his expectations about a blaze of glory would have been fulfilled.

Ironically, the BA of the Cincy players were below .300 except Joe Tinker, who finished with a .317. And it was Tinker that may have lowered player morale by the statements he gave to the *Cincinnati Enquirer.* Just another day in baseball.

Once home, Kling learned that Tinker, his best friend, would no longer be manager of the Cincinnati team. He had jumped into the new Federal League and was going to manage the Chicago Whales in 1914.

As for himself, Noisy John had definitely decided that he would no longer don his mask, grab his mitt, squat low behind the bat and begin his chatter, trying his darndest to distract the batter as the ball sped toward the plate. He would now keep his eye on business.

As such, John G. Kling demonstrated what an amazing individual he was. He had his fingers on the pulse of all the goings on in the world of business. Not long after the season was over, he introduced August Herrmann, his former boss, to the National Electric Ticket Register Co., of which he was a stockholder and an officer.

A machine made by this company printed and delivered baseball tickets along with a rain check stub, to be used if needed, directly into the patrons' hands at the rate of 10,000 per hour. One had already been installed in the Brown's Park in St. Louis and it handled the bleacher crowd perfectly.

Mr. Herrmann was encouraged to talk to Mr. Hedges and learn that one cashier with this machine would do the work of two. The Cincinnati magnate was assured that if he installed the machine in his ballpark, he would receive a contract, with a guarantee that the unit would be kept in repair and replaced when worn out, and that the company would sell him tickets for the machine at the same price as he currently was paying.

Kling closed his letter by saying, "We want to arrange a demonstration of this machine before members of the National League at such time as will meet their convenience and I will appreciate any assistance you can render me in this direction."[17]

Mr. Herrmann's reply to this letter is not known. But he did ask Johnny Kling to rejoin the Reds for the 1914 season. The former catcher's response was, "I don't think there is a chance of my playing ball again. Sorry to hear you are having trouble with your players but hope you will succeed in rounding out a winning club for the coming season as you justly deserve a winner."[18]

On January 21, 1914, Johnny Kling again wrote to August Herrmann regarding the unconditional release he had received from the Cincinnati club, thanking him for the way he had been treated and assuring him that "if at any time I may be of any service to you, don't fail to call upon me" (see Appendix B, item J).

The contrast between Kling and Herrmann and Kling and Murphy is interesting. There was respect and a high regard for Herrmann. For Murphy, the opposite.

Murphy's focus was money. After the Cubs lost the inter-city series to the Sox in 1913, losing in six instead of seven games, Murphy blamed Evers, his manager, saying that not playing game 7 cost him $10,000. He fired Evers several months later. Johnny knew it was going to happen and that he was to be traded. So, he threatened to jump to the Federal League, a third major league that was then being formed.

Johnny Kling, a Redleg in 1913 at West Side Grounds (*Chicago Daily News*).

 The other National League club owners who were gearing up to do battle with the newcomers (whom they viewed as brazen interlopers and worse) were appalled at the idea that one of the league's top stars was being forced into the ranks of the "outlaw" league. So Murphy was summoned to a meeting in the office of the league president John Tener. He was told that baseball no longer needed his services. Murphy's dignity was comforted by approximately $500,000.

So much for the man who had given Johnny Kling such a difficult time. For Noisy there would be no further difficulties as a major leaguer. He was through with the game, having quit as a Cincinnati Redleg.

14

Rest and Relaxation

Leaving baseball may not have been easy. Then again, John Kling was a "brainy" guy, and probably knew that it was time to move on, to engross himself in his business ventures. He and Bennie already had the Hotel Dixon.

The structure began its rise after Johnny Kling and his partner Bennie Allen bought from A.C. Bilicke a 125 by 25 foot tract just south of the Sexton Hotel for $45,000, and built a seven-story annex to the hotel. It was announced that they would occupy the second and third floors with their billiard parlor, considered to be one of the best in the world.[1]

The hotel had 212 guest rooms, all with tile bath and radio. It was located in a neighborhood of hotels, in the heart of the theater and shopping district. It established a standard for other grand hotels that were to follow. Baseball and billiards were motifs for the hotel. It had huge chandeliers that were made of a dozen baseball bats and the lights at the bottom looked like baseballs.

The elegant pool hall, complete with carpet and immense walnut tables, was a favorite hangout for bankers and lawyers who could take off work in the afternoon. It also was a mecca for husbands who needed a diversion while their wives shopped downtown in the evenings.[2] Diagonally across the street was the old Glennon Hotel, famous for housing Harry Truman's Haberdashery, and where Mr. Truman started his political career.[3]

The corner came alive under the control of Kling and Allen. Their names were for many years synonyms for the art of billiards, in which both these men excelled. Each had captured a national cue title, and the deluxe billiard establishment, in which alcohol was taboo, played host to stars of stage, screen and the billiard world. World tournaments and matches were held there. Its luminaries numbered from E. H. Sothern to Bob Hope to Willie Hoppe, and many others in its long and useful life of raising the splendid sport from the status of a game for bums to a diversion for gentlemen ... and ladies, too.[4]

14. Rest and Relaxation

Hotel Dixon at 12th and Baltimore, completed 1912 (courtesy Don Brink).

The Kling and Allen rooms became the location for world championship tournaments. A gallery ran around the edge of the room, free of posts, and for some of the feature games, hundreds would gather to watch the action. The contestants wore tuxedos, and there was an atmosphere of quiet charm about the event. The audience was hushed and all that was heard was the clicking of the balls. Once in awhile one of the trick artists would appear to make the balls do extraordinary things and, after the visit, there would be a rash of imitators for a time.[5]

The billiard emporium became famous and was the finest world wide, and was advertised as such:

JOHN KLING
World's Greatest
Backstop

BENNY ALLEN
Pocket Billiard Champion of
the World

Kling's Billiard Emporium
FINEST IN THE WORLD

39 Kling's Specially Designed Tables

12th AND BALTIMORE AVE.   KANSAS CITY, MO.

Kling's Billiard Emporium advertisement (Kansas City Library Special Collections).

A number five 5 by 10 Kling billiard table (Brunswick Corporation).

The billiard emporium made the 5 by 10 Brunswick-Balke-Collender billiard tables famous, since there were 39 tables in each of its rooms, and the "world" came, saw them and bought them. In recognition of the contribution made to the Brunswick Corporation's bottom line, they named the table after Johnny Kling.

Additions and changes were made to the hotel and the billiard emporium over the years, and on May 19, 1945, the articles of incorporation were changed to Kling and Allen Billiard and Bridge Club, Inc.[6]

One aspect of the hotel that may have existed from early on, and never advertised openly, was revealed in an interview on September 1, 2004, with 92-year-old Helen Allen, Bennie Allen's daughter-in-law. She talked about her husband, Hollie, telling her never to go down into the basement of the Hotel Dixon.

Curiosity got the best of her, and she crept down a stairway until the lighted room was open to her. She saw men sitting around a table playing cards. Others were shooting dice. And still others were up front betting on horses. She never went back.

If you think Helen's 92-year-old memory was faulty, it was verified by information about T.J. Pendergast's reign over Kansas City. It talked about gambling. It said, "Despite being illegal, gambling went on with the full knowledge of almost everyone, as it did at the Dixon Hotel at 12th and Baltimore."[7]

Johnny Kling must have been happy, enjoying life, running a hotel and a billiard emporium for years in Kansas City, and merrily shooting the little ball into the little pocket, and the nickels and quarters and dimes into the cash register. Little did he dream the deal would turn out to be such a moneymaker. Now, he and Allen decided to add several stories to the Dixon. Once completed, they would clear $200,000 in 12 years, not including billiard hall income.[8]

With such projections, Kling was exhilarated. He talked with Messrs.

Strand Hotel and theater in Chillicothe, Missouri (Kansas City Library Special Collections).

Cuff and Reed, two of his partners in a new corporation. Kling proposed a hotel in Chillicothe. On September 3, 1924, the idea came alive under Cuff-Kling Enterprises, Inc.[9]

Chillicothe was experiencing one of the biggest building booms in years. The most costly structure was the Strand Hotel, at an approximate cost of $100,000.[10] Work began in early November 1924, and it was anticipated that it would take 120 working days to complete, but because of winter setting in, the completion date was set for the following spring.[11]

On a Friday nine months later a front-page headline read: "The Public May See New Hotel Sunday Evening."

Come and see the new Strand Hotel Sunday evening, a modern fireproof structure with 69 guest rooms, circulating ice water, hot water, telephone and electric fans in every room.

The lobby will compare in beauty and accommodations with any in the state. Furnishings are all of the best, including tapestries, velours, needlepoint and velvet finished chairs that are large and restful.

A ladies rest room is provided off the lobby and is equipped with every convenience.

There are 30 local shareholders, John G. Kling of Kansas City and Mr. Cuff being the principal stockholders.

The officers in the Cuff-Kling Enterprises Inc. are W. P. Cuff, President and General Manager, W. Haley Reed, Vice President and John G. Kling, Secretary and Treasurer.[12]

Thousands of Chillicotheans passed through the Strand and had nothing but words of praise for the new structure. They learned that the traveling public was about to receive first class service from the Chillicothe Transfer Co. They had signed a contract with Cuff and Kling to meet all trains and provide buses and taxicabs for hotel patrons.[13]

After years of outstanding service, the Strand Hotel became known for its fine hospitality. It was such a success, Kling added another story to the building and made several changes inside the hotel. The Strand Coffee Shop was also enlarged.[14]

When Chillicothe and Livingston County celebrated their one-hundredth birthday, John G. Kling and his staff celebrated their eleventh anniversary of service to the community.

15

DINNER AND THE THEATER

Guests at the Dixon must have been enchanted by the fairytale-like surroundings. They had the finest, most luxurious accommodations, a game of cards, or rolling the dice, or betting on a favorite horse in the basement, and come evening, dinner at the Pennant Café.

The café was the brainchild of Gerald Hayes, an umpire in the American Association club. W. H. Dixon, owner of the Sexton Hotel, picked up on the idea and had plans drawn up. It was located in the basement of the Sexton and completed in 1911.

After Kling and Allen bought a 125 by 25 tract of land in 1912 immediately south of the Sexton and built the Dixon as a seven-story annex to the Sexton, the two buildings became known as the Kling-Allen building. But the Sexton Hotel and the Pennant Café remained under the management of the Sexton Hotel Company and was not owned by Kling and Allen, as some people believed.

Nevertheless, the idea of a baseball motif for the Pennant Café came about because of Johnny Kling's fame as the greatest backstop in baseball. The café had two rooms with mahogany woodwork, light fixtures of baseball bats, masks, shoes and balls. The tile floor in the barroom was solid green to represent grass. And there were two baseball diamonds set in white tile. The café floor had the same white tile, and every six feet there were different colored tiles of bats, masks and balls.

The decorations in the café were reproductions of baseball parks throughout the country. In one booth was the White Sox Park showing the grounds, grandstand and bleachers, in another booth, the Kansas City Park, and so on around the room. The chairs had legs that looked like baseball bats, and the back of each chair looked like a baseball.

At the grand opening, it was next to impossible to get into the place. The tables had been reserved weeks and weeks before. The menu was printed on a pennant, and they gave as souvenirs baseball replicas filled with chocolates. "The Pennant" was a high-class café with a cabaret show from

Left: Pennant Café advertisement (Kansas City Library Special Collections).

6 to 1 o'clock, and it was a saying around Kansas City that an outsider could not consider his visit complete without seeing the Pennant Café.[1]

For guests staying at the Strand Hotel in Chillicothe, they too had a wonderful place to dine — the completely air-conditioned Strand Coffee Shop. The popularity of this eatery was indicative of the wide approval of John Kling's efforts to please his customers. Menus offered a variety of deliciously prepared foods which were served attractively.

After an elegant dinner at the Pennant or the Strand, it was time to sit back and enjoy a movie at the Strand Theater. The theater was built sometime after September 18, 1913, when Johnny Kling was finishing his career in baseball with the Cincy Reds. It was then that the Cuff-Kling Enterprises Inc. started in business. Johnny became a stockowner and officer of Cuff-Kling and it was the corporation that constructed the Strand Theater, one of the finest moving picture theaters in Missouri.[2] A movie back then was *Princess Jones*, an absorbingly interesting comedy drama by Joseph Franklin Pollard. It was a Vitagraph production.[3]

Johnny Kling branched out and operated other motion picture theaters in Chillicothe.[4] On April 21, 1931, it was announced: "A deal has just been consummated by the Glen W. Dickenson Theaters, Inc. and John G. Kling, owner of the Strand Hotel and the Strand and Empire theaters, for a new twenty-year lease, and $50,000 will be spent immediately on improvements at the Strand Theater."[5]

On March 29, 1933, the Dickinson Theater burned to the ground. The interior of the building was a roaring furnace and flames

15. Dinner and the Theater

reached the Strand Hotel, while the firemen battled the flames for 7 hours. When the firefighters left the scene at three-o'clock in the morning, the front wall supported by a mass of twisted steel was all that remained of the beautiful theater. The damage to the theater and contents was estimated at $150,000, partially covered by insurance.[6]

When the Dickinson Theater was destroyed, Kling intended to build a bigger and better theater for Chillicothe, but changed his mind. With the remodeling of his old Empire Theater, he concluded that the town had all the theaters it could support.

The press reported: "John G. Kling, Kansas City capitalist and owner of the Strand Hotel and Dickinson theater site, said today, he had definitely decided to build a new building, five stories high, the same as the Strand Hotel. The ground floor will be used for a coffee shop, small shops, and the other four floors will be divided into hotel guest rooms and small apartments. In the basement, there will be a large banquet room and kitchen. The space occupied by the coffee shop in the Strand Hotel will be converted into an extension of the main lobby of the hotel."[7]

Work on the building had been delayed for eight months due to the failure of the insurance companies to adjust their losses on the theater building and on the hotel that was damaged by the fire when the Dickinson burned down. But work had begun.[8]

On April 1, 1936, the Strand Hotel's new Coffee Shop and Fiesta Room beneath it opened its doors for business. The enlarged, redecorated and refinished lobby and the new rooms in the annex had also been completed. "All will be open to visitors," said John G. Kling.[9]

16

PEANUTS AND CRACKER JACK

Since 1908 Johnny Kling cherished the idea of owning a baseball team. He offered to quit the Cubs and manage the Kansas City Blues, then owned by George Tebeau, but Johnny could not get his release from the Cubs.[1]

When he was not selected as the winning bidder to purchase the Boston Braves after the death of W. Hepburn Russell in 1911, the desire to own a team lingered, and probably simmered on the back burner for many years.

When he finally quit baseball at the end of the 1913 season, the catcher vowed to have nothing further to do with the national pastime. But he succumbed to the lure in early 1933 when he rescued E. Lee Keyser after the latter had floundered as owner of the Kansas City Blues.[2]

Brewery owner George Muehlebach had owned controlling interest in the team, and in 1923 he built a ballpark for the Blues and named it after himself. Fans packed the stadium. But by 1930 the fans seemed to lose interest. Ticket sales dropped. Muehlebach tried to resuscitate the franchise by playing night baseball. But at the end of the 1932 season, he sold the Blues and the stadium to a partnership that included the radio and movie comedian Joe E. Brown, Tris Speaker and Lee Keyser. The group grew disenchanted with baseball as the Depression had hit the area hard.[3]

Johnny Kling purchased Speaker's interest in the club and other holdings and now controlled the Blues in partnership with E. Lee Keyser. The team was wallowing in last place, going nowhere.

"We're going to rebuild the team," Kling said. "In order to put the Blues up where we want them in the 1934 pennant race, we'll probably need eight or ten new players."[4]

But before doing anything, one of the first things Kling changed was a practice that had existed since the park opened. When Muelebach Field first opened its gates, seating was segregated when the Blues played, but the White and Colored signs came down for Monarchs games (an all Negro team). Kling refused to segregate seating as long as he owned the club no matter who played. It was goodbye to the signs.[5]

This change occurred shortly after Kling took control of the team. The date was fixed by a newspaper story that told of Dutch Zwilling, the new Blues manager, going to Mobile on March 12, 1933, to whip a team together out of baseball material that Kling was going to send him. And of Kling's intention to join him shortly.[6]

The date is important because March 29, 1933, was the date the Dickinson Theater, a property under lease by Cuff-Kling Enterprises, burned to the ground. Was it arson? Was it related to anger at what Kling had done in desegregating seating at the Blues Stadium? There are no records regarding an investigation back then.[7]

But what was widely known back then was the activities of the Ku Klux Klan. This was a group of white Protestant men who wanted to rid the country of what they considered un–American: Jews, Catholics, leftists, blacks, and those who did not speak English. To accomplish their "sacred" task, the Klansmen dressed up in white sheets and followed their wizard to beat-up, lynch, and bully the undesirables out of the country.

The popularity of the Klan reached its zenith in 1937 in the U.S.A. with a membership of over 2 million, including judges, police chiefs and local politicians.[8] So why did Kling desegregate seating at the ballpark? It was unheard of at the time. Opposition to this must have been rampant. Was it because he was Jewish and had also suffered discrimination? Was it because he could empathize with blacks and was determined to right an injustice? A good possibility. At any rate, he did it.

The next thing he did, as he acquired new ballplayers and got rid of old ones, was to issue stock certificates in his ball club as a newly formed corporation.[9]

After that, Kling gathered support from the business community and accepted an invitation to attend a meeting of the South Central Business Association (S.C.B.A.).[10] He received their full support. They encouraged more than thirty clubs and civic organizations to participate in a citywide contest. Each group sold tickets to the Blues' opening game. The group that sold the most would win the Johnny Kling trophy.[11]

In addition to a single group prize, there were ten season passes to the ten individuals who sold the most tickets to the season opener.[12]

Johnny Kling's efforts began to manifest itself in 1934. A news item announced: "Johnny Kling Has Fans Pulling for His Team."

> Johnny Kling, the fellow who caught for the Chicago Cubs back in the days of that famous double play combination, Tinker to Evers to Chance, is wearing his best baseball grin again.
> The Kansas City American Association club which he took over last year when

Stock in Kansas City Baseball Club, Inc. (Kansas City Library Special Collections).

it was wallowing in last place is kicking up dust in the first division and the rabid fans are trooping back to Muehlebach Field.

Already more than 110,000 have poured through the turnstiles to see the Blues in contrast to 71,000 for all of last season and six home games remain to be played.

"If we draw 125,000 we'll break even," said the man who once swung his bat at the offerings of Christy Mathewson.

"That's more then the club has done in five years. But we've got a long way to go to get back to the old crowds of 400,000."[13]

But the team finished the year in last place with a 65–88 record. Kling continued to make changes and give support, and his effort continued to grow.

As the opening game of the 1935 season drew near, ticket sales were brisk, with 3,000 advance purchases by April 12 and still climbing. Several block sales had been reported to firms distributing tickets as rewards to employees. The Lions Club cancelled its weekly luncheon and distributed tickets to its members. More than thirty civic groups and district associations made block reservations for the opening game.[14]

Many people and organizations were vying for the coveted John G. Kling Trophy. The contest had become an annual event, something everyone looked forward to.

Opening day was April 16. A crowd of 12,000 was expected. And although a holiday had not been declared, Mayor Bryce Smith declared a half-holiday. He was going to pitch the first ball and wanted as many supporters to watch him as possible.[15]

Neighboring townsfolk came, as did mayors of nearby towns. The preliminaries for the game had all been laid out. It included a band concert, flag raising and tossing out the first ball. And the team that had just returned from Memphis, along with Manager Dutch Zwilling and President John Kling, were invited to be guests of the S. C. B. A. at a luncheon at the LaSalle Hotel.[16]

Kling's boys jump-started the season and it was obvious to all that they were going to make a race of it. Even into early September, the news media recognized what the owner of the team had done with the wreck he had purchased just two years earlier.

A story appeared and the headline told it all: "Kling Making Good as Baseball Prexy."[17]

As hard as John G. Kling had tried, the Blues did not capture the brass ring. But they did finish in the first division, coming in third with a win-loss of 84–70, only seven games behind first place Minneapolis.

Still, Kling tried. He and Zwilling toured the southern baseball leagues

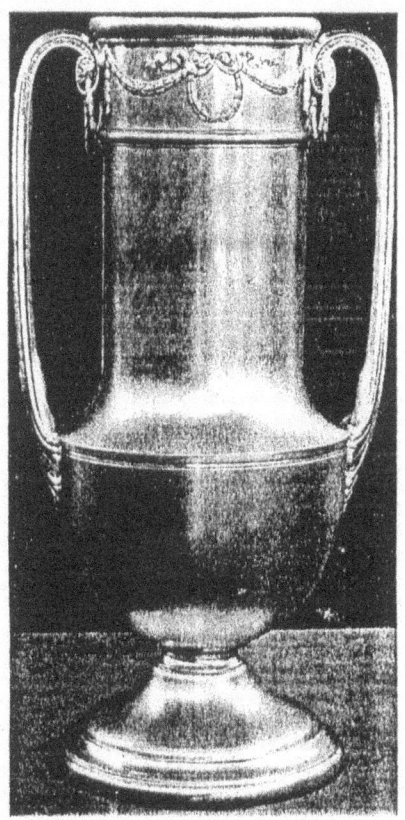

John G. Kling Trophy

Won by South Central

THE baseball opening day campaign was climaxed with the awarding of the John G. Kling trophy at Muehlebach Field to the South Central Business Association by Albert H. Wood, chairman of the Chamber of Commerce committee directing that affair, just before the season's initial contest between the Kansas City Blues and St. Paul.

May, 1934

John G. Kling trophy (Kansas City Library Special Collections).

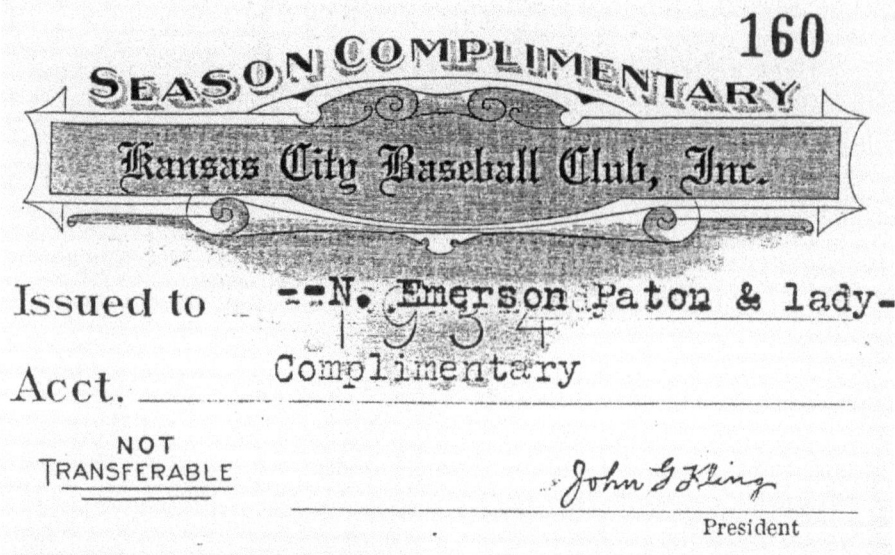

Season pass to Kansas City Blues' games (Kansas City Library Special Collections).

in an effort to secure new material. They were on the lookout for young players who could go to the training camp come next spring.[18]

Johnny tried to obtain playing strength from major league clubs and was baffled by his inability to do so. He then considered hiring a scout and met with Pat Monyhan, who was the trusted and highly helpful scout for the Giants in 1933 when Manager Terry won the pennant that year.[19] Nothing came of it. Nevertheless, the Blues made a fairly good showing in 1936, again coming in third with 84–69, only 5 and one half games behind first place Milwaukee.

Still determined, John Kling continued to find new players for his team in preparation for 1937. Just prior to the season opener, a news article gave the Kansas City fans something to look forward to. The headline read, "Blues Play Minneapolis Opening Game Here Friday. Blues Look Like Pennant Contenders."

> John Kling is deserving of considerable credit for the seemingly high class team which he has assembled for this year's pennant drive. It is believed that Kansas City has the strongest pitching department of any team in the League and from the defensive standpoint, is in a class by itself.
>
> On the attack the Kansas City outfit possibly does not compare with advance dope of some of the other teams in the League, but it is believed that with warm weather near, the artillery will soon get in form and will immediately start upwards the winning of the pennant.

At the regular meeting of the S.C.B.A., Zwilling said he was satisfied with the outlook for the Blues for the 1937 season. Club members urged support for the Blues because of the loyalty Kansas Cityans owe Mr. Kling and his team.[20]

The press then reported: "John Kling, owner of the Blues, will be unable to watch his team open Friday. The magnate, who became ill two months ago, has been ordered by his physician to remain at home for another week.

"'This was bad news for Mr. Kling,' said Charles Burrell, business manager. 'He has gotten together by far the strongest club since he took over the franchise and he is anxious to see the athletes perform.'"[21]

Unfortunately, he did not see his athletes perform. On July 25, 1937, the *Kansas City Star* reported:

> John Kling is selling the Blues in mid-season after ill health has prevented him from seeing the 1937 team in action or having a hand in its business management.
>
> The Kansas City baseball team will pass into ownership of the New York American League club August 1 and become a part of a "chain" of minor league clubs owned by the Yankees from coast to coast.
>
> All that remains to conclude the deal is the signature of Col. Jacob Ruppert, owner of the Yankees. The purchase price, including both franchise and park, is understood to be $235,000.

No sooner had the ink on the contract dried than Jacob Ruppert changed Kling's policy. Segregation was reinstituted. The White and Colored signs went back up for all Blues' games. This decision caused a great deal of bitterness in the black community.[22]

Change in ownership and change in policy probably stirred up feelings in Blues' players, feelings that interfered with their style of play. The team finished fifth in 1937 with a record of 72–82, eighteen games behind first place Columbus.

The "ill health" that was given as the reason for selling the Blues was not clearly spelled out. One article said, "This return to baseball as a clubowner, they say, had a disastrous effect on Kling's health since he found a great many worries attendant to the ownership of a ball club."[23]

The worries were not defined. One possible worry was the consequences of taking down the White and Colored signs when he purchased the Blues. There must have been some resentment on the part of whites, and it seems reasonable to say, that given the climate of the times regarding race relations, Kling heard from some people in one way or another. But he must be applauded for keeping Muehlebach Field desegregated as long as he was owner of the club.

Did he pay a price healthwise due to extremes of stress? No one knew for sure. But as soon as his deal with Jacob Ruppert was concluded, he and his wife sailed off to Hawaii for a much needed rest. On his return, he was met by a reporter on board the ship, and he allowed himself to be interviewed and photographed, something he seldom did.[24]

17

Sugar and Spice

Johnny Kling was a difficult man to know. Throughout his life, be it in baseball, billiards or business, he established his goals and pursued them with conviction and a firm determination, not easily swayed by arguments contrary to his beliefs. And yet, as difficult as he was to really know, Johnny had the faculty of making friends and holding them. Once the shell around him was broken and the reserve dropped, he was found to be one of the most delightful persons one could meet. He was sugar and spice and everything nice.[1]

Ford Frick, former National League president, a commissioner of baseball and the man who played a role in the founding of the Hall of Fame, had a tale to tell in 1973:

> In the summer of 1907, the champion Chicago Cubs stopped off in Indiana for an exhibition game with our Kendalville, Blues. Clubhouses were unheard of in those days. Visiting players donned their uniforms at the local tavern, then walked the short distance to the ballpark through an excited honor guard of juvenile worshippers. You can be sure that I wasn't going to miss that.
>
> Among the last players to come along was a smiling, darkly handsome chap. He spotted me, big-eyed and mouth agape, watching in awed silence as the athletes walked past. He grinned, and beckoned.
>
> "Hi, kid," he said, "want to go to the ballgame?"
>
> I gulped, and managed to convey the idea that I would.
>
> "Tell you what to do. Just carry these shoes for me, and when we get to the gate you just walk in with us. Maybe the gateman will let you by."
>
> I did exactly as he told me, and the miracle happened: I walked right into the ballpark with the players. Furthermore, I was permitted to sit on the ground alongside the player's bench. I could see Mordecai Brown and Ed Reulbach in person. I could hear Schulte and Tinker and Chance and Evers and Steinfeldt talking on the bench between innings. What a moment.
>
> Years later, I had the opportunity to meet and chat with the Crown Prince of Japan. On another occasion, as a newspaperman, I spent several days with the Prince of Wales when he attended the international polo matches at Meadowbrook, Long Island. Through the years, I've been privileged to chat with Presidents at the White House; to hobnob with renowned figures in sports, in finance,

science, and all phases of public life. But these were routine workday assignments, to be taken in stride as part of a newspaperman's days. That ballgame was different. For the rest of the summer, I lived in a dreamworld. I was the hero of the village, the envy of every kid in the community, the hometown boy who, for a few fleeting minutes, had hobnobbed with greatness.

It was not until 1937, thirty years later, that I had an opportunity to meet and talk again with my hero of the shoes. Older, grayer, and heavier than I remembered, he still retained that same friendly smile. There was the same warm, friendly twinkle in his eyes that I recalled from the day of my biggest boyhood thrill. He didn't remember the incident, but seemed to enjoy the story.

One thing sure. That day in 1907 convinced me that baseball was the greatest game in the world, and he its greatest player. Now, more than half a century later, mature judgement and the leavening experience of years dims somewhat my childish enthusiasm. In my mind I know that there must have been others greater — but in my heart he will remain forever the greatest catcher who ever lived.

His name? Johnny Kling.[2]

Frank Kling, of Livingston, New Jersey, also had a story to tell on May 24, 2000:

As a young boy living in Orange, New Jersey I was a rabid baseball fan. My favorite team was the New York Giants of Mel Ott, Carl Hubbell etc. playing in the Polo Grounds in New York City. I was very fortunate to get to the Polo Grounds occasionally to see the great stars of yesteryear and especially the NY Giant–Brooklyn Dodgers Series.

I checked the Box Scores religiously of all the Major League Teams. One day I came across the name of John Kling, Catcher for the Chicago Cubs. Having the same last name, and also my confirmation name was John, I wondered if we might be related. Kling did not seem to be a common name at that time. I was awestruck as a young lad to find a major league ballplayer with the same name as mine. I wrote to John Kling c/o of the Chicago Cubs and asked if he would send me an autographed picture of himself. I was never able to ascertain whether or not we were related somewhere down the line.

The picture enclosed is a copy of that same picture that I

John Kling photo mailed to Frank Kling in 1935 (courtesy Frank Kling).

received from John Kling some 65 years ago. I may be off on the exact date, as I will be 75 years old this June and I must have been around ten years old when I received the picture.

I have the original autographed picture and have kept it in good condition all these years. I am extremely happy to share my story and this picture with the Legacy of John Kling, Catcher Chicago Cubs. Please keep me informed of the events surrounding the Cooperstown installation [see Appendix B, item K].

Johnny Kling was not only helpful to youngsters with a passion for the national pastime, but also to his community when civic responsibilities were called for. In October 1913, when Noisy John quit baseball, the Commercial Club in Kansas City planned for a celebration of the new Union Station. It was an enormous task. Money was needed to complete an assortment of plans connected with the festivities. There wasn't time, so a Finance Committee was named to obtain funds quickly.

John Kling was a member of this sizeable committee. The tasks were doled out to a number of smaller committees and the accruing of the required money was speedily accomplished.[3]

Johnny Kling also remembered friends, according to Dutch Zwilling, manager for the Kansas City Blues, the one St. Joseph man who knew him best.

"I was in his office one day," Dutch recalled, "when he got an appeal for help from a baseball immortal in the Hall of Fame, one of the men he played with on the Chicago Cubs. While Kling was letting me read the letter, he was writing a check for $100. "He never mentioned the incident to me again, but I am sure that this was just one of the charities he extended to men with whom he had played."[4]

Chillicotheans awakened to an astonishing bit of news on November 9, 1942. Front page headlines announced, "Johnny Kling has patriotically turned over the Strand Hotel, including the coffee shop and the hotel garage to the Army Air Force."[5]

The Strand? The hotel providing all modern comforts for its guests? The popular hotel with a regular following? The one on the front cover of the *Southern Hotel Journal* showing Kling and his hotel manager, Sam Gorman?[6]

Yes. That's the one.

Months earlier, Mr. Gorman became a private in the army and went off to fight a war. Kling never managed the Strand, but became temporary manager. He looked for someone to replace Sam. His wife came in to help, but she had no experience.[7]

Come November, the military needed space to house three hundred ninety-five men who were to be trained by the Chillicothe Business College to carry out a variety of jobs. Kling turned over the Strand, coffee shop, garage, the whole kit and caboodle to the college.

The question was raised as to whether or not Kling benefited financially. This question was put to Jeffrey Sahaida, military historian at Maxwell Air Force Base. This question made its way to Washington, D. C. and a reply from the Pentagon said, "The history does not indicate what the Army Air Forces paid for the hotel."[8]

Based on this reply, it is possible that the *Chillicothe Constitution Tribune* was correct in saying that Kling turned over his hotel as a patriotic gesture. Be that as it may, on June 19, 1943, all of the students graduated and were shipped out. The detachment was inactivated by Richard T. Pendleton, captain, Air Corps.[9]

The Strand was returned to Johnny Kling. He kept it closed for a thorough redecoration and a conversion back to civilian use at a cost of $20,000. He then sold the hotel to M. M. Carder and B. T. Clark, owners of the Leeper Hotel in Chillicothe.[10]

It was said that he sold the Strand because of illness, the same reason given when he sold the Kansas City Blues in 1937. Rumors were that his illness had become worse by 1943 and he could not handle the stress of managing the Strand. This argument did not hold up.

An explanation for the sale could not be found. Perhaps it was no longer profitable. Perhaps he could not find a manager. But whatever the reason, in all probability it was not sold because of illness, just as the K. C. Blues were not sold because of illness.

During an interview with Parke Carroll, it was learned that "Kling sold the Kansas City baseball club to New York because he couldn't stand to lose. Johnny was not as sturdy as a stevedore when he took over the property from Lee Keyser, but his health was good. His trouble dated from that day. He worried about the weather and gate receipts, but it was when the club had bad days on the diamond that the old Cubs' catcher sat in his box back of the first base dugout and suffered.

> He tore himself apart and replayed the situations during sleepless nights. Eventually, it broke down his resistance, undermined his health and a physician forced him to sell the property.
>
> "I quit because I couldn't stand to lose," Johnny said. "It was that way when I played with the Cubs, but I was younger then. It was harder taking it in a box seat than it would have been on the field. I wanted to give Kansas City a winner. I wanted to win every game.
>
> "There have been a lot of times when I was sorry I sold the club. Kansas City is the greatest minor league town in the country. It's a big league town, but you are better off with the Yankees than you are with me. They are big operators, they have the players and they know how to build teams."[11]

After selling the club, Johnny was 62 years of age. His business activities were many. On any given day he was hard to locate because he was operating his billiard hall, running two hotels and managing theaters, and at times he could be found on the links.

His hobby turned to golf and he admitted scoring in the seventies occasionally, usually in the eighties. He claimed he would rather be on the golf course than in the grand stands, although the attraction of baseball found him in attendance at the home games of the Kansas City Blues.[12]

Johnny Kling was engaged in more activities than a college youngster. The rigors of a busy city life were not as relaxing even with time on the links. So Johnny began to plan for a life in the country. He decided it was time to move.

18

THE GENTLEMAN FARMER

In 1912, Johnny Kling bought 300 acres in Hickman Mills, Missouri. It was a tract of land in the country, and that same year, he leased 247 acres to T. M. Godfrey, who built a home on the land, went into the dairy business, and raised virtually everything the family ate.[1]

After more than two decades, the Hickman Mills dairy farm ceased to be. Sometime later, after Kling sold the Kansas City Blues, he built a ranch style home on a knoll overlooking the countryside and began another career as a gentleman farmer.[2]

It wasn't long after Kling sold the Strand Hotel that the *Chicago Daily News* greeted Chicago baseball fans with a headlined question: "Where Is Catcher Johnny Kling Today?"

Clyde Brown, dean of newspaper photographers, traveled to Kansas

Kling's hilltop home dominating his 300 acre farm (*Chicago Daily News*).

18. The Gentleman Farmer 211

City, drove to Hickman Mills, and photographed Johnny Kling leading two Percheron mares.

Brown then captured Kling on camera helping to round up a herd of cows for the late afternoon milking — a chore that Johnny usually left to his ranchhands. But he often did this after a day in town. He also captured the 68-year-old former ballplayer and his daughter Jerre as they strolled down the hill from their home.

These photographs and comments were published on page 11 of the *Chicago Daily News*, Saturday November 27, 1943.

Kling leading two Percheron mares on his Hickman Mills farm (*Chicago Daily News*).

19

BREAD AND BUTTER

In 1908 Charles Kling was a baker. One year later, Gould's *1909 Kansas City Directory* listed him as a bookkeeper for John G. Kling's pool hall. For the rest of his life, up until he died in 1922, he worked for his brother doing a variety of jobs in the Billiard Emporium. His last job was manager. For Charles, brother John was indeed rock solid in his financial support, the bread and butter for family members.

For William, it was initially different. As the oldest boy in the family, he tried to make it on his own. He tried baseball, but it didn't work for him. As a saloonkeeper for nineteen years, he finally branched out into the theater business in 1917, closed his saloon two years later and continued on in the moving picture business for three more years. He then began working for brother John in the billiard hall in 1923 and stayed on until he died in 1934 — another example of John's close knit ties and support for family.

Sister Lizzie was something else. She rented out furnished rooms for eleven years, was not listed as employed for the next five years, and in 1917, at the age of fifty-four, she became a stenographer. Throughout her life, her name in the directory was Elizabeth Kling. In 1919 she became a widow of John W (last name not listed). Prior to this, no mention was ever made of Lizzie's husband. Did he provide support even though they may have been separated? It's hard to say. But one thing seems certain. Lizzie seems to have had a fair amount of independence until she died in 1949. She never depended on brother John for anything.

One son-in-law did. After Sam Gorman married Kling's oldest daughter Virginia, he became manager of the Strand Hotel. After their divorce, he continued managing until he entered the military during World War II. Sam depended on Kling for a livelihood and proved his worth by retaining his job when he and Virginia were no longer married.[1]

Throughout his business career, "Brainy John" had the Midas touch. It didn't seem to matter what he did or what he invested in, including a barber shop (Kling's, in the Dixon), a baseball club (K.C. Blues), a baseball supply company, billiards, a bowling alley (replaced Pennant Café after it closed in 1918), breeding Angus cattle on his farm, a bridge club, gambling (at Dixon, even though illegal), hotels, investment property, Kling's Dairy Farm, Percheron horses, a race horse (at one time), and theaters.

In addition, he held or had held stock in Bryan Oil & Products Co. (defunct), K.C. Tire & Rubber Co. (defunct), Summe Products (defunct) and Trustee Realty Co.[2]

With all of his wealth, Johnny Kling always seemed willing and ready to help a family member or friend when the need arose. What more could one ask of anyone?

20

MEAT AND POTATOES

Johnny Kling became wealthy, some say a millionaire. But as diligently as he pursued his business interests, he also pursued values that encompassed his personal life. Kling was unorthodox from the start and remained so. In an era when professional baseball players were men about town, Johnny made and saved every cent he could. He invested it and was as shrewd in business matters as he was in things baseball.[1]

He did not smoke, drink, chew or swear. Instead of sounding off at umpire Klem, calling him a liar, or even a damned liar during a game, Kling chose to call him a "prevaricator." How's that for a swear word? In regard to drinking, he was described as "strait-laced." His wife enjoyed a late day high ball, but had to hide it from the Cub backstop.[2]

During his lifetime, he was sued three times:

January 25, 1917, Vermont Marble Company, Inc., Plaintiff, vs. John G. Kling, et al. Defendant, Case No. 93937. Judge Ray G. Cowan awarded plaintiff $1,449.00.

December 1, 1934, Midwest Creamery Supply Company, Plaintiff, vs. John G. Kling, d/b Westport Dairy, Defendant, Case No. 435,192. Judge Ray G. Cowan ruled in favor of plaintiff, no details available. Reportedly, records destroyed.

January 25, 1935, "L. H. Nothnagel, through his attorneys, filed suit in the Livingston County Circuit Court for $25,000 damages for injuries and false arrest. Defendants named were Sam Gorman, Donald McElvain, Fred Walker, John Kling and the Cuff-Kling Enterprises, Inc.

"Plaintiff claimed he was thrown violently to the floor of the Strand Hotel lobby on December 26 last, that he was falsely arrested and maliciously charged with robbing a "slot machine."[3] The case did not come to court.

Considering the diversity and complexity of involvement in corporate and non-corporate investments all of his life, it is remarkable that he had such little involvement with the legal system. And no involvement with the criminal justice system. This attests to the line he learned to walk in growing up.

The elder John Kling taught his youngest son well, especially so after Johnny had been given the job of "bread wagon chauffeur." By abandoning the horse and wagon in favor of playing baseball on a corner lot, and responding to the urging of a teammate to "sticker over the ol' oyster," an irate housewife, who did not receive her delivery, went to another baker. She had been the down-to-earth means of support, the meat and potatoes for the Kling family, and the young Johnny Kling probably never forgot the meaning of responsibility.

Throughout his life, Kling was a doting parent and his wife and two daughters never wanted for the basic comforts, even during the height of the Great Depression.[4] His nephew, Bennie Allen, was taken under Kling's wing as an eighteen-year-old youngster, and at that age had become a partner in the Hotel Dixon. Bennie had the freedom to nourish his talent in pool and billiards, then went onto the world stage in winning successive championships due to his wonderful talent, but also due to a doting, loving and caring uncle. Their relationship lasted a lifetime.

Lifetime relationships and connections beyond were commitments Johnny made with family members early on. Kling was a Mason. As such, he was entitled to burial at Mount Moriah, a cemetery dedicated for burial of Freemasons and their relatives. But burial beneath ground was not what John G. Kling had in mind.

In 1925 the Mount Moriah Cemetery Association decided to erect a mausoleum building, a luxurious and expensive undertaking to provide a permanent structure. It came to be known as the Temple Mausoleum. It was made of marble, inside and out, and inscribed above two massive, front doors, on the face of the building, were the Masonic symbols, the compass and the square.

To be buried at this cemetery, one had to be a Mason or a family member. And those who could afford the expense purchased space within the building and had it customized into a family section, the dimensions determined by the amount of space the owner desired. John G. Kling had such a section. The floor and walls were made of beautiful marble. The rear wall had a vertical cutout with a light above. The sidewalls were divided into horizontal units, each designed to hold an individual's remains upon interment.

Johnny Kling knew who he wanted with him after he left for his eventual journey to the far beyond. For them there was a place. He also added additional units for others he had not planned for, knowing that that decision would be made by family members who would one day follow him. In planning for this occasion, Johnny Kling emphasized the value he placed on a close knit family and togetherness even after death.

John Kling's section inside the Masonic Temple building (photograph by author).

Along with this, there came the pride he must have felt in being able to afford and to build such a family resting place with the name of John G. Kling on a beautifully designed solid brass door guarding the entryway.

His pride in doing things involving money was obvious when he posed for a photo alongside his new Pierce Arrow automobile.[5] The stone-brick home in the background was at 1220 W. 62nd St. in Kansas City. The city directory placed Johnny Kling at that location between 1929 and 1931. After that, he was listed at 1224 W. 62nd St. through 1937.

This seeming confusion in the address was cleared up by Bernice Fromm, the current resident at 1224. She said the building is a duplex, and it would have been a simple matter to move from 1220 to 1224. She also said, after viewing the photograph of Kling alongside the automobile, that the house in the background was the 1220 address.

How did having values allow Johnny Kling to reap such obvious rewards? The answer to this question can best be understood by returning to the days when he was a major league player, to the days when he believed that idleness did not pay.

"A ballplayer has considerable spare time when he is on the road," said Kling in telling about his good fortune. "It is a fact that some of them spend the mornings in bed and the evenings in the hotel lobbies, cafes or theaters. I don't want to say that it does them any particular harm to loaf and have a good time, but it produces laziness.

Johnny Kling alongside his Pierce Arrow automobile (courtesy James Dickerson).

"I liked billiards when I was young and devoted my spare time to that game. I did not do it merely as recreation, but with the idea that I would learn the game and the business and devote my time to it in the off season and when I quit baseball.

"I always picked up the right sort of friends, congenial fellows who liked billiards, and we spent pleasant and helpful evenings at the green table. Billiards is a scientific pastime, requiring a good eye and steady nerve. It is an ideal recreation for a ballplayer."[6]

Making money in baseball or in billiards had its place. But the basic part of Johnny Kling, the essence of his soul and his existence, were his values. Near the top of his list was family. Caring for one another. Raising children, providing for them and loving them. Eventually arranging for the marriage of his daughters, Virginia on June 16, 1937, to Jerome Jacobson, and Geraldine, four months later to William Jacobstein. Each meant a gala celebration at the Blue Hills Country Club where family and friends would gather to wish the couple well.[7]

Caring for siblings, other family members and friends, helping them as best he could, was the *sine qua non* that Kling adhered to. The same went for the needs of his community as well as his country. And his social conscience was obvious when he refused to continue on with the injustice of segregated seating at the ballpark even though the climate of his time demanded otherwise. In addition, he did not drink, smoke or swear. This was a moral value that he believed in and followed, something not often seen in ballplayers of his era.

Another value of a personal nature was being rewarded for a job well done. This meant enshrinement in Baseball's Hall of Fame. It was something he yearned for. After all, he had been a premier catcher. One of the best if not the best. He followed his vote count. He saw other catchers, two of his contemporaries allowed into the hallowed Hall. His teammates, Tinker, Evers and Chance, were allowed into the Hall by the Veterans Committee, all at the same time. Between 1936 and 1946 his vote count went up and down. The Veterans Committee never gave him the nod. Would he ever get in?

21

Just Another Day

When Johnny Kling built a home on a knoll overlooking the countryside and became a gentleman farmer, he had farmhands do the work, and it seems fair to say that his involvement with horses and cattle was a hobby. It was something he could do after a busy day in town. It should have been relaxing.

In an interview with Lillian Kling, Dick Farrington took copious notes for an article he planned to write. He had just jotted down the fact that Johnny raised Angus cattle for market and had something like 60 head, when the man himself walked onto the veranda, seated himself and listened.

"Oh, it's grand out here," said Mrs. Kling. "But let me tell you something," she added seriously. "I agreed to Johnny building the house and moving here because he said it would add ten years to his life…. What's happened, though, is that it has already taken ten years off both our lives, the help situation being what it is. Why, we can't keep a resident manager and to tell the truth, I'm doing every bit of the housework. That's how hard it is to get and keep help.

Johnny only laughed, shooed his two Doberman pinscher dogs away from the front veranda and said: "Well, I feel good enough since being out here to rejoin the Cubs."[1]

Although Noisy John may have been feeling good at the moment, his health began to decline. In 1946, he went to Miami, Florida, for the winter. He spent most of his time in the company of other old baseball men, taking in the sun, even engaging in almost daily games of catch. While returning home, he suffered a heart attack.[2]

Johnny was admitted at the Menorah Hospital in Kansas City, Missouri. He had almost recovered and was scheduled to leave the hospital when he suffered a setback on January 23, 1947.[3]

To sadden his last days came the news that Tinker had undergone an operation for the amputation of a leg and that Sheckard, the outfielder, had been killed in a motor car accident. It was while thinking of these and the others of a matchless team that the end came to Johnny — just another day, as he might have said, in the life of a ballplayer.[4]

John G. Kling was interred on the upper floor, Tier North, Room P, Crypt D at the Mount Moriah Temple, to be followed by his 8-year-old granddaughter, his 2-day-old grandson, his wife Lillian, his daughter Virginia Jacobson, his daughter Jerre Ann Kling, and his son-in-law Jerome Jacobson.[5]

Johnny had planned for his afterlife quite well. He was now in heaven, talking with Chance, jawing about the old days. He was waiting for his dear friend Joe Tinker, knowing he would soon be joining the team. Johnny Kling had already suited up, put on his spikes, donned his mask and picked up his mitt. He was looking forward to once again crouching low behind the bat, sizing up his man and starting his chatter. All he needed was to hear the umpire holler, "play ball!"

John G. Kling knew that some day, he would have his own cheering section up in the stands — family.

22

JEWISH ANCESTRY, PART ONE

Throughout his baseball career, Johnny Kling's teammates knew him as "the Jew."[1] Sportswriters also referred to him as a Jew.[2] Braven Dyer of the *L.A. Times* said, "Probably the greatest Jewish player in the big leagues was Johnny Kling, catcher and 'brains' of the famous old Chicago Cubs of the Frank Chance era."[3] Shirley Povich of the *Washington Post* said, "The only Jewish player of any fame until Hank Greenberg came along was Johnny Kling, the Cubs' catcher of the Tinker-to-Evers-to-Chance era."[4] Books and articles about him said he was Jewish.[5] No record was found showing that Kling ever denied any of this.

In 1965 Abraham Ribicoff, a U.S. senator from Connecticut and former secretary of the Department of Health, Education and Welfare, wrote the Foreword for a book titled *Encyclopedia of Jews in Sports*. He said, "This volume has been compiled with care, dedication and professional skill...."[6]

John G. Kling was seen as a Jewish ballplayer. The Acknowledgement page of the *Encyclopedia* said, "The authors owe a special debt of gratitude to four men who helped make this volume possible. One of the men was Lee Allen, Historian of the Baseball Hall of Fame at Cooperstown, New York, for his assistance with the research on the baseball section...." It was he who wrote the bio of Kling on pages 42 to 45.

Steve Gietschier, director of Historical Records for the *Sporting News*, knew Allen. In the Introduction to Allen's book, *Cooperstown Corner: Columns from The Sporting News, 1962–1969*, Gietschier said, "At the time of his death in 1969, Allen had for ten years been the Historian at the Hall of Fame's National Baseball Library. He was widely celebrated for his encyclopedic recall of persons, famous and obscure, events large and small. 'I care very little for statistics as such,' he always said. 'My concern is the players. Who are these men? What are they? What problems have they faced? Where are they now?' Allen dedicated his life to asking these questions and then to answering them. He demonstrated his knowledge on radio programs and television shows and was a prolific writer whose books and articles marked him as baseball's foremost historical expert."[7]

As the expert, Allen contributed 139 Jewish ballplayer bios to the baseball section of the *Encyclopedia of Jews in Sports*. And up until February 12, 1969, all the players were regarded as Jewish, including Kling. But after February 12, John G. Kling began to lose his Jewish identity while the other 138 continued to be Jews. Was Lee Allen wrong in his assessment of Kling? If so, how did it happen? How and why did Kling go from being a Jew one day to not being a Jew the next day?

When Roy Silver of NBC, one of the authors writing in the *Encyclopedia of Jews in Sports*, wanted confirmation about Kling's ancestry, he asked Lee Allen, who said, "It was widely believed in baseball that Kling was Jewish. An old trainer for the Cubs of the Kling era stopped in my office at the Hall of Fame one afternoon and I asked him. 'I think he was Jewish,' the trainer said. 'I remember Joe Tinker always called him by a Yiddish name.'"[8]

Roy Silver published Kling's bio as submitted by Allen. But since the question had been raised, Lee Allen wanted more evidence. In *Cooperstown Corner* he said, "The truth had to wait until I located Mrs. Kling." After retiring, he found and wrote Lillian Kling. She replied February 12, 1969:

Mr. Lee Allen
Boca Raton, Fla

In reply to your letter received yesterday, I am happy to give you the following information with the hope that the erroneous reports as to Johnny's religion may be cleared up.

Johnny was baptized in the Lutheran Church but I doubt he ever attended church; at least I know he didn't from the time we met. I think all the confusion probably was due to the fact that I am Jewish and we were married at my parents' home by a Rabbi.

I was born in Salena Kansas in 1881 and there was no Temple there, so consequently I would attend Sunday school with my girl friends at the Catholic Church, Methodist and others. We moved to Kansas City when I was fifteen but my parents didn't join the Temple here, so as a result I continued to go to Sunday school and church here with my new friends.

I often tried to get Johnny to deny rumors that he was a Jew but he said he didn't care what was written about his religion. Enough of this. I hope I have been able to get the situation straightened out. So far as the information as to Johnny's religion, you need not consider it confidential should you care to use it.

Sincerely,
Mrs. John G. Kling[9]

Did Lillian Kling lie? Consider this. On December 2, 1948, more than twenty years earlier, Lillian responded to questions from Hy Turkin in the sports department of the *Daily News* in New York.[10] Turkin wanted to know

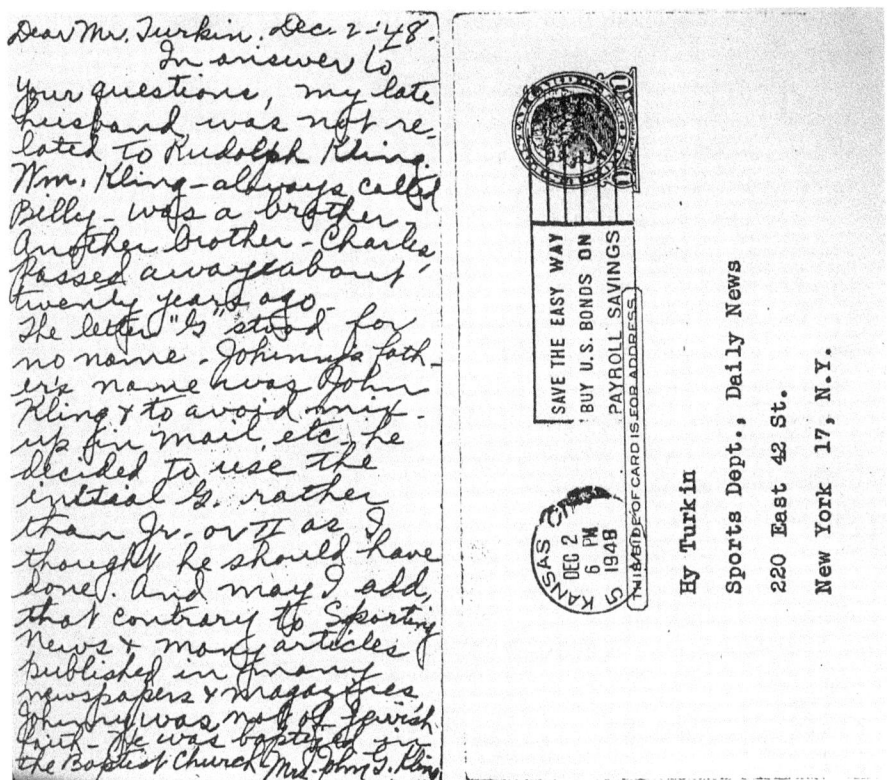

A 1948 postcard from Lillian Kling to Hy Turkin (National Baseball Hall of Fame).

if Rudolph Kling was Johnny Kling's brother. Lillian replied in the negative and gave Mr. Turkin the names of Johnny's brothers. She then told Mr. Turkin that the G. her husband used as a middle initial was not a name, and that he used it to avoid a mix up in the mail, and preferred it instead of Jr. or II after Kling.

Without any further questions, Lillian launched into a remark that had nothing to do with Turkin's questions. She said, "And may I add, that contrary to *Sporting News* and many articles published in many newspapers and magazines, Johnny was not of Jewish faith. He was baptized in the Baptist Church."[11]

This uninvited remark puts her 1969 Lee Allen letter into question. Putting it more bluntly, her Allen letter can be viewed as pure fabrication.

According to Lillian Kling, her husband was a Baptist in 1948, and a Lutheran in 1969. If Johnny had truly been baptized a Baptist, it seems reasonable to expect her to remember his religion. And her story in 1969 should have been no different than it was in 1948. But if the 1948 story was a lie, being forgetful 20 years later is easy to understand.

It is interesting that Lillian's comment came out of the blue. It was something she wanted the sports world to know. Why? Why now in 1948, decades after Johnny quit baseball? To answer this, consider whom she was talking to. Consider her motivation.

Hy Turkin was a sportswriter. The New York newspaper had a wide circulation. That meant publicity, possibly influence. And there should be no question as to who she was trying to influence. It was the Baseball Writers Association of America (BBWAA), the sportswriters who vote and decide on who gains entry into Baseball's Hall of Fame in Cooperstown. She had been praying for this for years.

Her letter to Joseph Simenic in Cleveland, Ohio, on January 5, 1969, five weeks before she responded to Lee Allen, shows that her desire for her husband's enshrinement in the hallowed hall had been ongoing for years. She said:

> Your most valued letter enclosing a questionnaire to be filled in concerning the life of my late husband, received yesterday and I am so very grateful for the interest you have taken and hope and trust your efforts will bring results in getting Johnny's name enshrined in the Hall of Fame at Cooperstown. I have hoped and prayed this would come to pass while I'm still alive....
>
> Gratefully yours,
> Mrs. John G. Kling.[12]

Why now in 1948, decades after Johnny quit baseball? The answers to these questions must be put within the context of Kling's yearly vote count for admission to the Hall of Fame and the count for some of his teammates and his contemporaries who were enshrined there.

	1936	1937	1938	1939	1942	1945	1946	1948	1953
Kling	8	20	26	14	15	12	20	2	1
Ewing	0	0	0	2	1939, enshrined by Veterans Committee				
Bresnahan	47	43	67	67	1945, enshrined by V.C.				
Tinker	0	15	16	12	1946, enshrined by V.C.				
Evers	6	44	91	107	1946, enshrined by V.C.				
Chance	5	49	133	158	1946, enshrined by V.C.				
Brown	6	31	0	54	1949 enshrined by V.C.				
Schalk	4	24	45	35	1955 enshrined by V.C.				

In 1936, Johnny Kling out-polled his teammates and contemporaries except Bresnahan. Although their vote count rose after that, they never received enough votes for admission to the hall and were eventually enshrined by the Veterans Committee, also known as the Old Timers' Committee.

After failing for two years to add a single bronze plaque to the shrine at Cooperstown, the committee broke the stalemate with a vengeance in 1946. No fewer than eleven of the diamond's great were selected for immortality in the brown brick museum in the Leatherstocking village at the foot of Lake Otsego.[13]

Three of Kling's teammates, Tinker, Evers and Chance, were selected. Kling was not. Mordecai Brown, another Kling teammate who couldn't garner enough votes, finally made it in after fourteen years. Buck Ewing was selected in 1939 after receiving only two votes in four years. Ray Schalk was selected in 1955 after failing to be voted in over a nineteen year span. Bresnahan too didn't receive enough votes, and was allowed in after six years. All three were catchers.

Kling also had a greater vote total than others in 1937, '38, '39, '42, '45, and '46, but it ended there. All of these others made it into the Hall of Fame. Kling did not. In 1948, Kling's numbers nose dived and never recovered.

When her husband's vote count plummeted in 1948 to 2, it seems fair to say that Lillian Kling was more than troubled. She knew that some of his teammates had been enshrined. Why not Johnny? After all, he had received so many accolades. Johnny Kling had been regarded as a premier catcher. He had led the team to four pennants and two World Series championships. He was the best. That's what top ranking baseball men said. That's what Steven Riess said in *Sports and the American Jew*.[14] That's what an unidentified baseball book said when it talked about the Chicago Union Giants, the best nonwhite team in the Chicago area, and then went on to mention Johnny Kling as the Chicago Cubs catcher who was organized baseball's first Jewish star.[15] In addition, the *New York Times* did a piece on Mickey Cochrane and reported that he belonged among the best catchers baseball has known, including Roger Bresnahan, Gabby Hartnett and Johnny Kling.[16] As late as 1987, Kling was repeatedly referred to as a Jewish player in a baseball Judaica question and answer text.[17]

Was he not allowed in because he was Jewish? This was a logical question. And with all the publicity about his being Jewish, in Lillian's mind the answer was yes.

Lillian Kling tried to change history. She seized upon the opportunity to convince Hy Turkin and his newspaper that her husband was a Baptist. She did this without ever being questioned by Turkin as to her husband's religion. Nothing came of it. In 1953, Kling's vote count went from 2 to 1. After that, none.

When Lee Allen raised the question as to Kling's religion in 1969, more than twenty years later, she again wanted to change history. She must have still held onto the belief that her husband was not in the Hall of Fame because of his Jewish heritage. She now claimed her husband was Lutheran.

This time, she changed history. Allen bought her story. He wrote about it. Being who he was, the baseball world believed it. Since then, Kling has been viewed as Lutheran, even though a few writers still claimed he was Jewish.

Although Lillian Kling was successful in stripping her husband of his Jewish ancestry, she was not successful in getting him into the Hall of Fame. The BBWAA no longer voted for him. And she learned that when members of the Old Timers' Committee met to consider their selections, Johnny Kling was never considered as a serious candidate for the Hall of fame.[18] Although he was nominated along with hundreds of other players, he never made the final cut, and was never in contention for a bronze plaque in the hallowed hall.

23

Jewish Ancestry, Part Two

Where are the documents to prove Kling was Jewish? Did he observe Yom Kippur, the Day of Atonement, the holiest Jewish holiday of the year? It was a time for prayer, a time to ask for forgiveness for all of his sins committed that year. A time to say L'Shanah Tovah to family and friends, which means a good year, and refers to the year that is about to begin.

Sandy Koufax and Hank Greenberg, two Jewish players, refused to play on Yom Kippur. But Johnny Kling did. Box scores for the Chicago Nationals for Oct. 1, 1903 (city series with White Sox), Sept. 29, 1906, and Sept. 18, 1907, showed Kling playing all 3 days. That means he wasn't Jewish, or he wasn't a religious Jew. If Jewish, in all probability, he was not raised in a home where this holiday was observed.

Yet, another Jewish tradition and custom was observed by the Kling family, such as following law number 206, one of the 613 Laws of the Torah. This law dealt with the prohibition for a man to have sex with the sister of his wife. But upon his wife's death, Jewish law permitted him to marry the sister.

In the author's discussion with rabbi Lawrence Rigal in 2004, he affirmed the practice. He said that after the death of Caroline, "Rabbis deemed it praiseworthy for Louise, the oldest non-married sister to marry Mr. Schutte, now a widower, since no other woman would show the same affection for the orphaned Victor as that of an aunt."[1]

It was also a custom for Jewish families to have their children marry Jews, and the wedding ceremony had to be conducted by a rabbi. John G. Kling and his wife Lillian were married by Rabbi Harry H. Mayer on January 27, 1904, in Kansas City (Marriage License No. 28780). His daughter Virginia was married to Jerome L. Jacobson by Rabbi Mayer on June 16, 1937 in Kansas City (License No. A 67329). Daughter Jerre Ann was married to William Jacobstein by the same rabbi on Oct. 21, 1937, in Kansas City (License No. A 68948).

B'nai Jehudah membership record for Jerome and Virginia Jacobson (American Jewish Archives).

Virginia had married previously on July 18, 1930, in Kansas City. The groom was Samuel Paul Gorman. (License No. A42253). The ceremony was conducted by a justice of the peace, not a rabbi. But they were divorced and Samuel Paul Gorman is buried in the Rose Hill Cemetery, an all–Jewish Cemetery in Kansas City.

In pursuing the religion of Samuel Paul Gorman, Temple B'nai Jehudah, who owns Rose Hill, was contacted via e-mail. A reply on June 28, 2004, from Sheilah Kocherov, the synagogue's secretary, said, "The rules of Rose Hill state that to be buried there you must be a member of the synagogue, or a relative, such as mother, father, son, daughter of a member or one already buried there."

Confirmation of the religion for William Jacobstein was obtained from the 1920 U.S. Census, Jackson County, Missouri. Jacob Jacobstein, his wife Minnie, and two sons, William, age 10, and Louis, 4, were listed. Under column 20, titled "Mother tongue," it said, "Yiddish" for the father and mother.

For proof closer to home, the document above shows Kling's daughter, Virginia, and her husband as members of Congregation B'nai Jehudah. Their address, the Dixon Hotel at 12th and Baltimore, was Kling's hotel. But he had died and his wife Lillian was in charge.

An interesting piece of information was found in *Oldtyme Baseball News*, Vol. 6, Issue 6, page 14, in an article titled, "Baseball's Greatest

Dynasty" by John Infanger. He did a piece on Johnny Kling and explained that Johnny was called "The Jew" because of "the fact that he was conversant in Yiddish." The source for this statement was not mentioned and confirmation could not be found.

But an interview with Helen Allen, a 92-year-old daughter-in-law of Kling's partner Bennie Allen, can be viewed as valid. She met Johnny Kling and remembers her mother, Rose Corrigan Murray, telling her that Kling was Jewish.

In addition, a written statement from Kling's grandson can be accepted as valid. On Jan. 29, 2004, an e-mail from John Kling, the grandson, said, "By the way, to clear up my grandfather's status as being Jewish, he positively was Jewish." Johnny Kling's grandson would have known this only if it had been handed down from one generation of the family to another, from his grandfather or his grandmother to his mother Geraldine, and she to him.

The grandson's affirmation that his grandfather was positively Jewish supports the idea that Lillian Kling lied in 1969 when she wrote to Lee Allen claiming her husband had been baptized Lutheran. And there is reason to believe that in doing so, she believed that anti–Semitism played a role in keeping Johnny Kling out of the Hall of Fame. And as she said, she wanted him inducted before she died.

Having said all of this, there is still a wrinkle in the fabric of Johnny's Jewish heritage. Rabbi Harry H. Mayer, who conducted the marriage ceremony for Johnny Kling, may have conducted the ceremony even if he was not Jewish.

Rabbi Mayer participated in a debate in 1909 and spoke against the adoption of a resolution whereby a rabbi would not officiate at a marriage between a Jew or a Jewess if one or the other professed a religion other than Judaism. The resolution passed by a vote of 42 to 2. Rabbi Mayer was one of the two who objected to this resolution. So the possibility exists that he may not have followed the adopted resolution, and could have conducted the wedding ceremony if Kling was not Jewish. But he would have conducted the ceremony in the Jewish tradition with all of its symbolism.[2]

24

JEWISH ANCESTRY, PART THREE

There is additional information showing Johnny Kling to be Jewish, but it is based on circumstantial evidence. He had Jewish friends. Mrs. Louis Stein visited Kansas City and stayed at his home for the weekend.[1]

His mother died May 3, 1905. When his father died August 7, 1906, the elder Kling was interred next to his wife, but the obituary did not reveal the cemetery. Three months later, November 14, 1906, Charles Kling hired the J. C. Duffy Company and had his parents dug up and moved to Forest Hill, a non-denominational cemetery.

In an interview with Patty Scholl, manager at Forest Hill, she had no record as to where Mr. and Mrs. Kling had come from. She wondered if the bodies had been moved from Rose Hill, an all Jewish cemetery directly across the street. It was owned and is still owned by B'nai Jehudah, the synagogue whose rabbi conducted the wedding ceremonies for Johnny and Lillian Kling and their two daughters.

Sheilah Kocherov, secretary at B'nai Jehudah, had no records for John and Caroline Kling at Rose Hill, but she did provide the names of eight other Klings interred there. She also provided the names of seven former Lorch members of the synagogue at Rose Hill. All were Jewish.

Why would Charles Kling do this? Since he and his sister Elizabeth are buried alongside their parents, it seems reasonable to believe that he and his sister wanted to be interred with their parents but did not wish to be buried in a Jewish cemetery, if in fact the parents were buried at Rose Hill. The issue of assimilation into the acceptable culture and hiding their Jewish heritage had been the practice of Johann Kling since coming to America. And Charles and Elizabeth may have wanted to continue this practice even after death.

William Kling, Johnny's brother, took it one step further. He and his wife chose to be interred at Calvary, an all Catholic cemetery in Kansas

24. Jewish Ancestry, Part Three

Charge for moving parents to Forest Hill cemetery (Jackson County Courthouse).

City. But he had always been the rebel in the family, like becoming a saloon-keeper when his father had been against the use of alcohol.

Even today, the issue of being Jewish for a Kling granddaughter seems to be a problem. A friend sent the author two e-mails. On August 2, 2003, one e-mail said, "She [name confidential] said her parents worried when her last name being Jacobstein, as to College. They changed it back to Kling.... This issue happened within my own family, she was murdered here in KCMO in the late 80s. And yes, some still hate Jews."

On August 2, 2003, a second e-mail said, "[name confidential] is already worried, being a church elder, what people will say behind her back if the word got out she was 100% Jewish. A damn shame."[2] The granddaughter's problem shows the continuation from one generation to the next of a kind of struggle in accepting the idea that the entire family was and is Jewish.

In digging for this kind of information on Kling's mother's side of the family, it was mentioned in Chapter 1 that Kling's father-in-law, Charles Lorch, was interred at Palm Grove Cemetery in Cincinnati. It is under the United Jewish Cemeteries but non–Jews are interred there also.

Charles Lorch may have come to America in 1831–1832, since his daughter Caroline was born in Cincinnati in 1833, and there was no Lorch family in the city directory prior to that time. He may have arrived in America with a wife and a son, Benedict, but the ship manifest could not be found. Benedict died in 1849 at the age of 22 as a result of the cholera scourge in Cincinnati. He was interred at the Chestnut Street Cemetery. His gravestone, as well as all the others, have Hebrew inscriptions, proving that the people interred there were Jewish.

Another circumstance is related to the son Charles, who was listed in the Federal Census in 1850, age 16. Although it was easy to follow his sister Caroline, who became Johnny Kling's mother, her brother vanished. He could not be found in any records. But in tracking the Lorch name, a Charles Lorch appeared two generations later in the *Lima News,* Oct. 22, 1960, page 8. He was in Louisville, next door to Cincinnati. He was the chairman of a regional Hebrew convention. The guest speaker announced was a professor from the Hebrew Union College in Cincinnati. The topic for discussion was "Education Beyond Confirmation." This demonstrated that the Lorch name was intimately tied to Jewish organizations and topics.

Benedict Lorch gravesite at Chestnut Street Cemetery (Dr. Leonard Lipton).

Another bit of circumstantial evidence is

24. Jewish Ancestry, Part Three

the caricature of Johnny Kling shown in chapter 9, leading his KC All Stars for a series of games in Chicago. His profile depicts him to have a large hooked nose. In the 19th century this physical characteristic portrayed its owner as "typically" Jewish in order to suggest that Jews can be identified by this nose. It stigmatized Jews and assigned to them a feature that has been called the "treacherous" nose even though the anthropological studies by Maurice Fishberg proved that the "Semitic" nose was found in 30 percent of the non–Jewish population in the alpine region of Germany. In portraying Johnny Kling this way, it gave him a negative stereotype. It symbolized him as "evil." It also supported the widespread belief in the baseball world that he was Jewish.[3]

25

BASEBALL AND ANTI-SEMITISM

1900 to 2004

For all the years Kling played in the major leagues, and with all the accolades he received, he never made it into Cooperstown. Did anti–Semitism play a role?

Throughout his life, and long after he died, the sports world saw him as one fantastic player. They also saw him as a Jew. In the 1906 World Series with the White Sox, in a day when hitting .300 was a tremendous feat, Kling batted .312. And a series historian, writing at that time, called him "the matchless Kling."[1]

Barry Schweiker, who claimed to be the number one authority on Jewish players in the majors, picked an All-Jewish team. He said, "I could select Moe Berg and Joe Ginsberg for catcher. But the spot belongs to Johnny Kling, a Cub immortal after the turn of the Century. And the back-up man would be Harry Danning."[2] Barry justified his number one pick by listing "exclusive statistics on catchers who had caught the most 20-game winners":

1. Jim Hegan (20)	Indians 1941–'57	Lemon 7, Wynn 4, Feller 4, Garcia 2
		Score 1, Bearden 1
	Giants 1959	Sam Jones 1
2. Roger Bresnahan (18)	Giants 1903–1908	Mathewson 6, McGinnity 4, Taylor 1
		Ames 1, Wiltze 1
	Cardinals 1909–1912	Harmon 1
	Cubs 1913–'15	Cheney 2, Vaughn 2
3. Johnny Kling (17)	Cubs 1900–1911	Brown 6, Taylor 3, Overall 2, Weimer 2
		Cole, Reulbach, Pfister, Nickel 1

25. Baseball and Anti-Semitism

4. (Tied) Del Crandell (16)	Braves 1949–1963	Spahn 12, Burdette 2, Sain 1
	Giants 1964	Marichal 1
4. (Tied) Lou Criger (16)	Clv. NL, 1896–'98	Cy Young 2, Powell, 1
	St. Louis NL, 1899–1900	Powell 1, Cy Young 1
	Red Sox AL 1901–1908	Cy Young 5, Dinenen 3 Tinnell 2, Houghe 1
5. (Tied) Ray Schalk (15)	White Sox 1912–1928	Faber 4, Cicotte 3, Scott 2, Williams 2
		Kerr 1, Russell 1, Lyons 1, Thurston 1
6. (Tied) Mickey Cochrane (15)	Athletics 1925–1933	Grove 7, Earnshaw 3, Walberg 1, Rommell 1
	Tigers 1934–1937	Bridges 2, Rowe 1

With all that's been said about Johnny Kling, a concerted effort was made to find information that reported anti-Semitism during the years he played. An article by Roger Kahn cited a 1912 book calling Kling "the Jew." Kahn went on to say, "persistent anti-Semitism pervaded baseball."[3]

The *Chicago Tribune* and *Chicago Daily News* were reviewed for all the years Kling played, from Sept. 11, 1900, through June 11, 1911. An item found in the *Chicago Tribune,* "Notes of the Cubs," July 20, 1908, page 8, said, "Mr. Kling is not a Jew. He is a professional pool shark and backstop with a bum thumb, spotting a few trial heats in right field for his batting. He got three yesterday."[4]

This comment was meant to be a compliment to Johnny Kling's ability as demonstrated by shooting pool and playing ball. But it was a slur against Jews. It referred to the stereotypical Jew, who was viewed as athletically inept, uninterested in sports, someone who preferred books over sports. It was thus asking, how could Kling be a Jew if he was so good at baseball? This reflects the view and feelings toward Jewish ballplayers, Kling being one of them.

There is also much evidence for anti-Semitism when Hammerin' Hank Greenberg broke into major league baseball — his first full year was 1933. In his autobiography, he reported hearing, "Jew bastard" or "kike son of a bitch" from the stands. He had to eat those words, or else he would be out of every game he played.[5]

"Sure, there was added pressure being Jewish," he said. "How the hell could you get up to home plate every day and have some son of a bitch call you a Jew bastard and a kike and a sheenie, and get on your ass without feeling the pressure. If the ballplayers weren't doing it, the fans were. I used to get frustrated as hell. Sometimes I wanted to go up in the stands and beat the shit out of them."[6]

Greenberg, as a club executive, ran into another problem:

"One winter, after we bought the club," recalled Nate Dolin, who became one of the directors of the Indians after Bill Veeck sold the team in 1949, "we went to Phoenix for the winter meetings. The American League clubs were staying at a big hotel there. We checked in and the fellow said to me, 'Mr. Dolin, I want to tell you something. We have a problem.'
I said, 'What's the problem?'
He said, 'Mr. Greenberg can't stay at this hotel.'
I said, 'Why can't he stay?'
He said, 'Because he's Jewish.'
I said, 'Well, we're all Jewish.'
And he said, 'I didn't know by your name.'
Well, the National League was staying at the Arizona Biltmore, which was owned by the Wrigleys, and the Cubs got us rooms in that hotel. I called Bill Harridge, who was president of the American League, and I told him under no circumstances were we going to go to any meetings at that first hotel.
Oh, we had a lot of anti–Semitism from some of those owners. We were just about the first Jewish owners in baseball. But we fought for our rights. You had some of these guys with their fancy clubs and all that stuff. It was just a matter of our not going to any private clubs for meetings. The same thing happened in Cleveland. I refused to have a board of directors meeting at the Union Club because of prejudice in Cleveland. No Jews allowed there.
Later, I told Hank about what had happened in that hotel in Phoenix. He was shocked, and angry. We all were.[7]

Even sportswriters displayed anti–Semitic attitudes:

After Hank joined Detroit mid-season in 1945, upon returning after a four year military stint, he found himself at the plate, top of the ninth, bases loaded, needing one more win to go to the World Series. The Browns were ahead 4–3. The count was 1–1 when Greenberg met the next pitch head on, sending it into the left field bleachers and clearing the bases. Detroit won the game, and the pennant, and all the players charged the field when he reached home plate, pounding him on the back and carrying on like he was a hero. Wow! What a story!
"There was almost nobody in the stands to pay attention," Greenberg said, "and there were few newspapermen, just the ballplayers giving me a hero's welcome." The absence of newspapermen can be viewed as a reluctance to glorify a Jew.
"When we returned home to Detroit there were thousands of people in the train station giving me a big hand," Greenberg explained. "But the best part of that home run was hearing later what the Washington players said: 'Goddamn that dirty Jew bastard, he beat us again.' They were calling me all kinds of names behind my back, and now they had to pack up and go home [Washington came in 2nd], while we were going to the World Series."[8]

Johnny Kling never wrote his autobiography. But the social climate during his day and long after he played was written by the country's leading newspaper and others:

Jews denied admission to health resorts in the Caucasus, and Jewish musicians barred from playing in government orchestras.[9]

Russian Mobs Kill Jews.[10]
Y.M.C.A. Board of Directors Rejects Jews.[11]
Jews discriminated against in Army and Navy.[12] Nationwide boycott of theatres presenting "scurrilous and debasing impersonations of Hebrew type."[13]
Poles and Cossacks Massacre Jews.[14]
Millions of Jewish men, women and children slaughtered.[15]
Those who proclaim Four Freedoms do little to rescue 6,000,000 Jews from Nazi torture and butchery.[16]
U.S. and Britain Apathetic on Jews.[17]

Throughout America, doors were closed for Jews. They were barred from elite schools, country clubs, employment and certain neighborhoods. Ivy League schools introduced Jewish quotas.[18]

Ideally, the world of athletic competition is the proverbial level playing field, where every athlete is judged fairly and excels according to his or her ability. But African Americans experienced exclusion and prejudice. And so did Jews, particularly from the 1880s through the 1940s. At the end of the nineteenth century, Jews were barred from the American Jockey Club. The situation was similar for the New York Athletic Club–so much so, that by the 1930s even an Olympic contender, a relay runner who was Jewish, was not allowed to come in with a friend and train.

Avery Brundage, then president of the American Olympic Committee, who praised Hitler's government, who spoke at Bund rallies and who, in 1939, was accusing Jews of poisoning American attitudes against Germany, this same man owned a club in Santa Barbara and he excluded Jews and Blacks throughout the late 1960s.[19]

And what about Henry Ford, who did his best to mass-produce hatred of Jews, beginning in 1920, blaming all of America's problems on Jews? Hitler described him in his book, *Mein Kampf*, as the only American "who truly understands what we are trying to accomplish."[20]

In the midst of the social turmoil and upheaval, there were claims that sports were above it all. These legendary claims for the virtue of sport had been that "besides its character-building and morally uplifting nature, it was a reasonably just world sensibly separated from the often harsh and unfair ordinary world. In sport, so the claim implied, performance, not social background or special privilege or race, mattered most. But when this rhetoric was stripped away, the actual conduct of sport wasn't particularly exceptional at all — at least when equal opportunity was the issue. Sport was just as real-world as the real-world. It was segregated as well."[21]

Did anti–Semitism play a role in keeping Johnny Kling out of the Hall of Fame? It seems reasonable to say it did. Was it the only thing that kept him out? Based on the bad PR he received, the answer must be no.

26

SETTING THE RECORD STRAIGHT

For 100 years or so, Johnny Kling has been painted with the broad brush of a holdout, wanting more money when it came time to sign his 1909 baseball contract.

February 26, 1936, saw an article by John Kieran titled "The Holdout Situation." "If any fervid fan is worrying about the holdout situation as it affects his favorite team," Kieran said, "there is comfort in history. Few holdouts hold on. The only case that comes to mind of a holdout with a really good grip was the case of Johnny Kling, great catcher of bygone days. Johnny held out for a full season, which is par for the course."[1]

March 11, 1937, Allan Gould wrote a gossip column of the "Affairs of Sport." He said, "Baseball's most conspicuous holdouts won't get all the money they are demanding but they can't complain about publicity this spring.... Major league openings are still more than a month off and there is little danger that any of the hefty performers will emulate Johnny Kling who made his argument stick in bygone days by staying out for all or part of the full season."[2] On the day Kling died, Jan. 1, 1947, Fred Lieb wrote a lengthy obituary saying Johnny was a "brilliant first-string catcher of the team." "One of the foremost backstops of all time," he went on, "known particularly for his brainy work behind the plate, and given credit for much of the effectiveness of the famous Cub pitching quartette of Mordecai Brown, Orval Overall, Ed Reulbach and Jack Pfiester."

But then he said, "The Cubs' failure to make it five pennants in a row was charged to Kling's season-long holdout in 1909. Johnny wanted a substantial raise after a fine season in 1908, but Charley Murphy, then the Cub owner, agreed to meet Kling's demand only to the extent of a few hundred dollars. After that, neither the catcher nor club owner would budge, with Johnny sitting out the entire campaign. Kling was one of the few top-ranking players who carried a holdout through an entire season."[3]

26. Setting the Record Straight

A little more than a year after Kling died, the baseball world continued to read about his 1909 holdout situation. "The late Johnny Kling whose name is always somewhere near the top when great catchers are listed was ostensibly a holdout for financial reasons," Bill Bryson said.[4]

Almost 20 years later in another article, George Vass said, "Kling, the catcher on the Cub team, may have been the holdout who had the greatest effect on his team's performance after he decided to sit it out. Without him, the Cubs finished second. From a team's standpoint, Kling's holdout had to be the costliest in the history of baseball."[5]

In 1993, a newly released baseball book had a photo of Kling. Beneath the photo it said, "After the Cubs won the 1908 World Series, catcher Johnny Kling decided to hold out for a big raise in 1909. This was a big mistake."[6]

Before responding to a century's worth of bad PR, it is important to understand the kind of man Johnny Kling had to deal with. This can best be done by listening to what two Cub managers and the National League president had to say about Charles Webb Murphy.

October 8, 1912. Frank Chance was in charge of the Cubs in the City Series against the White Sox. The Cubs were leading three games to one with only one more game needed for them to claim the town's championship. The Sox tied it 3–3, and in the final game the White Sox hammered the Cubs into a disgraceful 16–0 loss.

Murphy was so furious, he came down from his box seat to the bench and fired his manager. Frank Chance gave vent to his feelings. "No manager can be a success without competent players, and some of these I had are anything but skilled. In all the time I have been with this club I have had to fight to get players I wanted. Murphy has not spent one-third as much for players as have other magnates. How can he expect to win championships without ballplayers?"[7]

According to Chance, when he told Murphy what the other owners were spending for new players, Murphy told him, "If they want to be suckers and pay for it, they can, but I won't."[8] Before leaving, Chance said that he had to operate under Murphy's cheap reign for the past three years. He said his players would often complain of the low salaries that Murphy was paying them.

Johnny Evers took over as manager. But in 1913, Sam Weller of the *Chicago Tribune* wrote, "He had several run-ins with Murphy and only the success of the Cubs during the last six weeks of the season kept Evers from being fired." Wrote Weller, "Long before the season was over, Evers confided to some of his friends that he didn't feel sure of his job and in reality was manager in name only because he dared make no move of consequence without the sanction of Murphy. He explained that his financial condition compelled him to stick to the job no matter how unpleasant it might be."[9]

But after the Cubs lost the City Series to the White Sox, Murphy fired Evers, declaring that his bad judgement enabled the White Sox to defeat the Cubs in the fall series of 1913. Evers was as mad as a wet hen and made no pretext to hide his true feelings. "Frank Chance had the right dope on Murphy," said Evers, "only Chance did not put it half strong enough. I will not play for Murphy again under any condition and that goes."[10]

Charles Murphy eventually had to pay the piper. He was seen as a disturbing element in the National League, flouting an ethical contract, firing his manager with scant ceremony. In doing so he overreached himself. It was Murphy who was banished from the game. He was summoned to a meeting in the office of league president John Tener. Present at the meeting was Charles Taft, who had originally bankrolled Murphy in the Cubs venture. Tener, Taft and other league officials informed Murphy that baseball no longer needed his services. Murphy's dignity was comforted by approximately $500,000 that Taft coughed up for Charley's 53 percent interest in the club.[11] This is the kind of man Kling had to deal with — an owner who bickered with him every year about his salary. An owner who nickeled and dimed him to death by pointing out that he was getting free uniforms worth $30.00. An owner who had the audacity to tell him that his winnings in pool on the road was $1800.00 and that it should be considered as part of his salary. An owner who told him he was fat and out of condition, and that the club could get along without him. An owner who made other disparaging remarks about one of the greatest backstops of all time.

Unlike other players, Kling had other sources of income. He didn't want to play for Murphy. Why should he play for such a man? He wanted the Cubs to trade him away since other clubs wanted him. He was not a holdout for more money, as has been cited for 95 years. He was a disgruntled player who had had more than enough of Murphy and he had the courage to stand up for what he thought was right.

Also to be taken into consideration was the fact that Murphy gave Kling an indefinite leave of absence for 1909. With that in hand, it seems reasonable to assume that Johnny Kling had sufficient reason to believe he was not in violation of his contract. And for decades, the articles that were published about his being a holdout made no mention of the indefinite leave of absence. This information was buried away in major league archives, in the 1910 investigative report, released in 1911. The investigation came about after Johnny Kling applied for reinstatement. Why was this information not widely reported? And why did it take so many years for the truth to come out? We will never know.

In 1910, during and after the World Series between the Cubs and the Athletics, Johnny Kling was once again the recipient of bad publicity: unfounded bad publicity.

26. Setting the Record Straight

Philadelphia was clobbering Chicago, and Frank Chance got it into his head that Kling was allowing Mack's boys to steal his signs. Convinced he was correct without any proof, Chance refused to allow Kling to conduct his usual campaign behind the bat and removed him from the last two games. Kling was thus singled out as the scapegoat for the loss, as discussed in chapter 10.

Christy Mathewson talked about how the Cub team blamed Kling, hardly talking to him and fixing the loss of the series on him. Christy also pointed out that Kling changed the signs three times. He talked about Connie Mack's clever strategy and pointed out what really happened and why the Cub pitchers lost the World Series, not Kling. Nevertheless, the bad PR followed Kling.

Although there is no hard evidence, it is not difficult to surmise the thinking and feelings that Kling generated in 1933 when he bought Muehlebach Field and the Kansas City Blues and immediately desegregated seating. White and colored signs had been ongoing since the inception of the ballpark, and now Kling refused to segregate seating. The signs came down.

Two weeks later, a Kling property, the Dickinson Theater, burned to the ground. Ray Elder, historian and archivist for the Kansas City Fire Department, checked Chillicothe newspapers two weeks after the fire looking for mention of the cause or an investigative report of the fire. He found none.

Imagine, a seven hour fire where firemen from adjacent towns had to help put out the flames of a blaze that left the theater a mass of twisted steel and damaged the adjacent Strand Hotel—no report of a cause and no remarks about a pending investigation.

Also imagine the Ku Klux Klan at a time when its membership was climbing to two million with judges, police chiefs and local politicians as members. The reason for the absence of an investigation or the mention of a cause is left to your imagination.

When Kling sold the K.C. Blues to Col. Jacob Ruppert, owner of the Yankees, the White and Colored signs went right back up, and it wasn't until Jackie Robinson came along almost 30 years later that the color barrier was broken. It seems fair to say that Kling's integration of seating at the Kansas City ballpark did not sit well with the baseball establishment. His act was significant in light of the times and it is indeed unfortunate that this has been overlooked by many baseball historians.[12]

Did this generate bad publicity for Johnny Kling? A good possibility. But in view of his courageous position, a position that attacked discrimination, he should be recognized and applauded for what he did. He truly was a man before his time.

In regard to Kling's ancestry, his Jewish heritage was amply discussed in previous chapters and it is only appropriate to say that he should once again be recognized as the first Jewish ballplayer of the 20th century.

The history of a major league player must be preserved in a factual manner. It simply does not make sense to alter history because of a single letter, no matter who wrote it. Lillian Kling's claim should have been pursued. The facts were out there. All one had to do was to dig deep and find them.

If not, it is easy to see the consequences. The course of events resulting from Lillian's letter in 1969 stripped Johnny Kling of his Jewish ancestry. Prior to Lillian's letter, he was listed in *The Jew in American Sports* as a member of the Hebrew race. The 1985 edition published by Hippocrene Books no longer listed Johnny Kling. It is time to restore his ancestry.

Conclusion

Before answering that essential question as to whether Johnny Kling was great enough to be in the Hall of Fame, it is important to understand why he is not. Once this is done, his achievements will be cited, and the question one must then ask is, does he deserve entry?

Years before the Hall of Fame became a reality, and years before the first player entered the sacred shrine, Kling went from fame to infamy when baseball's National Commission submitted its *Seventh Annual Report* in 1911. This report was promulgated to the president of the National and American leagues, to the president of each National and American League club, and to the secretary of the National Association.

Page 37 said, "This case has been given so much attention by the press and the baseball public in general, that the Commission in passing thereon, deems it advisable to go into all of the details in connection therewith." But Messrs. Lynch and Herrmann, who signed the report, did not go into all of the details. If they had, they would have found proof that Kling did not violate his 1909 contract.

The commission reported that on April 26, 1909, President Murphy granted Kling "an indefinite leave of absence." They also cited testimony from Murphy and concluded that he gave Kling a verbal indefinite leave, and followed it up in writing on or about March 4, 1909. Messrs. Lynch and Herrmann could not explain why there were two leaves of absence on two different dates. They said, "But be this as it may, this purported leave of absence should have no bearing whatever in this case."

They were wrong. The two dates had everything to do with the contract violation aspect of this case. All Lynch and Herrmann had to do to understand the significance was to examine Kling's contract that Murphy dated March 19, 1907. (Item C of that contract can be seen in Appendix B.)

Since Kling had to report 40 days prior to April 15, he would have had to report on or about March 6, but since he was given an indefinite leave of absence on that date, Kling did not have to report. He was therefore not in violation of his contract because in accordance with the terms of the contract, President Murphy had the authority to grant him indefinite leave. By giving Kling a second leave on April 26, Murphy managed to confuse the commission regarding the contract violation issue.

The commission members went so far as to say, "The absence of this player from the team, no doubt, would, and in fact did, in our judgement, affect the standing of the club in the championship race." This statement has been oft repeated in baseball literature, and to this day, Kling has been the fall guy for the Cubs' failure to win the 1909 pennant. And for over 90 years, baseball articles and texts have given Johnny Kling a bad rap by consistently claiming he refused to honor his 1909 contract unless he was paid more money.

In addition to the bad press about his 1909 contract, Johnny Kling was blamed, and received bad press for, the Cubs' loss of the 1910 World Series. As discussed in Chapter 10, the Cubs lost the series for other reasons. But Kling was singled out as the scapegoat, and it seems fair to say that his teammates still harbored resentment against him for the 1909 loss of the pennant, thus making it easier for them to blame him for the 1910 loss of the World Series.

When Kling desegregated seating at Muelebach Field in 1933, something unheard of back then, he must have raised a great deal of resentment from the world of baseball. This speculation, although not proven, is supported by the reintroduction of the black and white signs as soon as the he sold the Kansas City Blues and the ballpark to the Yankees. It seems reasonable to say that Kling's act of defiance towards the accepted practices of white and black seating in ballparks was not forgotten by those with the power to influence the acceptance or rejection of candidates for the Hall of Fame.

In addition to bad PR, Kling was a Jew. And anti–Semitism was, in all probability, a factor when consideration was given as to who was in and who was out when candidates were selected.

With all that's been said, it is important to remember that baseball can be cruel and unforgiving once a great player is viewed as having besmirched his reputation as well as the national game. Consider Pete Rose. The likelihood that he will gain entry into the Hall of Fame appears to be remote. Perhaps that is the way it should be, who knows? But Rose committed an act that was a clear violation, and initially he tried to squirm out from under the charge of betting on his own team by lying about it. Kling, on the other hand, was falsely accused. And it is time to reconsider the facts of his case, to look at his record and to judge from that alone as to whether or not he deserves entry.

Although we cannot crawl into the minds of everyone who was anyone in baseball during the deadball era, historical records clearly show that

Conclusion

Johnny Kling was recognized as the premier catcher of his day. The very best. Everyone wanted him.

He was hailed as one of the smartest backstops the game ever produced. His knowledge of batting weaknesses of opposing teams was little short of uncanny. He likewise was a veritable wonder at pegging the hit-and-run play, base stealing, and breaking up those offensive methods by opposing teams.

From 1902 through 1908 Kling led the National League in fielding percentage four times, putouts six, assists twice and double plays once. He stole 23 bases twice — the only National League catcher to top 20 steals more than once. He led the Cubs in triples twice. Although not a slugger, he often got timely hits to win ball games. Kling's reputation for throwing out runners trying to steal has not been overexaggerated. He was the only catcher who stopped Ty Cobb's base running, who pinned Ty down.[1] He had a club record of 189 assists in 1903 and it is still a team record. His strong throwing arm established a lifetime record of assists in major league play and it has not been matched by Hall of Fame catchers who played more seasons than Kling.

	Seasons Played	Lifetime Assists
Johnny Bench	17	982
Yogi Berra	20	693
Roger Bresnahan	17	1235
Roy Campanella	10	384
Mickey Cochrane	13	721
Bill Dickey	18	804
Carlton Fisk	19	916
Gabby Hartnett	20	1125
Johnny Kling	13	1546
Ernie Lombardi	17	717

He was the most important cog in the Cub machine, the Mr. Brains who led the team to four pennants and two World Series championships in five years. His handling of pitchers and overall field generalship was superb. With Kling behind the plate, the Cubs led the National League in ERA seven times in nine years, and Noisy John's masterful handling of the great Chicago pitching staff was an extremely important factor.[2]

His teammate, Johnny Evers, known for being one of the smartest players of all time, was asked to name the greatest players of that era. He put Kling on the list with Hall of Fame immortals Honus Wagner, Christy Mathewson, Ty Cobb, Tris Speaker and Mordecai Brown.

"He was a holler type guy and expert at the snap throw from the crouch," Evers said. "In the particular of catching runners in crucial moments of games, John Kling was the best in the business."[3]

What the quarterback is to the football team, the catcher is on the diamond, except that one directs his team while attacking and the other while on defense. Brains are the chief essential. Unless a man can think fast and clearly, can watch with instinctive intelligence his opponents' every little movement, many of which really do have a meaning of their own, and can anticipate any play that is likely to come up, he is not a star catcher.[4]

But Johnny Kling had all of these things and more. He was the secret weapon of the Cubs' dynasty of 1906–1910. With his brains and ability behind the bat in 1906, the Chicago National team established an amazing win-loss record of 116–36 (.763). The best the great Philadelphia Americans could do in 1929 with Jimmie Foxx, Al Simmons and Mickey Cochrane was 104–48 (.693). The best the great Yankee teams could do: in 1939 with Joe DiMaggio, Lou Gehrig and Bill Dickey, 104–45 (.702); in 1956 with Mickey Mantle and Yogi Berra, 97–57 (.630).

In 1906–1907, the Cubs went on to win a consecutive two-year record of 223 games. It still stands. The years 1906, '07 and '08 saw the Cubs win 322 games—another record. And although Kling did not play in 1909, he was back in 1910 and a five year record of 530 wins was established. The six-year tally, 1905–1910, was chalked up at 622. After 93 years and despite the addition of more games to the schedule, the Cubs still hold all of those records.

And they did it without a "Sultan of Swat," without a "Jolting Joe DiMaggio" and without a 565-foot blast from a Mickey Mantle bat. Based on this, it seems fair to say that the Cubs of 1905–1910 had one of the most outstanding teams in the history of baseball. And Johnny Kling's brilliant leadership led that team into the record books. In essence, he was its heart and soul.

Consider the number of pennants and World Series championships won by teams with the following Hall of Fame catchers leading the way, as compared to Johnny Kling:

	Pennants	*World Series*
Johnny Bench	0	0
Roger Bresnahan	1	1
Roy Campanella	5	1
Mickey Cochrane	5	0
Carlton Fisk	1	0
Gabby Hartnett	3	0
Johnny Kling	4	2
Ernie Lombardi	2	1
Ray Schalk	1	1

Having said all of this, and with available records showing the impact Johnny Kling had on his team's success, it seems fair to say that Kling belongs in the Hall of Fame. After all, when it comes down to it, baseball, as once defined, is not about "a bunch of durn fools hittin' a ball and a bunch of other durn fools chasin' it." It is about winning and losing. It is about coming down to the wire and taking home the flag. It is about fighting it out for the number one spot. It is about winning the world championship. Johnny Kling helped the Cubs do that. If that ain't great, what is? And if that doesn't entitle him to entry into the Hall of Fame, what will?

APPENDIX A: A WRITER'S REGARD

William F. Kirk, a nationally known poet and humorist, was born in Mankato, Minn., April 29, 1877. He was a graduate of the Chippewa Falls, Wis., high school. He was well known in his early days as a writer of verse and as a writer of baseball. Coming out of the northwest, where he had built a reputation for himself for his verses of folklore in Swedish dialect, he began his career in New York, with the Hearst organization, writing baseball and other sports for the New York American *and the* New York Evening Journal. *He put into verse many episodes of sport life and competition, and some of his baseball poems were widely copied and quoted. His verses were syndicated by the International Features Syndicate for a number of years. His health declined in 1923, and he died in his hometown of Chippewa Falls at age 50. The Eastern-based Kirk held Midwesterner Kling in high regard, as the pieces below demonstrate, and suggest that Kling's fame extended beyond the region he played in.*

Strolls Through Sportville

By William F. Kirk

A Marvelous Backstop

During the first few years of this well-known and justly celebrated twentieth century, baseball was rich in catchers of extraordinary skill. Three were operating at the same time in those days—Lou Criger, John Kling and Roger Bresnahan.

Criger and Bresnahan were splendid backstops in every sense, but we always thought Johnny Kling was about the smoothest piece of machinery that ever worked behind the bat. He was not so aggressive as Roger Bresnahan—nobody ever was. He might have lacked a little of Criger's grace now and then. But he was aggressive enough, and he was graceful—and he was STEADY.

Kling was at the zenith of his fame when the great THREE-FINGER Brown was shining, and he handled Mordecai's offerings with masterly skill and cooperation. His throwing to bases was as near perfect as human throwing could possibly be. Time and again he pegged to second base the second he caught the ball, throwing from the position he had assumed before the catch and thus not wasting a second of valuable time. He was crafty and cool and courageous, and he never gave up the ship.

It is small wonder that so brainy a ballplayer has been successful in the bigger game of life. During his active years on the diamond he easily earned a place among the Immortals of Baseball.

Billiards and Kling

Some very good persons teach youngsters at school
To beware of such evils as billiards and pool.
That talk would not go with one catcher of fame
For John Kling thinks billiards a mighty good game.
When John quit the Cubs in a distant year
And wound up a glorious baseball career,
For some walk in life he proceeded to scout
And in a short time he had figured it out.
At this time he is flush, sitting tight in K. C.
With a billiard and pool hall from mortgages free.
He came to the front as his friends knew he would
And he's two hundred thousand or more to the good.
If you make Kansas City drop in and see Kling,
Once famous Cub catcher now billiard ball king.
This may sound like an ad, but 'tis written to show
That sometimes ex-ball players clean up real dough!
Our head would become too large for our hat
If an ex-baseball writer could clean up like that!
Great stars, when they quit, do not fade out like dubs.
Which is proven by Kling, once a star with the Cubs!

Appendix B:
Documents and Letters

Charles W. Murphy
PRESIDENT
CHICAGO LEAGUE BALL CLUB
CHICAGO

1115 Masonic Temple, Feb. 1st, 1906.

John Kling, Esq.,
   1000 Monroe Ave.,
      Kansas City, Mo.

My dear Kling:--

    In response to your letter of Jan. 31st, permit me to say that I am glad you are pleased with the diamond-studded emblem which you received from the National Commission for the triumph of the Chicago Club in the post season series with the White Sox. It is also a pleasure to know that Mrs. Kling and your daughter are in good health.

    In reference to salary I desire to say that when I sent you a contract for $3500.00, I did so against the advice that I had received, as I had been told that you should play for $3000.00. However, I took it upon myself to send you a contract for the same salary,--by far the largest that any man on our club receives,-- that you received in 1905. As you doubtless know, most of the clubs are cutting down salaries, and if it were not for the fact that you have rendered such loyal service to the Chicago Club, and keep yourself in such good condition, I most certainly would have expected you to have signed for a great deal less than what your contract calls for. I wish to request in this connection that the terms of your contract be kept to yourself, as it would cause endless illfeeling, perhaps, among the other members of the club, if they knew you were receiving $3500.00. Of course you know

A Page 1, February 1, 1906, letter from Murphy to Kling (courtesy James Dickerson).

...at in addition to this you will have your post season money, which will probably bring your entire earnings up over the sum you say you thought you should get. I do not desire to start in with the Chicago Club by cutting salaries, but I wish to tell you, from the knowledge that I have of the New York, Cincinnati and other club pay rolls, that you are receiving princely pay, compared to what other men are getting in the same line of work. I have a very high regard for you personally and look upon you as one of the best men in the country in your position, and in Moran you will doubtless have a good running mate for 1906. I wish it were in my power to pay you five or six thousand dollars a year, but the salaries of the players must be regulated by the amount of money that comes in at the gates, and the Chicago Club is paying you all now, if not a little more, than it really can afford to pay. However I will stand by the contract that was previously made with you, because, as I said, I do not want to begin to cut salaries, even if you are receiving so much more than any of the other players.

Trusting that you are well and happy and that you will sign your contract some time between now and March 1st and send same to me, I am,

       Very truly yours,

          Charles W. Murphy,
            President.

T.

A Page 2, February 1, 1906, letter from Murphy to Kling (courtesy James Dickerson).

B Kling's March 29, 1906, contract signed by Ted Sullivan for Chicago (courtesy James Dickerson).

Articles of Agreement, between the

Chicago League Ball Club,

of the city of Chicago, in the State of Illinois, a club member of a League known as the "National League of Professional Base Ball Clubs," party of the first part, and

John G. Kling, of the city of

Kansas City, in the State of Missouri, party of the second part,

Witnesseth:

1. That in consideration of the faithful performance, by party of the second part, of the conditions, covenants, undertakings and promises hereinafter set forth, including the option in first party to terminate this contract, the said party of the first part agrees to pay unto second party the sum of Three Thousand Dollars, per season, payable as follows: In semi-monthly instalments on the first and fifteenth of each month during the period covered by this contract; unless this contract shall be terminated by the first party while second party be "abroad" with the ball club of the first party for the purpose of playing games, in which event the instalment then falling due shall be paid on the first week day after the return "home" of the ball club.

2. Said party of the second part agrees to perform for party of first part, and for no other party during the period of this contract (unless with the consent of said first party) such duties pertaining to the exhibition of the game of base ball as may be required of him by said party of the first part, at such reasonable times and places as said party of the first part may designate, for the National League season for the year 1907, beginning on or about the fifteenth day of April, 1907, and ending on or about the fifteenth day of October, 1907, which period of time shall constitute the life of this contract, unless sooner terminated in accordance with the further provisions of this contract.

3. Party of the first part may, from time to time, during the continuance of this contract, establish reasonable rules for the government of its players "at home" and "abroad" and such rules shall be a part of this contract as fully as if herein written, and binding upon second party hereto; and for violation of these rules and for any conduct impairing the faithful and thorough discharge of the duties incumbent upon second party, may impose reasonable fines upon second party and deduct the amount thereof from any money due, or to become due, second party herein.

4. It is further agreed that should second party be disabled or his ability to perform his duties be impaired at any time during the term herein prescribed, the said party of the first part may deduct from the amount then due or to become due under this contract, such proportion thereof as the period of said disability or impairment may bear to the term herein prescribed; but no such deduction shall be made by reason of any accident or injury received by second party while in performance of his regular duties under the direction of first party, unless such injury or accident shall wholly or partially incapacitate second party for a period of fifteen days, in which event this contract may be terminated at the option of first party.

5. It is further agreed, should party of the second part become disabled, as provided in the preceding section, that he will submit himself to medical examination and treatment by a regular physician, in good standing, to be selected by the first party, and such examination when made at the request of first party, shall be at the expense of said first party, unless made necessary by some act or conduct of second party contrary to the terms of this agreement or rules and regulations made under it.

6. It is further understood and agreed, that the said party of the first part shall furnish the said party of the second part with two complete uniforms, exclusive of shoes, for which the said party of the first part shall be allowed the sum of $30 toward the cost thereof, to be deducted from the wages or salary herein prescribed. And the said party of the first part shall provide and furnish the said party of the second part, while "abroad" or traveling with the "nine" or team in other cities, with proper board, lodging, and pay all proper and necessary traveling expenses.

7. In order to enable the party of the second part to fit himself for the duties necessary under the terms of this contract, the said party of the first part may require the said party of the second part to report for practice at such place as the party of the first part may designate and participate in such exhibition contests as may be arranged by said party of the first part for a period of 40 days prior to the 15th day of April, the party of the first part to pay the actual hotel and traveling expenses of the said party of the second part, from the city of Chicago during said period. In event of the failure of the party of the second part to report for practice a penalty of at least one hundred dollars may be imposed by party of first part, same to be deducted from the compensation stipulated in this contract.

8. It is further understood and agreed, that the party of the first part may, at any time after the beginning and prior to the completion of the period of this contract, give the party of the second part ten days written notice to end and determine all its liabilities and obligations under the contract, in which event all liabilities and obligations undertaken by said party of the first part, in this contract, shall at once cease and determine at the expiration of said ten days; the said party of the second part shall thereupon be also freed and discharged from compensation. If such notice be given to the party of the second part while "abroad" with the club, he shall be entitled to his necessary traveling expenses to the city of Chicago.

9. It is further understood and agreed between both parties to this contract that they will respect all of the provisions and conditions of the National Agreement.

In Witness Whereof, The said party of the first part hath hereunto caused its common seal to be affixed and these presents to be subscribed by the president of said club, and the said party of the second part has hereunto set his hand and seal this 19th day of March, A.D., 1907.

[signature: Charles W. Murphy], President.

COMMON SEAL

Chicago League Ball Club.

_____, Player.

WITNESSES PRESENT:

C Kling's March 19, 1907, contract signed by Charles W. Murphy (courtesy James Dickerson).

LAW OFFICE OF
D... GEAR
... BLDG.
AN ...TY, MO.

June 17, 1907

Mr. John G. Kling,
1115 Masonic Temple,
Chicago, Illinois.

Friend John,-

Yours at hand. I enclose herein the real estate contract signed by you and Mr. Heidleberger which reads that you are to pay so much and assume the interest from November 19, 1906. I went to see him when he first called me up and before ever I wrote you about pro rating the interest, but he called attention to this clause and said that you were to step right into his shoes as this was the way the entire piece of property was taken and he was merely turning so much of it over to you. He has paid the city tax for 1907 in amount $11.61, so send me your check for $29.25 to cover the taxes and interest $17.64.

I thought it was understood at the time we made the deal that we were to divide the net profits on account of the low figure at which the property was bought, but if you did not so understand it, why make the contracts you now have read onethird for my part, as per your letter, and we will be satisfied. You and Mrs. K. both better sign one of the contracts and return to me, also return the enclosed contract unless you want to keep it there, but better keep all the papers together here in the vault.

I am working on the horse matter. Saw a horse man at Lees Summit yesterday and he is coming in to look at your horse. There is not much of a market for this class of horses, unless you get a party who wants fast horses.

We go down to City Hall Friday to pass the ordinances opening both Broadway and Washington streets through the 43d street property, and will get at things later. This vacation of streets with the City seems to be a slow matter.

With best wishes,

Dale Gear

D June 17, 1907, letter from Dale Gear to John Kling (courtesy James Dickerson).

Chicago Ills. 5-27-1908

Mr. Aug. Herrmann,
Cincinnati Ohio.

My dear Mr. Herrmann:-
While talking to Chance a few days ago, I informed him that I would like to go to Cincinnati, providing my deal with Mr. East goes through all O.K. He didn't seem at all favorable when I first approached the subject but after talking with him awhile and telling him of my future plans. He warmed up a little saying he didn't want to stand in my way, and that he would like to favor me in any way he possibly could providing he could make a satisfactory trade.
I sincerely hope he will make a deal with you in the near future, as I am

E Page 1, May 27, 1908, letter from Kling to Herrmann (courtesy National Baseball Hall of Fame).

anxious to come to Cincinnati. I have been expecting to hear from you regarding the trade, but suppose Mr. East has neglected to send it over, or it wasn't made out properly.

Hurrah for the "Reds." hope they keep up the good work, and finish next to the "Cubs."

Waiting an early reply, and with kindest regards, I am

Very truly yours,

John G. Kling

P.S. 230 Ashland Blvd.

E Page 2, May 27, 1908, letter from Kling to Herrmann (courtesy National Baseball Hall of Fame).

Articles of Agreement, between the ....
.... Chicago League Ball Club, ...
of the City of ... Chicago, ..., in the State of ...... Illinois, ...
a club member of a League known as the "National League of Professional Base Ball Clubs," party of the first part,
and .... John G. Kling, ... of the City of
. Kansas City, ... in the State of .... Mo., ... party of the second part.

Witnesseth:

1. That in consideration of the faithful performance, by the party of the second part, of the conditions, covenants, undertakings and promises hereinafter set forth, including the option in first party to terminate this contract, the said party of the first part agrees to pay unto second party the sum of ....
. Forty-Five Hundred Dollars, ($4500.00) .... per season, payable as follows: In semi-monthly installments on the first and fifteenth of each month during the period covered by this contract; unless this contract shall be terminated by the first party while the second party be "abroad" with the ball club of the first party for the purpose of playing games, in which event the installment then falling due shall be paid on the first week day after the return "home" of the ball club.

2. Said party of the second part agrees to perform for party of first part, and for no other party during the period of this contract (unless with the consent of said first party) such duties pertaining to the exhibition of the game of base ball as may be required of him by said party of the first part, at such reasonable times and places as said party of the first part may designate, for the National League season for the year 1910, beginning on or about the ..... 14th .... day of .... April ...., 1910, and ending on or about the ... 15th .... day of October, 1910, which period of time shall constitute the life of this contract, unless sooner terminated in accordance with the further provisions thereof.

3. Party of the first part may, from time to time, during the continuance of this contract, establish reasonable rules for the government of its players "at home" and "abroad" and such rules shall be a part of this contract as fully as if herein written, and binding upon second party hereto; and for violation of these rules and for any conduct impairing the faithful and thorough discharge of the duties incumbent upon second party, may impose reasonable fines upon second party and deduct the amount thereof from any money due, or to become due, to second party herein. Party of the first part may also suspend the party of the second part for violation of any rules so established and during such suspension the party of the second part shall not be entitled to any compensation under this contract.

4. It is further agreed that should second party be disabled or his ability to perform his duties be impaired at any time during the term herein prescribed, the said party of the first part may deduct from the amount then due or to become due under this contract, such proportion thereof as the period of said disability or impairment may bear to the term herein prescribed; but no such deduction shall be made by reason of any accident or injury received by second party while in performance of his regular duties under the direction of first party, unless such injury or accident shall wholly or partly incapacitate second party for a period of fifteen days, in which event this contract may be terminated at the option of first party.

5. It is further agreed, should party of the second part become disabled, as provided in the preceding section, that he will submit himself to medical examination and treatment by a regular physician, in good standing, to be selected by the first party, and such examination when made at the request of the first party, shall be at the expense of said first party, unless made necessary by some act or conduct of second party contrary to the terms of this agreement or rules or regulations made under it.

6. It is further understood and agreed, that the said party of the first part shall furnish the said party of the second part with two complete uniforms, exclusive of shoes, for which the said party of the first part shall be allowed the sum of $30 toward the cost thereof, to be deducted from the wages or salary herein prescribed. And the said party of the first part shall provide and furnish the said party of the second part, while "abroad" or traveling with the "nine" or team in other cities, with proper board, lodging, and pay all proper and necessary traveling expenses.

7. In order to enable the party of the second part to fit himself for the duties necessary under the terms of this contract, the said party of the first part may require the said party of the second part to report for practice at such place as the party of the first part may designate and participate in such exhibition contests as may be arranged by said party of the first part for a period of .... days prior to the .... day of
............................, the party of the first part to pay the actual hotel and traveling expenses of the said party of the second part, from the city of .... during said period. In event of the failure of the party of the second part to report for practice a penalty of at least one hundred dollars may be imposed by party of first part, same to be deducted from the compensation stipulated in this contract.

8. It is further understood and agreed, that the party of the first part may, at any time after the beginning and prior to the completion of the period of this contract, give the party of the second part ten days written notice to end and determine all its liabilities and obligations under this contract, in which event all liabilities and obligations undertaken by party of the first part, in this contract, shall at once cease and determine at the expiration of said ten days; the said party of the second part shall thereupon be also freed and discharged from compensation. If such notice be given to the party of the second part while "abroad" with the club, he shall be entitled to his necessary traveling expenses to the city of .... Chicago.

9. The party of the second part will not be permitted at any time, either during the playing season, or before the commencement or after the close thereof to participate in any exhibition base ball games, indoor base ball, basket ball, or football, except that the consent of the party of the first part has first been secured in writing.

10. It is further understood and agreed between both parties to this contract that they will respect and abide by the Constitution, rules and edicts of said League, subject only to an appeal for final adjudication to the National Commission, and also respect and abide by all of the provisions and conditions of the National Agreement and rules of the National Commission.

In Witness Whereof, The said party of the first part hath hereunto caused its common seal to be affixed and these presents to be subscribed by the president of said club, and the said party of the second part has hereunto set his hand and seal this ...... 4th .... day of .... May, ... A. D. 1910.

.... Charles W. Murphy ...., President,
.... Chicago League Ball Club ....

[SEAL]

.... John G. Kling ....
Player. [SEAL]

WITNESSES PRESENT:

F   May 4, 1910, one-year contract signed by Murphy and Kling (courtesy James Dickerson).

Kling's Billiard Parlors
12th and Baltimore

JOHNNY KLING

BENNIE ALLEN

PHONES: HOME 2815 MAIN
BELL 2815 MAIN

Kansas City, Mo., March. 20th. 1912.

Mr. August Herrmann.
    Wiggins Block.
        Cincinnati, Ohio.

My Dear Mr. Herrmann:-

    As I wired you last night it is simply out of the question to leave here and join your team at this time. I have exhausted every effort to secure the only man here capable of handling my affairs, but he insisted upon a five years contract at such an exhorbitant figure, that it was absolutely impossible to do business with him. I regret exceedingly my inability to help you out this year, as I think you have a club that will be up in the race, and know that I could have been of great assistance to you, but my business here demands my first consideration and simply can't leave it at present. However if I can see my way clear and you should still want me, might help you out later in the season.

    Wishing you a most successful season and with kindest regards, I am,

                Yours very truly,

                John G Kling.

G March 20, 1912, letter from Kling to Herrmann (National Baseball Hall of Fame).

JOHNNY KLING   BENNIE ALLEN

Kling's Billiard Parlors
12th and Baltimore

PHONES: HOME 2815 MAIN
        BELL 2815 MAIN

Kansas City, Mo., April. 17th. 1913.

Mr. August Herrman,
    Wiggins Block,
        Cincinnati, Ohio.

My Dear Mr. Herrman:—

    I have at last arrainged my business so that I could join your club about the 25th. should you still desire my services. I have been training the past week, and another week will put me in first class shape.

    As per my conversation with Mr. Williams, I would only consider playing this year. So if you will give me my unconditional release at the close of this season I will accept your terms. I may want to buy a club next season in the Western League and that is my reason for asking for my release. Should I continue to play Major League ball I would naturally play with your club.

    Hoping to hear from you at your earliest convience,
I remain,

                            Yours very truly,
                            John G. Kling

H April 17, 1913, leeter from Kling to Herrmann (National Baseball Hall of Fame).

OFFICE OF
CUBAN CIGAR CO.
J. ADAM SCHMIDT, PROP.

Manufacturers of **High Grade Havana Cigars**
Telephone Canal 635

2nd, 3rd, 4th and 5th Floors Ohio Building,
111 SIXTH AVENUE, EAST
Office: Second Floor Front

Cincinnati, Ohio, May 2nd, 1913.

Hon. Aug. Herrmann.

Dear Sir:-

    I am delighted that you were successfull in getting Johnny Kling, If there is anything in a pitcher he will get it out of him, This is the first catcher that you have since you are President and I hope that you will develope two more like him.

    Pay attention to the catching department and you will finally land the championship, with best wishes.

    I am.

I May 2, 1913, letter from Schmidt to Herrmann (National Baseball Hall of Fame).

JOHNNY KLING   BENNIE ALLEN

Kling's Billiard Parlors
12th and Baltimore

PHONES: HOME 2815 MAIN
        BELL 2815 MAIN

Kansas City, Mo., Jan. 21, 14.

Mr. Garry Herrmann,

    Cincinnati, Ohio.

My dear Mr. Herrmann:-

    Your very kind favor of the 16th inst. and notification, under date of Jan. 19th, of my unconditional release by the Cincinnati Club duly received and wish to thank you and assure you of my appreciation of your very kind treatment of me. If at any time I may be of any service to you, don't fail to call upon me.

    With kindest regards and very best wishes, I am,

            Very truly yours,

                John G. Kling.

J January 21, 1914, letter from Kling to Herrmann (National Baseball Hall of Fame).

MAY 24, 2000

As a young boy living in Orange, New Jersey I was a RABID BASEBALL FAN. My FAVORITE TEAM THEN WAS THE NEW YORK GIANTS OF MEL OTT, CARL HUBBELL etc. playing in The Polo Grounds in New York City. I was very fortunate To get To The Polo Grounds occasionally To see the great stars of YESTERYEAR and especially the NY Giant - Brooklyn Dodger Series.

I checked The Box Scores religiously of all the major League Teams. One day I came across the name of JOHN KLING, CATCHER for the CHICAGO CUBS. Having the same last name, and also my confirmation name was John, I wondered if we might not be related. Kling did not seem to be a common name at that time. I was awe struck as a young lad To find a MAJOR League ball player with the same name as mine. I wrote to JOHN KLING c/o of The CHICAGO CUBS and asked if he would send me an autographed Picture of himself. I was never able To ascertain whether or not we were related somewhere down the line.

The Picture enclosed is A copy of that same picture that I received from John Kling some 65 years ago. I may be off on the exact date as I will be 75 years old this June and I must have been around Ten years old when I received the Picture.

I have the original autographed Picture and have kept it in good condition all these years. I am extremely happy To share my story and this picture with the Legacy of John Kling CATCHER CHICAGO CUBS. Please keep me informed of the events surrounding the Coopers Town installation.

Sincerely yours
Franklin Kling
107 SYCAMORE AVE
LIVINGSTON, NJ 07039

K May 24, 2000, letter from Frank Kling (courtesy Frank Kling).

Chapter Notes

Introduction

1. Kirk, William F., "Old Stars." *New York Evening Journal* (Jan. 2, 1923).
2. Grayson, Harry, "Johnny Kling Considered Smartest Catcher of All." *Zanesville Signal* (June 18, 1943).
3. Evers, John J., and Hugh S. Fullerton. *Touching Second* (Chicago: Reilly and Britton, 1910), p. 91.
4. *Ibid.*, pp. 91–99.
5. Honig, Donald. *The Greatest Catchers of All Time* (Dubuque: Wm. C. Brown, 1991), p. 9.
6. Hirshberg, Al. *Baseball's Greatest Catchers* (New York: G.P. Putnam's Sons, 1966), p. 22.
7. Postal, Bernard, Jesse Silver and Roy Silver. *Encyclopedia of Jews in Sports.* (New York: Bloch Publishing, 1965), p. 44.
8. Wagner, Hans., "My Grand All-American Team." *Los Angeles Times* (January 8, 1924).
9. Dickerson, James, Park Ranger. U.S. Army Corps of Engineers, Longview–Blue Springs Project Office, Kansas City, Missouri. Scrapbook items, Kling Collection. Uncredited (undated). "Johnny Kling Was Uncanny Judge of Pitcher's Condition — Wagner." By Hans Wagner. Donated by Mr. and Mrs. Ken Eccles.
10. *Ibid.*
11. *Ibid.*
12. Ribalow, Harold U., and Meir Z. Ribalow. *Jewish Baseball Stars* (New York: Hippocrene Books, 1984), p. 18.
13. Barton, George A., "Johnny Kling Bobs Up in Limelight." *The Minneapolis Tribune* (May 10, 1930).

Chapter 1

1. 1880 U.S. Census. Westport, Jackson, Missouri Family History Library Film 1254694, NA Film Number T9-0694, p. 257 B.
2. Website, http://www.springgrove.org. Interment Record No. 4123, Lorch, Charles.
3. E-mail, July 25, 2004. Phil Nuxhall, Historian, Heritage Foundation, Spring Grove Cemetery.
4. LDS Microfilm, Marriages 1855–1856, Batch No. M869146, Source Call No. 0344469V. B 9-10.
5. Herbert, Jeffrey G. *Index of Death Notices and Marriage Notices Appearing in the* Cincinnati Daily Gazette, *1827–1881* (Cincinnati: Hamilton County Chapter, The Ohio Genealogical Society, 1992).
6. Website. "Germany Research Outline." http://www.familysearch.org/Eng/Search/guide/Germany14.asp.
7. Sarna, Jonathon D., and Nancy H. Klein. *The Jews of Cincinnati* (Cincinnati: Center for the Study of the American Jewish Experience, 1989), p. 3.
8. E-mail address, Bavarian-ancestors-d@rootsweb.com.
9. Marcus, Jacob Rader. *The American Jew: 1585–1990* (New York: Carlson Publishing, 1995), p. 93.
10. Sarna, Jonathon D., and Nancy H. Klein. *The Jews of Cincinnati* (Cincinnati: Center for the Study of the American Jewish Experience, 1989), p. 34.
11. Marcus, Jacob Rader. *The Jew in the American World* (Detroit: Wayne State Univ. Press, 1996), p. 190.
12. LDS Microfilm Reel FHL 175474, New York Passenger List, 11 Aug.–31 Aug. 1852.
13. Microfilm reel 175474. *Passenger lists 11 Aug. 1852–31 Aug. 1852.* (National Archives, Family History Library Catalogue, 2002.)

Chapter 2

1. Sarna, Jonathon D., and Nancy H. Klein. *The Jews of Cincinnati* (Cincinnati: Center for

the Study of the American Jewish Experience, 1989), p. 7.
2. *Ibid.*, pp. 3–7.
3. Williams, C.S. *Cincinnati Phone Directory* (Cincinnati: Williams College Hall Publishers, 1855), p. 123.
4. Herbert, Jeffery G. *Restored Hamilton County, Ohio Marriages, 1850–1859* (Bowie: Heritage Books, 1999), p. 203.
5. Sarna, Jonathon D., and Nancy H. Klein. *The Jews of Cincinnati* (Cincinnati: Center for the Study of the American Jewish Experience, 1989), p. 14.
6. Kurzweil, Arthur. *From Generation to Generation* (New York: Schocken Books, 1980), p. 156.
7. Website, www.jewishgen.org/cemetery/northamerica/ohcinn.html.
8. Sadleir, Steven S. *The Spiritual Seeker's Guide* (Costa Mesa: Allwon Publishing Co., 1992), p. 72.
9. LDS Microfilm Reel # 1510039. *St. John's Unitarian Baptismal Records, 1859.* Baptism Numbers 246 and 247.
10. Eban, Abba. *My People: The Story of the Jews* (New York: Behrman House Inc., and Random House, 1968), p. 265.
11. 1880 U.S. Census. Westport, Jackson, Missouri Family History Library Film 1254694, NA Film Number T9-0694, p. 257 B.
12. Sarna, Jonathon D., and Nancy H. Klein. *The Jews of Cincinnati* (Cincinnati: Center for the Study of the American Jewish Experience, 1989), p. 9.

Chapter 3

1. *Ballenger and Hoye's Kansas City Directory*, 1876, p. 194.
2. Dennis, Clifford, Registrar. Certified Copy of Death Record. Office of Vital Statistics, Kansas City, Missouri.
3. *Ibid.*
4. Telushkin, Rabbi Joseph. *Biblical Literacy* (New York: William Morrow and Company, Inc., 1997), pp. 543–544.
5. Dickerson, James. Scrapbook news item and photo. Uncredited (undated). "John Kling." Donated by Ken and Bev Eccles.
6. *Kansas City Journal* (June 22, 1890), p. 2.
7. *Ibid.* (June 23, 1890), p. 2.
8. *Ibid.*
9. *Ibid.*
10. "Blues Management Builds for Championship," *Parkview Party News*, Muehlebach Field, Kansas City, Mo. (May 6, 1936).
11. Honig, *The Greatest Catchers of All Time*, p. 11.
12. *Chicago Tribune* (July 14, 1912), p. B 2.
13. Jackson, David, Director of Archives. Jackson County Historical Society. *Surveys and Plats of Properties of Kansas City, Mo.* (Philadelphia: G. M. Hopkins, 1891), plat 14 and 20.
14. Schechter, Gabriel, Library Associate. National Baseball Hall of Fame.
15. "Blues Management Builds for Championship," *Parkview Party News,* Muehlebach Field, Kansas City, Mo. (May 6, 1936).
16. Baseball Hall of Fame, Scrapbook article. "Kling, John Gradwohl 'Johnny,' 'Noisy.'" By David L. Porter. *Biographical Dictionary of American Sports, Baseball* (Cooperstown, Society for American Baseball Research, 1986), p. unlisted.
17. *Ibid.* "Famous Catcher Tells of His Holdout That Lasted All Season." By Dick Farrington (undated).
18. Baseball Hall of Fame Library, Scrapbook article. Uncredited (undated). "Daguerreotypes, John G. Kling."
19. *Tribune* (July 14, 1912), p. B 2.
20. *Ibid.*
21. Baseball Hall of Fame, Scrapbook bio from *Biographical Dictionary of American Sports.* By David L. Porter (undated). "Kling, John Gradwohl 'Johnny,' 'Noisy.'"
22. Baseball Hall of Fame Library, Scrapbook informational item. Uncredited (undated), "Johnny Kling."
23. Johnson, Lloyd, and Miles Wolff. *The Encyclopedia of Minor League Baseball.* (Durham: Baseball America, Inc., 1997), p. 91.
24. Baseball Hall of Fame Library, Scrapbook news item. Uncredited (undated). "Daguerreotypes, John G. Kling."
25. Honig, *The Greatest Catchers of All Time*, p. 23.
26. *Tribune* (July 14, 1912), p. B 2.
27. Golenbock, Peter. *Wrigleyville: A Magical History Tour of the Chicago Cubs* (New York: St. Martin's Griffin, 1999), p. 97.
28. *Chicago Daily News* (Oct. 4, 1910). "How I Got My Start," by John Kling.

Chapter 4

1. *Tribune* (Sept. 12, 1900), p. 6.
2. Evers, John J., and Hugh S. Fullerton. *Touching Second.* (Reilly and Britton, 1910), pp. 90–91.
3. *Ibid.*, pp. 89–92.
4. *Sporting Life* (Aug. 5, 1899), p. 1.
5. Golenbock, *Wrigleyville*, p. 113.
6. *Tribune* (Sept. 13, 1900), p. 8.
7. *Ibid.* (Sept. 12, 1900), p. 6.
8. *Ibid.*
9. *The Chicago Daily News* (Oct. 4, 1910), p. 6.
10. *Ibid., Sporting Extra* (Sept. 12, 1900), pp. 1–2.

11. *Tribune* (Sept. 13, 1900), p. 8.
12. Evers, John J., and Hugh S. Fullerton. *Touching Second* (Reilly and Britton, 1910), pp. 88–89.
13. *Tribune* (Sept. 14, 1900), p. 8.
14. *Ibid.* Sept. 16, 1900, p. 18.
15. *Ibid.* Sept. 17, 1900, p. 8.
16. "Johnny Kling's Views on Catching." *Baseball Magazine* (May 1911), p. 72.
17. *Ibid.*
18. *Ibid.* Sept. 23, 1900, p. 18.
19. *Ibid.* Sept. 26, 1900, p. 6.
20. *Ibid.* Oct. 1, 1900, p. 8.
21. *Ibid.* Oct. 7, 1900, p. 19.
22. Holtzman, Jerome, and George Vass. *The Chicago Cubs Encyclopedia* (Philadelphia: Temple Univ. Press, 1997), p. 22.
23. *Ibid.* Oct. 9, 1900, p. 6.
24. Hirshberg, Al. *Baseball's Greatest Catchers* (New York: G. P. Putnam's Sons, 1966), p. 24.
25. *Hoye's Kansas City Directory*, 1900, p. 567.
26. Baseball Hall of Fame Library, Scrapbook news item. Uncredited (undated). "Final Game, John G. Kling."

Chapter 5

1. *Tribune* (April 1, 1901), p. 8.
2. *Ibid.* April 11, 1901, p. 6.
3. *Ibid.* April 16, 1901, p. 6.
4. *Sunday Tribune*, Part Three, Sporting (April 14, 1901), p. 2.
5. *Ibid.*, p. 17.
6. *Tribune* (April 16, 1901), p. 6.
7. *Ibid.*, April 20, 1901, p. 4.
8. *Sunday Tribune* (April 21, 1901), pp. 17–18.
9. *Tribune* (April 28, 1901), p. 18.
10. Evers, John J., and Hugh S. Fullerton. *Touching Second*, pp. 97–98.
11. *Tribune* (April 30, 1901), p. 6.
12. *Tribune* (April 21, 1901), p. 6.
13. *Ibid.*
14. *Tribune* (June 7, 1901), p. 6.

Chapter 6

1. Golenbock, *Wrigleyville*, p. 97.
2. Stang, Mark. *Cubs Collection — 100 Years of Chicago Cubs Images* (Orange, Frazer Press, 2001), p. 8.
3. Bogen, Gil. *Tinker, Evers and Chance: A Triple Biography* (Jefferson, NC: McFarland, 2003), p. 39.
4. *Tribune* (April 7, 1902), p. 6.
5. *Ibid.* (April 10, 1902), p. 13.
6. *Chicago Daily News*, Sporting Extra (April 15, 1902), p. 1.
7. *Tribune* (April 4, 1902), p. 6.
8. *Ibid.* (April 17, 1902), p. 6.
9. *Ibid.* (April 13, 1902), p. 9.
10. *Ibid.*
11. Bogen, Gil. *Tinker, Evers and Chance* (Jefferson, NC: McFarland, 2003), p. 41.
12. *Ibid.*, p. 42.
13. *Chicago Daily News, Sporting Extra* (Jan. 26, 1903), p. 8.
14. *Washington Post*, "Gossip of the Diamond" (Feb. 1, 1903), p. E 32.
15. *Tribune* (Jan. 27, 1903), p. 8.
16. *Los Angeles Times* (March 25, 1903), p. 4.
17. *Tribune* (April 5, 1903). Part two, Sporting, front page.
18. Drebinger, John. "The Super-Catcher." *Baseball Magazine* (Jan. 1939), pp. 339–342.
19. *Tribune* (April 16, 1903), p. 13.
20. *Ibid.* (April 29, 1903), p. 7.
21. *Ibid.* (May 23, 1903), p. 7.
22. *Ibid.* (May 26, 1903), p. 8.
23. *Ibid.* (Sept. 25, 1903), p. 8.
24. *Ibid.* (Sept. 27, 1903). Front page, Sporting section.

Chapter 7

1. *Ibid.* (Jan. 19, 1904), p. 10.
2. *Los Angeles* Times (Feb. 24, 1904), p. B 2.
3. *Ibid.* (Feb. 26, 1904), p. 10.
4. *Tribune* (April 3, 1904). Part two, Sporting.
5. *Ibid.* (April 13, 1904), p. 9.
6. *Ibid.*
7. *Ibid.* (April 19, 1904), p. 6.
8. *Ibid.* (April 20, 1904), p. 6.
9. *Ibid.*
10. *Sandusky Evening Star* (May 13, 1904). Sports page.
11. *Tribune* (June 1, 1904), p. 10.
12. *Tribune* (July 30, 1904), p. 6.
13. *Ibid.* (Aug. 8, 1904), p. 8.
14. *Kansas City Star* (Feb. 3, 1947). "The Sport Dial."
15. *Washington Post* (April 10, 1904), p. S3.
16. Richards, Paul. *Modern Baseball Strategy* (New York: Prentice Hall, 1955), p. 69.
17. *Tribune* (Oct. 9, 1904), p. A 2
18. Brown, Warren. *The Chicago Cubs* (New York: Putnam, 1946), p. 18.
19. Evers, *Touching Second*, p. 65.
20. *Tribune* (May 4, 1905), p. 10.
21. *Ibid.* (May 5, 1905), p. 8.
22. Grant, Roger. *Corn Belt Route Great Western* (DeKalb: Northern Illinois University Press, 1984), p. 157.
23. *Tribune* (May 17, 1905), p. 8.
24. Bogen. *Tinker, Evers and Chance: A Triple Biography*, p. 59.
25. *Tribune* (July 1, 1905), p. 10
26. Copy of Suit filed in Probate Court of

Jackson County, Kansas City, Missouri against Charles Kling, Number 7912.

27. Letters to John Kling had the return address: President, Chicago League Ball Club, 1115 Masonic Temple, Chicago, Illinois.

Chapter 8

1. Case No. 7944, filed in the Probate Court of Jackson County, Missouri.
2. Dickerson, James. Jan. 1, 1906, letter from Charles Murphy to John Kling. Donated by Mr. and Mrs. Ken Eccles.
3. *Ibid.* Feb. 25, 1906, letter from Murphy to Kling.
4. *Ibid.* March 26, 1906, letter from Murphy to Kling.
5. *Ibid.* March 27, 1906, letter from Murphy to Kling.
6. *Chicago Daily News* (March 31, 1906), p. 8.
7. Rice, Grantland. "Tinker to Evers to Chance." *Collier's* (Nov. 29, 1930), p. 11.
8. Pietrusza, David, Matthew Silverman and Michael Gershman. *Baseball: The Biographical Encyclopedia.* (New York: Total Sports Publishing, 2000), p. 39.
9. *Daily News* (April 21, 1906). Sporting News, p. 2.
10. *Ibid.*
11. *Ibid.* Also, *Tribune* (April 22, 1906). Front page, Part Two, Sporting.
12. *Tribune* (May 3, 1906), p. 6.
13. *Ibid.* (May 4, 1906), p. 6.
14. "The Most Important Cog in the Baseball Machine," *Baseball Magazine* (October 1922), p. 489.
15. *Tribune* (May 23, 1906), p. 6.
16. *Ibid.* (June 5, 1906), p. 10.
17. *Daily News* (June 7, 1906), p. 6.
18. *Daily News* (June 8, 1906), p. 6.
19. *Tribune* (July 14, 1906), p. 10.
20. *Kansas City Star* (Aug. 8, 1906), p. 4.
21. *Tribune* (Sept. 2, 1906), Part Two, Sporting.
22. Last will and testament of John Kling, filed with the Probate Court of Jackson County, Missouri.
23. Dickerson, James. Kling's acknowledgement letter, donated by Ken and Bev Eccles.
24. *Tribune* (Sept. 2, 1906), Part Two, Sporting.
25. *Ibid.*
26. Baseball Hall of Fame Library, Scrapbook news item. Uncredited (Oct. 13, 1906), "Modest Champions."
27. *Daily News* (Sept. 20, 1906), p. 6.
28. *Tribune* (Oct. 7, 1906), p. B 4.
29. Hirshberg, Al. *Baseball's Greatest Catchers* (New York: G. P. Putnam's Sons, 1966), p. 22.
30. Wallace, Joseph. *Baseball: 100 Classic Moments in the History of the Game* (New York: Dorling Kindersley, 2000), pp. 26–27.
31. Brown, Warren. "Heading for Greatness." *The Chicago Cubs* (New York: Putnam, 1946), pp. 31–32.
32. *Liberty* (1936, Vol. 13, Issue No. 35).
33. *Washington Post* (Feb. 7, 1907), p. 8.
34. *Ibid.* (Feb. 9, 1907), p. 8.
35. Dickerson, James. Five letters from Kling collection, donated by Ken and Bev Eccles.
36. *Washington Post* (May 26, 1907), p. S 2.
37. *Tribune* (May 8, 1907), p. 12.
38. *Ibid.* (June 9, 1907). Part Two, Sporting.
39. *Ibid.*
40. *Ibid.* (June 24, 1907), p. 11.
41. *Ibid.* (July 31, 1907), p. 6.
42. *Ibid.* (Aug. 18, 1907). Part Two, Sporting.
43. *Ibid.* (Aug. 22, 1907).
44. *Ibid.* (Aug. 28, 1907), p. 6.
45. *Daily News* (Sept. 7, 1907), p. 6.
46. *Ibid.* (Oct. 2, 1907).
47. *Ibid.*
48. *Ibid.* (Oct. 7, 1907). Sporting Extra.
49. *Ibid.* (Oct. 9, 1907). The World of Sports section.
50. *Ibid.* (Oct. 10, 1907).
51. Baseball Hall of Fame Library, Scrapbook news item. Uncredited (Dec. 26, 1936), "Johnny Evers Speaks."
52. *Daily News* (Oct. 14, 1907), p. 6.
53. *Ibid.*
54. *Washington Post* (Feb. 29, 1908), p. 8.
55. *Ibid.* (March 13, 1908). "Sporting Comment" by J. Ed Grillo.
56. *Ibid.*
57. *Tribune* (April 13, 1908), p. 12.
58. *Ibid.* (April 15, 1908), p. 11.
59. *Ibid.* (April 17, 1908), p. 9.
60. *Ibid.* (April 23, 1908), p. 8.
61. *Ibid.*
62. *Ibid.* (May 10, 1908). Part 3, Sporting.
63. *Ibid.* (May 14, 1908), p. 6.
64. *Ibid.* (May 18, 1908), p. 10.
65. *Daily News* (May 20, 1908), p. 6.
66. *Tribune* (May 29, 1908), p. 10.
67. *Daily News* (July 3, 1908). The World of Sports section.
68. Ribalow, *Jewish Baseball Stars*, p. 15.
69. *Tribune* (July 19, 1908). Sporting, Part 3.
70. *Ibid.* (July 20), p. 8.
71. *Ibid.* (July 21, 1908), p. 6.
72. *Ibid.* (July 29, 1908), p. 12.
73. *Daily News* (July 31, 1908), p. 6.
74. *Ibid.* (Aug. 15, 1908), p. 6.
75. *Ibid.* (Aug. 21, 1908). The World of Sports section.
76. *Ibid.*
77. *Tribune* (Aug. 25, 1908), p. 6.
78. *Daily News* (Aug. 25, 1908), p. 6.

Chapter Notes 269

79. *Tribune* (Aug. 27, 1908). Front page
80. *Tribune* (Sept. 13, 1908). Sporting, Part 3.
81. *Ibid.* (Sept. 14, 1908), p. 12.
82. *Daily News* (Sept. 19, 1908), p. 6.
83. *Tribune* (Sept. 22, 1928), p. 8.
84. Bogen. *Tinker, Evers and Chance: A Triple Biography*, pp. 88–90.
85. *Tribune* (Sept. 27, 1908). Sporting, Part 3.
86. *Ibid.* (Sept. 30, 1908), "Notes of the Cubs," p. 14.
87. *Ibid.* (Oct. 4, 1908), p. B 1.
88. *Ibid.* (Oct. 5, 1908). Front page.
89. *Daily News* (Oct. 5, 1908). The World of Sports section.
90. *Tribune* (Oct. 8, 1908), p. 12.
91. Bogen, p. 92.
92. *Harper's Weekly* (May 25, 1912), p. 9.
93. Carmichael, John P. *My Greatest Day in Baseball* (New York: Grosset and Dunlop, 1968), pp. 28–29.
94. *Tribune* (Oct. 9, 1908), p. 2.
95. Golenbock, *Wrigleyville*, p. 151.
96. *Tribune* (Oct. 10, 1908), p. 6.
97. *Ibid.*
98. *Ibid.*
99. *Ibid.* (Oct. 11, 1908), p. B 2.
100. *Ibid.*
101. *Ibid.* (Oct. 12, 1908), p. 1.
102. *Ibid.* (Oct. 14, 1908), p. 6.

Chapter 9

1. *Daily News* (Jan. 1, 1909), p. 8.
2. *Ibid.* (Dec. 22, 1908), p. 19.
3. *Ibid.* (Jan. 5, 1909), p. 8.
4. "Kling Is in Hard Luck," *The Washington Post* (Feb. 25, 1909), p. 8.
5. *The Washington Post* (Jan. 27, 1909), p. 8.
6. *Kansas City Times* (Feb. 25, 1909), p. 10
7. *Tribune* (Feb. 27, 1909), p. 7.
8. *The Sheboygan Daily Press* (Jan. 28, 1909).
9. *Tribune* (March 20, 1909), p. 10.
10. Baseball Hall of Fame Library, Scrapbook news item. Uncredited (undated), pp. 46–48.
11. *Tribune* (March 21, 1909). Front page, Sporting (Part 3).
12. *Ibid.* (March 22, 1909), p. 14.
13. *Washington Post* (May 16, '09), p. S4
14. *Kansas City Star* (Jan. 10, 1909), p. 4.
15. *Tribune* (March 22, 1909), p. 14.
16. *Ibid.*
17. *Ibid.*
18. *Fort Wayne Journal-Gazette* (March 23, 1909), p. 6.
19. Dickerson, James. Scrapbook article, Uncredited (March 27, 1909). "Bank Roll Retires Kling." Donated by Ken and Bev Eccles.
20. *Tribune* (March 24, '09), p. 12.
21. *Ibid.* (March 8, '09), p. 8.
22. *Ibid.* (April 7, 1909), p. 14.
23. *Ibid.*
24. *Ibid.* (Jan. 31, 1909).
25. *Ibid.* (April 7, 1909), p. 14.
26. *Ibid.* (April 9, 1909), p. 8.
27. *Ibid.* (April 17, 1909), p. 8.
28. *Ibid.* (April 19, 1909), p. 12.
29. Baseball's Seventh Annual Report by the National Commission came out in 1911.
30. *Ibid.*
31. *Tribune* (March 20, 1909), p. 10.
32. *Kansas City Times* (Jan. 25, 1909), p. 8.
33. *Tribune* (April 4, 1909). Sporting, Part 3.
34. *Ibid.* (June 3, 1909), p. 8.
35. *Reno Evening Gazette* (July 20, 1909), p. 6.
36. Grillo, J. Ed. "Sporting Comment." *The Washington Post* (Sept. 2, 1909), p. 8.
37. *Ibid.* (Sept. 3, 1909), p. 12.
38. Grillo, Ed, "Sporting Comment." *Washington Post* (July 21, '09), p. 8.
39. *Ibid.* (Sept. 3, 1909), p. 12.
40. *Ibid.* (Sept. 8, 1909), p. 10.
41. *Ibid.* (Sept. 10, 1909), p. 14.
42. *Ibid.* (Sept. 12, 1909), p. C 2.
43. *Tribune* (Sept. 19, 1909), p. 2.
44. Grillo, Ed. "Sporting Comment." *Washington Post* (Sept. 29, 1909), p. 16.
45. Brink, Don, Scrapbook news item. The *Kansas Cityan* (undated). "J. G. Kling, Pool Champion."
46. *Washington Post* (Oct. 10, 1909), p. S 4.
47. "Johnny Kling Incorporates Company." *Washington Post* (Aug. 29, 2909), p. S 2.
48. *Kansas City Post* (Sept. 2, 1909), p. 7.

Chapter 10

1. Grillo, J. Ed. "Sporting Comment." *Washington Post* (Oct. 19, 1909), p. 8.
2. *Washington Post* (Jan. 4, 1910), p. 8.
3. *Ibid.* (Jan. 5, 1910), p. 8.
4. *Ibid.*
5. *Ibid.* (Jan. 12, 1910), p. 8.
6. "Kling Wants to Play Ball." *Washington Post* (Jan. 19, 1910), p. 8.
7. Baseball Hall of Fame, Scrapbook news item. Uncredited (March 31, 1910). "National Commission Hands Down Decision in Kling Case."
8. "Fans Want Kling." *Washington Post* (Jan. 23, 1910), p. S 3.
9. *Washington Post* (Jan. 27, 1910), p. 6.
10. Grillo, J. Ed. "Sporting Comment." *Washington Post* (Jan. 27, 1910), p. 6.
11. Baseball Hall of Fame Library, Scrapbook news item. Uncredited (March 31, 1910). "National Commission Hands Down Decision in Kling Case."
12. *Washington Post* (Feb. 8, 1910), p. 8.
13. *Ibid.*

14. *Ibid.* (Feb. 13, 1910), p. M 5.
15. *Ibid.* (Feb. 16, 1910), p. 6.
16. *Ibid.* (March 1, 1910), p. 8.
17. *Ibid.* (March 3, 1910), p. 8.
18. *Daily News.* (March 19, 1910), p. 1, Sporting Extra.
19. *The Washington Post* (March 20, 1910), p. MS 5.
20. *Ibid.* (March 23, 1910), p. 9.
21. *Ibid.* (March 24, 1910), p. 8.
22. *Tribune* (March 26, 1910), p. 14.
23. *Washington Post* (March 29, 1910), p. 9.
24. *Ibid.* (April 1, 1910), p. 9.
25. *Ibid.* (April 2, 1910), p. 9.
26. *Ibid.* (April 5, 1910), p. 8.
27. *Ibid.* (April 7, 1910), p. 8.
28. *Ibid.* (April 10, 1910), p. MS 7.
29. *Ibid.* (April 20, 1910), p. 9.
30. *Ibid.* (April 21, 1910), p. 8.
31. *Ibid.* (April 22, 1910), p. 8.
32. *Ibid.*
33. *Ibid.* (April 24, 1910), p. S 1.
34. *Ibid.* (April 25, 1910), p. 9.
35. *Ibid.* (May 3, 1910), p. 8.
36. *Tribune* (May 5, 1910), p. 13.
37. *Ibid.* (May 6, 1910), p. 12.
38. *Ibid.* (May 7, 1910), p. 16.
39. *Ibid.* (May 9, 1910), p. 12.
40. *Ibid.*
41. *Ibid.* (May 7, 1910), p. 16.
42. *Ibid.* (June 13, 1910), p. 8.
43. *Chicago Daily News* (June 30, 1910), p. 6.
44. *Ibid.* (July 27, 1910), p. 6.
45. *Tribune* (Aug. 26, 1910), p. 10.
46. *Ibid.* (Oct. 14, 1910), p. 24.
47. *Newsweek* (Sept. 25, 1950), p. 78.
48. *Tribune* (Oct. 2, 1910). Sporting, Part 3.
49. *Ibid.* (Oct. 18, 1910), p. 21.
50. *Ibid.* (Oct. 19, 1910), p. 21.
51. *Ibid.* (Oct. 21, 1910), p. 21.
52. *Ibid.* (Oct. 22, 1910), p. 19.
53. Bogen, Gil. *Tinker, Evers and Chance: A Triple Biography* (Jefferson, NC: McFarland, 2003), p. 112.
54. *Tribune* (Oct. 19, 1910), p. 21.
55. Wallace, Joseph, *Baseball: 100 Classic Moments in the History of the Game* (Dorling Kindersley, 2000), pp. 26–27.
56. *Fort Wayne Daily News* (Feb. 14, 1911).
57. Mathewson, Christopher. *Pitching in a Pinch* (Briarcliff Manor, N.Y.: Scarborough House, 1977), pp. 140–143.
58. *Washington Post.* (Nov. 20, 1910), p. S 3.
59. *Washington Post* (March 29, 1910), p. 9.
60. *Los Angeles Times* (April 24, 1910), p. V119.

Chapter 11

1. *Fort Wayne Daily News* (Feb. 14, 1911).
2. *New York Times* (Feb. 5, 1911), p. C 7.
3. *Tribune* (March 31, 1911), p. 21.
4. *Ibid.* (April 9, 1911). Sporting, Part 3, p. 2.
5. *Chicago Daily News* (April 12, 1911). Sporting Extra, front page.
6. *New York Times* (June 10, 1911), p. 7.
7. *Ibid.* (June 11, 1911), p. C 5.
8. *Sporting Life,* June 17, 1911, article published from a June 12, 1911, Chicago publication.
9. *Washington Post* (June 13, 1911), p. 8.
10. *Ibid.* (June 14, 1911), p. 8.
11. *Ibid.* (June 15, 1911), p. 8.
12. *New York Times* (June 11, 1911), p. C 5.
13. *Washington Post* (July 18, 1911), p. 8.
14. *Kansas City Times* (Nov. 25, 1911), p. 8.
15. *Ibid.*
16. *Ibid.*, p. 15.
17. *Ibid.*, p. 9.
18. *Washington Post* (Dec. 6, 1911), p 8.
19. *Sporting Life* (Dec. 9, 1911). Vol. 58, No. 14.
20. *Daily Northwestern* (Dec. 5, 1911), p. 11.
21. *Sporting Life* (Dec. 9, 1911). Vol. 58, No. 14.
22. *Ibid.* (Dec. 23, 1911), p. 7.
23. *New York Times* (Dec. 11, 1911), p. 15.

Chapter 12

1. *The Western Contractor* (Jan. 3, 1912), p. 18.
2. *Indianapolis Star* (Jan. 6, 1912), p. 10.
3. *New York Times* (Jan. 20, 1912), p. 11.
4. *Tribune* (Jan. 28, 1912), p. C 3.
5. *Sporting News* (Feb. 15, 1912), p. 2.
6. *Tribune* (March 1, 1912), p. 13.
7. *Washington Post* (March 20, 1912), p. 8.
8. *Boston American* (March 23, 1911).
9. *New York Times* (April 7, 1912), p. C 7.
10. *Los Angeles Times* (April 11, 1912), p. III 1.
11. *New York Times* (April 16, 1912), p. 14.
12. *The Sporting News* (April 18, 1912), p. 2.
13. *The Western Contractor* (June 5, 1912), p. 16.
14. *Los Angeles Times* (Oct. 6, 1912), p. VII 12.
15. *Ibid.*
16. *New York Times* (Aug. 16, 1912), p. 7.
17. *Sheboygan Press* (Nov. 19, 1912).
18. *The Sporting News* (Oct. 17, 1912).
19. *Sandusky Star-Journal* (Oct. 23, 1912), p. 7.
20. *Decatur Review* (Nov. 13, 1912), p. 5.

Chapter 13

1. Dickerson, James. Jan. 1, 1906, letter from Charles Murphy to John Kling.
2. Bogen, p. 126.
3. Brown, Warren. "Heading for Greatness."

The Chicago Cubs (New York: Putnam, 1946), p. 19.
  4. Bogen, p. 127.
  5. *Washington Post* (Feb. 5, 1913), p. 8.
  6. Kansas City, Missouri Library, Scrapbook news item. Uncredited (Feb. 19, 1913): "A Final Bid For Kling."
  7. *Ibid.*
  8. National Baseball Hall of Fame Library, Scrapbook collection, letter from Kling to Herrmann, March 3, 1912.
  9. *Washington Post* (May 2, 1913), p. 8.
  10. *Ibid.* (June 8, 1913), p. S 4.
  11. *Ibid.* (June 23, 1913), p. 5.
  12. *Sheboygan Press* (July 3, 1913), p. 8.
  13. *Cincinnati Enquirer* (July 30, 1913), p. 6.
  14. *Ibid.* (Aug. 14, 1913), p. 8.
  15. *Ibid.* (Aug. 15, 1913), p. 8.
  16. *New York Times* (May 5, 1913), p. 7.
  17. National Baseball Hall of Fame Library, Scrapbook collection, letter from Kling to Herrmann (Nov. 6, 1913).
  18. *Ibid.* (Jan. 14, 1914).

Chapter 14

  1. Dickerson, James. Uncredited (April 29, 1914). "Forty Years Ago in Kansas City." Donated by Ken and Bev Eccles.
  2. *Kansas City Star* (May 2, 1935), p. 10A
  3. Website: www.kclibrary.org.
  4. The Kansas City Centennial Association. "Stars Abound at Kling and Allen Recreation." (1950), p. 27.
  5. *Kansas City Star* (May 7, 1921). "A Sport Demanding Steady Nerves."
  6. State of Missouri, Certificate of Incorporation No. 66096.
  7. Website: http://www.kcstar.com.
  8. Kansas City, Missouri, Library, Scrapbook news item. *Life* (March 11, 1916). "That's What Lease Is Doing for Famous Johnny Kling."
  9. State of Missouri, Certificate of Incorporation No. 43024.
  10. *Chillicothe Constitution* (Aug. 7, 1925). Front page.
  11. *Ibid.* (Nov. 8, 1924). Front page.
  12. *Ibid.* (Aug. 14, 1925). Front page.
  13. *Ibid.* (Aug. 17, 1925). Front page.
  14. *Ibid.* (May 5, 1939), p. 2. "Looking Back—Ten Years Ago."

Chapter 15

  1. *Baseball Magazine Advertiser* (July 1913), pp. 106 and 108.
  2. *Chillicothe Constitution* (Aug. 14, 1925). Front page.
  3. *The Daily Constitution* (Oct. 19, 1921). Society section.
  4. Anderson, J. H. "Ex-Cub Catcher Now in Business." Associated Press (Feb. 11, 1929). Reprinted, *Chillicothe Constitution*.
  5. Ripley, Catherine Stortz. *Dateline Livingston County* (Chillicothe, Mo.: Constitution Tribune, 2001), p. 93.
  6. *Ibid.*, p. 97.
  7. *Ibid.*
  8. *Ibid.*
  9. *Ibid.*, p. 102.

Chapter 16

  1. Kansas City Library Special Collections, Scrapbook article. Cochrane, Edward W. (April 2, 1936). "Johnny Kling Sought to Own Kansas City Club in '08, but Didn't Realize Ambition Until 1934."
  2. *Ibid.* Scrapbook news item. Uncredited (undated): "Lured Back into Baseball."
  3. Johnson, Lloyd, Steve Garlick and Jeff Maglif. *Unions to Royals: The Story of Professional Baseball in Kansas City* (Jefferson, NC: McFarland, 1996), p. 2.
  4. *Zanesville Times Recorder* (Oct. 14, 1933), p. 5.
  5. Ritter, Lawrence S. *Lost Ballparks: A Celebration of Baseball's Legendary Fields* (New York: Viking, 1992), pp. 131–132.
  6. Kansas City Library Special Collections. Scrapbook news item. Uncredited (undated).
  7. Rinehart, Joe. Chief of Fire Department in Chillicothe (Nov. 30, 2004, Interview). All records prior to 1970 had been destroyed.
  8. Website: http://www.dingwall.bc.ca/history/main. 20th Century History Glossary: Ku Klux Klan.
  9. Kansas City Library Special Collections. Stock Certificate No. 24, signed by John Kling, President.
  10. *Ibid.* Scrapbook news item, "Kling in a Luncheon." Uncredited (Sept. 10, 1933).
  11. *Ibid.* "Competition Keen in Chamber of Commerce Contest." Uncredited (April 4, 1934).
  12. *Ibid.* "Civic Clubs Turn in Blues' Ticket Sales." Uncredited (April 13, 1934).
  13. *Ibid.* "Johnny Kling Has Fans Pulling for His Team." Uncredited (undated).
  14. *Ibid.* "Advance Purchases for Opening Game Now 3000." Uncredited (April 12, 1935).
  15. *Ibid.* "The Opening Game of A. A. Season at Muehlebach Field with Milwaukee." Uncredited (April 16, 1935).
  16. *Ibid.* "Baseball at High Pitch." Uncredited (April 14, 1935).
  17. *Washington Post* (Sept. 6, 1935), p. 14.
  18. *Chillicothe Constitution Tribune* (Aug. 13, 1935), p. 4.
  19. Kansas City Library Special Collections,

Scrapbook news item. McBride, C. E. (April 27, 1935). "Sporting Comment."
20. *Kansas City Star* (April 14, 1937). "Blues Play Minneapolis Opening Game Here Friday."
21. *Ibid.* "The Blues Home Today."
22. Kansas City Library Special Collections, Vertical File. "Municipal Stadium, Kansas City." Uncredited (undated), p. 132.
23. *Ibid.* News item. "Lured Back into Baseball." Uncredited (undated).
24. *Los Angeles Times* (Aug. 27, 1937), p. A 16.

Chapter 17

1. Kansas City Library Special Collections, Scrapbook article. *Kansas City Times* (Feb. 3, 1947). "The Sport Dial."
2. Frick, Ford C. *Games, Asterisks, and People.* (New York: Crown, 1973), pp. 4–5.
3. Forsee, G. H. *The Kansas Cityan.* (Kansas City: The Commercial Club of Kansas City, 1914), p. 233.
4. *St. Joseph News-Press* (Feb. 2, 1947), p. 18 A.
5. *Chillicothe Constitution Tribune* (Nov. 9, 1942). Front page.
6. *Ibid.* (Feb. 14, 1934). Front page.
7. *Ibid.* (July 8, 1942). Front page.
8. E-mail reply, Jan. 6, 2004, from afhso.research@pentagon.af.mil.
9. June 1, 1943, letter to Commanding General, Army Air Force Technical Training Commanding.
10. *Chillicothe Constitution Tribune* (Nov. 8, 1943). Front page.
11. Kansas City Library Special Collections, Scrapbook article. Carroll, Parke (undated). "Truth About Johnny Kling."
12. *Salisbury Times* (Feb. 11, 1930), p. 7.

Chapter 18

1. Ballou, M. E. *Jackson County: Its Opportunities and Resources.* (Jackson County, Mo.: Historical Society, 1926), p. 65.
2. Longview Recreation Park — Blue Springs Project Office, Kansas City, Missouri, Kling Collection, Scrapbook news article, by Dick Farrington (undated). "Turning Back Time." Donated by Ken and Bev Eccles.

Chapter 19

1. *Chillicothe Constitution Tribune* (July 8, 1942). Front page. "John Kling, Owner, Manages the Strand."
2. John Kling's Will, No. 59,885. Probate Court of Jackson County, Missouri.

Chapter 20

1. *St. Joseph News-Press* (Feb. 2, 1947), p. 18 A.
2. Anderson, David. "John Kling, Cub Stalwart." *The National Pastime # 31* (Cleveland: The Society for American Baseball Research, 2001), p. 49.
3. *Chillicothe Constitution Tribune* (Jan. 25, 1925). Front page.
4. Anderson, Dave. "John Kling. The Modest Hero." Comments from interview of Kling's two granddaughters.
5. Rosencranz, Robert, Highland Park, Ill. Antique auto buff. Auto identified by headlights on front fenders, hub caps and bumper.
6. Baseball Hall of Fame, Scrapbook news item. Uncredited (undated). "Kling Reaping His Reward."
7. *Chillicothe Constitution Tribune* (Oct. 21, 1937), p. 3.

Chapter 21

1. Dickerson, James (undated). "Turning Back Time." By Dick Farrington. Donated by Ken and Bev Eccles.
2. Carberry, Jack. "The Second Guess." *The Denver Post.* (Feb. 1, 1947), p. 9.
3. *Kansas City Times* (Feb. 3, 1947).
4. *Ibid.* "The Sport Dial."
5. Entombment records, Mount Moriah cemetery.

Chapter 22

1. *Los Angeles Times* (Dec. 26, 1936). "Johnny Evers Speaks."
2. *Ibid.* (July 20, 1908), p. 8.
3. *Ibid.* (July 5, 1936), p. A 13.
4. *Washington Post* (March 18, 1941). "This Morning," p. 22.
5. Drebinger, John. "The Super Catcher." *Baseball Magazine* (January 1939), pp. 339–342.
6. Postal, Bernard, Jesse Silver and Roy Silver. *Encyclopedia of Jews in Sports* (New York: Bloch Publishing Co., 1965), p. vii.
7. Allen, Lee. *Cooperstown Corners: Columns from* The Sporting News (Cleveland: Society for American Baseball Research, 1990), p. 1.
8. *Ibid.*, p. 168.
9. Baseball Hall of Fame Library, Letter from Lillian Kling to Lee Allen, Feb. 12, 1969.
10. *Ibid.* Letter from Lillian Kling to Hy Turkin, Dec. 2, 1948.
11. *Ibid.* Postcard, Dec. 2, 1948, from Lillian Kling to Hy Turkin, Sports Department, *Daily News*, 220 E. 42 St., New York 17, N.Y.
12. *Ibid.* Letter from Lillian Kling to Joseph E. Simenic, Jan. 12, 1969.

13. Danzig, Allison, "Sports of the Times." *New York Times* (April 25, 1946).
14. Dickerson, James. Page 391 of *Sports and the American Jew* by Steven A. Riess. Donated by Ken and Bev Eccles.
15. *Ibid.* Uncredited (undated). Page title "The Outsiders," p. 99.
16. Danzig, Allison, "Sports of the Times." *New York Times* (April 25, 1946), p. 28.
17. Lynn, Erwin. *The Jewish Baseball Hall of Fame* (New York: Shapolsky Publishers, 1987), pp. 49, 62, 90, 182.
18. *New York Times* (January 23, 1946), p. 32.

Chapter 23

1. Rigal, Rabbi Lawrence. "A Jewish Custom," e-mail (Jan. 31, 2004).
2. Adler, Frank J. *Roots in a Moving Stream* (Kansas City: The Temple, Congregation B'nai Jehudah, 1972), p. 89.

Chapter 24

1. *Chillicothe Constitution Tribune* (Jan. 28, 1933). "Personals." p. 5.
2. E-mail from Bevjean @aol.com.
3. Website http://www.mumi.org/etranger/en/st5.htm.

Chapter 25

1. Ribalow, Harold U. *The Jew in American Sports* (New York: Bloch Publishing Co., 1949), p. 15.
2. Levitt, Ed. "How About a Matzo Ball Nine?" *Baseball Digest* (Sept. 1971), p. 21.
3. Kahn, Roger. "Humor's Raw Edges." *New York Times* (Jan. 30, 1978), p. C 8.
4. Microfilm at the Chicago Historical Society and the Harold Washington Library, both in Chicago.
5. Greenberg, Hank. *Hank Greenberg: The Story of My Life* (New York: Times Books, 1989), p. 103.
6. *Ibid.*, p. 116.
7. *Ibid.*, pp. 207–208.
8. *Ibid.*, p. 155.
9. *New York Times* (April 9, 1909), p. 6.
10. *Ibid.* (July 7, 1909), p. 1.
11. *Ibid.* (May 11, 1910), p. 4.
12. *Ibid.* (June 9, 1911), p. 16
13. *Ibid.* (April 25, 1913), p. 3.
14. *Ibid.* (Jan. 8, 1915), p. 3.
15. *Ibid.* (March 2, 1943), p. 1.

16. *Ibid.*
17. *Ibid.* (Nov. 26, 1943), p. 17.
18. Jaher, Frederic Cople. "Anti-Semitism in American Sports." *Shofar Fall,* Vol. 20, No. 1 (2001), pp. 61–73.
19. *Ibid.*
20. Website. "How Henry Ford hoped to mass-produce hatred of Jews." www.philly.com/mld/inquirer/entertainment/books.
21. Harper, William A. *How You Played the Game: The Life of Grantland Rice.* (Columbia: Univ. of Missouri Press, 1900), p. 160.

Chapter 26

1. Kieran, John. "Sports of the Times." *New York Times* (Feb. 26, 1936), p. 25.
2. Gould, Allan. *The Helena Daily Independent* (March 11, 1937), p. P-2.
3. Baseball Hall of Fame Library, Scrapbook article. "One of Few Stars Who Held Out Entire Season." By Fred Lieb (Jan. 31, 1947).
4. Bryson, Bill. "Holdouts Who Meant It." *Baseball Magazine* (May 1948), p. 413.
5. Vass, George. "Holdouts Aren't What They Used to Be." *Baseball Digest* (April 1966), pp. 15–16.
6. McCabe, Neal and Constance McCabe. *Baseball's Golden Age* (New York: Harry Abrams, Inc., Publishers, 1993), p. 161.
7. Bogen, Gil. *Tinker, Evers and Chance: A Triple Biography* (Jefferson, NC: McFarland, 2003), pp. 125–126.
8. Brown, Warren. *The Chicago Cubs* (New York: Putnam, 1946), p. 23.
9. Lane, Frank C., "The Gamest Player in Baseball." *Baseball Magazine* (Sept. 1913), pp. 51–61.
10. Baseball Hall of Fame Library, Scrapbook news item. Uncredited (undated).
11. Bogen, p. 136.
12. Personal communication from SABR member Dave Anderson, Feb. 21, 2004.

Conclusion

1. *Soda Springs Sun* (March 2, 1944).
2. Postal, *Encyclopedia*, p. 43.
3. Shalin, Mike and Neil Shalin. *Out by a Step* (Chicago: Diamond Communications, 2002), p. 182.
4. Sanborn, I. E. "Catcher Is Brain Center of Club; Most Important Factor in Defense. *Chicago Tribune* (Dec. 10, 1911), p. C4.

Bibliography

Books

Adler, Frank J. *Roots in a Moving Stream*. Kansas City: Congregation B'nai Jehudah, 1972.
Allen, Lee. *Cooperstown Corner: Columns from* The Sporting News. Cleveland: Society for American Baseball Research, 1990.
Anderson, David W. *The National Pastime*. Cleveland: The Society for American Baseball Research, 2001.
Ballou, M. E. *Jackson County: Its Opportunities and Resources*. Jackson County, Mo.: Jackson County Historical Society, 1926.
Bogen, Gil. *Tinker, Evers and Chance: A Triple Biography*. Jefferson, N.C.: McFarland, 2003.
Brown, Warren. *The Chicago Cubs*. New York: Putnam, 1946.
Caren, Eric C. *Baseball Extra*. Edison, N.J.: Castle, 2000.
Carmichael, John P. *My Greatest Day in Baseball*. New York: Grosset & Dunlap, 1968.
Eban, Abba. *My People: The Story of the Jews*. New York: Behrman House & Random House, 1968.
Evers, John J., and Hugh S. Fullerton. *Touching Second*. Chicago: Reilly & Britton, 1910.
Forsee, G. H. *The Kansas Cityan*. Kansas City: The Commercial Club of Kansas City, 1914.
Frick, Ford C. *Games, Asterisks, and People: Memoirs of a Lucky Fan*. New York: Crown, 1973.
Glazier, Ira A., and P. William Filby. *Germans to America: Lists of Passengers Arriving at U.S. Ports*, Vol. 3.
Golenbock, Peter. *Wrigleyville: A Magical History Tour of the Chicago Cubs*. New York: St. Martin's Griffin, 1999.
Grant, Roger. *Corn Belt Route Great Western*. DeKalb: Northern Illinois University Press, 1984.
Greenberg, Hank. *The Story of My Life*. New York: Times Books, 1989.
Harper, William A. *How You Played the Game: The Life of Grantland Rice*. Columbia: University of Missouri Press, 1900.
Herbert, Jeffery G. *Restored Hamilton County, Ohio Marriages, 1850–1859*. Bowie, Md.: Heritage, 1999.
Hirshberg, Al. *Baseball's Greatest Catchers*. New York: Putnam, 1966.
Holtzman, Jerome, and George Vass. *The Chicago Cubs Encyclopedia*. Philadelphia: Temple University Press, 1997.
Honig, Donald. *The Greatest Catchers of All Time*. Dubuque: Wm. C. Brown, 1991.
Jackson County, Missouri. *Surveys and Plats of Properties of Kansas City, Mo*. Philadelphia: G.M. Hopkins, 1891.

Johnson, Lloyd, Steve Garlick and Jeff Magliff. *Unions to Royals: The Story of Professional Baseball in Kansas City*. Jefferson, N.C.: McFarland, 1996.
Kurzweil, Arthur. *From Generation to Generation*. New York: Schocken, 1980.
Levine, Peter. *Ellis Island to Ebbets Field*. New York: Oxford University Press, 1992.
Marcus, Jacob Rader. *The Jew in the American World*. Detroit: Wayne State University Press, 1996.
_____. *The American Jew, 1585–1990*. New York: Carlson, 1995.
Mathewson, Christopher. *Pitching in a Pinch*. Briarcliff Manor, N.Y.: Scarborough House, 1977.
McCabe, Neal, and Constance McCabe. *Baseball's Golden Age*. New York: Harry Abrams, 1993.
Neft, David S., and Richard M. Cohen. *The Sports Encyclopedia: Baseball*. New York: St. Martin's Press, 1994.
Pietrusza, David, Matthew Silverman, and Michael Gershman. *Baseball: The Biographical Encyclopedia*. New York: Total Sports Publishing, 2000.
Porter, David L. *Biographical Dictionary of American Sports: Baseball*. Cooperstown, N.Y.: Society for American Baseball Research, 1986.
Postal, Bernard, Jesse Silver and Roy Silver. *Encyclopedia of Jews in Sports*. New York: Bloch, 1965.
Ribalow, Harold U. *The Jew in American Sports*. New York: Bloch, 1949.
Richards, Paul. *Modern Baseball Strategy*. New York: Prentice Hall, 1955.
Ripley, Catherine Stortz. *Dateline Livingston County*. Chillicothe, Mo.: Chillicothe Newspapers, 2001.
Ritter, Lawrence S. *Lost Ballparks: A Celebration of Baseball's Legendary Fields*. New York: Viking, 1992.
Sadleir, Steven S. *The Spiritual Seeker's Guide*. Costa Mesa: Allwon, 1992.
Sarna, Jonathon D., and Nancy H. Klein. *The Jews of Cincinnati*. Cincinnati: Center for the Study of the American Jewish Experience, 1989.
Telushkin, Rabbi Joseph. *Biblical Literacy*. New York: Morrow, 1997.
Wallace, Joseph. *Baseball: 100 Classic Moments in the History of the Game*. London: Dorling Kindersley, 2000.

Articles, Letters and Poetry

"Again." *Fort Wayne Daily News* (Feb. 14, 1911).
Anderson, David W. "John Kling, Cub Stalwart." *The National Pastime* (2001).
Anderson, J. H. "Ex-Cub Catcher Now in Business." Associated Press (Feb. 11, 1929).
Baseball Hall of Fame scrapbook articles (chronological order):
    "Johnny Kling Has Fans Pulling For His Team." Uncredited (undated).
    "Kling Reaping His Reward." Uncredited (undated).
    "Modest Champions." Uncredited (Oct. 13, 1906).
    Letter from John Kling to August Herrmann (May 27, 1908).
    "Daguerrotypes, John G. Kling." Uncredited (Jan. 1912).
    Letter from John Kling to August Herrmann (Nov. 6, 1913).
    Letter from John Kling to August Herrmann (Jan. 14, 1914).
    Letter from John Kling to August Herrmann (Jan. 21, 1914).
    "Johnny Evers Speaks." Uncredited (Dec. 26, 1936).
"Boston Club's Status." *Sporting Life* Vol. 58, No. 14 (Dec. 9, 1911).
Bradford, Paul. "Johnny Kling's Neighbor — The Pennant Café." *Baseball Magazine Advertiser* (July 1913).
Carberry, Jack. "The Second Guess." *Denver Post* (Feb. 1, 1947).
"Catcher Kling Signs Cincinnati Contract." *Washington Post* (May 2, 1913).

Drebinger, John. "The Super-Catcher." *Baseball Magazine*, Vol. 62, Issue 2 (Jan. 1939).
"Emerged." *Cincinnati Enquirer* (July 30, 1913).
Evers, Johnny. "Tinker to Evers to Chance." *Liberty*, Vol. 13, Issue No. 35 (1936).
Gould, Allan. "Allan Gould's Gossip of Affairs of Sport." *The Daily Helena Independent* (March 11, 1937).
"Half Million Dollars is Being Spent Here on Building." *Chillicothe Constitution* (Aug. 7, 1925).
Herrmann, August, and Thomas J. Lynch. *National Commission's Seventh Annual Report* (March 31, 1910).
"Johnny Kling Is Dead." *Kansas City Times* (Feb. 3, 1947).
"John Kling Is President." *Washington Post* (Nov. 29, 1910).
"Johnny Kling, Once Famous Catcher, Now Likes Golf Better." *Salisbury Times* (Feb. 11, 1930).
"Johnny Kling, Owner, Manages the Strand." *Chillicothe Constitution Tribune* (July 8, 1942).
"Johnny Kling's Views on Catching." *Baseball Magazine,* Vol. 7, Issue No. 1, (May 1911).
Kahn, Roger. "Humor's Raw Edges." *New York Times* (Jan. 30, 1978).
Kansas City Centennial Association, Souvenir Program. "Stars Abound at Kling & Allen Recreation." Uncredited (1950).
Kansas City, Missouri Library, Scrapbook articles:
    Carroll, Parke. "Truth About Johnny Kling." Sport News (undated). p. 12.
    Farrington, Dick. "Turning Back Time." Uncredited (undated).
    "Johnny Kling Has Fans Pulling for His Team." Uncredited (undated).
    "Lured Back into Baseball." Uncredited (undated).
    "A Final Bid for Kling." Uncredited (Feb. 19, 1913).
    "Kling in a Luncheon." Uncredited (Sept. 10, 1933).
    "Twenty Clubs Are Selling Tickets." Uncredited (Apr. 4, 1934).
    "Civic Clubs Turn in Blues' Ticket Sales." Uncredited (Apr. 13, 1934).
    "Blues Ticket Sales Good." Uncredited (Apr. 12, 1935).
    "Baseball at High Pitch." Uncredited (Apr. 14, 1935).
    "Blues Off Today." Uncredited (Apr. 16, 1935).
    "Sporting Comment." McBride, C. E. (Apr. 27, 1935).
    Cochrane, Edward W. "Johnny Kling Sought to Own Kansas City Club in '08 but Didn't Realize Ambition Until 1934." (Apr. 2, 1936).
    "The Blues Home Today." *Kansas City Star* (Apr. 14, 1937).
    "Blues Play Minneapolis Opening Game Here Today." *Kansas City Star* (Apr. 14, 1937).
    "The Sport Dial." *Kansas City Times* (Feb. 3, 1947).
Kieran, John. "Sports of the Times: Holdout Situation." *New York Times* (Feb. 26, 1936).
Kirk, William F. "A Marvelous Backstop." *New York Evening Journal* (Jan. 2, 1923).
_____. "Old Stars" & "Billiards and Kling."
"Kling Affirms Old Story." *Washington Post* (July 18, 1911).
"Kling After Boston Club." *Kansas City Star* (Nov. 25, 1911).
"Kling On His Way to Boston." *Washington Post* (Dec. 6, 1911).
"Kling to Join Reds Here." *New York Times* (May 5, 1913).
"Kling's Elephant Story." *Washington Post* (April 10, 1904).
"Kling's Presence Aids Reds." *Sheboygan Press* (July 3, 1913).
Lane, Frank C. "The Gamest Player in Baseball." *Baseball Magazine* (Sept. 1913).
Lardner, John. "Who Goes There." *Newsweek* (Sept. 25, 1950).
Levitt, Ed. "How About a Matzo Ball Nine." *Baseball Digest* (Sept. 1971).
Lieb, Fred. "One of Few Stars Who Held Out Entire Season." Uncredited (Jan. 31, 1947).

"Local Men Get Contract for New Hotel." *Chillicothe Constitution* (Nov. 8, 1924).
Longview Recreation Park, Kansas City, Missouri, Kling Collection, letters and articles donated by Ken and Bev Eccles: "Forty Years Ago in Kansas City." Uncredited (April 29, 1914).
Letters from Charles Webb Murphy to John Kling.
"Looking Back—Ten Years Ago." Uncredited (May 5, 1939).
Moss, Edward Bayard. "The Rewards of Baseball." *Harper's Weekly* (May 25, 1912).
"Public May See New Hotel Sunday Evening." *Chillicothe Constitution* (Aug. 14, 1925).
Rice, Grantland. "Tinker to Evers to Chance." *Collier's* (Nov. 29, 1930).
Ripley, Catherine Stortz. "Fifty Thousand Dollars to Be Spent on Strand Theater." *Dateline Livingston County* (Apr. 21, 1931).
_____. "Fire Destroys Dickinson Theater." (Mar. 29, 1933).
_____. "Hotel Strand Coffee Shop Will Open Wednesday." (Mar. 31, 1936).
_____. "Modern Shops, Apartment Hotel Annex on Site of Old Dickinson." (Dec. 7, 1933).
Sanborn, I. E. "Catcher Is Brain Center of Club; Most Important Factor in Defense." *Chicago Tribune* (Dec. 10, 1911).
_____. "The Most Important Cog in the Baseball Machine." *Baseball Magazine* (Oct. 1922).
"A Sport Demanding Steady Nerves." *Kansas City Star* (May 7, 1921).
"Stopped Speedy J. Kling." *Kansas City Times* (Nov. 25, 1911).
"Strand Hotel an Army Barracks in Air Program Here." *Chillicothe Constitution Tribune* (Nov. 9, 1942).
"Strand Hotel Inspected by Thousands." *Chillicothe Constitution* (Aug. 17, 1925).
Sullivan, Gene. "The Wise Owl." *St. Joseph News-Press* (Feb. 2, 1947).
"Surprising Results of Having 'Grandest Name.'" *Daily Constitution* (Oct. 19, 1921).
Vass, George. "Holdouts Aren't What They Used to Be." *Baseball Digest* (April 1966).

City Directories
Chicago, Illinois
Cincinnati, Ohio
Kansas City, Missouri

Newspapers and Periodicals
Baseball Digest
Baseball Magazine
Baseball Magazine Advertiser
Brooklyn Daily Eagle
Chicago Daily News
Chicago Tribune
Chillicothe Constitution
Chillicothe Constitution Tribune
Cincinnati Daily Gazette
Cincinnati Enquirer
Daily Constitution
Daily Northwestern
Decatur Review
Denver Post
Fort Wayne Daily News
Fort Wayne Journal-Gazette
Helena Daily Independent
Indianapolis Star
Kansas Cityan
Kansas City Journal
Kansas City Star
Kansas City Times
Liberty
Los Angeles Times
Minneapolis Tribune
New York Evening Journal
New York Times
Newsweek
Parkview Party News, Muehlebach Field, Kansas City, Missouri
Reno Evening Gazette
Salisbury Times
Sandusky Evening Star
Sandusky Star-Journal

Sheboygan Daily Press
Soda Springs Sun
St. Joseph News-Press
Washington Post
Western Contractor
Zanesville Signal
Zanesville Times Recorder

Websites and E-mail Addresses

afhso.research@pentagon.af.mil
http://memory.loc.gov
http://www.baseballhalloffame.org/history/hofvoting
http://www.dingwall.bc.ca/history/main
http://www.familysearch.org/Eng/Search/rg/guide/Germany14.asp
http://www.glorecords.blm.gov
http://www.kclibrary.org
http://www.kcstar.com
http://www.mumi.org/etranger/en/st5.htm
http://www.philly.com/mld/inquirer/entertainment/books
http://www.SABR.org
http://www.springgrove.org
lawrence@rigal.freeserve.co.uk
pressbox@website.mlb.com
sean-forman@baseball-reference.com

INDEX

Adams, Babe 184
Allen, Bennie 126, 164, 182–183, 190–191, 215, 229
Allen, Helen 192, 229
Allen, Hollie 173, 182–183, 192
Allen, Lee 221–222, 225, 229
Alperman, Whitey 97
Altrock, Nick 89–90
American Association 32, 41, 68, 149, 157, 165, 195
American Jockey Club 237
American Music Hall 154
Ames, Red 71, 95
Anson, Cap 34, 101, 155
Anti-Semitism 11, 15–16, 234–237, 244
Archer, Mrs. James 168
Archer, Jimmy 136, 140, 152, 157, 161, 169
Army Air Force 207–208
Arndt, Harry J. 80
Association Park in Kansas City 75

Barry, Jack 68, 79, 112
Baseball Hall of Fame 205, 217, 221, 224–225, 247
Baseball Writers Association of America 3, 224–225
Batch, Heinie 97
Bates, Johnny 184
Bavaria 9, 11
Beaumont, Ginger 100
Beck, Erve 50
Beckley, Jake 51
Bench, Johnny 6, 245–246
Bender, Charles "Chief" 161
Benjamin, I. J. 14
Bennett, Titus 80, 104–105
Berg, Moe 234
Bergen, Bill 169
Berger, Clarence 50

Berra, Yogi 245–246
Bescher, Bob 184
Bilicke, A.C. 190
Billiards and Kling 250
Biographical Dictionary of American Sports—Baseball 22
B'nai Jehudah Temple 61, 228, 230
Boston American 176
Boston Beaneaters 32, 52, 172
Boston Doves 171, 175
Boston Nationals 31, 41, 48, 167, 176, 180
Bradley, Bill 34–35, 37
Bread Wagon chauffeur 18, 215
Bresnahan, Roger 5–6, 71, 94–95, 100, 119, 158, 172, 224–225, 234, 245–246, 249
Bridwell, Al 112, 114, 120
Briggs, Buttons 61, 67
Briggs, Caricaturist 126, 128
Brink, Don 21, 191
Brooklyn Nationals 46
Brown, Buster 172
Brown, Clyde 210
Brown, Joe E. 198
Brown, Mordecai "Three Finger" 3–4, 59, 61, 63, 65, 77, 84, 88–90, 93–95, 103, 107–108, 113, 117–120, 123, 130, 156–157, 160, 162, 169, 184, 205, 224–225, 245, 250
Brown, Mrs. Mordecai 168
Brundage, Avery 237
Brunswick-Balke-Collender billiard table 192
Brush, John T. 35, 115, 121
Bryan Oil & Products Co. 213
Bryson, Bill 239
Burkett, Jesse 43
Burrell, Charles 203
Byrne, Bobby 184

Callahan, Nixey 37
Calvary Cemetery 230
Campanella, Roy 6, 245–246
Campbell, Bill 105
Campbell, Vin 178–179
Carder, M. M. 208
Carey, Max 184
Carroll, Parke 208
Casey, Doc 60, 64–65, 69, 97
Champaign, Illinois 77
Chance, Frank 25, 27, 34, 39–42, 44, 49–54, 56, 58–59, 63–65, 69, 71–72, 75, 78–79, 81–84, 86–93, 97–99, 101–105, 107–108, 112–115, 117–122, 124, 126–130, 132–133, 135–136, 140, 149–152, 156–162, 167–172, 181–182, 199, 205, 217, 220, 224–225, 239, 241
Chance, Mrs. Frank L. 168
Chase, Hal 155
Chestnut Street Cemetery 232
Chicago City Directory, 1901 38
Chicago Colts 39, 47–48, 52–53, 57–59, 63, 71
Chicago Cubs 25, 48, 63, 72, 89, 103, 162, 199, 207
Chicago Daily News 23, 30, 35, 63, 75–77, 82, 84, 88, 96, 99–101, 107–108, 117, 178, 188, 210–211, 235
Chicago Masonic Temple 72
Chicago Orphans 23, 27, 31–32, 37
Chicago Times 173
Chicago Tribune 29–30, 32, 34, 39, 41, 55, 57, 61, 65, 68, 77, 84–86, 92–93, 95, 100, 106, 109–110, 112–113, 116–117, 121–122, 124, 127, 129, 131–132, 134, 138–139, 145, 150, 153, 155–158, 162, 169, 178, 235, 239
Chicago Whales 186
Chicago White Sox 59, 89–90, 182
Childs, Clarence "Cupid" 29, 32–33, 37, 40, 42
Chillicothe Business College 207
Chillicothe Constitution Tribune 10, 208
Cincinnati, Ohio 9
Cincinnati Daily Gazette 10
Cincinnati Enquirer 159, 185
Cincinnati Nationals 47
Clark, B. T. 208
Clarke, Fred 100, 157, 182
Clarke, Tommy 184–185
Clingman, Billy 37
Coakley, Andy 106
Cobb, Ty 6, 100–103, 123–124, 144, 245
Cochrane, Mickey 225, 235, 245–246

Cole, King 156–157
Cole, Mrs. King 168
Coleman, Bob 184
Collins, Eddie 31, 163
Comiskey, Charles 39
Commercial Club 207
Congalton, Bunk-William 49, 51
Coogan's Bluff 26
Coombs, Jack 161–162
Cooperstown Corner 222
Corridon, Frank 61, 63
Cote, Henry 21
Cowan, Judge Ray G. 214
Crandell, Del 235
Crawford, Sam 100, 122–124
Criger, Lou 100, 235, 249
Crisp, Joe 176
Crohn, R. S., Public Administrator 73
Cross, Montgomery 46
Cuff, W. P. 192, 194
Cuff-Kling Enterprises 192, 194, 196, 199, 214

Dahl, Lena 85
Dahlen, "Bad Bill" 94, 184
Danning, Harry 234
Dell, Harry 138
Denver Western League 56
DeOro, Alfred 91, 143
Detroit Tigers 6
Devlin, Art 112, 114, 119–120
Devore, Josh 184
Dexter, Charley 27, 32, 39–40, 49–51
Dickerson, James 217
Dickey, Bill 6, 245–246
Dickinson Theater 196–197, 199, 241
DiMaggio, Joe 246
Dixon, W.H. 195
Dixon Hotel 181, 190, 192, 195, 215, 228
Dobbs, John 54
Dodge, John 184
Dolin, Nate 27, 41, 236
Donlin, Turkey Mike 112, 114, 119
Donough, Jiggs 47
Donough, Rhoderick Dhu 46
Donough, Tim 35, 39
Donovan, "Wild Bill" 34, 102–103, 122
Dooin, Charlie 174
Doyle, Jack 160–161
Doyle, Larry 120, 172
Dreyfuss, Pres. Barney 93
Duffy, Hugh 31
Dyer, Braven 221

Index

Eason, Mal 34
Ebbets, Charlie 136
Elder, Ray 126, 241
Ellick, Joe 19
Ellis, Rube 168
Empire Theater 196–197
Emporia 22
Emslie, Umpire Bob 27, 29, 31–32, 43–44, 94, 97, 115
Encyclopedia of Jews in Sports 221–222
Evans, Steve 158
Evers, Mrs. John 168
Evers, Johnny 52–53, 56, 59, 65, 78–79, 84, 90, 101, 103, 105–107, 111–112, 14–116, 119–122, 124, 136, 141, 158–160, 172, 182, 187, 199, 205, 217, 224–225, 239, 245
Ewing, Buck 104–105, 224–225
Exposition Park 18–19

Federal League 185, 187
Fez cigarettes 171
Fiesta room 197
Fishberg, Maurice 233
Fisk, Carlton 6, 245–246
Flannagan Bros. Mfg. Co. 179
Flanner, Joe 148
Flynn, Jack 157
Ford, Henry 237
Forest Hill Cemetery 230
Foxx, Jimmie 246
Fraser, Chic 94, 106–109
Frick, Ford 205
Fromm, Bernice 216
Fullerton, Hugh 177, 179

Gaffney, Jmes E. 174–177, 179–180
Ganzel, John 105, 108
Gardner, Jimmy 48
Garvin, Ned 37
Gear, Dale 96
Gehrig, Lou 246
Germans to America: Lists of Passengers Arriving in U.S. Ports 12
Gessler, Doc 87
Giants, National League 6, 23, 27
Gibson, George 144
Gietschier, Steven P. 221
Ginsberg, Joe 234
Glazier, Ira A. 12
Glennon Hotel 190
Golden Eagles 18
Gorman, Sam 207, 212, 214, 228
Gould, Allan 238

Grace, Kevin 15
Gradwohl, Julia 173
Gradwohl, Lillian May 55, 60–61
Grady, "Mich" 30, 80
Graham, "Peaches" 171
Green, Danny 35, 46
Greenberg, Hank 221, 227, 235–236
Griffin, Hank 168
Griffith, Clark 27–29, 32, 37, 147, 172
Grillo, J. Ed 104, 136, 144
Groh, Heinie 184

Hahn, "Noodles" 33, 67
Hamilton, Ohio 9
Hamilton County 11, 15
Hanlon, Felix 174
Hannibal Meat Market 20
Hardy, Jack 98
Harley, Dick 60
Harper, Jack 87–88
Harridge, Bill 236
Harrison, Mayor Elect Carter H. 168
Harry Truman's Haberdashery 190
Hart, James A. 27, 35, 37, 39, 47–48, 50, 54, 57–58, 68–69, 72, 84, 106
Hartnett, Gabby 6, 225, 245–246
Hartsel, "Topsy-Tully" 41–43, 46, 163
Hauser, Arnold 158, 178
Haverlys 18–19, 21
Hayes, Gerald 195
Hebrew Union College, Cincinnati 232
Hegan, Jim 234
Heidrick, Emmet 42–43
Herrmann, Garry 106, 108, 134, 138–140, 146, 150, 155, 162, 182–187, 243
Herzog, Buck 6, 119–120
Heuston, Thomas 54, 104, 144
Heuston Building 125, 131
Heyden, Jack 114
Hickman Mills 29, 210–211
Hippodrome 127
"Hitless Wonders" 89–90, 99, 162
Hofman, Solly 67–68, 87, 96–97, 107, 113–114 119, 122, 140, 158–161, 170–171
Honig, Donald 5, 20, 22
Hope, Bob 190
Hoppe, Willie 190
Houston Buffs 22
Houston Texas League 21–22
Howard, Del 103, 111–112, 119
Howe, Henry 13
Hoy, Dummy 50–51
Huff, George 40, 51, 54, 69, 71, 78
Huggins, Miller 65, 78, 107, 158, 168

Index

Hulswitt, Rudy 107, 140
Hundt, Hartwig 11
Infanger, John 229
Israelites 13

Jackson, George 178
Jacobson, Jerome 217, 220, 227
Jacobstein, Jacob 228
Jacobstein, Louis 228
Jacobstein, Minnie 228
Jacobstein, William 217, 227–228, 231
J. C. Duffy Company 230–231
Jennings, Manager Hughey 100–102, 104–105, 123–124, 144
The Jew in American Sports 242
Jews 11–16
Johnny Kling Baseball Supply Co. 142–143
Johnny Kling trophy 199, 201
Johnson, Ban 39, 106, 148, 150, 164–165
Johnson, Claude 133
Johnson, Walter 5, 56
Johnston, Artie 40
Johnstone, Umpire Jim 79
Jones, Fielder 49, 54, 58, 60, 65, 69, 91, 161

Kahn, Roger 235
Kahoe, Mike 46, 49, 92, 99
Kansas City All Stars 134, 137, 140, 149, 233
Kansas City American Association 180, 199
Kansas City Baseball Club, Inc. 200, 202–203
Kansas City Blues 149, 165, 198, 207–210, 212, 241
Kansas City Directory 86, 212
Kansas City Journal 19, 134
Kansas City Post 134
Kansas City Schmeltzers 21–23, 48
Kansas City Star 126–127, 130, 203
Kansas City Times 126
Kansas City Western League 22
Kansas State Agricultural College 69
Karger, Ed 96
K.C. Tire & Rubber Co. 213
Kelley, Mike 104–105
Keyser, E. Lee 198, 208
Kieran, John 238
Killian, Ed 102
Kirk, William 249
Klem, Umpire 97, 119, 123, 214
Kline, Johnny 22
Kling, Amelia 15, 73, 164

Kling, Caroline 16–17, 72–73, 227, 230
Kling, Caroline (Carrie) 15
Kling, Charles 15, 18, 21, 72–73, 85, 91, 103, 164, 175, 212, 230
Kling, Elizabeth (Lizzie) 15, 18, 73, 85, 91, 104, 175, 212, 230
Kling, Frank 206
Kling, George P. 14
Kling, Geraldine "Jerre Ann" 211, 217, 220, 229
Kling, Johannes (John Sr.) 12–13, 15–18, 85, 230
Kling, John (grandson) 229
Kling, Johnny: baseball 3–7, 9–10, 17–37, 39–58, 60–61, 63–114, 116–125, 128–133, 135–142, 144–165, 167–189, 195, 198, 205–207, 216, 220, 234–235, 243–247, 249–250; billiards 54–56, 61, 75, 86, 91, 96, 104, 106, 108–109, 113, 116, 125–127, 129, 131, 141–144, 148, 155, 164, 175–176, 181–182, 190–192, 195–196, 209, 212, 217, 235; business 91, 95, 106, 108–109, 125–126, 129–131, 143, 181, 187, 190, 193–194, 197–203, 207–215; declining years 220; gentleman farmer 211, 219; Jewish heritage 56, 109–110, 221–224, 227, 229–230, 233–234, 242
Kling, Lillian 76, 164, 220, 222–226, 229–230, 242
Kling, Louise 15, 17, 227
Kling, Magdalene (Lena) 15
Kling, T. 13
Kling, Virginia 73, 164, 176, 212, 217, 220, 227–228
Kling, William (Bill) 15, 18, 20–21, 73, 85, 91, 104, 175, 230
Kling-Allen Building 195
Kling and Allen Billiard and Bridge Club 192
Kling's barber shop 212
Kling's Billiard Emporium 191, 212
Kling's dairy farm 213
"Kling's Elephant Story" 66
Kocherov, Sheilah 228, 230
Koufax, Sandy 227
Kroh, Rube 114
Ku Klux Klan 199, 241

L.A. Times 221
Lane, Dan 174
Lanigan, Ernest 5
Lardner, R. W. 156–157
Laws of the Torah 227
Leach, Tommy 107, 157

Leeland Giants 139
Lieb, Fred 238
Lilienthal, Rabbi Max 13
Lima News 232
Lincoln Giants 19
Lobert, Hans 105–107
Loftus, Tom 27, 30, 32, 35, 39–40, 43
Lombardi, Ernie 6, 245–246
Loney, D. J. 125
Lorch, Benedict 232
Lorch, Caroline 9, 12, 14
Lorch, Charles 9, 232
Lorch, Theresa 9
Lowe, Bobby 31, 49, 51–54
Lumley, Harry 97
Lundgren, Carl 52, 78–80, 82, 94
Lynch, Thomas J. 150, 155, 165, 243

Mack, Connie 39, 161–163
Maloney, Billy 69
Mantle, Mickey 246
Marquard, Rube 179
Marshall, Doc 109
Masons 215
Mathewson, Christy 83, 88, 97, 111, 114–115, 118–120, 162, 178–179, 200, 241, 245
Mayer, Rabbi Harry H. 61, 227, 229
McBreen, Hugh 174
McChesney, Harry 67–68
McCormick, Barry 37, 42–43, 46
McCormick, Moose 29, 31, 114, 120
McCourt, Charles 173
McDonald, Ed 179
McElvain, Donald 214
McGann, Dan 94–95
McGill, J.G. 174
McGinnity, "Iron Man" Joe 82–83, 114, 118
McGraw, John 5, 39, 83, 111, 113, 115, 118, 120–121, 146–147, 182
McIntyre, Matty 122, 162
McKibben, Manager 22, 55
McLean, Larry 95, 100, 106
McPhee, Biddy 50
McQuillen, George 113
Mein Kampf 237
Menefee, Jocko 30–31, 33, 41, 46, 53, 56
Menorah Hospital 219
Merkle, Fred 114–115, 121
Meyer, Charles 175
Meyers, Chief 178
Midwest Creamery Supply Company 214
Miller, John 157, 159, 169
Missouri Valley Athletic Club 131, 149, 164

Monyhan, Pat 202
Moran, Pat 78–79, 86–87, 89, 92–93, 96–99, 109, 129, 132, 140, 152
Mostov, Stephen 14
Mount Moriah Cemetery 215
Mount Moriah Temple 215, 220
Mowrey, Mike 158, 168
Muehlebach, George 198
Muehlebach Field 198, 200, 203, 243
Murphy, Charles Webb 72–76, 79, 87–88, 92–93, 100, 104, 106, 109, 115, 118, 121–122, 124, 126–127, 130, 132–137, 139–140, 144, 146–150, 152, 154, 156, 167, 176, 181–182, 187–189, 243–244
Murray, Manager Bill 103
Murray, Rose Corrigan 229

National Baseball Hall of Fame 25, 41
National Commission 140, 146–152, 155–156, 162
National Commission's Seventh Annual Report 243
National Electric Ticket Register Co. 187
National League 6, 20, 23, 39, 41, 155, 187
National League Board of Directors 117
Needham, Tom 100, 132, 137, 140, 152, 156
New York American League club 180, 203
New York Athletic Club 237
New York Giants 37
New York Herald 118
New York Times 179, 185, 225
Nichols, "Kid" 43, 68, 131, 133
Noonan, Pete 79
Nothnagel, L. H. 214
Nuxhall, Phil 9

Oakes, Rebel 158
O'Day, Umpire Hank 34, 93, 112, 115–116, 158
O'Hagen, Hal 51
Old Mill cigarettes 171
Oldfield, Barney 173
Oldtyme Baseball News 228
O'Leary, Charley 123
O'Rourke, Frank 179
Overall, Orval 4, 54, 94, 97, 105–106, 111–113, 115–116, 122, 124, 160

Packard, Gene 185
Padden, Dick 43, 56
Page, L. Coues 174
Palm Grove Cemetery 232
Payne, Freddie 101
Pendergast, T.J. 192

Pendleton, Captain Richard T. 208
Pennant Café 195–196, 213
Pentagon 208
Percheron horses 213
Perdue, Hub 180
Petway, Bruce 28
Pfeffer, Jeff 69
Pfiester, Jack 4, 80, 89, 94, 101–102, 112, 114, 118–119, 123, 160, 162
Philadelphia Athletics 27, 162
Philadelphia National League 103, 144
Philadelphia Telegraph 161
Pierce Arrow 216–217
Pittsburgh Nationals 47
Plum Street Universalist Church 13
Pollard, Joseph Franklin 196
Polo Grounds 6, 23, 26, 29, 94, 206
Portland Pacific Northwest League
Povich, Shirley 221
Prager, Josh 163
Protestants 14
Pulliam, Pres. Harry C. 115–116

Raber, Charles 20, 22
Raub, Tommy 58
Reed, W. Haley 192, 194
Reiman, Richard J. 14–15
Remnants 39–40, 42, 44, 46–47, 49
Reulbach, Ed 4, 71, 89, 91, 102, 110, 158, 160, 162, 168, 176, 205
Rhenish Palatinate 11
Ribalow, Harold 3
Ribicoff, Abraham 221
Rice, Grantland 5
Richard, Dick 138
Richie, Lew 167
Riess, Steven 225
Rigal, Rabbi Lawrence 227
Rigler, Umpire Cy 168
Robinson, Jackie 241
Robison, Stanley 168
Rockford, Illinois 22–23
Rohe, George 90
Rose, Pete 244
Rose Hill Cemetery 228, 230
Roseman, Claude 124
Roth, Adam 9
Rucker, Nap 108, 169
Ruppert, Col. Jacob 203, 241
Russell, Henry (né Levy) 12
Russell, Mary G. 173
Russell, Pres. W. Hepburn 170, 173–174, 198
Ryan, James 32

Sadleir, Steven S. 15
Sahaida, Jeffrey 208
Saier, Vic 168
St. John's Unitarian Church 14–15
St. Joseph 22–23
St. Louis Browns 56, 126
St. Louis Cardinals 21, 34, 42–43, 53
St. Louis Star 57
Schaefer, Germany 50, 51, 54, 101
Schalk, Ray 5, 224–225, 235, 246
Schmidt, Boss 124
Scholl, Patty 230
Schulte, Frank "Wildfire" 66, 68, 78, 83, 87, 97, 99, 107–108, 119–120, 122, 157–158, 160, 205
Schutte, Caroline (Carrie) 17
Schutte, Louise 18, 85
Schutte, Sigesmund Z. 17–18, 85, 227
Schutte, Victor 17, 73, 85
Schutte, Zacheriah 17
Schweiker, Barry 234
Selee, Frank 48, 50–54, 56, 58–59, 61, 63–64, 67–69, 71–72
Sexton Hotel 190, 195
Seymour, Cy 29, 65, 78, 84, 119
Shannon, "Spike" 80, 98
Sheboygan Press 180
Sheckard, Mrs. James 168
Sheckard, Jimmy 78, 98, 105, 107–108, 122, 157–158, 160–162, 168, 185, 219
Shivah 71, 85
Shriner, Secretary of Kansas City Blues 75
Siber, John R. 20
Siber baseball team 20–21
Silver, Roy 222
Simenic, Joseph 224
Simmons, Al 246
Slagle, Jimmy 49, 53–54, 60, 63, 65, 78, 78, 93, 95, 97, 105, 107, 116
Smith, Alec 29
Smith, Mayor Bryce 201
Sothern, E.H. 190
Southern Central Business Association 199, 201, 203
Southern Hotel Journal 207
Spalding Guide 21
Spaulding, Reverand 13
Speaker, Tris 198, 245
Sporting Life 170
Sporting News 10, 90, 175–176, 180, 221, 223
Sports and the American Jew 225
Spring Grove Cemetery 9, 14
Stallings, George 180

Stein, Mrs. Louis 230
Steinfeldt, Harry 78, 82–83, 96–97, 101, 103, 105, 107–108, 111–112, 116, 119, 122–123, 133, 158, 160, 205
Strand Coffee Shop 194, 196–197, 207
Strand Hotel 192–194, 196–197, 207–208, 210, 212, 214, 241
Strand Theater 192, 196
Strang, Sammy 23, 30, 33–34, 39, 57, 77, 84
"Strolls Through Sportville" 249
Strunk, Amos 161
Sullivan, Ted 23, 76–77
Summe Products 213
Summers, Ed 122
Sweeney, Bill 174, 178

Taft, Charles 239
Taylor, Dummy 82
Taylor, Jack 30, 37, 41–43, 50–52, 59, 94
Tebeau, George 127, 198
Tener, John 188, 239
Tenney, Fred 119–120, 167, 172, 174
Thompson, W. A. 154
Tinker, Joe 48–54, 56, 59, 63, 65, 78–79, 84, 94, 103, 105, 107–108, 111–114, 116, 119–120, 122–124, 135, 140, 152, 154, 158, 160–161, 172, 183–186, 199, 205, 217, 219–220, 222, 224–225
Titus, John 179
Toney, Fred 168–169
Topeka Western League 176
Torah law 206
Troy, New York 52
Truman, Harry 190
Trustee Realty Co. 213
Turkey Red cigarettes 171
Turkin, Hy 222, 224

Union Club 236
Union Station 207

Unitarians 13–14
United Jewish Cemeteries 14, 232
University of Cincinnati, Archives and Rare Books Department 15
University of Illinois 39–41, 49, 51, 54, 77
Up and On to America 12
Upper Franconia 11

Vass, George 239
Veeck, Bill 236
Vermont Marble Company 214
Veterans Committee 224

Waddell, Rube 37, 41, 125
Wagner, Honus 5, 58, 81, 101, 157, 184, 245
Walker, Fred 214
Walsh, Ed 89–90
Walsh, Tom 79
Ward, John M. 174–177, 179–180
Washington Post 54–55, 58, 61, 69, 71, 91, 100, 140, 144, 152, 221
Weart, William G. 161
Weaver, Orlie 168
Weller, Sam 239
West Side Grounds 46, 53, 59, 68, 72, 92, 99, 101, 106, 111, 122, 188
Western Association 22, 30, 165
Weston, "Cowboy" 141–143
Westphalia 12
Westport Dairy 214
Wicker, Bob 63–65, 80–81
Williams, Otto 54, 65, 68
Wiltse, Hooks 111–112
Winslow, Beverly 174
Wise, Rabbi Mayer 13

Zalusky, John 49
Zimmerman, Heinie 106, 113, 167, 169
Zwilling, Dutch 199, 201, 203, 207